JAPANESE
AND
ENGLISH
IDIOMATIC EQUIVALENTS

A DICTIONARY OF JAPANESE

AND

ENGLISH

IDIOMATIC EQUIVALENTS

和英熟語慣用句辞典

Charles Corwin, Ph. D.
General Editor

Lincoln Saito, M. A.
Associate General Editor

Jiro Takenaka, Ph. D.
English Editor

Norikazu Shioda, A. B.
Japanese Editor

Takaaki Hitotsuyanagi, M. A.
Associate English Editor

KODANSHA INTERNATIONAL LTD.
Tokyo, New York and San Francisco

Distributors:
UNITED STATES: Kodansha International/USA Ltd., through Harper & Row, Publishers, Inc., 10 East 53rd Street, New York, New York 10022. SOUTH AMERICA: Harper & Row, Publishers, Inc., International Department. CANADA: Fitzhenry & Whiteside Limited, 150 Lesmill Road, Don Mills, Ontraio M3B 2T5. MEXICO AND CENTRAL AMERICA: HARLA S.A. de C.V., Apartado 30–546, Mexico 4, D.F. UNITED KINGDOM: Phaidon Press Limited, Littlegate House, St. Ebbe's Street, Oxford OX1 1SQ. EUROPE: Boxerbooks Inc., Limmatstrasse 111, 8031 Zurich. AUSTRALIA AND NEW ZEALAND: Book Wise (Australia) Pty. Ltd., 104–8 Sussex Street, Sydney 2000. THE FAR EAST: Toppan Company (S) Pte. Ltd., No. 38, Liu Fang Road, Jurong Town, Singapore 2262.

Published by Kodansha International Ltd., 2–12–21 Otowa, Bunkyo-ku, Tokyo 112 and Kodansha International/USA Ltd., 10 East 53rd Street, New York, New York 10022 and 44 Montgomery Street, San Francisco, California 94104. Copyright in Japan 1968 by Kodansha International Ltd. All rights reserved. Printed in Japan.

LCC 68–11818
ISBN 0–87011–111–6
JBC 1581–787893–2361

First edition, 1968
Fifth printing, 1980

CONTENTS

To Elouise
Beloved wife, mother, missionary
Who entered the Japanese idiom world
Along another route—sitting where they sit

INTRODUCTION

KIPLING'S adage "never the twain shall meet" is being challenged by history. Today as foreign visitors browse through Japan's dazzling department stores, glide along on her two-mile-a-minute streamliners, and view her vast apartment house complexes, they will conclude that the modernization of Japan is virtually complete. Those differences of food, clothing, living standards, and customs that prevailed 100 years ago have all but disappeared. Yet a formidable wall still stands between Japanese and Westerners. As long as they avoid serious interaction and conversation with each other, as long as they simply ask directions and prices, say "thank you" and "goodbye," this barrier goes unnoticed. But when either Japanese or Westerner steps beyond the rudiments of the other's language, he is immediately deluged by a never ending cataract of words, idioms, and syntactical forms that defy systematic arrangement. This language barrier can be traced to (1) the basic linguistic differences between Japanese and English, (2) the confusion added to the Japanese language by the adoption of Chinese ideographs during the Nara-Heian periods (A.D. 710–1159), and (3) the non-technical, emotive character of the Japanese language.

The Japanese people have taken a serious approach to this language barrier since the Meiji Restoration. The study of English is required in all Japanese middle schools and is now being introduced at the elementary level. Modern language-learning techniques are being employed at advanced levels, and electronic language laboratories are springing up at cultural centers across the nation. Since World War II, more Westerners have come to serious grips with the Japanese language. Those who apply themselves at professional language schools can be speaking, reading, and even writing with some facility within two years. However, if freedom in the target language has been the goal of this linguistic enterprise, perhaps in no other field of scholarship has so much effort gained so few results. In relation to the populations involved, the number of Japanese or Westerners who can move freely in the others' idiomatic world is next to zero. Recognizing this, the editors of the *Dictionary* have taken upon themselves the task of exploring a new approach to the learning of idiomatic expressions. The plan and layout of the *Dictionary* can be best understood by describing its range, purpose, and presentation. Briefly, the range of entries is limited to the world of human relationships; the purpose of the *Dictionary* is to generate good idiomatic speech; and the presentation of over ten thousand expressions is organized neither alphabetically nor according to Chinese character, but under 222 General Thought Categories ranging from AI (love) to ZOKUAKU (vulgarity).

RANGE

The editors selected lexical data from a limited range of sources. Though word density is not directly proportional to a dictionary's usefulness, frequency is a good criterion. The usage frequency list of the National Language Research Institute (*Vocabulary and Chinese Characters in Ninety Magazines of Today*, Tokyo, 1962) was employed to check our range of entries. Only those words found in at least four of the five categories of magazines, which fell within our " human relationships " field of research, and had a relative usage frequency[1] of .045% and above, were checked against the General Japanese Index. This frequency list, however, did not serve as the basic means of selecting words and phrases. Rather, having compiled our lexical data from Japanese literature and textbooks, the frequency list was checked to discover serious omissions. Next, the lexical data was categorized according to meaning, not alphabetically nor according to Chinese character. Alphabetical word lists simply do not increase the facility of a speaker in a foreign tongue. The cate-

---

1 The relative usage frequency is based on the number of times an individual word appears in everyday usage. For example, if a word in Japanese has a relative usage frequency of about 1.8%, for every 1,000 words used in general speech, it would appear about 18 times in one form or another.

gories selected—a total of 222—are from the provinces of life or human endeavor. We consulted classification systems such as the *Syntopicon* of *Great Books* of *the Western World, Roget's Thesaurus*, and others. The provinces are those which may occur in a single person's life in his relationships with others or as he encounters the vicissitudes of life. Thus the English sentences used as examples are sometimes based on incidents which occurred in the life of Abraham Lincoln, not only because of the interest they have for Japanese students, but also to demonstrate the point that each category touches upon some aspect of one human life. Putting it another way, the provinces do not range from beauty operators to mechanics, from doctors to zoo keepers; rather, they cover the range of possibilities of human experience irrespective of formal profession.

PURPOSE

For native speakers of English whose target language is Japanese, the *Dictionary* fulfills two major functions: (1) it serves as a quick guide for locating idiomatic equivalents in Japanese, and (2) it enables one to familiarize oneself with the correct use and selection of Japanese idioms. It is designed for those who have grasped the basic structure of the language and are attempting to express ideas in Japanese. The *Dictionary* is a shortcut to finding Japanese idiomatic expressions hitherto found only through the reading of Japanese books—a laborious and frustrating task that left the reader unsure whether the expression was in common use or was simply a phrase coined by the author. The phrases found in the *Dictionary* have been checked by scholars to insure that they are, in fact, part of general Japanese speech. The *Dictionary* also serves as a reference which provides a systematic form for finding expressions one has heard but cannot recall. It is a memory aid, showing the range of possibilities for expressing ideas and encouraging the reader to employ his working knowledge of Japanese in the actual use of the expressions. The *Dictionary* is not a word list; rather it is designed for penetration into idiom study through perusal, memorization, and usage, and can be used as a systematic guide to building one's command of Japanese idiom.

PRESENTATION

1. TYPES OF ENTRIES

Single words—Nouns, verbal adjectives, noun-adjectives, verbs, and adverbs are presented for three reasons: (1) to indicate the semantic spectrum within each category, (2) to delimit meaning from synonymous terms, and (3) to serve as core words around which derivative words and phrases are built.

Colloquial expressions—Phrases which are characteristic of conversation and informal writing, and which assume a certain intimacy between speakers.

Idiomatic expressions—Phrases which have a meaning other than the total sum of the literal meanings of their component parts.

Proverbial expressions—Set Japanese phrases, derived from history or literature. These are not so much bits of philosophical advice but fixed phrases, often derived from some historical incident, which precisely fit certain situations. They exist in the warp and woof of Japanese culture and flow effortlessly from Japanese lips when the phrases describe situations in daily life. They are included primarily for native speakers of English, and their English equivalents serve as definitions rather than options for the Japanese-speaking user.

Phrases—Those words which are neither colloquial nor idiomatic but whose choice of words would not be anticipated by the native speaker of English. For example, *ai o uchiakeru* (confess one's love) is neither idiomatic nor colloquial, but an English-speaking person would not anticipate the co-occurrence of this noun and verb.

Bible verses—These occur in English and Japanese and are introduced to acquaint the native Japanese speaker with the Hebrew-Christian concepts which have molded Western literature and art for centuries. Until Japanese students of English familiarize themselves with Biblical thought, the Western mind, and hence Western literature, will abound with unintelligible phrases and allusions.

2. CLASSIFYING OF ENTRIES UNDER 222 GENERAL THOUGHT CATEGORIES.

These General Thought Categories serve as semantic dividers of our lexical data. Because they are chosen from provinces of life and because human experience may be sliced as thin or as thick as one wishes, these categories are arbitrary. We do not mean to imply that they exhaust the classification options or that all possible entries have been found, but for classifying words and phrases found in our Japanese sources they proved satisfactory. Nearest equivalent Japanese words were found for these larger categories without concern for the characters appearing in these words. The Thought Categories are listed alphabetically in the front of the *Dictionary* both in romanized Japanese and in English, and the *Dictionary* itself is divided alphabetically under these categories from AI (love, #1) to ZOKUAKU (vulgarity, #222).

3. SUBCLASSIFICATION UNDER GENERAL THOUGHT CATEGORIES

Japanese entries related to the Thought Category in meaning—irrespective of Chinese character—are grouped alphabetically under the categories to the far left of each column. English equivalents are listed to the right. These entries are of four types:

(a) *Core words*—Words related to the title word of the Thought Category by meaning but peculiar to themselves. For example, the core words under the Thought Category AI (love) are AI, JŌ, KOI, KOKORO. From these core words other words are derived or phrases are built around them.

(b) *Sense-related words and phrases*—Entries, unrelated by Chinese character to the Thought Category title words or core words but which have a certain sense relationship to the meaning of the Thought Category. They are listed alphabetically between the core words and appear as single entries, though occasionally derived words and phrases appear with them. They are also on the extreme left of each column. For example, some sense-related words and phrases under the category AI, are *chiya hoya suru, furareru, itoshisa o kanjiru.*

(c) *Derived words*—Words related to the core words or sense-related words in meaning and by Chinese character. They are listed alphabetically to the right and below the core words to which they are related. For example, some derived words of the core word

KOI in the category AI are *hatsukoi, koibito, koiwazurai, shitsuren.*

(d) *Phrases built around the above three types*—These are phrases related to the Thought Category in meaning, built around the three types of words listed above, viz., core words, sense-related words, derived words. The phrase consists of the noun to the left and above (indicated by ∼), plus a particle and a verb. For instance, a phrase built around the derived word *aijō* of the core word AI, of the category AI, is *aijō ni oboreru.*

4. METHODS OF ENTRY AND DESIGNATIONS

Nouns—Without designation. No meaning discriminations are given in our presentation for this reason : discriminations have already been made in the source language (Japanese) by a word or phrase being entered under the Thought Category. When a noun is a verbal noun (that is, a noun to which *suru* can be added, thus making it a verbal phrase), *suru* is listed in parentheses and its English equivalent verbal phrase also appears in parentheses.

Verbs—Without designation, in the neutral form. " One's " or " one " is often given in the English equivalent. When the equivalent English verb takes a particular preposition (fixed by usage), this preposition will be given in brackets unless it is used with that verb in all cases.

Adjectives—Japanese descriptive words are not technically adjectives. They are called adjectives for convenience, but there is no formal correspondence with English adjectives. Descriptive words which inflect we shall call verbal adjectives. They are listed without designation. This means they may be inflected, e.g., *samui, samuku, samukereba, samukatta,* etc. If the adjective precedes a noun, it may be used just as it appears on the English side. If it is inflected in Japanese, corresponding helping verbs, such as " is ", " was ", must precede the adjective in English. The other type of descriptive word is the noun-adjective, such as *yūryoku* or *kirei.* *Yūryoku* is similar to a noun in its form but never appears with such particles as *wa* or *ga*. *Na* (or *no*) makes it adjectival, e.g., *yūryoku na hito* (influential person) ; *ni* makes it adverbial ; *da* makes it a predicate adjective. These noun-adjectives cannot be inflected as the verbal adjectives. They are designated by *da*. The English equivalents will be either the adjectival translation or both the noun and adjectival forms, the latter being marked off by parentheses.

Colloquial expressions—Designated by [c]. When an English slang expression renders the Japanese phrase, it is designated [s]. We have eliminated slang and vulgarisms from the Japanese entries.

Proverbial expressions—Designated by [P]. When an equivalent English proverb is given, it is also designated by [P]. Where no English proverb could be found, the nearest equivalent English phrase is listed without designation.

Bible verses—Designated by the Biblical reference, including chapter and verse. Those appearing at the end of each category give the Biblical view of the category.

English translations—Where one-to-one correspondence occurs and equivalent usage can be anticipated, no English sentences are given as examples. Usually context can be ascertained by checking the source language entry. If the user will keep in mind what Thought Category he is in and consider the context in which the source language entry is usually found, he will be safe in using the target language entry in the same context. However, since most colloquial, idiomatic, and proverbial expressions are difficult to use in context, English equivalent sentences appear with these three types of entries (except in some cases of single-word entries.) Only those words in italics are directly related to the Japanese counterpart, but the sentences themselves have been chosen to convey a common contextual setting. For verb renderings in English, we have found that the past tense lends itself to sentences more easily; thus tense correspondence with the source language (Japanese) is not maintained.

General Japanese Index—Core words, sense-related words and phrases, and derived nouns—the first three types of entries discussed above are the only ones found in the General Japanese Index. Numerals indicate where the entry may be found: 144.2 means that the entry will be found on the second column of page 144.

Miscellaneous—[L] designates a word or phrase not normally spoken but employed in the written style. No pronunciation aids are given. ～ designates an omission; the noun to which it refers is found above and to the immediate left. Parentheses are used to designate an alternative form which can be used interchangeably with the word or phrase immediately preceding it. Particles within brackets mean that the word following usually takes the particle included in the brackets: [. . . ni] fureru. Words which show the context of a word are also given in brackets: execution [of a plan]. Numbers at the bottom of each category refer the user to related Thought Categories. Long vowels have macrons over them: ō, ū, etc. Double consonants stand for assimilated sounds: *akka, itta,* etc. ' is put after n when n closes a syllable: *an'i.* Words or phrases which have an antonymic relation to the Thought Category appear without designation.

HOW TO USE THE DICTIONARY

How to find an idiomatic equivalent in Japanese
Assume you wish to find the Japanese idiomatic equivalent of the English phrase " to come down to earth."

1. You have already used English as the source language in thinking of the phrase. Now think of the general idea the phrase conveys. Is it related to "truth," "reality?"

2. "Reality" seems closer. Turn to Reality in the English-Japanese Thought Categories List. Reality is Category 41.

3. Run down the English entries under REALITY, page 50. Soon you come across "come down to earth." To the left you find the Japanese equivalent *genjitsu ni modoru.*

4. Compose your sentence. "He was hoping to go abroad but has come down to earth and given up the plan." *Kare wa kaigai ryokō o shiyo to omoi tatta ga, genjitsu ni modotte, sono keikaku o yameta.*

5. Thus we move in this order:
General English Thought—Specific English Thought—Actual Japanese Expression

How to familiarize yourself with the use and selection of Japanese idioms

1. Become familiar with the 222 General Thought Categories so that you know the range of expressions to be covered.

2. Attempt to read over one new category every day.

3. Keep the English equivalents in mind. If you can use a particular English expression in its given context, then feel safe in using the Japanese entry likewise.

4. Study the use of particles.

5. Try composing a Japanese sentence, either patterning it

after the English model sentence or actually translating the English sentence into Japanese.

6. Check your sentence with a Japanese speaker to make sure you are correctly using particles, verbal inflections, contexts, etc.

ACKNOWLEDGMENTS

WITHOUT the sacrificial help of many friends and scholars this *Dictionary* could not have been completed. In addition to my associate editors, whose names appear on the title page, my deep appreciation goes also to Miss Kimiko Takahara, Associate Professor of Japanese Language, U.C.L.A., Dept. of Oriental Languages (1964–1965) for hammering out a sound linguistic basis for presenting the lexical data, to Donald Boone of Encyclopedia Britannica (Japan), for his painstaking editorial labors and sound advice, to Toshi Imai, for bringing his bilingual genius to bear on matching Japanese-English equivalents, to Mrs. Lincoln Saito, for checking Japanese entries, to Misses Kobayashi and Gunji, for transcribing romaji entries into Japanese, to Miss Marjorie Bower of Christian Academy in Japan and Mr. Kurt Ribi for proofreading, to Terataka Yakuwa for his pioneering research, and finally to the Christian university students of Tyrannus Hall for their enthusiastic help right from the beginning of the project.

CHARLES CORWIN, *General Editor*
Tokyo, 1968

ま え が き

　この辞典は，私たちが日ごろ使いなれている日本語の知識をもと
にして，自分の気持ちにピッタリ合った「生きた」英語の使い方を知
り，また相手の心をとらえる適切な表現がすぐ引用できるように，
数年間にわたる日米の言語学の専門家たちの努力によって完成され
た，これまでにない画期的な辞典です。

　とくに英語の実力が一目でわかる英会話，英文の手紙，英作文な
どで，すぐ役にたつ「生きた」英語を，もっとも効果的に学んでみ
ようという人たちに，ひろくおすすめします。

　この本は私たちが常時これを読み，暗記し，利用することによっ
て，「英語のイディオムの正しい使い方」また「文章の構成」に親し
むことができるいままでにない独特な辞典といえるでしょう。英会
話や，実用英語に強くなるため，多くの学生や，海外交流の尖端を
ゆく若い商社マンに，広く活用され，より新しく，より適切な英語
の表現が生み出される機縁ともなれば，編者にとって望外の喜びで
あります。

　　　1968 年 3 月　　　　　　　　チャールス・コーウィン

凡 例

語句の種類

単語——名詞，形容詞，副詞，動詞は主として次の三つの観点から取りあげました。

(1) 各カテゴリーの意味の範囲がわかる。

(2) 同義語間の意味のちがいを明らかにする。

(3) 派生語や派生語句を作る核として役立つ。

口語表現——会話とか，文章でも相手に親しみを感じさせる表現。

イディオム表現——語句の文字どおりの意味とはちがった内容の表現。

ことわざ表現——英語国民の見方，考え方をよりよく理解するためのものです。

聖書の引用——英語，日本語のいずれにも出ています。聖書を紹介した大きな目的は，何世紀にもわたって西洋文芸の鋳型となったキリスト教的概念を，日本人の利用者に知っていただきたいからです。西洋の精神または文学の根源を知るためには，聖書の思想に親しまなければなりません。各カテゴリーの最後に聖句をのせたのも，そのカテゴリーに関する概念を知るとともに，日本の思想との比較をも試みていただきたいと願うからです。*The New English Bible* (Oxford University Press, 1961) は聖書本文の意味を美しいイディオムで表現しています。

カテゴリーの分類

本書に収めた約 1 万語は 222 のカテゴリーに分類してあります。各カテゴリーは日常生活を中心に，人生や人間の思想，感情（喜怒哀楽），行動などあらゆる人間的行為の分野から選びました。したがって鉄，羊毛，建物，ラジオ，飛行機など具象的なカテゴリーは意識的にはぶいてあります。カテゴリーの配列は AI (愛, 1) から ZOKUAKU (俗悪, 222) までのアルファベット順とし，索引も巻頭にローマ字と英語でやはりアルファベット順にならべました。

各カテゴリー内の分類

単語，口語表現，イディオム表現，ことわざ表現——これらはその意味内容によって（漢字にかかわりなく）アルファベット順に各欄の左側にならべ，その英訳をつぎに続けてあります。その意味内容には四種類あります。

(1) **中核語**——意味の上から各カテゴリー内の中心となることばであり，主項目として，各欄の左に大文字でアルファベット順にのせました．たとえばカテゴリー AI (愛, 1) に属する中核語は，AI, JŌ, KOI, KOKORO です。

(2) **類義語**——これも主項目として，中核語と中核語の間にアルファベット順に（ただし小文字で）のせました。漢字の上ではカテゴリーの表題語とつねにつながっているとは限りませんが，なんらかの関係があります。類義語は主項目として独立させてはありますが，派生語と同じ性質のものもあります。カテゴリー AI (愛, 1) に属する類義語は，chiyahoya suru, furareru,

itoshisa o kanjiru などです。

　(3)　**派生語**──意味と漢字の上から主項目（中核語と類義語）に従属させ，1 段下げてのせてあります。例として中核語 KOI の派生語は koibito, koiwazurai, shitsuren などです。

　(4)　**上記の3種を中心に組み立てられた語句**──すなわち中核語，類義語，派生語をもとにしてできたことばです。たとえば，中核語 AI の派生語 aijō から発した aijō ni oboreru などで，主項目より2段下げてのせてあります。

　ことわざ表現──ことわざには〔P〕を付け，これに対応する英語のことわざにも〔P〕をつけました。対応する適当な英語のことわざがない時にはふさわしい英文をのせましたが〔P〕はつけてありません。

　聖書の引用──引用した聖句の末尾に（　）の中に引用箇所の章節を示しました。

　英訳──日本語と英語とは一対一で対照させましたが，簡単に英訳できるものは語句にとどめ，文章は示しませんでした。誤った英語の表現をさけるために，日本語で示した状況にご注意ください。ただし，口語表現，イディオム表現，ことわざ表現などでは状況を示しにくいので，ふさわしい英文をあげて，日本語がわに対応する部分をイタリックにしました。しかし英文そのものはふつうの文脈をつくるためにえらんだので，時制が日本語といつも対応しているとは限りません。

　日本語総索引──日本語総索引には，中核語，類義語，派生語の3種をのせました。144.1 は 144 ページの左欄，144.2 は同ページの右欄にあることを示します。

　その他──〔L〕は話しことばにはふつう用いられず，書きことばにだけ用いられる文語体，〔c〕は口語体，〔s〕は俗語を示します。発音は表示してありません。〜は省略を意味します。（　）内のことばは，直前の単語や語句と入れかえて用いる場合を表わします。［　］の中の助詞は，次の語がふつう"[…に]ふれる"というように助詞を伴うことを示します。英語の単語の場合には execution [of a plan] のように［　］でその単語の用法を示しました。カテゴリーと反意語の関係にある語句もあわせてのせてある場合もありますが，記号は付けませんでした。

活　用　法

イディオムに習熟するために
　1.　毎日一つずつ新しいカテゴリーを通読し，特に英語の文章全体を記憶すること。
　2.　対応する日本語を心にとめておくこと。

英語の語句の見つけ方
　日本語の「現実にもどる」という語句に相当する英語の表現を見つけたいとする。
　1.　語句の中の主要な単語は**現実**ということばです。
　2.　カテゴリー表（　）の中の GENJITSU か，日本語総索引の中の**現実**を引く。どちらの索引でもカテゴリー番号 41，GENJITSU—REALITY (50ページ) が出てきます。
　3.　そして簡単に "come down to earth" を見つけることができます。
　4.　時制(tense)や数などを考慮して英文を書く。たとえば，"After talking about that trip abroad, she finally *has come down to earth* and has given up the plan."

JAPANESE-ENGLISH THOUGHT CATEGORIES LIST

ENGLISH-JAPANESE THOUGHT CATEGORIES LIST

APOLOGIA

The editors of the *Dictionary* realize that an undertaking of this sort is open to many omissions and errors. Any suggestions the reader may have to improve the book by way of additions, deletions or corrections will be greatly appreciated. Help us to close the "idiom-gap" between Japanese and English by dropping a postcard to: *Charles Corwin*
Tyrannus Hall
6–2–30 Higashi Fushimi
Hoya-shi
Kitatama-gun
Tokyo

GENERAL THOUGHT CATEGORIES

1 AI 愛 LOVE, AFFECTION

AI (suru) 愛(する) love (love ; be fond of)

~ **ni afureru** ～にあふれる overflow with love

~ **ni mukuiru** ～に報いる He *rewarded* his mother's *love* by taking good care of her when she was old.

~ **ni somuku** ～にそむく betray one's love

~ **no shirushi** ～のしるし token of love ; symbol of love

~ **o eru** ～を得る gain one's love

~ **o isshin ni ukeru** ～を一身に受ける be the sole object of one's love ; monopolize one's love

~ **o sasayakiau** [L] ～をささやきあう The young couple stood under the tree, *speaking words of love.*

~ **o shimesu** ～を示す express one's love ; demonstrate one's love

~ **o tsugeru** ～を告げる tell of one's love [for]

~ **o ubau** ～を奪う steal one's love away [from]

~ **o uchiakeru** ～を打ち明ける She *confessed* her *love for him* while they were walking home.

~ **o ushinau** ～を失う lose one's love [for]

aichaku o kanjiru 愛着を感じる feel an attachment for

~ **o oboeru** をおぼえる be fond of

aidokusha 愛読者 reader ; bibliophile

aijin 愛人 lover

aijō 愛情 affection

~ **ni oboreru** ～におぼれる He *is* so *infatuated with* her that he visits her daily.

~ **o komete** ～をこめて affectionately ; with affection

~ **o motomeru** ～をもとめる crave one's affection

~ **o sasageru** ～をささげる devote one's affection to

~ **o sosogu** ～を注ぐ pour out one's affection on ; shower one with affection

nikushin no aijō 肉親の愛情 parental love

aikō suru 愛好する be fond of ; have a love of [pictures, mountains, etc.]

aikoku no jō ni moeru 愛国の情に燃える *Burning with patriotism*, he led the Satsuma troops into battle.

aikokushin 愛国心 patriotism

aikōsha 愛好者 lover of [books, art, etc.]

aikurushii 愛くるしい charming ; sweet ; cute [baby, etc.]

aiyoku 愛欲 passion

boseiai 母性愛 motherly love

choai (suru) [L] 寵愛する favor ; good graces (grant favor to)

fūfuai 夫婦愛 conjugal love

jiai 慈愛 charity ; merciful love

~ **ni tomu** ～に富む The apostle Peter *was full of compassionate love for* the lame beggar.

jinruiai 人類愛 humanitarian love

keiai (suru) 敬愛(する) love and respect (have love and respect for)

manamusume 愛娘 favorite daughter

mōai 盲愛 blind love

netsuai (suru) (熱愛する) ardent love ; fervent love (love fervently)

on'ai 恩愛 kind affection

seiai 性愛 erotic love

seishinteki ai 精神的愛 platonic love

shin'ai 親愛 affection; dearness

sōai no naka (da) 相愛の仲(だ) They *are in love* with each other.

yūai 友愛 friendship

chiya hoya suru [C] ちやほやする She is quite spoiled because her Dad *pampers* her.

furareru [C] ふられる Alice has been unhappy ever since she *was jilted* by Bob.

hitomebore suru [C] 一目ぼれする He *fell in love with* her *at first sight.*

[...ni] horeru [C] [...に] ほれる I think she has *really fallen for (fallen head over heels in love with)* him.

[...ni] iiyoru [...に] 言い寄る John tried to *woo (court)* Betty, but she was indifferent to him.

itoshigo いとし子 beloved child

itoshisa o kanjiru いとしさを感じる She *was endeared (was close)* to her lame boy.

itsukushimi (mu) いつくしみ(いつくしむ) loving kindness (love compassionately)

JŌ ni moroi 情にもろい Be careful not to upset her; she's *quite emotional (easily swayed by her emotions).*

  ~ no komotta ～のこもった It was a *warm-hearted* letter.

  jōji 情事 love affair; romance

  jōnetsu 情熱 passion; warm affection

  shikijō 色情 carnal lust

kawaigaru かわいがる hold dear; treat kindly; pet

kobonnō (da) 子ぼんのう(だ) He *is crazy about kids (is indulgent with his children).*

KOI (suru) 恋(する) love (between man and woman) (be in love [with])

  hatsukoi 初恋 first love; puppy love

  koibito 恋人 lover; sweetheart; suitor

  koikogareru 恋いこがれる pine away for

  koiwazurai (suru) 恋煩い(する) lovesickness (be lovesick for)

  ren'ai (suru) 恋愛(する) love (be in love; fall in love [with])

  rembo (suru) 恋慕 (する) attachment

(feel an attachment for; be enamored of)

shitsuren (suru) 失恋(する) disappointment in love (be disappointed in love)

KOKORO ga hikareru 心がひかれる one's heart is drawn to

  ~ ga muku ～が向く I don't know why, but she *goes for* (her *heart is set on*) him.

  ~ o yoseru ～を寄せる one's heart warms to; have a crush on

konomi (mu) 好み(好む) liking; fancy (like; have a fancy for)

[...ni] kubittake [C] [...に]首ったけ He *is head over heels in love with* (*is crazy about*) her.

[...ni] me ga nai [...に]目がない My husband *has a weakness for* chocolate cake and always eats too much.

  ~ ni irete mo itakunai ～に入れても痛くない Tad could enter Lincoln's office any time, for he was *the apple of his* father's *eye.*

misomeru 見そめる love one at first sight; be captivated at first sight

natsukashii なつかしい beloved; longed for

[...o] nikukarazu omou [...を] 憎からず思う I *have taken a liking to* her.

[...ni] omoi o yoseru [...に] 思いを寄せる have a crush on

  kata omoi 片思い Abe was sad over his *unrequited love (one-sided love)* for Mary Owens.

shitau 慕う long for; yearn for

shūchaku (shūjaku) 執着 attachment

Sumeba miyako [P] 住めば都 *Once I get accustomed to it, any place is good to live in.*

tsurenai つれない cold hearted; indifferent

[...ni] utsutsu o nukashite iru [...に] うつつを抜かしている He *is crazy about* jazz. She *is nuts about* him.

yoromeku [c] よろめく She is suing for divorce because he *has been unfaithful* (*has committed an act of infidelity*). ⇨ 212

私たちが神を愛したのではなく，神が私たちを愛し，私たちの罪のために，なだめの供物としての御子を遣わされました．ここに愛があるのです．　（ヨハネ I 4 ¹⁰)

2　AKIRAME あきらめ
RESIGNATION

AISŌ ga tsukiru あいそうが尽きる Because of his careless ways she *became disenchanted* with him.

　~ o tsukusu ~ を尽くす I tried to help him stop drinking but finally *became disgusted* (*got fed up with him*; *gave it up as a bad job*).

AKIRAME (**ru**) あきらめ(あきらめる) resignation (resign oneself [to]; give up)

　~ ga ii ~ がいい He will take the disappointment all right because he *has learned to accept situations* (*knows when to quit; knows when he's whipped*).

　~ ga tsukanai ~ がつかない She *cannot resign* herself *to* the fact that her husband has cancer.

　fuun to akirameru 不運とあきらめる He lost his wallet on the train but *dismissed it as bad luck*.

dannen (**suru**) 断念(する) despair (despair [of]; abandon; give up)

　kannen (**suru**) 観念(する) resolution (resign oneself to)

MIKIRI (**ru**) 見切り(見切る) forsaking (forsake; cut relations with)

　~ o tsukeru ~ をつける After failing three times, I *gave up* trying to enter Tokyo University.

　mikagiru 見限る forsake; give up

　misuteru 見捨てる desert; turn one's back on

omoikiri (**ru**) 思い切り(思い切る) giving up (give up; relinquish)

　~ ga warui ~ が悪い He *was a bad loser* and kept arguing with the referee.

　~ ga yoi ~ が良い The umpire made a bad decision, but Suzuki *was a good loser* (*took it in stride*).

[...ni] miren ga aru [...に] 未練がある He was forced to retire but still *had a longing for* the classroom.

　~ ga nai ~ がない I left Tokyo for the country *without any regrets*.

Nagai mono ni wa makarero [P] 長いものには巻かれろ Give way to the strong.　Yield to the inevitable.

omoitodomaru 思いとどまる put out of one's mind; drop from one's thinking

oteage suru お手上げする I tried to reason with him but finally *threw up my hands* (*gave it up*).

saji o nageru さじをなげる I tried to teach him English but finally *threw up my hands*.

shikata ga nai しかたがない it can't be helped; there's no way out

　shiyō ga nai しようがない there's no way out

shinde mo shinikirenai 死んでも死にきれない Some suggested Lincoln resign, but he *felt he could not quit* until the Union was restored.

un o ten ni makaseru 運を天に任せる He was worried about passing the exam, but I told him to *do his best and leave the matter*. ⇨ 182, 190

私たちは非常に激しい，耐えられないほどの圧迫を受け，ついにいのちさえも危くなり，ほんとうに自分の心の中で死を覚悟しました．これはもはや自分自身を頼まず死者をよみがえらせてくださる神により頼む者となるためでした．　（コリント II 1 ⁸, ⁹)

3 AKU 悪 EVIL

AKU 悪 evil

- **~ ni makeru** ~ に負ける Do not let *evil conquer* you, but use good to defeat evil. (Romans 12:21)
- **~ ni ochiiru** ~ に陥る lapse into evil; fall into sin; go wrong
- **~ ni somaru** ~ に染まる be infected with evil; be contaminated by evil; sink into vice
- **~ no chimata** ~ のちまた skid row
- **~ o issō suru** ~ を一掃する The mayor pledged to use every means to *root out evil* (*eradicate evil*) from the labor unions.

akka suru 悪化する deteriorate; get worse; worsen; go from bad to worse

akkanjō o idaku 悪感情をいだく harbor ill feelings towards; there is bad blood between [them]; feel animosity towards

akkō o iu 悪口を言う revile

akudō 悪童 naughty boy

akueikyō o oyobosu 悪影響を及ぼす I believe that the general run of movies *has a bad influence on* youth.

akufū 悪風 bad custom; evil practice

akugyō 悪行 misdeed

akuhei o kuitomeru 悪弊を食い止める check evil [influences]; put a stop to the evil

akuheki 悪癖 vice; bad habit

akui 悪意 malice

- **~ kara suru** ~ からする do for spite; do out of malice
- **~ ni kaisuru** ~ に解する take [it] the wrong way
- **~ o idaku** ~ をいだく harbor ill feelings; bear ill will [against]

akuji 悪事 evil deed

- **~ ni fukeru** ~ にふける indulge in vice; give oneself over to evil
- **~ o hataraku** ~ を働く work evil; commit an evil deed
- **~ o kasaneru** ~ を重ねる commit one crime after another
- **~ o okonau** ~ を行なう practice evil; commit evil
- **~ senri o hashiru** [P] ~ 千里を走る Evil spreads fast. Ill news travels fast.

akujōken 悪条件 unfavorable conditions

akujunkan 悪循環 vicious circle

akuma 悪魔 devil

akunen [L] 悪念 evil thoughts

akuratsu (da) 悪らつ(だ) unscrupulous

akuryō (akurei) 悪りょう (悪霊) evil spirit of the dead [demon]

- **~ ni toritsukareru** ~ に取りつかれる be possessed by demonic spirits
- **~ ni uchikatsu** ~ に打ち勝つ conquer demons
- **~ o oidasu** ~ を追い出す drive out demons

akushin o okosu 悪心を起こす be taken up with a bad idea

akushitsu (da) 悪質(だ) malicious; wicked

akushū 悪習 bad habit

akutai o tsuku 悪態をつく use abusive language; rail against

akutō 悪党 punk; rascal; scoundrel

akutoku 悪徳 vice

akuyō (suru) 悪用(する) misuse; abuse (misuse; abuse)

akuyū 悪友 bad companion

kyōaku (da) 凶悪(だ) extremely wicked; vicious

saiaku no baai 最悪の場合 *If worse comes to worst*, we can always sell out.

warui 悪い bad; foul; ill

warujie o tsukeru 悪知恵をつける He *put* the child *up to* cheating on the examination.

warumono 悪者 bad "egg"; bad fellow

zaiaku 罪悪 vice

ankokumen 暗黒面 dark side [of life, of society, etc.]

baishun 売春 prostitution

fugi 不義 immorality; infidelity

fusei (da) 不正(だ) injustice (unjust; criminal)

haitoku [L] 背徳 corruption; demoralization

haraguroi 腹黒い evil-hearted; black hearted

heigai 弊害 abuses; evil influences

jadō (da) 邪道(だ) evil way; stray path (improper; unorthodox)

~ **ni ochiiru** ~ に陥る go astray; slip into evil ways

jaaku (da) [L] 邪悪(だ) wickedness (wicked)

kegare (ru) 汚れ(る) defilement (be defiled)

kusare en [C] くされ縁 He has many *evil connections* and cannot break away from the life he is leading.

[...**ni**] **ma ga sasu** [...に] 魔がさす *Something must have possessed him* to rob the school; he had been a model student.

mi o mochikuzusu 身を持ちくずす He began *living a fast life* away from home.

mimochi ga waruku naru 身持ちが悪くなる He *became dissolute* after taking to drink.

Shōjin kankyo shite fuzen o nasu [P] 小人閑居して不善をなす Idleness is the devil's workshop [P].

Shu ni majiwareba, akaku naru [P] 朱に交われば赤くなる One is easily tainted by bad companionships.

Bad company is the ruin of a good character. (I Corinthians 15 : 33)

⇨ **203, 222**

内側から，すなわち，人の心から出て来るものは，悪い考え，不品行，盗み，殺人，姦淫，貪欲，よこしま，欺き，好色，ねたみ，そしり，高ぶり，愚かさであり，こ

れらの悪はみな，内側から出て，人を汚すのです。(マルコ 7 21-23)

4 ANSHIN 安心 PEACE OF MIND, TRANQUILLITY

ANSHIN (suru) 安心 (する) peace of mind; tranquillity (have peace of mind [about]; feel relieved)

~ **saseru** ~ させる set one at ease; relieve one's anxiety

an'i (da) 安易(だ) With that retirement income, she *is living an easy life* (*is well off*).

annon (da) 安穏(だ) tranquil; quiet

anshinkan 安心感 sense of security

goanshin kudasai! ご安心ください Please don't worry about it.

chinchaku (da) 沈着(だ) composure; calmness (composed; calm)

goshimpai naku! ご心配なく Don't worry about it. There's no problem.

HEION (da) 平穏(だ) calmness (calm)

~ **buji (da)** ~ 無事(だ) Because our family lived in a small village, we came through the war *safe and sound*.

heisei 平静 tranquillity; serenity

~ **o torimodosu** ~ を取りもどす recover one's presence of mind

hotto suru ほっとする breathe a sigh of relief

~ **mune o nadeorosu** ~ 胸をなでおろす I *heaved a sigh of relief* when I heard they had found the lost girl.

igokochi ga yoi 居ごこちが良い This room *is* very *comfortable*.

kata ga karuku naru 肩が軽くなる He *felt relieved* when they told him the debt had been paid.

ki o shizumeru 気を静める calm one's feelings

kimochi ga ochitsuku 気持ちが落ち着

〈 When she heard that the children had returned safely, she *regained her composure.*

yuttari shita kimochi ゆったりした気持ち relaxed feeling; comfortable feeling

KOKORO ga hareru 心が晴れる After that hike to the mountains, I *felt refreshed.*

~ **ga yawaragu** ~ が和らぐ The criminal *was touched by* (*was moved by*) the warm letter from our pastor.

~ **jōbu da!** ~ 丈夫だ Now that he's going along on the trip with me, I *feel at ease* about it.

~ **o yurumeru** ~ をゆるめる relax

makura o takaku shite nemuru 枕を高くして眠る sleep peacefully

nodoka (da) のどか(だ) mild; calm

ODAYAKA (da) 穏やか(だ) calm; mild; peaceful

~ **ni hanasu** ~ に話す speak gently

~ **ni kurasu** ~ に暮らす The old couple *lived peacefully* in their mountain cabin.

omoni o orosu 重荷を降ろす *It's a load off my mind* not to have to watch the children in swimming today.

yasuraka (da) 安らか(だ) peaceful; restful

~ **na hi o okuru** ~ な日を送る He is now *quietly spending his days* collecting biological specimens.

⇨ **5, 156**

すべて, 疲れた人, 重荷を負っている人は, わたしのところに来なさい. わたしがあなたがたを休ませてあげます. (マタイ 11 28)

5 ANZEN 安全 SAFETY

ANZEN 安全 safety

~ **daiichi** ~ 第一 safety first

~ **garasu** ~ ガラス safety glass

~ **o ayauku suru** ~ を危うくする endanger; compromise the safety of

~ **o hakaru** ~ をはかる The school *took safety measures* to protect children using buses.

~ **o kisuru tame ni** [L] ~ を期するために to be on the safe side; as a safety measure

kōtsū anzen 交通安全 traffic safety

annei chitsujo o tamotsu [L] 安寧秩序を保つ maintain peace and order

ampi ga kizukawareru 安否が気づかわれる *There is much concern over the safety* of the children.

~ **o tazuneru** ~ を尋ねる I went to the hospital to *find out how* my sick friend *was getting along.*

antei (suru) 安定(する) stability; security (be stable; be secure)

~ **o kaku** ~ を欠く For a period after the war, Japan's economy *lacked stability.*

~ **o tamotsu** ~ を保つ The Yoshida cabinet *maintained* business *stability* by curbing inflation.

banzen (da) 万全(だ) sure; secure; perfect

BŌGO (suru) 防護(する) safeguard; protection (safeguard; protect)

bōgyo (suru) 防御(する) defense (defend)

yobō (suru) 予防(する) prevention; safeguard (prevent; safeguard)

BUJI (da) 無事(だ) safely; without incident

bunan (da) 無難(だ) safe; secure

shinai hō ga bunan da しないほうが無難だ *Play it safe and don't* (*Be on the safe side and don't*) send that letter.

daiji o toru 大事を取る *Be on the safe side* (*Play it safe*) and drive slowly in those narrow streets.

kiki o dassuru 危機を脱する The wounded soldier was running a high fever but *is now past the crisis* (*is now out of the* *woods*).

ōbune ni notta kimochi 大船に乗った気
持ち Since you are helping out, I *feel
secure* in this venture.

otagai no mi no tame ni お互いの身のた
めに for mutual protection...
⇨ 4

わたしは安らかに伏し，また眠ります．主よ，わたしを安
らかにおらせてくださるのは，ただあなただけです．
(詩篇 4 ⁸)

6 APPAKU 圧迫
OPPRESSION

APPAKU (suru) 圧迫(する) oppression
(oppress)
　〜o kuwaeru 〜を加える bring pres-
　sure upon
　〜o ukeru 〜を受ける be tyrannized;
　be under the pressure of
　genron o appaku suru 言論を圧迫す
　る suppress free expression
　tōkyoku no appaku 当局の圧迫 offi-
　cial pressure
appakukan 圧迫感 sense of oppression
assei (suru) 圧制(する) tyranny; despo-
tism (tyrannize; oppress)
atsuryoku 圧力 pressure
attō suru 圧倒する overwhelm; crush
chin'atsu (suru) 鎮圧(する) repression;
subjugation; suppression (repress;
subjugate; suppress)
dan'atsu (suru) 弾圧(する) suppression; oppression (suppress; oppress)
iatsu (suru) 威圧(する) overpowering;
coercion (overpower; coerce)
　〜o kanjiru 〜を感じる The soldier
　felt himself under pressure talking to
　the President, but Lincoln set him
　at ease with a witty joke.
juatsu 重圧 heavy oppression
　〜no moto de aegu 〜の下であえぐ
　The Israelites *sighed under the*

heavy oppression of Pharaoh.

yokuatsu (suru) 抑圧(する) restraint;
suppression; check (restrain; suppress; check)

gyakutai (suru) 虐待(する) cruel treatment (treat cruelly; mistreat)
　〜o ukeru 〜を受ける On his trip down
　the Mississippi River, young Abe
　saw Negro slaves *being mistreated*
　(*being treated cruelly*).

hakugai (suru) 迫害(する) persecution
(persecute)
　[...**no**] 〜**ni au** [...の] 〜にあう The early
　Christians *suffered persecution at the
　hands of* Hideyoshi.

happō fusagari (da) 八方ふさがり(だ) He
tried to get going on that new project,
but *everything was against* him (he *was
shut up on all sides*).

kenryoku ni mono o iwaseru 権力に物
を言わせる He *has been throwing his weight
around* since he became boss.

kuchidome sareru 口止めされる be
silenced

KYŌSEI (suru) 強制(する) coercion;
imposition; forcing (coerce; impose
upon; force one to; constrain one)
　seiyaku o ukeru 制約を受ける Foreign
　trade *is hampered* (*is hindered; is
　restricted*) by all sorts of regulations.
　yokusei (suru) 抑制(する) control;
　repression (control; repress)

obiyakasu 脅かす intimidate; infringe on
the rights of others

ōbō (da) 横暴(だ) tyranny; high-handed-
ness (tyrannical; high-handed)

odosu おどす browbeat; bully

osaeru 押える suppress; stifle

oshitsukeru 押しつける They *forced* (*foist-
ed*) the worst jobs on me.

semeru 責める, 攻める reproach; press for

shimen soka (da) [L] 四面楚歌(だ) In his
ban-the-bomb efforts, he felt that *the
whole world was against him* (he *was*

surrounded by opposition; there was opposition from all sides).

shiitageru しいたげる oppress

SOKUBAKU (suru) 束縛(する)restriction; restraint; bondage (restrict; restrain; bind)

    ~ o dassuru ~ を脱する The Israelites *became free of* Pharaoh's *restraint* and fled from Egypt.

    tachiba ni shibarareru 立場に縛られる The boss *was constrained by his position* so could not discuss it freely with us.

    takabisha ni deru 高飛車に出る act in a high-handed way

    [...no] toriko ni naru [...の] とりこになる Before he knew it, he *became a prisoner of* drink (*became captivated by* drink.)

    tsurushiage (ru) つるしあげ(つるしあげる) kangaroo court (victimize)

    yaridama ni ageru やりだまに上げる The newspapers immediately *victimized* the railway president (*made him the object of their attack*) for the train disaster.

⇨ 185, 220

わたしを人のしえたげからあがなって下さい. そうすればわたしは, あなたのさとしを守ります. (詩篇 119 ¹³⁴)

7 ARASOI 争い
DISPUTE, CONTENTION

ARASOI (u) 争い(争う) dispute; contention (dispute; contend [with])

    ~ ga okoru (shōjiru) ~ が起こる(が生じる) A *dispute arose* between them.

    ~ no moto (tane) ~ のもと (種) bone of contention; seed of trouble

    gakumonjō no arasoi 学問上の争い academic controversy

    habatsu arasoi 派閥争い factional dispute

    hōtei no arasoi 法廷の争い court case; legal dispute

yūretsu o arasou 優劣を争う The English contestants *are struggling for top honors.*

funsō 紛争 dispute; division

iiarasoi (u) 言い争い(言い争う) battle of words; quarrel (have a battle of words [with]; quarrel; argue)

kyōsō (suru) 競争(する) competition; contest (compete [against])

ronsō (suru) 論争 (する) discussion; contention (discuss; contend [with])

sōgi 争議 dispute [labor, etc.]

    ~ o chūsai suru ~ を仲裁する arbitrate a dispute

    gōhōteki sōgi 合法的争議 lawful dispute

    rōshikan no sōgi 労資間の争議 capital-labor dispute

sōten 争点 point of issue

    horitsujō no sōten 法律上の争点 legal issue

tōsō (suru) 闘争(する) struggle; combat (struggle [against]; combat)

bengo (suru) 弁護(する) defense (defend; speak on behalf of)

bunretsu(suru) 分裂(する)schism; disunity (split; have a falling out [with])

    ketsuretsu (suru) 決裂(する) breakdown (be broken off [negotiations, etc.])

    kaidan ga ketsuretsu suru 会談が決裂(する) negotiations break down

chūsai o suru 仲裁をする arbitrate a dispute; settle a dispute

dōshiuchi o suru 同志討ちをする argue among themselves; take different sides; have internal strife

fungi 紛議 dispute; dissension

gotagota [C] ごたごた problems; trouble; wrangling

    ~ o okosu ~ を起こす He is always *causing trouble* (*causing problems*) among his fellow students.

hatairo ga warui 旗色が悪い At first they

were winning, but now *the tide is turning against* the Giants.

herikutsu o iu へりくつを言う quibble; say it for argument's sake

igamiai o tsuzukeru いがみあいを続ける continue a dispute; keep on bickering

iibun ga aru 言い分がある Does the prisoner *have something to say?* Yes, he wants to *give his side of the story.*

inu to saru no aidagara いぬとさるの間柄 Don't put them in the same office; they get along *like cats and dogs.*

iron o dasu 異論を出す During the conference he *brought forward an objection* to the plan.

izakoza いざこざ trouble

  ~ ga taenai ~が絶えない *Petty troubles are never-ending* in that family.

jidan de kaiketsu suru 示談で解決する make a settlement out of court

kattō [L] かっとう dissension; discord; conflict

KENKA (suru) けんか(する) fight; quarrel (fight; quarrel)

  ~ ni hana ga saita ~に花が咲いた A minor difference *developed into a full blown argument.*

  ~ no sobazue o kuu ~のそばづえを食う While watching the fight, I *was struck by one of their blows.*

  ~ no tane o maku ~の種をまく sow seeds of strife

  ~ o fukkakeru ~を吹っかける pick a fight [with]

  ~ o kau ~を買う have it out [with]; go to it

  ~ o shikakeru ~をしかける pick a fight [with]; start a fight

  ~ o uru ~を売る look for a fight; spoil for a fight

kuchigenka o suru 口げんかをする have words with; quarrel

ōgenka 大げんか big row

kōron (suru) 口論(する) dispute (quarrel)

kujō o iu 苦情を言う I *complained to* my neighbor about his noisy dog.

momeru もめる wrangle

  momegoto もめごと trouble; strife; wrangling

mondai o okosu 問題を起こす take issue with

motsure (ru) もつれ(もつれる) tangle; complications (get entangled; get complicated)

naguriai o hajimeru なぐりあいを始める come to blows

naka ni tatte torimotsu 中に立って取り持つ mediate between (two parties); intervene

nakatagai (suru) 仲たがい(する) enmity; dissension among friends; personal rivalry (be at odds with each other; have a falling out with)

rantō 乱闘 free-for-all

rigai ga shōtotsu suru 利害が衝突する have a clash of interests

rikutsuppoi 理屈っぽい argumentative

shiai (suru) 試合(する) match; game (have a match; play a game)

shōbu (suru) 勝負(する) game (play a game; have a match)

  ~ nashi ni owaru ~なしに終わる The *game ended in a draw.*

tairitsu (suru) 対立(する) opposition; antagonism (oppose; be antagonistic [to]; be at odds [with])

tatakai (u) 戦い(戦う) struggle; fight; battle (struggle; fight; battle)

  shinogi o kezutte tatakau しのぎを削って戦う The Giants and the Hawks *were fighting desperately.*

torikumu 取り組む wrestle with [a problem, etc.]

yarikaesu やり返す When he criticized me, I *shot back at him (retorted)* that he was at fault too.

⇨ 44

主のしもべが争ってはいけません． むしろ，すべての人に

優しくし，よく教え，よく忍び，反対する人たちを柔和な心で訓戒しなさい．もしかすると，神は彼らに悔い改めの心を与えて真理を悟らせる．（テモテ II 2 ²⁴, ²⁵）

8 ASA, YORU 朝・夜
MORNING, EVENING

akatsuki 暁 sunrise
akegata 明けがた dawn
ASA 朝 morning
　～ **hayaku** 早く early in the morning
asahi 朝日 morning sun
ashita (asu) あした(あす) tomorrow
ashita [L] 朝 morning
maiasa 毎朝 every morning
sōchō 早朝 early morning
BAN 晩 evening; night
　hitobanjū 一晩じゅう all night long; the whole night
　komban 今晩 this evening; tonight
　myōban 明晩 tomorrow evening
　sakuban 昨晩 last night; yesterday evening
gogo 午後 afternoon; P.M.
　gozen 午前 morning; A.M.
HI 日 sun; day
　～ **ga katamuku** ～が傾く the sun begins to sink; the sun begins to go down
　～ **ga ochiru** ～が落ちる the sun is setting
　～ **ga shizumu** ～が沈む the sun is setting; the sun is going down
　～ **no de** ～の出 sunrise; sunup
　～ **no kurenai uchi ni** ～の暮れないうちに You'd better leave *while it is day* (before the sun goes down).
asatte あさって day after tomorrow
higure 日暮れ sunset; sundown; nightfall
kinō きのう yesterday
myōnichi 明日 tomorrow
nichibotsu 日没 sunset; sundown
ototoi おとつい day before yesterday

sakujitsu 昨日 yesterday
higashi ga shiramu koro 東が白むころ at daybreak
ippaku (suru) 一泊(する) night's lodging (stay overnight)
tasogare たそがれ dusk; twilight
usuguraku naru 薄暗くなる become dusk; grow dim
YORU 夜 evening
　～ **osoku made** ～ おそくまで until late at night
　shūya 終夜 all night
　tetsuya suru 徹夜する [study, work] all night
　yabun 夜分 night-time
　yakan 夜間 night-time; during the night
　yo ga akeru 夜が明ける day breaks
　　～ **ga fukeru** ～ がふける be far into the night
　　～ **o akasu** ～ を明かす stay up all night
　yodōshi 夜通し all night long
　yoi no kuchi (da) よいの口(だ) the night is young; early in the evening
　yonaka 夜中 midnight; middle of the night
YŪBE 夕べ evening; last night
　yūgata 夕方 evening; twilight
　　～ **made ni** ～ までに by evening
　yūgure 夕暮れ dusk; twilight; nightfall
　yūhi o abite iru 夕日を浴びている The bay was *bathed in the evening sun.*
　yūyake 夕焼け evening glow
　yūyami ga semaru 夕やみが迫る dusk gathers
　　～ **ni magirete** に紛れて be lost in the evening darkness

夜はふけて，昼が近づきました．ですから，私たちは，やみのわざを打ち捨てて，光の武具を着けようではありませんか．（ローマ ¹²）

9 AWAREMI あわれみ COMPASSION, MERCY

AWAREMI (mu) あわれみ(あわれむ) compassion; mercy (feel compassion for; have mercy on)

~ **o kōmuru**[L] ~をこうむる ... because I acted ignorantly in unbelief I *was dealt with mercifully;* the grace of our Lord was lavished upon me. (I Timothy 1 : 13, 14)

~ **o kou** を請う beg for mercy; seek pity

~ **o ukeru** ~ を受ける The drummer boy expected to be shot at sunrise, but he *received mercy* from Lincoln.

aware 哀れ sorrow; grief

~ **o moyōsu** ~ を催す Abe *was moved to pity* when he saw the chained slaves in Louisiana.

yo ni mo aware na[L] 世にも哀れな The refugees flowing into Hongkong are in an *extremely pitiable* condition.

awaremubeki mono ga aru あわれむべきものがある be deserving of sympathy

Dōbyō aiawaremu [P] 同病相あわれむ Misery loves company [P].

DŌJŌ (suru) 同情する sympathy (sympathize [with])

~ **ga nai** ~ がない be unsympathetic

~ **ni tayoru** ~ にたよる rely on the sympathy of; be at one's mercy

~ **o atsumeru** ~ を集める arouse sympathy; move to pity

~ **suru yochi ga nai** ~ する余地がない Dr. Wright had shot the Negro officer without reason, so Lincoln could *find no room for sympathy* (*find no grounds for sympathy*).

dōjōshin 同情心 sympathetic feeling

ninjō 人情 human feeling; kindness; warmheartedness

reikoku mujō na hito 冷酷無情な人 cold-blooded person

fubin ni omou ふびんにおもう feel sorry for; feel compassion for

itsukushimi (mu) いつくしみ(いつくしむ) loving kindness (love compassionately)

JIAI 慈愛 mercy; love

hakuai no seishin 博愛の精神 philanthropic spirit

jiaibukai 慈愛深い be full of compassion

jihi 慈悲 pity; mercy

jihishin 慈悲心 benevolence

ningenai 人間愛 humanitarian love; love for people

kaerimiru 顧みる regard; consider; think of

~ **hito mo nai** 人もない He *has been deserted by everyone.* He *has no one to look after him.*

kandaisa 寛大さ clemency; leniency

kawai sō ni omou かわいそうに思う feel sorry for; feel for

kinodoku ni omou 気の毒に思う feel sorry for

kokoro o itameru 心を痛める feel grieved at heart [over]

mendō o miru めんどうをみる look after; take care of; care for

NASAKE 情け pity; compassion

~ **ni hamukau mono nashi** [P] ~ にはむかうものなし Sympathetic love disarms all enmity.

~ **ni hodasareru** ~ にほだされる *Overcome by* Jesus' *compassion,* the cleansed leper threw himself down at his feet and thanked him.

~ **ni sugaru** ~ にすがる live on charity; rely on the sympathy of

~ **o kakeru** ~ をかける be kind to; show mercy toward

onasake de お情けで His grades were too low, but he was graduated *through the kindness* of the teachers.

omoiyari (ru) 思いやり(思いやる) thoughtfulness; consideration (be thoughtful of; consider)

rembin [L] れんびん pity; commiseration

setsunaku omou せつなく思う feel distressed about

⇨ **1, 97, 149**

主は彼の前を過ぎて宣べられた. 主, 主, あわれみあり, めぐみあり, 怒ることおそく, いつくしみと, まこととの豊かなる神 (出エジプト記 34 ⁶)

10   AYAMARI 誤り
ERROR, FAULT

ageashi o toru あげ足を取る The teacher grew angry when the students *tripped him up* on his wording.

AYAMACHI あやまち mistake; error

~ **ni ochiiru** ~ に陥る fall into bad ways

~ **o kurikaesu** ~ をくり返す repeat the same mistake

~ **o okasu** ~ を犯す People often *make mistakes* unintentionally. Boys sometimes *go wrong* without thinking of the consequences.

Hito tare ka ayamachi nakaran [P] 人たれかあやまちなからん To err is human [P].

kashitsu 過失 mistake; error; blunder

AYAMARI (ru) 誤り(誤る) error; fault (make a mistake)

~ **ga nai** ~ がない be free from mistakes

ippo ayamareba 一歩誤れば with one slight mistake

isshō no ayamari 一生の誤り the greatest blunder of one's life

Kōbō mo fude no ayamari [P] 弘法も筆の誤り Even the best make mistakes. Nobody is perfect.

mi o ayamaru 身を誤る Young Abe tasted whiskey but he knew he would *jeopardize himself* through drink.

michi o ayamaru 道を誤る get off on the wrong foot

shōrai o ayamaru 将来を誤る jeopardize one's future

gokai (suru) 誤解(する) misunderstanding (misunderstand; take [it; one] wrong)

gosan 誤算 miscalculation

goyaku (suru) 誤訳(する) mistranslation (mistranslate)

sakugo 錯誤 error; mistake

CHIGAI (u) 違い(違う) mistake (be wrong)

okado chigai (da) お門違い(だ) You're *barking up the wrong tree (knocking at the wrong door)*; I had nothing to do with it.

sore wa chigaimasu! それは違います！ That's wrong!   「guess

kanchigai 勘違い mistaken idea; wrong

kangaechigai (suru) 考え違い(する) misapprehension (have a mistaken impression)

~ **o shite iru** ~ をしている You *are under a wrong impression.*

kokoroechigai o suru 心得違いをする act ill-advisedly; misbehave

kuichigai (u) 食い違い(食い違う) discrepancy; inconsistency (be inconsistent)

machigai (u) まちがい(まちがう) mistake (make a mistake)

yoku aru machigai よくあるまちがい Mispronouncing "L" *is a common mistake.*

mimachigae (u) 見まちがえ(見まちがう) mistaken identity (mistake for someone [something] else)

sujichigai 筋違い absurdity; illogicality

fuchūi 不注意 carelessness; oversight; mistake

FUKAKU 不覚 blunder; defeat

~ **o toru** ~ を取る fail; suffer a defeat

shūsei no fukaku 終生の不覚 tragic error; greatest blunder of one's life

gohei ga aru 語弊がある be misleading (phraseology); be cause for misunderstanding

hema [c] へま You sure made a *mess* of things.

~ **o yaru** ~ をやる upset the applecart; make a mess of things

hi o tadasu 非をただす reprove; set straight

kega no kōmyō けがの功名 He backed away from the ball, but it struck his bat and went for a hit; what a *lucky break* (*fluke*)!

kentō hazure (da) 見当はずれ(だ) His supposition *is off the point* (*is wide of the mark*).

Mi kara deta sabi [P] 身から出たさび A man reaps what he sows.

miso o tsukeru みそをつける You can't leave him alone on the job; he'll *make a mess of it* (*blunder; fumble*) every time.

misokonai (u) 見そこない(見そこなう) mistaken impression (take for someone [something] else)

yarisokonai (u) やりそこない(う) bungle; blunder (bungle; blunder; muff)

OCHIDO おちど fault

~ **no nai** ~ のない be without fault; be faultless

Saru mo ki kara ochiru [P] さるも木から落ちる To err is human [P]. Even the best make mistakes.

[...no] sei ni suru [...の]せいにする lay the blame on

Seite wa koto o shisonjiru [P] せいては事をし損じる Haste makes waste [P].

shikujiri (ru) しくじり(しくじる) blunder (make a blunder; fail)

SHIPPAI (suru) 失敗(する) failure; bungle (fail; bungle; make a mistake)

~ **wa seiko no moto** [P] ~ は成功のもと We learn by trial and error.

shissaku 失策 failure; error

shitsugen (suru) 失言(する) slip of the tongue (put one's foot in one's mouth)

tenukari 手抜かり oversight; slip-up

teochi 手落ち omission; oversight

torikaeshi no tsukanai koto 取り返しのつかない事 To fail to remove the cancer at once would be *an irrevocable error* (*a costly mistake*).

ukkari suru うっかりする forget oneself; slip up

zensha no tetsu o fumu [L] 前車の轍を踏む Don't *repeat the same mistake* as your brother and drop out of school early.

⇨ 203

だれが自分のあやまちを 知ることが できましょうか. どうか, わたしを隠れたとがから解き放ってください. (詩篇 19 ¹²)

11 AZAWARAI あざ笑い RIDICULE

azakeri (ru) あざけり(あざける) scorn; ridicule (scorn; ridicule; deride)

~ **no mato ni naru** ~ の的になる become the target of scorn

AZAWARAI (u) あざわらい(あざわらう) ridicule (ridicule; jeer [at]; scoff at; make fun of)

chōshō (suru) [L] 嘲笑(する) sardonic smile (sneer [at])

~ **o kau** ~ を買う be ridiculed

hana no saki de warau 鼻の先で笑う sneer [at]

monowarai no tane ni naru 物笑いの種になる Lincoln's gaunt frame and stove-pipe hat often made him the *butt of jokes*.

reishō (suru) 冷笑(する) cold sneer (make a wry smile)

seserawarai (u) せせら笑い (せせら笑う) sneer; derision (sneer at; deride; laugh scornfully [at])

baka ni suru ばかにする make a fool of

chakasu ちゃかす They *made fun of* the new girl at the office.

chōrō (suru) 嘲弄(する) ridicule (ridicule; mock; make fun of)

gurō suru 愚弄する make sport of; mock

hana de ashirau 鼻であしらう The wealthy woman *turned up her nose at* the beggar's plea for help.

hiyakasu ひやかす tease; jeer at; make fun of

ijimeru いじめる be hard on

KARAKAU からかう tease; make fun of

  karakai hambun ni からかい半分に jokingly; teasingly; half in fun

moteasobu もてあそぶ make sport of; trifle with

naburu なぶる make fun of; mock; gibe

  naburimono ni suru なぶり物にする make an object of ridicule; poke fun at

⇨ **25, 48, 99**

悪しき者のはかりごとに歩まず，罪人の道にたたず，あざける者の座にすわらぬ人はさいわいである．（詩篇 1 ¹)

12 BI 美 BEAUTY

AIKYŌ 愛きょう attractiveness; charm

  ~ ga aru ~ がある She *is a charming* girl.

  ~ ga nai ~ がない There *is nothing winsome* (*is nothing charming*) about her.

  ~ o furimaku ~ をふりまく At the party, she *spread her charm around* (*was all smiles*).

akanuke shita あかぬけした polished; refined; sharp

beppin [C] べっぴん a belle; a peach; a knockout

BI 美 beauty

  ~ ni utareta ~ に打たれた I *was struck by the beauty of* that girl.

  ~ no tankyū [L] ~ の探求 pursuit of beauty

  ~ o miru me ~ を見る目 an eye for the beautiful

  shinsen na bi 新鮮な美 fresh beauty

  shizen no bi (kan) 自然の美(観) nature's beauty; the beauties of nature

bibō 美ぼう beauty; good looks

  ~ o hokoru ~ を誇る She *is proud of* her *beauty*.

bidan 美談 beautiful story

binanshi 美男子 handsome man

bifū 美風 beautiful custom

bigaku 美学 aesthetics

biganjutsu 美顔術 beauty (facial) treatment

biishiki 美意識 aesthetic sense

bijin 美人 beautiful woman; a beauty

  hyōban no bijin 評判の美人 a recognized beauty

  mizu no shitataru yōna bijin 水のしたたるような美人 She *is a dazzling beauty.*

  zessei no bijin 絶世の美人 a peerless beauty; a real knockout

bijireiku 美辞麗句 flowery words

bijutsu 美術 fine arts

bika (suru) 美化(する) beautification (beautify)

bikan (bikei) 美観(美景) beautiful sight (picturesque scene)

  ~ o kizutsukeru ~ を傷つける mar the scenery; spoil a beautiful view

biteki (da) 美的(だ) aesthetic

  ~ kankaku (kannen) ~ 感覚(観念) sense of beauty

danseibi 男性美 masculine beauty

joseibi 女性美 feminine beauty

keitaibi 形態美 beautiful lines [building, etc.]

utsukushii 美しい beautiful; pretty

  utsukushiku kazatte aru 美しく飾ってある be beautifully decorated

  utsukushiku yosou 美しく装う be beautifully attired

  utsukushisa 美しさ beauty

nan to mo ienai utsukushisa なんとも言えない美しさ indescribable beauty

tatoeyō mo nai utsukushisa たとえようもない美しさ incomparable beauty

gōka (da) 豪華(だ) gorgeousness (gorgeous)

kawaii かわいい cute; sweet; pretty

kebakebashii けばけばしい showy; gaudy; all dolled up

kikishi ni masaru [L] 聞きしにまさる Yellowstone Park *was better than I expected.*

kinsei ga toreta 均整がとれた well proportioned

kirei (da) きれい(だ) pretty; nice; clean

~ **ni mieru** ~に見える look pretty; be lovely to look at

KIRYŌ 器量 facial beauty

~ **ga yoi (warui)** ~が良い(悪い) good looking; attractive (homely)

~ **jiman no musume** ~自慢の娘 nice looking girl

jūnin nami no (kiryō) 十人なみの(器量) ordinary (beauty)

kiryōgonomi 器量好み love of fair looks

kiwadatta mehanadachi きわ立った目鼻立ち extremely beautiful facial features

kōdanshi 好男子 handsome man; fine fellow; lady killer

miharashi ga yoi 見晴らしが良い good view; fine vantage point

miryoku 魅力 appeal; fascination; charm; attractiveness

myōrei no 妙齢の marriageable [girl]

seiso (da) 清素(だ) neat and graceful

sōrei (da) 壮麗(だ) grandeur (grand; imposing)

tansei (da) 端正(だ) decorous; graceful

uruwashii 麗しい lovely; beautiful

wakaku mizumizushii kao 若くみずみずしい顔 youthful and fresh-looking face

あなたがたは，髪を編んだり，金の飾りをつけたり，着物を着飾るような外面的なものでなく，むしろ，柔和で穏やかな霊という朽ちることのないものを持つ，心の中の隠れた人がらを飾りにしなさい。これこそ，神の御前に価値あるものです。（ペテロ I 3 ⁸, ⁴）

13 BINSOKU 敏速
QUICKNESS, HASTE

'A' to iu ma ni 'あっ'と言う間に right away; in an instant; quick as a wink

BINKATSU 敏活 quickness; promptness; alertness

~ **ni shori suru** ~に処理する I hope you *will dispose of* the matter *right away (will deal quickly with* the matter).

binshō 敏しょう alacrity; agility

kibin (da) 機敏(だ) sharp; keen

dashinuke ni iu だしぬけに言う announce suddenly; blurt out

datto no gotoku [L] 脱兎のごとく like a scared rabbit

denkō sekka 電光石火 as quick as lightning

dondon どんどん steadily; rapidly; quickly

hakabakashiku nai はかばかしくない The doctor said she cannot leave the hospital yet because her *progress is slow* (*progress is not good*).

hakadoru はかどる move at a good pace; move with dispatch

hashiru 走る run; dash

idatenbashiri ni 韋駄天走りに [run] as quick as greased lightning

HAYAI 早い quick; fast; speedy

~ **mono gachi** ~者勝ち First come, first served.

hayaku! 早く! Hurry up! Make it snappy!

dekiru dake hayaku できるだけ早く Please do that *as quickly as possible* (*as fast as you can*).

ichihayaku いち早く right away

ichinichi mo hayaku...suru 一日も早く...する We must solve the problem *as quickly as possible (without losing any time)*.

hayameru 早める hasten; hurry one up
ashi o hayameru 足を速める hasten; start hurrying

Hayaoki wa sammon no toku [P] 早起きは三文の得 The early bird catches the worm.

jiki shōsō no kan ga aru 時期尚早の感がある I *feel it is still too premature*.

me ni mo tomaranai hayasa de 目にもとまらない早さで at a speed quicker than the eye can see

sakkyū (ni) 早急(に) urgent; pressing (urgently; immediately)

sassoku 早速 at once; right now; immediately

subayai 素早い quick; agile

tebayai 手早い nimble

tettoribayaku katazukeru 手っ取り早くかたづける It seemed like a hopeless mess, but John *made short work of* it.

hitoiki ni 一息に in one spurt; in one breath

iki tsuku ma mo nai 息つく間もない I've been doing so many things lately that I *haven't had time to breathe*.

ikinari いきなり suddenly; without notice

ikkoku o arasou 一刻を争う There is no time to lose. There is not a minute to spare.

ISOGU 急ぐ hurry; be in haste
Isogaba maware [P] 急がば回れ Make haste slowly. The long way around is often the fastest.

isogaseru 急がせる expedite; hurry one along

isogashii 忙しい busy; in a rush

Isoge! 急げ Hurry up! Shake a leg! Step on it!

Zen wa isoge [P] 善は急げ There's no time like the present. Seize the opportunity to do good.

kinkyū (da) 緊急(だ) urgent
~ sochi ~ 措置 emergency measure

kyū (da) 急(だ) sudden; quick
~ o yōsuru mondai ~ を要する問題 urgent matter; matter requiring haste

kyūsoku (da) 急速(だ) rapid

ōisogi de 大急ぎで in a big hurry

shikyū (da) 至急(だ) prompt; urgent

issoku tobi ni 一足飛びに with one bound; at a bound

itsu no ma ni ka いつのまにか We were talking, and *before we knew it*, the train arrived in Tokyo.

kakeru 駆ける run
kakeashi (da) 駆け足(だ) on the run; on the double
kaketsukeru 駆けつける run up to; hasten to

kanhatsu o irezu ni 間髪を入れずに When the soldiers rushed to kill the old Indian, *without a moment's hesitation* Lincoln jumped to his side.

kibikibi shita kōdō きびきびした行動 spirited action; snappy action

ma mo naku まもなく shortly; soon

miru miru uchi ni 見る見るうちに in the twinkling of an eye; before one's eyes

shiranai uchi ni 知らないうちに before one knows it

SOKUDO 速度 speed; velocity
~ seigen ~ 制限 speed limit
jinsoku 迅速 speediness
kōsoku dōro 高速道路 freeway
sokuryoku 速力 rate; speed; velocity

masshigura ni まっしぐらに in a bee line; at full tilt

mezatoi 目ざとい quick-eyed

sumiyaka (da) すみやか(だ) quick

tachimachi たちまち instantly; in a moment; instantaneously

tadachi ni 直ちに immediately; right away

toki o utsusazu ni 時を移さずに without losing any time

yatsugibaya ni shitsumon suru やつぎばやに質問する During the debate, the students *fired questions one after another at the speaker* (*plied* the speaker *with questions*).

⇨ 102, 187

わたしはあなたの戒めを守るのに，すみやかで，ためらいません。 (詩篇 119 ⁶⁰)

14 BŌKYAKU 忘却
FORGETFULNESS

BŌKYAKU (suru) 忘却(する) forgetfulness (forget)

dowasure (suru) ど忘れ(する) lapse of memory (have a lapse of memory; [it] slips one's mind for the moment)

kenbōshō 健忘症 absent-mindedness; amnesia; forgetfulness

monowasure (suru) 物忘れ(する) forgetfulness (be forgetful)

okiwasureru 置き忘れる forget; leave behind

wasuremono 忘れ物 something forgotten; lost article

wasureppoi (wasuregachi no) 忘れっぽい (忘れがちの) forgetful; absent-minded

wasureru 忘れる forget

  kirei ni wasureru きれいに忘れる completely forget; [it] completely slips one's mind

  nete mo samete mo wasurenai 寝てもさめても忘れない I *can't get* that horrid accident *out of my mind.*

  Nodo moto sugireba atsusa o wasureru [P] のどもとすぎれば熱さを忘れる Danger past, vows forgotten.

  sappari to wasureru さっぱりと忘れる completely forget about [it]

  sukkari wasureru すっかり忘れる I

forgot all about that engagement.

tō ni wasurareta とうに忘られた My experiences as a child are *long forgotten.*

torimagirete wasureru 取り紛れて忘れる I *got involved* with little details *and forgot* to make the hotel reservations.

ukkari wasureru うっかり忘れる It *slipped* my *mind.*

usa o wasureru うさを忘れる He went out to the mountains and tried to *forget his troubles* (*drown his cares*).

ware o wasurete 我を忘れて Seeing the girl go under, the mother *forgot herself* and jumped into the swirling flood waters.

wasurenai uchi ni 忘れないうちに *Before I forget*, let me give you his telephone number.

wasurenai yōni suru 忘れないようにする keep in mind; try not to forget

wasurerarenai hito 忘れられない人 unforgettable person

wasureta koro ni 忘れたころに Trouble knocks at the door *when least* expected.

wasurete wa naranai 忘れてはならない We *mustn't lose sight of the fact* that economics and diplomacy are related.

zengo o wasurete 前後を忘れて *Being completely engrossed* in the game, I played without taking a break.

iiotosu 言い落とす forget to mention; leave [something] out

otoshimono 落とし物 lost article

kioku ga nai 記憶がない I *have no recollection* of seeing him there.

~ sōshitsu ~ 喪失 loss of memory

mizu ni nagasu 水に流す You were in the wrong, but *let's let bygones be bygones* (*let's forget it*).

nentō o hanarenai 念頭を離れない The *memory* of those pathetic children *never left* him. The *memory* of those pathetic children *was ever present with* him.

shitsunen suru [L] 失念する forget; let [something] slip one's mind

oboe ga nai 覚えがない have no memory of

monooboe ga warui 物覚えが悪い have a poor memory; be forgetful

Saru mono hibi ni utoshi [P] 去る者日々にうとし Out of sight, out of mind.

⇨ 147

兄弟たちよ，私は，自分はすでに捕えたなどと考えてはいません．ただ，この一事に励んでいます．すなわち，うしろのものを忘れ，ひたむきに前のものに向かって進み，キリスト・イエスにおいて上に召してくださる神の栄冠を得るために，目標を目ざして一心に走っているのです．（ピリピ 3 ¹³, ¹⁴）

15 BŌRYOKU 暴力
VIOLENCE

BŌRYOKU 暴力 violence

~ kōi ~行為 terrorism; act of violence

~ ni sarasareru ~にさらされる be wide open to violence; be exposed to violence

~ ni uttaeru ~に訴える No country should *resort to violence* in achieving its goals.

~ ni yotte ~によって by force; by strong-arm methods

~ o furuu ~を奮う use violence; employ violence

~ shudan ~手段 strong-arm methods

abaredasu あばれ出す go wild; run wild

abaremono あばれ者 rowdy

bōdo 暴動 riot; disturbance; violence

~ o okosu ~を起こす raise a riot; cause an uproar

bōfū 暴風 storm

bōgen 暴言 abusive language

bōkan 暴漢 hoodlum

bōkō (suru) 暴行(する) act of violence; outrage (molest)

~ o kuwaeru ~を加える do violence to; commit an outrage [against]; molest [a girl]

gokuaku hidō na bōkō 極悪非道な暴行 *Horrible atrocities* were committed at the Jewish extermination camps.

bōkun 暴君 tyrant

bōkyo 暴挙 violence; disturbance

bōryokudan (gurentai) 暴力団(愚連隊) gangsters; terrorist group

bōto 暴徒 rioters; insurgents

buryoku 武力 force; military power

~ ni kussuru [L] ~に屈する We must not *yield to the military might* of the aggressor.

~ ni uttaeru ~に訴える resort to military might

chikarazuku de 力ずくで by sheer force

rambō (suru) 乱暴(する) violence; rudeness (be rough)

~ ni atsukau ~に扱う The police were criticized for *manhandling* the demonstrators (*handling* the demonstrators *roughly*).

rannyū (suru) [L] 乱入(する) intrusion (intrude; trespass)

rantō 乱闘 free-for-all

wanryoku (de) 腕力(で) by brute force; by brawn

~ ni uttaeru ~に訴える resort to physical force

fundari kettari suru 踏んだりけったりする kick and trample; manhandle

kigai 危害 personal harm

~ o ukeru ~を受ける suffer personal loss

mōi o furuu [L] 猛威を奮う The typhoon *wrought havoc* everywhere.

naguru なぐる strike; punch

ryakudatsu (suru) 略奪(する) plundering (plunder; ransack)

sonshitsu o kōmuru 損失をこうむる suffer loss; undergo loss

teara na koto o suru 手荒な事をする rough up; manhandle

~**na toriatsukai** ~な取り扱い rough physical treatment

tero テロ terrorism

udezuku de (mo) 腕ずくで(も) (even) by strong-arm methods

⇨ 172

...イエスは彼に言われた.「剣をもとに納めなさい. 剣を取る者はみな剣で滅びます...」(マタイ 26 ⁵²)

16 BUNKA 文化 CULTURE

BUNKA 文化 culture

~**dantai** ~団体 cultural organization

~**ga shintō suru** ~が浸透する Buddhist *culture has permeated* Japan.

~**ga susumu** ~が進む be culturally advanced

~**kaihatsu** ~開発 development of culture

~**kesshō** ~結晶 fruit of culture

~**kokka** ~国家 advanced nation; civilized country

~**no hattatsu (hatten)** ~の発達(発展) cultural development

~**o fukyū suru** ~を普及する diffuse culture

~**seikatsu** ~生活 cultural life; modern way of life

~**no shimpo ni kōken suru** ~の進歩に貢献する Fukuzawa *contributed* much *to* Japan's *cultural advance* during the Meiji era.

atarashii bunka o moriageru 新しい文化を盛り上げる stimulate a new culture

genshi bunka 原始文化 primeval culture; primitive culture

kaigai bunka o toriireru 海外文化を取り入れる The "kaikoku" faction wanted Japan to *adopt foreign culture*.

mikai bunka 未開文化 barbaric culture

sekai no bunka kara torinokosareru 世界の文化から取り残される lag behind the times; be out of touch with the times

bunkajin 文化人 civilized person; cultured man

bunkasai 文化祭 cultural festival

bunkateki isan 文化的遺産 cultural inheritance; cultural monument

~**ni tachiokureru** ~に立ちおくれる be culturally retarded; trail behind culturally

bunkazai 文化財 cultural property; cultural heritage

bunkyō 文教 culture and education

bummei 文明 civilization

~**no riki** ~の利器 modern conveniences

busshitsu bummei 物質文明 materialistic age

kikai bummei 機械文明 machine age

Seiyō (Tōyō) bummei (bunka) 西洋(東洋)文明(文化) Western (Oriental) civilization (culture)

senshinkoku no bummei 先進国の文明 culture of advanced nations

hirakeru 開ける open up; become modernized; become civilized

jidai okure (da) 時代遅れ(だ) obsolescence (obsolete; out of date; outdated; outmoded)

~**sakugo** ~錯誤 anachronism

kōshinkoku 後進国 backward nation; underdeveloped country

kyōyō 教養 culture; education; refinement

~ **no aru** ~ のある cultured; educated; refined

~ **no hikui hito** ~ の低い人 uncultured person

seishin shūyō 精神修養 mental training

mikaihatsu chiiki 未開発地域 undeveloped area; backward region

yaban na jōtai o dassuru 野蛮な状態を脱する emerge from savagery

    yabanjin 野蛮人 savage

⇨ 133

正義は国を高くし，罪は民をはずかしめる．
(箴言 14 ³⁴)

17 BYŌKI 病気 SICKNESS

See Medical List, page 261

BYŌKI 病気 sickness

~ **ga omoi** ~ が重い be seriously sick; be dangerously ill

~ **ni naru** ~ になる get sick; become ill

~ **o naosu** ~ を直す make one well; heal the sickness

~ **o suru** ~ をする get sick; be sick

etai no shirenai byōki えたいの知れない病気 disease of an unknown origin; sickness of an unknown cause

byōin 病院 hospital

~ **ni kayou** ~ に通う She *is going to the hospital regularly* for treatments.

byōjō 病状 condition of the illness

~ **ga akka suru** ~ が悪化する condition worsens; take a turn for the worse

~ **ga susumu** ~ が進む condition gets worse

~ **ga tsunoru** ~ がつのる take a turn for the worse

~ **ga waruku naru** ~ が悪くなる condition gets bad

byōkon o kiritoru 病根を切り取る remove the cause of sickness

byōmei 病名 type of illness; name of a disease

byōnin 病人 sick person; the sick

    hinshi no byōnin ひん死の病人 person critically ill; dying person

byōsei 病勢 condition of the patient

byōshō 病症 nature of a disease

byōteki (da) 病的(だ) abnormal

densenbyō 伝染病 contagious disease; epidemic

ekibyō 疫病 epidemic

idenbyō 遺伝病 hereditary disease

jūbyō 重病 serious illness

~ **ni kakaru** ~ にかかる become dangerously ill; become critically ill

ryūkōbyō 流行病 epidemic

seishinbyō 精神病 mental illness

[nagai] tōbyō seikatsu [長い]闘病生活 [long] bout with sickness

chiryō (suru) 治療(する) treatment; medication (treat)

chinō shōgai 知能障害 mental retardation

chōkō 徴候 symptoms

chokusetsu densen 直接伝染 contagious disease

chūsha 注射 shot; injection

    chūshaki 注射器 syringe

    chūshabari 注射針 needle

fushō 負傷 injury

gen'in ga wakaranai 原因がわからない We still *don't know the root of* the trouble.

~ **ga fumei** ~ が不明 cause [of the sickness] is not clear

hōtai (suru) 包帯(する) bandage; dressing (bandage; dress)

ijō (da) 異常(だ) abnormal

    seijō (da) 正常(だ) normal

isha 医者 physician; doctor

    ganka'i 眼科医 oculist

    geka'i 外科医 surgeon

    haisha 歯医者 dentist

    ishi 医師 doctor

    meisha 目医者 eye doctor

shika'i 歯科医 dentist
jūtai (da) 重態(だ) serious condition (seriously ill)
kango (suru) 看護(する) nursing (nurse; care for)
  fuchō 婦長 chief nurse
  kangofu 看護婦 nurse
kanja 患者 patient
  gairai kanja 外来患者 outpatient
  nyūin kanja 入院患者 inpatient
kansetsu densen 間接伝染 infectious disease
kaze かぜ cold
  ~ ga hayaru ~ がはやる colds are prevalent
  ~ o hiku ~ をひく catch cold
kenkō o gaisuru 健康を害する injure one's health
  fukenkō na jōtai 不健康な状態 unhealthy condition
kibun ga sugurenai 気分がすぐれない be indisposed; feel bad; do not feel good
kitoku jōtai (da) 危篤状態(だ) be in a critical condition; be on the critical list
KUSURI 薬 medicine; medication
  ~ o nomu ~ を飲む take medicine
  kusuriya 薬屋 pharmacy
  yakkyoku 薬局 pharmacy; drug store
kyūsei (da) 急性(だ) acute
  kyūkyūbako 救急箱 first-aid kit
  kyūkyūsha 急救車 ambulance
mansei (da) 慢性(だ) chronic
mune o yarareru 胸をやられる be down with t.b.
naoru 直る get well; heal; be cured of
  naosu 直す cure; make well
NETSU 熱 fever; temperature
  ~ ga aru がある have a temperature; have a fever
  ~ ga deru ~ が出る have a temperature
  ~ o dasu ~ を出す run a temperature; have a fever
  hatsunetsu suru 発熱する come down with a fever

nyūin (suru) 入院(する) admission to a hospital (enter a hospital)
seki ga deru せきが出る have a cough; cough
SHINDAN (suru) 診断(する) diagnosis (diagnose)
  ~ o ayamaru ~ を誤る make a wrong diagnosis
  goshin (suru) 誤診(する) wrong diagnosis (make a wrong diagnosis)
  ōshin (suru) 往診(する) doctor's call (make a call)
  shindansho 診断書 medical certificate
  shinsatsu (suru) 診察(する) medical examination; consultation (examine)
  shinryōjo 診療所 dispensary
rinshō kensa 臨床検査 clinical investigation
shintai kensa 身体検査 physical examination
shohōsen 処方箋 prescription
shujutsu (suru) 手術(する) surgery; operation (operate)
  ~ o ukeru ~ を受ける go into surgery; be operated on
taionkei 体温計 clinical thermometer; thermometer
taiin (suru) 退院(する) release from a hospital (leave the hospital)
toko ni fuseru 床に伏せる go to bed
wazurai (u) わずらい(わずらう) illness; malady; sickness (suffer from a sickness)
yamai 病 illness; sickness
  fuji no yamai 不治の病 incurable disease
yamitsuku 病みつく get sick; be taken ill
[...ni] yarareru [...に]やられる be attacked [by]; be taken ill [with]
⇒ 211
...「彼が 私たちのわずらいを身に引き受け，私たちの病を背負った.」（マタイ 8 ¹⁷）

18　CHIE 知恵 WISDOM

ATAMA ga ii [hito] 頭がいい[人] smart; intelligent [person]

~ **no kaiten ga hayai** [c] 〜の回転が早い That young engineer is *quick-witted* (*a fast thinker*).

~ **no kireru [hito]** [c] 〜の切れる[人] At New Salem, Lincoln won many law cases because he was *a sharp thinker*.

~ **no saeta [hito]** 〜のさえた[人] clear-headed [person]

CHIE ga tsuku 知恵がつく The mother rejoiced when her little boy first *showed signs of intelligence*.

~ **no aru [hito]** 〜のある[人] wise [person]; intelligent [person]

~ **no nai [hito]** 〜のない[人] unwise [person], unintelligent [person]

~ **o kariru** 〜を借りる seek advice

~ **o kasu** 〜を貸す give advice

~ **o shiboru** [c] 〜をしぼる The authorities *racked their brains* for means to solve the Tokyo traffic problem.

~ **o tsukeru** 〜をつける He *gave* me *a hint* and I was able to solve the problem. Some comic books *give* children wrong *ideas*.

Sannin yoreba, Monju no chie [P] 三人寄れば文珠の知恵 Two heads are better than one [P].

chinō 知能 intelligence

~ **kensa (shisū)** 〜検査(指数) I.Q. (=Intelligence Quotient) test (I.Q.)

chiryoku 知力 mental capacity

chisei 知性 intellect

chiteki (da) 知的だ intellectual

Ichi o kiite, jū o shiru [P] 一を聞いて十を知る Given a part, he grasps the whole.

kichi 機知 wit; resourcefulness

~ **ni tomu** 〜に富む full of wit;

keen; sharp

monoshiri (da) 物知り(だ) He *is well informed* (*seems to know everything; is up on things*)

monoshirigao ni [c] 物知り顔に *With a wise look*, he held up the book to the professor.

richiteki (da) 理知的(だ) intellectual

sarujie さる知恵 shallow cunning; craftiness

tonchi とんち wit

warujie 悪知恵 cunning guile

funbetsu 分別 discretion

JŌSHIKI 常識 To pay him for his services is just *common sense*. Such a simple fact is *common knowledge* among students.

~ **ga aru** 〜がある have common sense; have horse sense

~ **o kaku** 〜を欠く lack common sense

hijōshiki (da) 非常識(だ) absurd; unreasonable; lacking in common sense

kashikoi 賢い clever; wise

warugashikoi 悪賢い crafty; wily; unscrupulous

KEMMEI (da) 賢明(だ) wise; judicious

senken no mei ga aru 先賢の明がある He *has insight into the future*.

sōmei (da) そうめい(だ) sagacious

KITEN 気転 tact; sharp-wittedness

~ **ga kiku** 〜がきく quick witted; tactful; have presence of mind

~ **o kikasu** 〜をきかす It was a difficult situation, but John *used his head on* (*applied his wits to*) the problem.

monowakari ga ii 物分かりがいい sensible; reasonable; understanding; rational

Nō aru taka wa tsume o kakusu [P] 能あるたかはつめを隠す A truly capable man does not flaunt his abilities.

nōmiso ga tarinai [c] 脳みそが足りない The foolish way he acts shows he is

short on gray matter (a simpleton).
nukeme no nai hito 抜け目のない人 a
shrewd man; a clever person
rikō (da) りこう(だ) clever; smart
SAICHI [L] 才知 wit
    saiki kampatsu no hito 才気煥発の人
    man of brilliant talent
    sainō 才能 ability; talent
    saishi 才子 clever man; talented person
satoi さとい sharp; smart; quick
    Zen ni satoku, aku ni utoi [P] 善にさ
    とく悪にうとい I hope when you grow
    up you will be *alert toward goodness*
    but ignorant of evil.
shiryobukai 思慮深い prudent
zunō 頭脳 brains
    ~meiseki (da) ~ 明晰(だ) brilliant;
    clearheaded
⇨ **21, 155**
事実、この世が自分の知恵によって神を知ることがない
のは、神の知恵によるのです。それゆえ、神はみこころに
よって、宣教のことばの愚かさを通して、信じる者を救
おうと定められたのです。(コリント I 1 ²¹)

19 CHIKARA 力
POWER, STRENGTH

CHIKARA 力 power; strength
    ~ga hakuchu suru ~ が伯仲する
    The two teams *are evenly matched.*
    ~ga minagiru ~ がみなぎる be full of
    vigor
    ~ga nukeru ~ が抜ける I carried that
    bag all the way from the station;
    my *strength is gone.*
    ~ga tsuku ~ がつく By studying on
    the side Abe *became* more *proficient*
    in mathematics.
    ~ippai ni ~ いっぱいに He pushed the
    car *with all his strength (with every-*
    thing he had).
    [...ni] ~ kobu o ireru [...に] ~ こぶを
    入れる The government *is laying*

great stress on the anti-violence
program.
    [...o] ~ ni suru [...を]~ にする He *was*
    encouraged by the word from the
    President and pressed on.
    ~ no aru kagiri ~ のある限り I will do
    all in my power (my utmost) to help
    you.
    ~ o dasu ~ を出す put forth effort
    [...ni] ~ o eru [...に] ~ を得る
    Encouraged by his team-mate's fine
    catch, the pitcher scored a shut-
    out victory.
    ~ o ireru ~ を入れる The President
    insisted that they *lay stress upon*
    (put effort into) solving the Negro
    problem.
    ~ o kasu ~ を貸す help; assist; aid
    ~ shigoto ~ 仕事 manual labor;
    physical work
hakarishirenai chikara はかり知れな
    い力 immeasurable power
hito o hikitsukeru chikara 人をひき
    つける力 Abe's plain speech and
    honesty became his *power to attract*
    people.
hōritsu no chikara 法律の力 the
    power of the law
jibun no chikara o shitte iru 自分
    の力を知っている It is a wise man
    indeed who *is aware of his own*
    limitations.
manshin no chikara o komete 満
    身の力をこめて with all one's might
bariki 馬力 horse power
buryoku 武力 military power
chikaramochi 力持ち strong man
chikarazukeru 力づける strengthen;
    encourage; cheer up
chikarazuyoku kanjiru 力強く感じる
    With three other good men on the
    relay team he *felt reassured.*
gendōryoku 原動力 motivating power
iryoku 威力 authority

~ o hakki suru ～を発揮する display power and might

jinryoku o tsukusu 人力を尽くす help all one can; exhaust all human resources

jitsuryoku 実力 real power; actual ability

~ ni uttaeru ～に訴える appeal to arms

keizairyoku 経済力 economic power

kenryoku 権力 influence; power

kiryoku 気力 spirit; vigor ·

~ ga otoroeru ～が衰える vitality declines; energy is sapped

~ no nai ～のない spiritless; enervated

nōryoku 能力 ability

seisanryoku 生産力 productive capacity

senzairyoku 潜在力 latent power

shiryoku 資力 financial means

~ no aru hito ～のある人 man of means

shiryoku o tsukushite 死力を尽くして Confederate defenders at Vicksburg *fought with everything they had* against Grant.

sokojikara ga aru 底力がある The Dodgers displayed *hidden strength* (*depth*) in winning the pennant.

suishinryoku to naru 推進力となる Atomic power *has become the propelling force* in many new submarines. The new director soon *became the driving force* needed to save the company.

tairyoku 体力 physical strength

~ o yashinau ～を養う Playing tennis is a good way to *build up one's physical strength.*

teikōryoku 抵抗力 power of resistance

~ o ushinau ～を失う When you have a cold, you *lose your power of resistance* to other diseases.

yūryoku (da) 有力(だ) powerful; influential

zenryoku o tsukusu 全力を尽くす do one's utmost

gaijū naigō no hito 外柔内剛の人 Southern leaders soon learned that Lincoln *looked gentle but was inwardly strong.*

IKIOI 勢い force; fortitude; vigor; spirit

seiryoku 勢力 influence; power; force

~ arasoi o suru ～争いをする They *are engaged in a power struggle* within the party.

kyodai (da) [L] 巨大(だ) colossal; huge; gigantic; massive

SEIRYOKU 精力 energy; vigor

~ o tsukeru ～をつける invigorate

~ o ushinau ～を失う lose one's vigor

~ ōsei (da) ～おうせい(だ) vigorous; energetic

seiippai no chikara o dasu 精いっぱいの力を出す exert all one's strength

seikon o uchikomu 精根を打ちこむ devote all one's energy [to]

seishinryoku 精神力 mental power; spiritual strength

TSUYOI 強い strong

jakuniku kyōshoku 弱肉強食 survival of the fittest

kyōkō shudan 強硬手段 strong measures

kyōkō suru 強行する enforce

kyōryoku 強力 power

tsuyomeru 強める strengthen; build up; make strong

⇨ **29, 135, 155**

私は福音を恥とは思いません。福音は、ユダヤ人をはじめギリシヤ人にも、信じるすべての人にとって、救いを得させる神の力です。(ローマ 1 ¹⁶)

20 CHINMOKU 沈黙 SILENCE, TACITURNITY

CHINMOKU 沈黙 silence; taciturnity

~ **o mamoru** ~を守る keep silent; keep quiet

~ **o yaburu** ~を破る break the silence

~ **wa kin nari** [P] ~は金なり Silence is golden.

omokurushii chinmoku ga tadayou 重苦しい沈黙が漂う As the accused man stood to receive the verdict, *a heavy silence filled the air.*

damaru 黙る become silent; hold one's tongue; shut up

muttsuri damaru むっつり黙る become sullen and silent

oshi no yōni damaru おしのように黙る shut up like a clam

mokumoku toshite 黙々として silently; tacitly

mokusatsu (suru) 黙殺(する) The boss *treated* the idea *with silent contempt.*

gobusata itashimashita ごぶさたいたしました Forgive my long silence!

henji ni komaru 返事に困る be lost for an answer

iki o koroshite 息を殺して I hid in the dark *with bated breath.*

koe o hisomete 声を潜めて in a low voice; in whispers

KOTOBA sukunaku 言葉少なく The astronauts reported on their great feat *in a few words and without ceremony.*

kaesu kotoba ga nai 返す言葉がない His accusations were true; *there was nothing I could say.*

genkyū shite inai 言及していない The senator *did not elaborate on* the new plan.

hitokoto mo iwanaide 一言も言わないで without one word

mugon (da) 無言(だ) silent; unspoken

KUCHI 口 mouth

~ **ga omoi** ~が重い The usually *taciturn* general was very talkative at the conference.

~ **ni dasenai hodo** ~に出せないほど The accident was *so* bad *that I can't talk about it.*

~ **ni shinai** ~にしない He simply *does not talk about* his past.

~ **o fusagu** ~をふさぐ *To silence (To shut the mouths of)* his younger brothers he gave them a quarter each.

~ **o kiru** ~をきる break the silence; break the ice

~ **o tojiru** ~を閉じる keep quiet

~ **o tsugumu** ~をつぐむ hold one's tongue

Shinin ni kuchi nashi [P] 死人に口なし Dead men tell no tales [P].

kuchidome (suru) 口止め(する) hushing up (hush up; squelch)

kuchikazu no sukunai hito 口数の少ない人 person of few words

mukuchi (da) 無口(だ) close-mouthed; taciturn; reticent

muttsuriya むっつり屋 silent fellow; glum person

ni no ku ga tsugenai 二の句がつげない When he said that, I *was dumbfounded (was stopped cold; was left speechless; was flabbergasted).*

seishuku ni 静粛に quietly and orderly

~ **ni negaimasu!** ~に願います Quiet please!

⇨ **167**

キリストは罪を犯したことがなく, その口に何の偽りも見いだされませんでした. ののしられても, ののしり返さず, 苦しめられても, おどすことをせず, 正しくさばかれる方にお任せになりました. (ペテロ I 2 ²², ²³)

21 CHISHIKI 知識
KNOWLEDGE

CHISHIKI 知識 knowledge
[...**no**] ~ **ga aru** [...の] ～がある have some knowledge of...
~ **ga masu** ～が増す knowledge increases
~ **kaikyū** ～階級 intelligentsia; intellectuals
~ **no aru hito** ～のある人 well-informed person
~ **no nai hito** ～のない人 ignorant man; uninformed person
~ **o ataeru** ～を与える Abe's stepmother *gave* him *a knowledge of* the Bible.
~ **o eru** ～得る gain knowledge [of]
~ **o fukyū suru** ～を普及する disseminate (spread) knowledge
~ **o hiromeru** ～を広める Abe *increased his knowledge* by reading *Pilgrim's Progress.*
~ **o kyūshū suru** ～を吸収する absorb knowledge
~ **o tsuikyū suru** ～を追求する pursue knowledge
~ **o yakudateru** ～を役立てる make use of (utilize) one's knowledge
ayafuya na chishiki あやふやな知識 fuzzy knowledge [of]; vague knowledge [of]
hyakkazenshoteki chishiki 百科全書的知識 encyclopedic knowledge
jitsuyōteki chishiki 実用的知識 practical knowledge
karimono no chishiki 借り物の知識 borrowed knowledge
kiso chishiki 基礎知識 basic knowledge; fundamental knowledge
semmonteki chishiki 専門的知識 specialized knowledge
shohoteki chishiki 初歩的知識 elementary knowledge
chinō 知能 intellect
chishikiyoku 知識欲 thirst for knowledge
jinchi [L] 人知 human knowledge
~ **o koeru** ～を越える be beyond knowledge; surpass human knowledge
jukuchi shite iru 熟知している He *knows* that subject *thoroughly.*
muchi 無知 ignorance
ninshiki (suru) 認識(する) understanding (appreciate)
~ **fusoku** ～不足 lack of understanding; ignorance
~ **o aratameru** ～を改める After getting into power the Chōshū leaders *saw* the foreign relations problem *in a new light.*
~ **o kaku** ～を欠く lack perception; be incognizant of
shiru 知る know
hiroku shirarete iru 広く知られている be commonly known; be common knowledge; be common parlance
jijō o yoku shitte iru 事情をよく知っている have thorough knowledge of
shirazu ni 知らずに unconsciously
shireru 知れる become known
shirewataru 知れ渡る become widely known
shittakaburi o suru 知ったかぶりをする He's *talking as if he knew all about it.*
shōchi (suru) 承知(する) awareness; consent (be aware of; agree to)
goshōchi no tōri ご承知のとおり as (you) well know
hyaku mo shōchi 百も承知 You've been here long enough to *know full well* what happens when you break a rule.
jūbun shōchi no ue (de) 十分承知のうえ(で) The soldiers attacked *knowing full well* that they were

outnumbered.

shūchi no 周知の commonly known
~ **no jijitsu** ~ の事実 generally known fact

yobichishiki 予備知識 advance knowledge; previous information

gainen o eru 概念を得る get the general outline [of]

gakushiki 学識 learning; scholarship
~ **keikensha** ~ 経験者 He is a *well-educated man of experience.*
~ **no aru hito** 学識のある人 learned person

gozonji desu ka? ご存じですか? Do you know…?

ikijibiki 生き字引き a walking dictionary

interi インテリ intellectual

jōshiki 常識 common knowledge
hijōshiki (da) 非常識(だ) lack of common sense; thoughtlessness

KEMBUN 見聞 information; knowledge; experience
~ **no hiroi** ~ の広い well-informed; has seen much of life
~ **o hiromeru** ~ を広める add to one's experience; enrich one's knowledge

kenshiki 見識 opinion; insight

kizuku 気づく be aware of

mimi ni hairu 耳にはいる I *happened to hear* that you were going abroad.

nama hanka na kangae 生半可な考え A plan based on such *shallow thinking (half-baked ideas)* will never succeed.

ninjō no kibi ni tsūjite iru 人情の機微に通じている Because Lincoln *had* such *keen insight into human nature*, people came in droves to the White House.

seitsū suru 精通する be well-versed in

sankō (ni suru) 参考(にする) reference (refer to)
[…o] ~ **ni suru** […を] ~ にする *Use* these figures *as reference* when you calculate the cost.

sanshō (suru) 参照(する) reference; comparison(refer to; compare[with]; consult)

unchiku うん蓄 stock of knowledge
~ **o katamukeru** ~ を傾ける The young scientist *poured his stock of knowledge into* the problem.

⇨ **19, 161**

知識は人を高ぶらせ，愛は人の徳を建てます。
(コリント I 8 ¹)

22 CHŌWA 調和
HARMONY

aiirenai mono ga aru 相いれないものがある In many ways the husband and wife *were incompatible.*

jidai to aiirenai 時代と相いれない be out of harmony (=step) with the times

AU 合う meet
hada ga au はだが合う He and I are very *compatible (congenial)* and have been close friends for years.
hochō o awaseru 歩調を合わせる The architect *worked in concert (fell into step)* with his engineers and the company made progress.
iken ga au 意見が合う be of the same opinion
~ **ga awanai** ~ が合わない do not see eye to eye [with]; disagree [with]
kokyū ga au 呼吸が合う Lincoln soon discovered he *saw eye to eye (clicked; got along)* with Grant.
uma ga au うまが合う Those two teachers *get along (hit it off)* with each other.

oriai 折り合い mutual relations; relationship
~ **ga umaku iku** ~ がうまくいく The young couple gradually learned to *get along with* their inlaws.
~ **ga warui** ~ が悪い Those two *do not get along very well.*

~ o tsukeru ~ をつける settle a matter; come to an understanding

shōgō (suru) 照合(する) verification; check (verify; check with)

tsuriai つり合い balance; proportion; harmony

    ~ no toreta ~ の取れた well balanced; well proportioned; well-matched [couple, etc.]

CHŌWA 調和 harmony

    ~ no torenai ~ の取れない out of keeping with; inharmonious

    ~ no toreta ~ の取れた harmonious; in keeping with

    ~ o kaku ~ を欠く The boss is concerned because the employees *lack harmony.*

    ~ o tamotsu ~ を保つ maintain harmony

    ~ o torimodosu ~ を取りもどす restore harmony

    ~ o yaburu ~ を破る create discord

    ~ shinai ~ しない doesn't harmonize

chōshihazure (da) 調子はずれ(だ) discordant; out of tune

kōchō (da) 好調(だ) favorable; smoothly

kyōchō (suru) 協調(する) cooperation; concord (cooperate; be in concord)

wagō (suru) 和合(する) harmony; concord; peace (be in harmony with; be in accord with; be at peace with)

yūwa (suru) 融和(する) harmony; reconciliation (melt; placate; reconcile)

    ~ o hakaru ~ をはかる promote harmony

CHŪDO o ayumu [L] 中通を歩む take the middle road; take the golden mean

chūkan 中間 middle; midway

chūyō [L] 中庸 middle of the road

CHŪSAI (suru) 仲裁する arbitration; mediation (arbitrate; mediate)

    arasoi o chūsai suru 争いを仲裁する arbitrate a dispute; settle an argument

nakanaori suru 仲直りする make up [with]; be reconciled; make peace [with]

enkatsu ni 円滑に smoothly; without a hitch

ikkansei ga nai 一貫性がない Your grammar is correct, but the whole theme *lacks consistency.*

ishi no sotsū o kaku 意志の疎通を欠く The two men *lacked mutual understanding* because their native languages were different.

issho ni yatte iku いっしょにやって行く work together; get along together

itchi shite 一致して unitedly; unanimously; harmoniously

junnō suru 順応する adapt to; adjust to

Ki ni take o tsugu yōna koto o suru [P] 木に竹をつぐようなことをする Those steel benches all over the wooded park *are quite out of place (are quite incongruous).*

kinsei ga torete iru 均整がとれている be well-proportioned [figure, picture, etc.]

kyōmei suru 共鳴する be in sympathy with

yori o modosu よりをもどす At long last the feuding parties *patched up their differences (restored relations)* and began working together.
⇨ **55, 74**

さて，兄弟たち．私は，私たちの主イエス・キリストの御名によって，あなたがたにお願いします．どうか，みなが一致して，仲間割れすることなく，同じ心，同じ判断を完全に保ってください．(コリント I 1 [10])

23　CHŪI 注意
CAUTION, ATTENTION

CHŪI (suru) 注意(する) caution (be careful [of])

    ~ ga tarinai ~ が足りない careless [of]; inattentive [to]

~ ga yukitodoku ~が行き届く Make sure *thorough care is taken* on the excursion trip to prevent accidents.

~ jikō ~事項 suggestion; word of caution

~ o harau ~をはらう After Lincoln had been shot at one night, Nichols told him to *give attention to* his personal safety.

~ o hiku ~を引く Abe's strange appearance *attracted* everyone's *attention.*

~ o mukeru ~を向ける direct one's attention to

~ o shūchū suru ~を集中する focus attention on

~ o sorasu ~をそらす The politician tried to *divert their attention away from* the real issues.

~ o suru ~をする I *cautioned* them *against* swimming without a lifeguard.

[...ni] ~ suru [...に] ~する *Watch* your step. *Be careful of* poisonous snakes. *Watch out for* falling rocks.

saishin no chūi o harau 細心の注意をはらう pay close attention to details; take infinite care; be meticulous

chūibukai 注意深い attentive; careful; conscientious

chūiryoku 注意力 attentiveness; power of attention; concentration

chūmoku (suru) 注目(する) attention (heed; observe; notice)

~ o abiru ~を浴びる become the object of attention

~ subeki ~すべき noteworthy; significant

chūshi (suru) 注視 (する) scrutiny (scrutinize)

ryūi (suru) 留意(する) wariness; heed (be wary [of]; take heed)

daiji o toru 大事をとる be on the safe side; play it safe

hairyo 配慮 consideration

Ishibashi o tataite wataru [P] "石橋をたたいて渡る" He *is extremely cautious (is overly cautious)* and refuses to make quick decisions.

KEIKAI (suru) 警戒(する) vigilance (be on the alert)

~ o gen ni suru ~を厳にする keep strict watch

~ o yurumeru ~をゆるめる When the soldiers *relaxed their vigilance (let down their guard)*, the enemy attacked.

kaikoku (suru) 戒告(する) warning (warn)

keikoku (suru) 警告(する) caution; warning (warn)

~ o mushi suru ~を無視する not heed one's warning

kunkai (suru) 訓戒(する) admonition; lecture (admonish; lecture to)

KI o kubaru 気を配る The sentry had to *keep on the alert (be on his toes)* for an attack.

~ o sorasu ~をそらす They *diverted* the enemy's *attention* and attacked from an unexpected quarter.

~ o torarete ~ を取られて The mother, *absorbed in* watching the children, let the cake burn.

~ o tsukeru ~をつける be careful; watch out [for]

~ o yurumeru ~をゆるめる be off one's guard; relax one's vigil

~ o yurusu ~を許す I *was off guard* for a minute and an accident occurred.

kizukaseru 気づかせる warn

KOKORO ni tomeru 心に留める keep in mind; bear in mind

kokoroe 心得 cautions; rules

kokorogake (ru) 心がけ (心がける) care; prudence (take care; be prudent)

~**no yoi (no warui)** ~のよい(の悪い) careful; prudent (careless; imprudent)

kokorozukai 心づかい consideration; thoughtfulness; advice

Korobanu saki no tsue [P] ころばぬ先のつえ Look before you leap [P].

Kunshi ayauki ni chikayorazu [P] 君子危うきに近寄らず A wise man will avoid danger.

ME ga todoku 目が届く be within sight of

~**o hanasanai** ~を離さない You'd better *keep an eye on* your children when they play in the park.

~**o hikarasu** ~を光らす I'm *keeping a watchful eye* on the new employees to see that they work their full time.

~**o kubaru** ~を配る keep a sharp lookout [for]; keep one's eyes peeled [for]

~**o samasu** ~をさます be on the alert; keep one's eyes open

~**o tsukeru** ~をつける keep an eye on

miharu 見張る keep one's eyes open [for]

mimamoru 見守る watch; guard

genjū ni mimamoru 厳重に見守る watch strictly; guard closely

mimi o katamukete kiku 耳を傾けて聞く They *listened intently* to the debate.

~**o sumashite kiku** ~をすまして聞く prick up one's ears to hear

NEN 念 attention; care

~**ga itte iru** ~がいっている well done; elaborately done

~**ni wa nen o irete** ~には念を入れて *Make doubly sure* that all the arrangements are taken care of.

~**no tame ni** ~のために *Just to make sure*, please consult the encyclopedia.

~**o osu** ~を押す make sure; confirm

neniri ni 念入りに carefully; with care

nentō ni oku 念頭に置く keep in mind

shisa (suru) 示唆(する) suggestion (suggest)

tsutsushimi (mu) 慎み(慎む) prudence; discretion (be prudent; be discreet)

kotoba o tsutsushimu 言葉を慎む weigh one's words; be careful of what one says

YŌJIN (suru) 用心(する) vigilance; care (be careful [of]; take care; guard [against])

hi no yōjin 火の用心 precaution against fire

yōjinbukai 用心深い careful

YUDAN (suru) 油断(する) inattention (be off guard)

~**dekinai** ~できない With the many pickpockets in the trains these days you *must be on your guard.*

~**taiteki** [P] ~大敵 Carelessness is the greatest danger.

⇨ **24**

身を慎み，目をさましていなさい．あなたがたの敵である悪魔が，ほえたけるししのように，食い尽くすべきものを捜し求めながら，歩き回っています．(ペテロ Ⅰ 5 ⁸)

24 CHŪKOKU 忠告 ADVICE

chie o kasu 知恵を貸す give advice

CHŪKOKU 忠告 advice

~**ni shitagau (o mamoru)** ~に従う(を守る) The student *followed the advice of* (*heeded the counsel of*) his teacher.

~**ni somuku** ~にそむく go against one's advice; disregard the counsel of

~**o motomeru** ~を求める seek advice

~**o mushi suru** ~を無視する ignore one's advice; not give heed to one's warning

kemmei na chūkoku 賢明な忠告 wise counsel; sound advice

tō o eta chūkoku 当を得た忠告

expedient advice; pertinent advice
kankoku (suru) 勧告(する) counsel
(advise)
~ **ni ōjiru** ~に応じる comply with
(respond to) one's advice
keikoku (suru) 警告(する) warning
(warn)
IKEN 意見 opinion; admonition
~ **o noberu** ~を述べる express one's
opinion
kōiteki ni iken suru 好意的に意見す
る give friendly advice
chūi (suru) 注意(する) caution (warn;
admonish)
**rōbashin nagara gochūi o mōshi-
ageru** 老婆心ながらご注意を申し上げ
る Perhaps this is superfluous, but
I would like to give a word of
caution...
imashime (ru) 戒め(る) admonition;
command (admonish; command)
isameru いさめる expostulate; admonish;
remonstrate
IU koto ga mi ni kotaeru 言うことが身に
こたえる *What he says* about loose morals
strikes home.
chūgen 忠言 advice
iifukumeru 言い含める instruct; give
counsel; inculcate; exhort
jogen (suru) 助言(する) word of advice
(counsel; advise)
kogoto o iu 小言を言う give a lecture
to; scold
kokorozoe 心添え advice
komon toshite 顧問として I am only
saying this *in an advisory capacity.*
kuchibashi o ireru 口ばしを入れる He's
always *poking his nose into other people's
business (butting in; giving uncalled-for
advice).*
kuchizoe (suru) 口添え(する) recommendation (recommend; put in a
good word for)
kunkai (suru) 訓戒(する) admonition
(caution)

junjun to kunkai suru じゅんじゅんと訓
戒する admonish one patiently
SATOSU さとす point out; teach
fukokoroe o satosu 不心得をさとす
point out one's error; admonish one
over his ill manner
shōrai o satosu 将来をさとす He
cautioned his son *about his future.*
sekkyō (suru) 説教(する) sermon (preach)
shimon kikan 諮問機関 advisory body
sōdan ni notte kureru 相談に乗ってくれる
We needed his advice on the project,
and he *was willing to talk about helping*
us on it.
~ **o mochikakeru** ~を持ち掛ける bring
up a matter for discussion
susume (ru) 勧め(勧る) recommendation
(recommend; urge)
⇒ 23, 70
高ぶりはただ争いを生じる. 勧告をきく者は知恵がある.
(箴言 13 ¹⁰)

25 CHŪSHŌ 中傷
SLANDER, CALUMNY

AKKŌ 悪口 abuse
~ **zōgon o abiseru** ~雑言を浴びせる
heap insults [on]; say all kinds of
foul things [to]
akutai 悪態 abusive language; abusive
remarks
~ **o tsuku** ~をつく Many letters *used
abusive language* against Lincoln,
calling him an idiot and an ape.
ashizama ni iu あしざまに言う speak
evil of
atekosuri あてこすり insinuating remarks
batō (suru) 罵倒(する) abuse (heap insults
on)
BŌGEN 暴言 strong words; wild words;
violent language
~ **o abiseru** ~を浴びせる heap scorn
upon

~ o haku ~ を吐く speak abusively

BUJOKU (suru) 侮辱(する) insult (insult)

~ o koraeru ~ をこらえる King David was reviled by old Shimei, but he *bore the affront.*

~ o kuwaeru ~ を加える heap insults upon

~ o ukeru ~ を受ける be insulted

DEMA ga tobu デマが飛ぶ ugly rumors spread

~ o tobasu ~ を飛ばす The Chicago Tribune *circulated a false report* (*spread a false rumor*) that Abe's health was shattered.

akushitsuna dema 悪質なデマ ugly rumor

dokuzetsu 毒舌 poisonous tongue

~ o furuu ~ をふるう wag a venomous tongue

gishō (suru) 偽証(する) perjury (perjure; bear false witness; falsify one's testimony)

gishōzai 偽証罪 perjury

hibō (suru) 〔L〕 ひぼう(する) slander (slander; abuse)

KAGEGUCHI 陰口 backbiting; malicious gossip

~ o iu ~ を言う She is always *talking about* her neighbor *behind her back.*

tsugeguchi 告げ口 tattler

warukuchi o iu 悪口を言う speak ill of; say bad things about; malign

sagesumi (mu) さげすみ(さげすむ) contempt (treat with contempt)

SOSHIRI (ru) そしり(そしる) slander; libel (vilify; libel)

~ o maneku ~ を招く lay oneself open to public criticism; incur public blame

~ o manukarenai ~ を免れない The senator felt he would *be open to slanderous charges* if he accepted the gift.

~ o ukeru ~ を受ける be spoken evil of; be maligned

nonoshiri (ru) ののしり(ののしる) slander; libel (rail against; inveigh against)

kuchigitanaku nonoshiru 口ぎたなくののしる say nasty things about; abuse; revile; defame [a person]

sutezerifu o nokosu 捨てぜりふを残す Because I refused to join his sect, that fanatic *made a parting threat* as he left my house.

toge no aru kotoba とげのあることば barbed words

ushiroyubi o sasu 後ろ指をさす point a finger of scorn at

⇒ **99, 206**

ひそかに, そのとなり人をそしる者をわたしは滅ぼします. 高ぶる目と高慢な心の人を耐え忍ぶことはできません. (詩篇 101 ⁵)

26 DAKYŌ 妥協
COMPROMISE

atozusari suru あとずさりする After receiving so many objections, the boss *backed down* on his plan.

ayumiyoru 歩み寄る make mutual concessions

binjō suru 便乗する take advantage of; get on the bandwagon.

chōshi o awaseru 調子を合わせる fall into line [with]; play along with

kyōchō (suru) 協調(する) conciliation; agreement (conciliate; agree)

DAKYŌ (suru) 妥協(する) compromise (compromise; reach an understanding [with])

~ no yochi ga nai ~ の余地がない *There is no room for compromise.*

dakyōan (dakyō saku) 妥協案(妥協策) compromise plan

~ o neru ~ を練る work out a compromise

dakyōsei no nai hito 妥協性のない人

intractable person; obstinate person; stubborn person

dakyōten o miidasu 妥協点を見いだす If you try to *find some common ground* (*meet them half-way*), I think you will reach an agreement.

emman ni kaiketsu suru 円満に解決する settle amicably

ga o oru 我を折る He was intransigent for hours but finally *gave in* (*backed down*).

~ **o tōsu** ~ を通す have one's own way; stick to one's guns

Gō ni itte wa, gō ni shitagae [P] 郷に入っては郷に従え When in Rome, do as the Romans do [P].

hanashi ga matomaru 話がまとまる the matter is settled; an agreement is reached

hōsaku o kōjiru 方策を講じる figure out a way

jidan 示談 private settlement

jiryū ni noru 時流に乗る Men feel they must *go along with the times* (*swim with the tide*) to get along in life.

jōho (**suru**) 譲歩(する) concession (concede; give ground)

sōgo no jōho 相互の譲歩 mutual concession

jōhoteki taido 譲歩的態度 Mr. Rusk revealed an *attitude of concession* to the African States.

kotonakareshugi 事なかれ主義 He failed as a politician because of his *do-nothing attitude.*

kussuru 屈する yield [to]; give in [to]

maruku osamaru まるく治まる come to an amicable settlement

~ **osameru** ~ 治める settle amicably

naka ni tatte torimotsu 中に立って取り持つ Shields challenged Lincoln to a duel with swords, but the lawyers *mediated between them.*

ORIAI (**u**) 折り合い(折り合う) compromise (give in on both sides)

~ **ga tsuku** ~ がつく come to terms; give in

~ **o tsukeru** ~ をつける strike a happy medium; split the difference

setchūan 折衷案 compromise plan

wakai (**suru**) 和解(する) reconciliation; amicable settlement (reconcile)

⇨ **22, 84**

この世と調子を合わせてはいけません．むしろ，神のみこころは何か，すなわち，何が良いことで，神に受け入れられ，完全であるのかをわきまえ知るために，心の一新によって自分を変えなさい．（ローマ 12 ²）

27 DOKURITSU 独立
INDEPENDENCE

DOKURITSU (**suru**) (独立する) independence (become independent)

~ **o mamoru** ~ を守る maintain one's independence

~ **o obiyakasu** ~ を脅かす threaten the independence [of]

~ **o sengen suru** ~ を宣言する declare one's independence

~ **o ushinau** ~ を失う lose one's independence

dokudan de 独断で on one's own authority; arbitrarily

~ **de kimeru** ~ 決める decide arbitrarily

dokuji no 独自の original

dokuritsudokkō [L] 独立独行 self-reliance; self-sufficiency

dokuritsudoppo [L] 独立独歩 standing on one's own feet; looking out for oneself; paddling one's own canoe

dokuritsukoku 独立国 independent nation ⌈Day

dokuritsusai 独立祭 Independence

dokuritsushin 独立心 spirit of independence

dokuryoku de 独力で by one's own efforts; singlehandedly; on one's own hook

dokusenteki (da) 独占的(だ) monopolistic

tandoku kōdō o toru 単独行動をとる act independently [of]

HITORI de tatte ikeru ひとりで立って行ける At the age of twenty, he felt he could *stand on his own two feet.*

    hitoridachi (suru) ひとり立ち(する) independence (become independent)

    hitoritenka ひとり天下 boss of the show

    ichininmae no 一人前の full-fledged

      ~ no shigoto ga dekiru ~仕事がでぎる At an early age, Abe proved to everyone that he *could do a man's work* (*could be on his own*).

JIKATSU (suru) 自活(する) self-support (become self-supporting)

      ~ no michi ~の道 way to economic independence; means of earning one's livelihood

    jikyū-jisoku (da) 自給自足(だ) self-sufficiency (on one's own)

    jiritsu 自立 self-reliance

    jishu 自主 self-governing

    jishuteki (da) 自主的(だ) independent

koritsu (suru) 孤立(する) isolation (be isolated; be alone)

⇨ 79

私は、人の金銀や衣服をむさぼったことはありません。あたながた自身が知っているとおり、この両手は、私の必要のためにも、私とともにいる人たちのためにも、働いて来ました。(使徒 20 ³³, ³⁴)

28 DONKAN 鈍感
DULLNESS

Baji tōfū [P] 馬耳東風 Telling him to change his ways is *just so many wasted words* (*like water off a duck's back*).

bonyari suru ぼんやりする be vague; be hazy

bōzen jishitsu (da) [L] ぼう然自失(だ) at a loss; at one's wits' end

chi mo namida mo、**nai** 血も涙もない Stanton was *cold-blooded* in his attitude toward the pathetic Confederates.

gori muchū (da) 五里霧中(だ) mystified; groping in the dark; at a loss

heiki (da) 平気(だ) unconcern (unconcerned)

    ~ no heiza [C] ~のへいざ No matter what happens, *nothing fazes him* (*he's as cool as a cucumber*).

hōshin (suru) 放心(する) absence of mind (be absent-minded; wool-gather)

ishiki ga naku naru 意識がなくなる become unconscious; pass out; black out

    ~ o kaifuku suru ~を回復する regain consciousness; come to (one's senses)

itaku mo kayuku mo nai 痛くもかゆくもない The bad election reports seemed to *have no effect upon Lincoln.*

kokoro ni mo nai koto o iu 心にもない事を言う He talks smoothly, but really he often *says things without meaning them.*

mukankaku (da) 無感覚(だ) insensibility (insensible)

mukandō (da) 無感動(だ) apathy (apathetic)

mushinkei (da) 無神経(だ) insensitiveness (insensitive)

mutonjaku (da) むとんじゃく(だ) unconcern (unconcerned)

nanige naku 何げなく with nothing particular in mind

nibui 鈍い numb; dull

    kankaku ga nibui 感覚が鈍い have dull senses

shibireru しびれる I've been sitting so long my legs *are asleep.*

    shibire ga kireru しびれがきれる (legs) get stiff; (legs) go to sleep

shōtai ga nakunaru 正体がなくなる The drunken man staggered into the room and *passed out.*

tamashii ga nuketa yōni 魂が抜けたように Failing in that venture *knocked the* *props right out from under him.*

Uma no mimi ni nenbutsu [P] 馬の耳に念仏 You can say it to him, but I'm afraid it will *be wasted advice* (*go in one ear and out the other*).

ware kansezu [L] 我関せず It's none of my affair.

zengo fukaku to naru 前後不覚となる lose consciousness

~ **o wasureru** ～を忘れる forget oneself ⇨ **147**

そこで私は、主にあって言明し、おごそかに勧めます。もはや、異邦人がむなしい心で歩んでいるように歩んではなりません。

彼らは、その知性において暗くなり、彼らのうちにある無知と、かたくなな心とのゆえに、神のいのちから遠く離れています。

道徳的に無感覚となった彼らは、好色に身をゆだねて、あらゆる不潔な行ないをむさぼるようになっています。

(エペソ 4 17, 18, 19)

29 DORYOKU 努力
EFFORT, ENDEAVOR

Amadare ishi o ugatsu [P] 雨だれ石をうがつ You can do almost anything if you stay at it long enough.

ashi o bō ni shite 足を棒にして I *worked* today *until my legs were stiff.*

dekiru dake no koto o suru できるだけの事をする do all one can; do one's best

DORYOKU (suru) 努力(する) effort; endeavor (make an effort; endeavor)

~ **no ato o miru** ～のあとをみる By the thorough way in which he answered the questions, *one can see that he worked hard* in preparation.

fudan no doryoku 不断の努力 constant effort

namidagumashii doryoku 涙ぐましい努力 heart-breaking effort

saidaigen (do) (no doryoku) o tsukusu 最大限(度)(の努力)を尽くす

do one's level best; leave no stone unturned

tayumazu doryoku suru たゆまず努力する make a constant effort

chikara o awaseru 力を合わせる combine efforts; unite efforts

~ **o ireru** ～を入れる put efforts into; exert strength

~ **o shūchū suru** ～を集中する concentrate one's efforts [on]

aran kagiri no chikara o tsukusu あらん限りの力を尽くす Lincoln told the nation that he would *exert all his strength* (*do all in his power*) to preserve the Union.

saigo no chikara o furishiboru 最後の力をふりしぼる *Putting forth one final effort*, Abe shoved the barge off the bank.

jinryoku (suru) 尽力(する) effort (strive; exert oneself)

zenryoku o tsukushite (o agete) 全力を尽くして(全力をあげて) I'll *do everything I can* (*make every possible effort*) to help you.

gamushara ni yaru がむしゃらにやる work like a house afire; work like mad

HATARAKI (ku) 働き(働く) work; labor (work; labor)

asemizu tarashite hataraku 汗水たらして働く He *worked hard* to support his family.

kage hinata naku hataraku 陰ひなたなく働く work faithfully

yo no me mo oshinde hataraku 夜の目も惜しんで働く work night and day; work without sleep

hagemu 励む strive for; work hard at

honeoru ほねおる exert effort; labor

hone no oreru shigoto ほねのおれる仕事 This *job takes a lot of elbow grease* [C].

honki de yaru 本気でやる If you want

to learn English, you had better *work at it seriously* (*dig into it*).

ishi ni kajiritsuite mo yaru 石にかじりついてもやる Despite the difficulties, I will *stick to it until my goal is reached.*

isshōkemmei ni yaru いっしょうけんめいにやる Lincoln's friends *did their best* (*went all out*) to get him elected.

Issun no kōin karonzubekarazu [P] 一寸の光陰軽んずべからず Don't waste a minute. Don't take even a minute lightly.

jinji o tsukusu 人事を尽くす exhaust human efforts

kimben (**da**) 勤勉(だ) diligence (diligent; industrious)

[...ni] mi o ireru [...に] 身を入れる He really *put himself into* that task and made a success of it.

ōwarawa ni naru 大わらわになる He worked *feverishly* (*frantically*) to meet the deadline.

oyobu kagiri o tsukusu 及ぶ限りを尽くす do one's best

rō o oshimanaide 労を惜しまないで without begrudging efforts; with no stint of effort

saizen o tsukusu 最善を尽くす put forth one's best effort

SEIKON o tsukusu 精根を尽くす do one's level best

~ **o uchikomu** ~ を打ち込む put one's soul into [it]

seirei (**suru**) 精励(する) diligence (be diligent; work hard)

kokku seirei suru [L] 刻苦精励する drive oneself hard; push oneself on

shigoto ni sei o dasu 仕事に精を出す He *has thrown himself into* his new *work.*

shōjin (**suru**) 精進(する) devotion; dedication; commitment (devote oneself to)

shinketsu o sosogu 心血を注ぐ put one's heart and soul into [one's work]; lay oneself out [for]

te o tsukusu 手を尽くす use all available means

tsutomeru 努める endeavor; do one's part

uchikomu 打ち込む devote oneself to; concentrate energy on ⇨ **19, 130**

すべてあなたの手のなしうる事は，力をつくしてなせ. (伝道の書 9 ¹⁰)

30 DŌSATSU 洞察
INSIGHT, PERCEPTION

DŌSATSU (**suru**) 洞察(する) insight; perception (have insight into; perceive)

dōsatsuryoku ga aru 洞察力がある He *has insight into* (*is able to perceive*) the various aspects of space technology.

~ **no aru hito** ~ のある人 man of insight

ganshiki 眼識 insight; discerning eye

gengai no imi o toru 言外の意味を取る read between the lines; catch the implied meaning; put two-and-two together

hakkiri to tsukamu はっきりとつかむ grasp well; really understand

kampa suru 看破する perceive; see through; penetrate; pierce

kaoiro o ukagau 顔色をうかがう Before asking the boss for a raise, I tried to *determine what mood he was in.*

~ **o kampa suru** ~ を看破する I *saw right through* his flattery; he wanted to borrow my car.

kyūsho o tsuku 急所をつく His remark *got to the crux of the matter* (*grasped the issue at stake*).

~ **o hazureru** ~ をはずれる I understand your words, but you *missed the point.*

ME ga kiku 目がきく have an eye for (a bargain); be a good bargainer

~ ga koete iru ~ が肥えている That buyer *has a discriminating eye* and only selects the finest products.

~ ga takai ~ が高い have a critical eye; have refined taste

~ ni kurui wa nai ~ に狂いはない have an unerring eye

MIRU 見る see

  ~ hito ga mireba ~ 人が見れば *If a discerning person were to see* it, he could tell that the property is valuable.

  ~ me ga aru ~ 目がある have perceptive eyes; have an eye for

  [...no] mi ni natte mireba [...の]身になってみれば *Put yourself in my place* and you will understand why I did it.

mikiwameru 見きわめる discern

minuku 見抜く see through; perceive

  kokoro o minuku 心を見抜く The boy tried to cover up his guilt, but his mother *saw right through* him.

  surudoku minuku 鋭く見抜く have full insight into

misadameru 見定める ascertain; make sure [of]

mitōsu 見通す see through; penetrate

  shōrai no mitōshi 将来の見通し It is difficult to *predict the future* (*foresee the future*).

miwakeru 見分ける distinguish; discern

nozokimiru のぞき見る peer into; look into; peep into

saguri o ireru 探りを入れる sound out; put out feelers

shikibetsu (suru) 識別(する) discernment; discrimination (discern; discriminate)

shinsō o kyūmei suru 真相を糾明する To *get to the bottom of* the swindle, the boss had all the financial records checked.

wakimaeru わきまえる discern; distinguish

yogen (suru) 予言(する) prophecy (prophesy; foretell)

  yohō 予報 prediction; forecast

  tenki yohō 天気予報 The *weather forecast* predicts rain tonight.

⇨ 92, 161

神のことばは生きていて，力があり，両刃の剣よりも鋭く，たましいと霊，関節と骨髄の分かれ目さえも刺し通し，心のいろいろな考えやはかりごとを判別することができます．（ヘブル 4 12）

31 DŌTOKU 道徳
MORALITY

biten 美点 virtue; merits

darashi ga nai だらしがない slovenly; loose; slipshod; sloppy

DŌTOKU 道徳 morality

  ~ ga chi ni ochita ~ が地に落ちた The government was concerned that *morality had disappeared* (*morality had lost its hold on people*) in towns near army camps.

  ~ ga fuhai suru ~ が腐敗する morals grow-corrupt

  ~ kannen ~ 観念 moral sense; moral convictions

  shakai dōtoku 社会道徳 social morals; social mores

akutoku 悪徳 vice

bitoku 美徳 virtue

dōgi 道義 moral principle

  ~ ni hansuru (motoru) ~ に反する(もとる) be against moral principle

  ~ ni motozuku に基づく He insisted that his views *were based on moral principle*.

  ~ o omonjiru を重んじる have a regard for morals

dōgishin 道義心 moral sense; moral scruples

  ~ no takai hito ~ の高い人 person of high moral character; person of high moral scruples

dōri ni kanau 道理にかなう Lincoln felt that Douglas' case for white supremacy didn't *stand to reason*.

~**o wakimaeru** ～をわきまえる Though Abe was uneducated, he became a skillful lawyer because he could *discern the right*.

dōtokugaku 道徳学 moral philosophy

dōtokujō (no) 道徳上(の) moral; from a moral standpoint

~**no gimu** ～の義務 moral obligation

dōtokuritsu 道徳律 moral code; moral law

dōtokushin ga tarinai 道徳心が足りない lack moral consciousness

~**o yashinau** ～を養う cultivate morals

dōtokuteki kijun 道徳的基準 moral standards

fudōtoku (da) 不道徳(だ) immorality (immoral)

futoku no itasu tokoro 不徳のいたす所 I *take full responsibility* for my son's behavior.

haitoku (kōi) 背徳(行為) moral depravity; moral anarchy (immoral conduct)

jindō 人道 humanity

~**ni somuku** ～にそむく be inhumane; be against humanity

kōtokushin 公徳心 common decency; public morality

~**ni kakeru** ～に欠ける lack common decency; be against public morality

michi ni hazureta okonai 道にはずれた行ない He did *something morally wrong* and will have to answer for it.

tokkō 徳行 morality

toku 徳 virtue

~**ga nai** ～がない be lacking in virtue

~**ga takai** ～が高い virtuous

~**o sonaeru** ～を備える possess virtue

~**o takameru** ～を高める edify

~**o yashinau** ～を養う cultivate moral character; cultivate virtue

fuhai shita shakai 腐敗した社会 corrupt society

fūki 風紀 public morals

~**o midasu** ～を乱す corrupt public morals

HINKAKU 品格 moral nature

hinkō ga warui 品行が悪い He *is conducting himself poorly* these days.

~**hōsei (da)** ～方正(だ) [person] of good conduct; [person] of irreproachable conduct

~**o tsutsushimu** ～を慎む be prudent

hinsei 品性 moral character

kihin 気品 moral tone

mimochi ga warui 身持ちが悪い She *is reputed to be a woman of loose morals*.

rinri 倫理 ethics

taihai 退廃 demoralization; degeneration; decay of public morals

すべてのことは、してもよいのです。しかし、すべてのことが有益とはかぎりません。すべてのことは、してもよいのです。しかし、すべてのことが徳を高めるとはかぎりません。(コリント I 10 ²³)

32 EIEN 永遠 ETERNITY

EIEN (da) 永遠(だ) eternity (eternal)

~**ni ikiru** ～に生きる live forever

~**no heiwa** ～の平和 lasting peace

~**no inochi** ～の命 eternal life

~**no shinri** ～の真理 eternal truth

~**no sonzai** ～の存在 eternal existence

~**no yorokobi** ～の喜び everlasting joy; eternal joy

eikyū (da) 永久(だ) permanence; eternity (permanent; eternal)

~**fuhen no** ～不変の everlasting

~**ni tsutaeru** ～に伝える transmit perpetually

eikyūteki (da) 永久的(だ) permanent

eizokusei 永続性 permanence
haneikyūteki (**da**)   半永久的(だ)
  semipermanent
  ~ **na shigoto** ~な仕事 a permanent
    job
fukyū 不朽 immortality; imperishability
fumetsu 不滅 immortality
[**furō**] **fushi** (**da**) [不老]不死(だ)
  agelessness; perpetual youth (ageless;
  immortal)
hateshi naku tsuzuku 果てしなく続く
  continue endlessly
itsu made mo いつまでも forever
kiri ga nai きりがない endless; be no end
  to; interminable [the problems, etc.]
kuchinai 朽ちない imperishable
mukyu (**da**) 無窮(だ) infinite time
  (permanent)
raise 来世 eternal (future) world
tokoshie (**da**) [L] とこしえ(だ) eternity
  (eternal; forever)
yūgen (**da**) 有限(だ) finiteness (finite;
  having limits)
  kagiri naku 限りなく endlessly; without
    end
  mugen (**da**) 無限(だ) infinity; bound-
    lessness (infinite; boundless)

その永遠のいのちとは, 彼らが唯一のまことの神であるあ
なたと, あなたの遣わされたイエス・キリストとを知ること
です. (ヨハネ 17 ³)

33 EIKYŌ 影響
INFLUENCE, EFFECT

EIKYŌ 影響 influence; effect
  ~ **o ukeru** ~を受ける The young
    men in Sapporo *were influenced*
    greatly *by* the Bible Class in Dr.
    Clark's home.
  warui eikyō o oyobosu 悪い影響を
    及ぼす have a bad influence on
  yoi eikyō o ataeru 良い影響を与える
    have a good influence on

[...**ni**] **hibiku** [...に]響く influence;
  effect
HAMON 波紋 response; repercussion;
  effect
  ~ **ga hirogaru** ~が広がる The arrest in
    the bribery case *caused repercussions*
    that spread to the top government
    offices.
  ~ **o makiokosu** ~を巻き起こす The
    arrest of the Canadian scientist
    created an uproar in the political
    world.
HANDŌ 反動 reaction
  hankyō (**suru**)   反響(する)   echo;
    response (echo; resound)
    ~ **o yobiokosu** ~を呼び起こす His
      novel *met with a* favorable *reaction*
      from the critics (*created a* great
      sensation).
  hannō (**suru**) 反応(する) reaction;
    response (react; respond)
KANKA (**suru**) 感化(する) influence;
  inspiration (influence; inspire)
  ~ **o ataeru** ~を与える have influence
    upon; exert an influence on
  ~ **o ukeru** ~を受ける be influenced by
KŌKA 効果 effect
  ~ **ga agaranai** ~が上がらない One
    English lesson a week will *have no
    noticeable results* (*will have little
    effect*).
  ~ **ga hayai** ~が早い have an
    immediate effect upon
  ~ **ga nai** ~がない be ineffective
  ~ **ga yoi** ~が良い have a good effect
    [upon]
  ~ **o ageru** ~を上げる yield results;
    produce the goods
  ~ **o arawasu** ~を現わす show the
    effects [of]
  ~ **o hakki suru** ~を発揮する become
    effective; come into effect
  ~ **o motarasu** ~をもたらす bring
    about the effect [of]

~o osameru ~をおさめる reap the fruits [of]; bring results

gyakkōka 逆効果 contrary effect; opposite effect

  ~o kitasu ~をきたす produce the opposite effect; bring about a contrary effect; boomerang

kekka 結果 effect; result

  sono kekka... その結果... the result being...; the upshot is...

kikime ききめ effect; efficacy

  ~ga nai ~がない be ineffective; be no good [for]

  ~no aru ~のある The druggist said this medicine *was effective (was efficacious)* for stopping colds.

kiku きく be effective; take effect

  haba ga kiku 幅がきく He *carries a lot of weight (has a lot of pull)* in that city.

  kusuri ga kiku 薬がきく This *medicine does something for you (medicine helps you)*.

  nirami ga kiku にらみがきく His *authority carries weight* in government circles.

kōnō 効能 virtue; effect; efficiency

kōryoku 効力 validity; efficacy; effectiveness

  ~ga oyobu ~が及ぶ have effect upon; effects extend to

  ~o hassuru ~を発する become effective; come into force

  ~o motsu ~を持つ Coffee often *has the effect* of a mild stimulant.

  ~o shōjiru ~を生じる come into effect; come into force

  ~o ushinau ~を失う lose its effect; become null and void

mukō (da) 無効(だ) invalidity (null and void; invalid)

  ~ni naru ~になる become null and void; come to nothing

yūkō (da) 有効(だ) validity; effectiveness (valid; effective)

  ~kikan o enchō suru ~期間を延長する I *extended* my membership.

  ~na shochi ~な処置 effective measures

oyobosu 及ぼす have effect [upon]

seiryoku 勢力 influence; power

  ~han'i 範囲 sphere of influence

settoku (suru) 説得(する) persuasion (persuade; talk into)

yoha 余波 after effect; consequences

  ~o ukeru ~を受ける This year's wheat crop *is suffering from the effects of* last summer's drought.

yūryoku (da) 有力(だ) influential

  yūryokusha 有力者 man of weight; influential person

⇨ **40, 72**

ですから、あなたがたは、互いに罪を言い表わし、互いのために祈りなさい。いやされるためです。義人の祈りは働くと、大きな力があります。（ヤコブ 5 [16]）

34 FUAN 不安 ANXIETY

ANJIRU (anzuru) 案じる(案ずる) be anxious [about, over]

  Anzuru yori umu ga yasui [P] 案ずるより産むが安い Things are never as hard as they seem.

  sue ga anjirareru 末が案じられる The boy has been seen in the bars, and there *is concern over his future*.

aoiki toiki (da) 青息吐息(だ) Due to the tight money policy, small business is *in a sad plight*.

Asu wa asu no kaze ga fuku あすは、あすの風が吹く "Tomorrow will look after itself; each day has troubles enough of its own." (Matthew 6 : 34)

dōki ga hageshiku naru 動悸が激しくなる one's heart begins to beat fast

dokitto suru どきっとする give a start; be startled

FUAN 不安 anxiety

~ na kaotsuki ~な顔つき an uneasy look

~ ni naru ~になる become uneasy

~ ni omou ~に思う Lincoln *felt uneasy* about the political maneuvering in Chicago.

~ ni osowareru ~に襲われる The President *was overcome with anxiety* over Grant's army at Vicksburg.

~ ni tsukimatowareru ~に付きまとわれる be haunted by anxiety

~ o kanjiru ~を感じる be disturbed [about]; feel anxious [about]; feel ill at ease

ichimatsu no fuan 一まつの不安 some concern; a touch of uncertainty

happō fusagari (da) 八方ふさがりだ *Everything seems to go against* me at the office.

hara hara suru はらはらする be uneasy; be in suspense; be on pins and needles

kenen (suru) 懸念(する) fear; worry (fear; worry about)

KI ga ki de nai 気が気でない be beside oneself; be full of anxiety; be on edge

~ ga momeru ~がもめる The train was about to leave without us, and we *were in a stew* (*were nervous*).

~ ga susumanai ~が進まない feel reluctant

~ ni kakaru ~にかかる be on one's mind

~ ni naru ~になる get on one's nerves; bother one; become sensitive about

~ ni suru ~にする He is always *worried about* his appearance.

~ ni yamu ~に病む As he grew older, he *became* very *self-conscious* about his height.

~ no yasumaru toki ga nai ~の休まる時がない have no time to relax

~ o momu ~をもむ His mother *was worried* (*felt anxious*) when he

was late coming home from the mountains.

kigakari 気がかり concern; apprehension

~ ni naru ~になる become a matter of concern; become concerned about

kizukai (u) 気づかい(気づかう) worry; concern (feel anxious about)

KOKORO ga kakimidasareru 心がかき乱される one's heart is troubled; be all upset

~ moto nai ~もとない I *feel insecure* traveling alone in a foreign country.

ikita kokochi ga shinai 生きたここちがしない After the bullet pierced his hat and the horse galloped away, Abe *felt more dead than alive*.

kokorobosoi 心細い helpless; forlorn

naishin odayaka de nai 内心穏やかでない I pretended not to notice but *felt uneasy inside*.

shimpai (suru) 心配(する) worry; anxiety (worry; worry about; be anxious about)

~ no amari ~のあまり Being *over-anxious* (*overly-worried*) about the children, she became exhausted and had to rest.

~ no tane ~の種 cause for worry

~ o kakeru ~をかける trouble one; cause anxiety [to]

yokei na shimpai o suru よけいな心配をする be overly-worried [about]; be unnecessarily concerned [over]

manjiri to mo shinai まんじりともしない I was concerned about her safety and *couldn't sleep a wink* last night.

munasawagi ga suru 胸騒ぎがする Since my boy had just walked to the railroad station, *a vague feeling of uneasiness came over me* when I heard the crash.

ochitsukanai 落ち着かない feel uneasy; be at sea

yoru mo ochiochi nemurenai 夜もおちおち眠れない can't sleep peacefully; can't get any sleep

omoiwazurai (u) 思い煩い(思い煩う) worry; anxiety (be anxious) [over]

ozuozu suru おずおずする be ill at ease

tameiki o morasu [L] ためいきをもらす heave a sigh; give a sigh of relief

tayorinai たよりない forlorn; undependable

te ni ase o nigitte 手に汗を握って I *sat on the edge of my seat* during the exciting auto race.

yūryo (suru) 憂慮(する) anxiety (dread)

zutsū no tane 頭痛の種 a headache
⇨ 150

何も思い煩わないで，あらゆるばあいに，感謝をもってささげる祈りと願いによって，あなたがたの願い事を神に知っていただきなさい．(ピリピ 4 ⁶)

35 FUHEI 不平
DISCONTENT, COMPLAINT

butsu-butsu iu [C] ぶつぶつ言う That old landlady is always *mumbling complaints (crabbing)* about the way we leave our rooms.

FUHEI 不平 discontent; complaint

~ **bunshi** ~分子 The *dissident group (dissatisfied element)* immediately raised an objection to the proposal.

~ **fuman ga aru** ~不満がある *There is malcontent and complaining* among the athletes staying at the hotel.

~ **no koe o kiku** ~の声をきく hear of complaints; receive complaints

~ **o idaku** ~をいだく feel discontented

~ **o iu** ~を言う complain; gripe

~ **o morasu** ~をもらす let out complaints

~ **o naraberu** ~を並べる make complaints

~ **o narasu** ~を鳴らす complain loudly; squawk

fufuku 不服 dissatisfaction

~ **o iu** ~を言う complain [of, about]; grumble [at]

~ **o tonaeru** ~を唱える lodge a complaint; complain [of]; protest [against]

fujūbun (da) 不十分(だ) insufficient; unsatisfactory

FUMAN 不満 discontent; malcontent

~ **ga tsunoru** ~がつのる dissatisfaction worsens; malcontent grows

~ **ni omou** ~に思う feel dissatisfied

~ **no hakeguchi o motomeru** ~のはけ口を求める The students did not like the professor and were *looking for an outlet for their complaints (seeking a vent for their dissatisfaction).*

~ **o buchimakeru** ~をぶちまける He came bursting into the president's office and *blurted out all his complaints.*

~ **o morasu** ~をもらす air grievances; complain

fumanzoku 不満足 dissatisfaction

fusoku 不足 insufficiency; inadequacy; shortage

GUCHI ぐち complaining; grumbling

~ **o kobosu** ~をこぼす pour out petty complaints; complain; gripe

guchippoi ぐちっぽい given to grumbling; always griping

guchippoku naru ぐちっぽくなる When people get older they *start moaning* about everything.

guzuguzu iu ぐずぐず言う Instead of getting the job done, he just keeps *grumbling about petty things (bellyaching* [S]).

guzuru ぐずる fret; murmur; complain

ii **kao o shinai** いい顔をしない When I suggested that he pay for all of us, he

didn't look very happy about it.
iibun ga aru 言い分がある Wait a minute, I *have something to say* about that.

iya na kao o suru いやな顔をする When I told him his English needed much improvement, he *looked hurt.*

kechi o tsukeru けちをつける When I showed him the new building, all he did was *find fault with it* (*pick flaws in it*).

ki ni iranai 気に入らない I *do not like* (*am dissatisfied with*) his way of teaching English.

~ ni kuwanai ~ にくわない I *can't stand* his attitude.

kokuso (suru) 告訴(する) legal complaint; (file a complaint [against])

KUJŌ 苦情 complaint
~ o iu ~ を言う lodge a complaint [against]; complain [of]
~ o mochidasu ~ を持ち出す bring out a grievance
~ o mōshitateru ~ を申し立てる file a complaint (against)

MONKU 文句 (verbal) complaint
~ o iu ~ を言う complain; grumble about
~ o tsukeru ~ をつける complain against; single out a complaint
kimarimonku 決まり文句 stock complaint; pet peeve; everyone's gripe

monotarinaku kanjiru 物足りなく感じる I *feel something is lacking* in the whole presentation.
monotarinai tokoro ga aru 物足りない所がある It is a good book on English study, but *something seems lacking* (*it leaves something to be desired*).

mushi ga osamaranai 虫がおさまらない They apparently tried their best to make up for it, but we *are still not happy.*

nakigoto 泣き言 tale of woes; complaint
~ o iu ~ を言う cry about; whine about

tsubuyaki (ku) つぶやき(つぶやく) murmuring (murmur; grumble)

uppun o harasu うっぷんを晴らす He *vented his anger on* them by reporting their actions to the boss.

乏しいからこう言うのではありません．私は、どんな境遇にあっても満ち足りることを学びました．
私は、貧しさの中にいる道も知っており、豊かさの中にいる道も知っています．また、飽くことにも飢えることにも、富むことにも乏しいことにも、あらゆる境遇に対処する秘訣を心得ています．（ピリピ 4 [11, 12]）

36 FUKANŌ 不可能
IMPOSSIBILITY

arienai あり得ない cannot be; impossible
DEKINAI できない cannot do
~ sōdan ~ 相談 On the subject of trade with Red China the Ambassador said *he couldn't talk about it* (*it was a useless discussion*).

tachiuchi dekinai たち打ちできない When skinny Abe faced the brawny wrestler, they thought he *would be no match for* him (*didn't have a chance*).

dō suru koto mo dekinai どうすることもできない Nothing can be done about it.

dō ni mo naranai どうにもならない Once the South fired on Fort Sumter, the situation *was beyond control.*

FUKANŌ na koto o kokoromiru 不可能な事を試みる try the impossible
~ na koto o nozomu ~ な事を望む hope for the impossible
~ na koto o yōkyū suru ~ な事を要求する ask the impossible
~ to minasu ~ とみなす look upon [something] as impossible
funō (da) 不能(だ) impossibility (impossible)

~ gatai ~ がたい hard to...
shinjigatai [etc.] 信じがたい[等] hard to believe

ikan tomo shigatai いかんともしがたい nothing can be done; there is no way to help

ha ga tatanai 歯が立たない The Americans *are no match for* (*can't compete with*) the British in soccer.

hanashi ni naranai 話にならない be absurd; be out of the question

hito wa dare demo ete fuete ga aru 人はだれでも得手不得手がある Everyone has his strong and weak points.

~ kaneru ~ かねる be unable to...

　dekikaneru [etc.] できかねる [等] be unable to do

　mōshiagekanemasu ga 申し上げかねますが It's difficult for me to say, but...

　mikomi ga nai 見込みがない He's going to try out for the Olympic team, but he *doesn't have a chance.*

　mondai ni naranai 問題にならない Concerning your request, I'm afraid *it's out of the question.*

rachi ga akanai らちがあかない There were so many conflicting opinions at the conference that we *got nowhere.*

seki no yama [P] 関の山 *It's all I can do* to pass my exams.

Sugitaru wa oyobazaru ga gotoshi [P] 過ぎたるは及ばざるがごとし Too much is as bad as too little.

te ni oenai 手に負えない unmanageable

tohō mo nai 途方もない His suggestion to tour America in three weeks was *absurd* (*wild; preposterous*).

tonde mo nai とんでもない That's out of the question.

⇨ **123**
神にとって不可能なことは一つもありません. (ルカ 1 ³⁷)

37 FUKUJŪ 服従
OBEDIENCE

chūjitsu (da) 忠実(だ) faithfulness (faithful; loyal)

FUKUJŪ (suru) 服従(する) obedience (obey)

　~ o shiiru ~ をしいる compel obedience

　kokoro kara fukujū suru 心から服従する yield whole-hearted obedience [to]

　zettai fukujū 絶対服従 absolute obedience

jūjun(da) 従順(だ) obedience; submissiveness (obedient; submissive; amenable)

kutsujū (suru) 屈従(する) submission (submit to)

mōjū (suru) 盲従(する) blind obedience (follow blindly)

shimpuku suru 心服する be devoted to

shitagau 従う obey; follow

　Kami no mikokoro ni shitagau 神のみ心に従う obey God's will

　kokuhō ni shitagau 国法に従う be obedient to the laws of the land

shōfuku suru 承服する give in [to]; go along with

gyoshigatai 御しがたい Lincoln found the many factions within his cabinet *hard to handle* (*hard to control*).

iu koto o kiku 言う事を聞く obey; mind; do as one says

iinari hōdai ni naru 言いなり放題になる He *has* the boss *wrapped around his little finger.*

kōkō (suru) 孝行(する) filial piety (fulfil one's obligations to one's parents)

　~ musuko (musume) ~ むすこ(むすめ) obedient son (daughter)

kussuru 屈する yield [to]; follow

ōjiru 応じる respond; comply [with]

　sunao ni ōjiru すなおに応じる The labor union *readily accepted* the management's proposal.

onjun (da) 温順(だ) docility (docile; compliant)

　onryō (da) 温良(だ) amiability (amiable; gentle)

somuku そむく disobey; go against
あなたがたはこのことを知らないのですか，あなたがたが自
分の身をささげて奴隷として服従すれば，その服従する
相手の奴隷であって，あるいは罪の奴隷となって死に至
り，あるいは従順の奴隷となって義に至るのです．
(ローマ 6 ¹⁶)

38 FUSHIGI 不思議 STRANGENESS

fu ni ochinai ふにおちない The explanation
he gave sounds plausible but there *are*
still *some doubtful points* about it.

FUSHIGI (da) 不思議(だ) strangeness
(strange; mysterious)
  ~ ni omou ~ に思う think it strange
  ~ sō na kao ~ そうな顔 mystified look;
  puzzled look

gara ni nai 柄にない *It's not like him* (*It's
out of character for him*) to use such bad
language.

HEN (da) 変(だ) strangeness; oddness
(strange; curious; odd; queer; bizarre)
  ~ na koto o iu ~ な事を言う *What
  you say sounds strange* to me.
  ~ ni omou ~ に思う think it strange
  [that]; be puzzled

fūgawari (da) 風変わり(だ) peculiarity
(peculiar; odd)

ippū kawatta hito 一風かわった人 a
somewhat queer person

kawarimono 変わり者 an odd
character

mesaki no kawatta mono 目先の変わ
ったもの This is *something one seldom
sees* (*a rarity*).

henkutsu na hito 偏屈な人 an eccentric

hitonami hazureta (ōkii; chiisai) 人並
みはずれた[大きい，小さい] Abe *had
extraordinarily* large hands.

IJŌ (da) 異状(だ) queerness (queer;
abnormal, unusual)
  ~ o mitomeru ~ を認める find something wrong; find something amiss

iyō (da) 異様(だ) strangeness (strange;
fantastic; odd)
  ~ na fukusō ~ な服装 She was
  wearing *outlandish clothes*.
  ~ ni kanjiru ~ に感じる *It was an
  odd feeling* (*It was a strange feeling*)
  to hear the boy speak so many
  languages.

KIBATSU (da) 奇抜(だ) unconventionali-
ty; novelty (striking; unconventional)
  ~ na koto o kangaeru ~ な事を考える
  He always *comes up with fantastic
  ideas* (*thinks up novel ideas*).

kii (da) 奇異(だ) peculiarity (peculiar;
queer; singular)

kikai (da) 奇怪(だ) grotesqueness
(grotesque)

kimyo (da) 奇妙(だ) strangeness
(strange; curious)
  ~ na dekigoto ~ なできごと a funny
  (odd; strange; freak) incident

kimi no warui 気味の悪い weird;
uncanny

mezurashii 珍しい rare; novel; curious

MYŌ (da) 妙(だ) strangeness (strange;
uncanny; queer)
  ~ na koto ni wa ~ な事には strange to
  say; strangely enough
  ~ ni kikoeru kamo shirenai ga... ~
  に聞こえるかもしれないが… This may
  sound strange to you, but…

okashii おかしい funny; strange; peculiar

tohō mo nai 途方もない outlandish;
ridiculous; absurd; bizarre

toppi (da) [c] とっぴ(だ) You'd better not
get involved with him; he is always
doing *wild* (*preposterous*) things.

toppyōshi mo nai [c] とっぴょうしもない
After the election, office seekers came
to Abe, making all sorts of *preposterous* (*extravagant*) demands.

⇨ 136
わが神，主よ，あなたのくすしきみわざと，われらを思うみ
おもいとは多くて，くらべうるものはない．わたしはこれを

語り述べようとしても多くて数えることはできない。
(詩篇 40⁵)

39 GANKO がんこ
OBSTINACY,
STUBBORNNESS

atsukamashii あつかましい brazen-faced; audacious

ekoji (da) [c] えこじ(だ) That old man is surely an *obstinate person.*

ga o haru 我を張る Even when we pointed out his error, he kept *asserting himself* and refused to listen.

GAN toshite kikiirenai がんとして聞き入れない refuse to listen to; remain impervious to reason; remain adamant
   ganbaru がんばる insist on; persist in
   gankoya がんこ屋 hard-headed person
   gankyō (da) がん強(だ) stubbornness (stubborn; dogged)
    ~ ni iitōsu ~ に言い通す We tried to talk him down, but he *doggedly maintained his position.*
    ~ ni teikō suru ~ に抵抗する resist stubbornly
   ganmei (da) がん迷(だ) bigotry (bigoted; obstinate)

gōjō (da) 強情(だ) obstinacy (self-willed)
   ~ o haru ~ を張る We hoped he would give in, but he *stuck to his position (refused to budge).*

goneru ごねる be cranky; be pig-headed

henkutsu (da) 変屈(だ) narrow-mindedness; bigotry (narrow-minded; bigoted)

ichizu ni omoikomu いちずに思い込む He *has a fixed idea (is unshakably convinced)* that he must study in Tokyo and won't listen to any other suggestion.

IJI o haru 意地を張る be unbending; be unpersuadable.
   ~ o tōsu ~ を通す In minor matters Lincoln did not *insist on having his own way.*

kataiji (da) 片意地(だ) intractability (intractable; stubborn; headstrong)

ikkoku(da) いっこく(だ) obstinacy(bigoted)

ippo mo yuzuranai 一歩も譲らない In the matter of preserving the Union, Lincoln *wouldn't give an inch (stood pat).*

ittenbari (da) 一点張り(だ) persistent; obstinate

ittetsu (da) 一徹(だ) doggedness (dogged; obstinate)
   oi no ittetsu 老いの一徹 old and stubborn
   ittetsumono 一徹者 dogged person; person of firm resolution; person set in his ways

iu koto o kikanai 言うことを聞かない I told the boy not to do it, but he *does not listen to me (is disobedient).*

katakuna (da) かたくな(だ) hardness (hardened; stubborn)
   kokoro o katakuna ni suru 心をかたくなにする Today, if you will hear His voice, do not *grow stubborn,* as in those days of rebellion...(Heb. 3:15)

kimuzukashii 気むずかしい hard to get along with; perverse; cranky
   kimuzukashiya 気むずかしや a crank

mimi o kasanai 耳を貸さない I tried to reason with him, but he *turned a deaf ear (refused to listen)* to me.

shibutoi しぶとい obstinate

shitsukoi しつこい persistent; troublesome; dogged
   shitsukoku iu しつこく言う We thought the matter was settled, but he *keeps harping on* it.
   shitsuyō (da) 執よう(だ) obstinacy (obstinate)

te ni oenai 手に負えない unmanageable
   ~ ni amaru hito ~ にあまる人 a hard person to deal with

tsumujimagari (da) [c] つむじ曲がり(だ) pig-headed person

wakarazuya [c] わからずや a crank; a hard

nut to crack

yutori ga nai ゆとりがない He won't listen to the plan, because he *has no latitude in his thinking.*

yūzū no kikanai 融通のきかない Judging by his attitude, he seems to be *an inflexible person.*

ところが，あなたは，かたくなさと悔い改めのない心のゆえに，御怒りの日，すなわち，神の正しいさばきの現われる日の御怒りを自分のために積み上げているのです。(ローマ 2 ⁵)

40 GEN'IN, KEKKA 原因・結果 CAUSE AND EFFECT

ashigakari o tsukeru 足がかりをつける He talked to the boss directly and *gained a foothold* for getting into the company.

dekibae できばえ result, workmanship

dōki 動機 motive; incentive

  [...ga] **dōki to naru** [...が]動機となる Studying English *became his motivation* for going abroad.

kien 機縁 chance; occasion; relation

GEN'IN 原因 cause

  ~ **fumei (da)** ~不明(だ) causes unknown

  ~ **o saguru** ~を探る search for the cause

  ~ **o tashikameru** ~を確かめる make sure of the cause

  [...ni] ~ **suru** [...に] ~する The rain showers today *are due to (are caused by)* the cold front from the west.

  [...no] ~ **to naru** [...の] ~となる become the cause of...

  ketteiteki gen'in 決定的原因 determining cause

  kore to iu gen'in ga naku これという原因がなく without any reasonable cause

  wake no wakaranai gen'in 訳のわからない原因 inexplicable cause; unknown cause

genshi 原始 beginning; origin

Hi no nai tokoro ni kemuri wa tatanu [P] 火のない所に煙は立たぬ Where there's smoke, there's fire [P].

jigō jitoku (da) 自業自得(だ) Your dismissal *serves you right;* you were always late to work.

jisseki o ageru 実績を上げる He is sure that this teaching method *will bring results.*

KEKKA 結果 result; effect

  [...no] ~ **to naru** [...の]~結果となる result in; effect; bring about the result of

  [...no] ~ **toshite** [...の]~結果として as a result of

  sono kekka... その結果... the upshot is...; as a result...

kihon 基本 foundation; basis; standard

  [...ni] **motozuku** [...に]基づく be based upon; be grounded on

kikime ききめ effect; efficacy

kikkake きっかけ opportunity

  ~ **o tsukeru** ~をつける He *found an occasion (created an opportunity)* for selling insurance to him by going to the baseball game with him.

kompon 根本 source; origin; basis; root

mi o musubu 実を結ぶ bear fruit; bring forth results

minamoto 源 source; spring

motarasu もたらす bring; bring about; effect

motomoto 元々 from the outset; by nature; in the beginning

NARITATSU 成り立つ materialize

  nariyuki 成り行き development; course; consequences

    shizen no nariyuki ni makaseru 自然の成り行きに任せる They decided to do nothing about the problem and just *let nature take its course.*

seika 成果 results

seiseki 成績 results

~ ga warui (yoi) ~が悪い(良い) bad (good) results

RIYŪ 理由 reason; cause

~ mo naku ~もなく without reason; without cause

~ o ageru ~をあげる give the reasons [for]

seitō na riyū 正当な理由 just cause; just reason

[...**no**] **sei** [...の]せい It was *because of* him that we failed.

shōjiru 生じる give rise to; bring about; cause

umidasu 生み出す give birth to; create; bring forth

shōko 証拠 proof; result [of]

tane 種 seed; cause; source

wake 訳 reason

yue ゆえ reason

⇨ **33**

なぜなら，万物は御子にあって造られたからです．天にあるもの，地にあるもの，見えるものまた見えないもの，王座も主権も支配も権威も，すべて御子によって造られたのです．万物は，御子によって造られ，御子のために造られたのです．

御子は，万物よりも先に存在し，万物は御子にあって成り立っています．（コロサイ 1 ¹⁶, ¹⁷）

41 GENJITSU 現実 REALITY

ari no mama ありのまま Don't color up the story; tell it *just as it is.*

chūshōteki (da) 抽象的(だ) abstract

GENJITSU 現実 reality

~ ga tomonawanai ~が伴わない Idealistically, a classless society sounds good, but it just *does not follow reality.*

~ kara yūri suru ~から遊離する flee from reality; run away from the truth

~ ni modoru ~にもどる come down to earth

~ ni mukau ~に向かう face reality

~ ni sokushite ~に即して be based on reality; be realistic

araware (ru) 現われ(現われる) manifestation; appearance (appear; emerge)

gen ni 現に really; actually

gemba ni iawaseru 現場に居合わせる happen to be at the actual spot

genjitsubanare shite iru 現実離れしている Your plan to start the project without any funds *is out of touch with reality.*

genjitsushugi (no hito) 現実主義(の人) realism (realist)

genjitsuteki (da) 現実的(だ) realistic

genjō 現状 present condition; status quo; existing order

~ iji ~維持 maintaining the status quo

~ no mama ni shite oku ~のままにしておく Since we don't have agreement, we had better *leave the matter as it is.*

~ o daha suru ~を打破する abolish the status quo; do away with the existing order

genjō 現場 the actual spot

genshō 現象 phenomenon

jijitsu 事実 fact

jikkan 実感 realization; real feeling

[...**no**] **~ ga deru** [...の]~が出る Seeing those beautiful paintings *makes me feel as if I were really* in the mountains.

jikken (suru) 実験(する) experimentation; test (experiment; test)

jikkō (suru) 実行(する) execution [of a plan] (execute; carry out)

jissai (wa) 実際(は) reality; actuality (as a matter of fact)

~ ni... 実際に... in practice...

~ ni sokushite ~に即して be in accordance with the facts; be pragmatic

~ no tokoro... ~のところ... **as a**

matter of fact...; to tell the truth...

jissaiteki (da) 実際的(だ) practical; down to earth

~ de nai ~でない isn't realistic

jissen (suru) 実践(する) practice (carry out)

jisshi suru 実施する put into operation; enforce; carry out

jisshitsu 実質 substance

jisshitsuteki (da) 実質的(だ) substantial

jissō [L] 実相 state of affairs

jitsugen (suru) 実現(する) actualization (actualize; realize)

jitsugensei no toboshii 実現性の乏しい unrealistic; lacking in reality; have little chance of being realized

jitsuzai (suru) 実在(する) real existence; actual being (have real existence)

jitsuzonshugi 実存主義 existentialism

jittai 実体 substance; substantiality

genri 原理 fundamental truth; principle

GUTAITEKI (da) 具体的(だ) concrete; definite

~ na katachi de arawareru ~な形で現われる appear in concrete form; take shape

gutaika (suru) 具体化(する) actualization; realization (actualize)

hommono 本物 the real thing; the real McCoy

honshitsu 本質 essence; intrinsic nature; essential qualities

jōtai 状態 condition; state of things

kyakkanteki (da) 客観的(だ) objective; matter of fact

mokuzen ni semaru 目前に迫る We were worried about finishing because the deadline *was drawing near* (*was pressing upon us*).

suikō (suru) [L] 遂行(する) performance (perform; carry out; execute)

yōsu 様子 situation; circumstances; state of things

~ o miru ~を見る Before you commit yourself, you'd better *see how the land lies* (*take stock of the situation*).

yume ga yaburareru 夢が破られる We hoped to take first place in the swimming meet, but our *dreams were shattered.*

~ monogatari ~物語 Talking about taking a world trip without any money is *an idle dream* (*a wild dream*).

⇨ **126, 175**

私たちは、あなたがたに、私たちの主イエス・キリストの力と来臨とを知らせましたが、それは、うまく考え出した作り話に従ったのではありません。この私たちは、キリストの威光の目撃者なのです。（ペテロ II 1 ¹⁶）

42 GIMAN 欺まん
FABRICATION, FALSEHOOD

demakase (da) 出任せ(だ) fabrication (fabricated; irresponsible [talk])

detarame でたらめ random talk; fib

~ o iu ~を言う say anything that comes into one's head; cook [it] up; talk through one's hat

detchiageru [C] でっち上げる The lawyers *trumped up a story* about his having been married before, but it was false.

itsuwari (ru) 偽り(偽る) lie, deception (lie; deceive)

~ o iu ~を言う lie

kotoba o nigosu 言葉をにごす When I asked him about last evening, he answered, *using evasive words* (*speaking ambiguously*).

kotobajiri o toraeru 言葉じりを捕える Don't try to *trap him in his words* (*find fault with his wording*) but listen to what he is trying to convey.

KUCHISAKI bakari keiki no ii koto o iu [C] ~口先ばかり景気のいい事を言う That politician *gives only the rosy side of things.*

~ **dake no** ~だけの insincere; with lip only

~ **de gomakasu** ~でごまかす He had obviously short-changed me, but he *quickly talked his way out of it.*

~ **no umai** ~のうまい smooth talking; honey-tongued

kōjitsu de 口実で on the pretext of…

kuchiguruma ni noserareru [c] 口車に乗せられる Be careful of that smooth salesman or you may be *talked into* (*be wheedled into*) buying something you don't need.

sorazorashii kuchi o kiku そらぞらしい口をきく make a circumlocution; make a fabrication

KYOGI 虚偽 fiction; fraud; falsehood

kyokō [L] 虚構 fabrication; fiction

kyosei o haru 虚勢を張る We thought he *was* just *bluffing* when he vowed to win in eight rounds.

makoto shiyaka ni iu 誠しやかに言う speak plausibly

mayutsuba mono [c] まゆつばもの That talk about cheap Tokyo land is *a cock and bull story* (is *suspect*).

mie 見え show

ne mo ha mo nai 根も葉もない Some charged the Lincoln family with treason, but *it was pure fabrication* (*there were no grounds whatsoever*).

nimaijita o tsukau hito 二枚舌を使う人 He's *a two-faced person*; he praises you to your face, then criticizes you in front of others.

ocha o nigosu お茶をにごす Don't *camouflage the issue* (*muddy the issue*) with irrelevant points.

okuba ni mono ga hasamatta yōna koto o iu 奥歯に物がはさまったような事を言う You *talk as if you were holding something back.*

teisai no ii koto o iu 体裁のいい事を言う He tried to calm the shareholders by

giving a rosy picture of the business.

~ **o tsukurou** ~を繕う put on an outward show; save appearances

tsukurigoe 作り声 falsetto

tsukurigoto 作り事 fabrication; falsehood

~ **o iu** ~を言う make up a story; concoct a story

tsukurou 繕う gloss over [the facts]

tsumi tsukuri na koto o suru 罪作りなことをする With tales like that, you'll *lead* that boy *astray.*

umai koto o iu うまい事を言う speak cleverly

umasugiru hanashi うますぎる話 talk that's too good; story too good to be true

USO うそ lie

~ **happyaku o naraberu** ~八百を並べる tell downright lies; tell a pack of lies

~ **kara deta makoto** [P] ~から出たまこと Truth born of falsehood. = There is some truth in every falsehood.

~ **mo hōben** [P] ~も方便 A lie is sometimes expedient. = A white lie doesn't hurt.

~ **no katamari** ~のかたまり Everything he told you was simply a *pack of lies.*

~ **o iu** (**tsuku**) ~を言う(をつく) lie; tell a lie

~ **o oshieru** ~を教える tell a lie; give one a bum steer

makka na uso 真赤なうそ That is an *outright lie* (*baldfaced lie*).

miesuita uso 見えすいたうそ obvious lie; clear lie

mottomo rashii uso もっともらしいうそ plausible lie

tachi no warui uso たちの悪いうそ evil lie

tsumi no nai uso 罪のないうそ white lie

usotsuke! [C] うそつけ! You're a liar! Don't lie!

usotsuki うそつき liar

~ wa dorobō no hajimari [P] ~ は どろぼうの始まり Show me a liar and I'll show you a thief.

[...no] wana ni hikkakaru [...の]わなにひっかかる be entangled in...

⇨ **46**

主の憎まれるものが六つある...すなわち, 高ぶる目, 偽りを言う舌... (箴言 6 ¹⁶, ¹⁷)

43 GIMON 疑問
DOUBT, QUESTION

ayashii 怪しい doubtful; far-fetched

ayashimu 怪しむ I *question (am dubious of)* his statements.

chūi jimbutsu 注意人物 suspicious person; a suspect

dōka to omou [C] どうかと思う He says he can pay it all in three months, but I *wonder.*

fu ni ochinai ふにおちない questionable; doubtful; be skeptical [of]

fukuzatsu na omomochi de 複雑な面持ちで He listened to the strange tale with a *bewildered look.*

fushigi (da) 不思議(だ) strangeness (strange; marvelous; miraculous)

~ ni omou ~ に思う be surprised [at]; think it strange

FUSHIN 不審 doubt; distrust

~ ni omou ~ に思う think it strange; suspect; be in doubt

~ no ten ga aru ~ の点がある *There are some questionable points* in his story.

~ o idaku ~ をいだく harbor doubts; have misgivings [over]

~ sō na yōsu o suru ~ そうな様子をする Everyone *looked doubtful* when he told his story.

~ sō ni ~ そうに inquiringly; suspiciously

GIMON 疑問 doubt, question

[...ka dōka] ~ da [...かどうか] ~ だ *It is questionable whether* his second play will be a success.

~ o idaku [L] ~ をいだく have doubts [about]; be wary [of]

ginen 疑念 doubt; suspicion; distrust; misgivings

~ o idaku ~ をいだく have doubts [about]; be uncertain

giwaku 疑惑 distrust; misgivings

~ no me de miru ~ の目で見る look [at] with doubtful eyes; look at suspiciously; take a dim view of

~ o idaku [L] ~ をいだく entertain doubts [about]; have qualms about

hanshin hangi de 半信半疑で When they told me that I had won the contest, I *could not quite believe it.*

kaigi 懐疑 unbelief; skepticism

~ ni torawareru ~ にとらわれる He *was seized with doubts* about his religious faith after studying all those philosophy books.

kaigiteki (da) 懐疑的(だ) skeptical

kengi けん疑 suspicion

[...no] ~ de [...の] ~ で He was arrested *on suspicion* of being a spy.

~ ga kakaru ~ がかかる After Lincoln's assassination, some members of his cabinet *came under suspicion.*

~ o kakeru ~ をかける suspect [a person]

utagai (u) 疑い(疑う) doubt; question (doubt; question; disbelieve)

~ ga hareru ~ が晴れる Upon discovering the facts, all the *doubts* about his story *were dissolved.*

~ no me de miru ~ の目で見る The policeman *looked at* me *with skeptical eyes.*

~ o harasu ~ を晴らす sweep away doubts; dissolve doubts

~o **idaku** [L] ～をいだく entertain doubts; be suspicious [of]

~o **kakeru** ～をかける throw doubt [on]; put a cloud over

~**yochi ga nai** ～余地がない *It is beyond the shadow of a doubt* (*There is no question*) that he had nothing to do with it.

jibun no me o utagau 自分の目を疑う When I saw the astronaut walking in space, I *could hardly believe my eyes.*

Nana tabi tazunete, hito o utagae [P] 七たび尋ねて人を疑え Perhaps you think he took your money, but *don't be too quick to judge.*

utagaibukai 疑い深い distrustful; overly suspicious

utagawashii 疑わしい doubtful; incredulous; questionable

~**baai ni** ～場合に *If in doubt*, don't pay him any money.

hammon(suru) 煩もん(する) inner struggle (have an inner struggle; question)

ikagawashii いかがわしい questionable; shady

kama o kakeru [C] かまをかける He *asked a leading question* to embarrass her, but she refused to answer.

kegen sō (da) けげんそう(だ) suspicious

kubi o kashigeru [C] 首をかしげる When I told him about the opportunities in Brazil, he *showed some doubts about* (*wondered about*) it.

kusai to omou [C] 臭いと思う *There is something fishy* about this deal.

madou 惑う be perplexed; be in a quandary

masaka to omou まさかと思う Did that dumbbell get into Tokyo University? I *can hardly believe it.*

mayoi (u) 迷い(う) illusion (be deluded; wander [off])

mayutsuba mono [C] まゆつば物 His

stories *should be taken with a grain of salt.*

mondai ni naru 問題になる become an issue; come into question

obotsukanai おぼつかない be doubtful; be uncertain

shinrai dekinai hito 信頼できない人 unreliable person

usankusai [C] うさん臭い suspicious looking

ushirogurai うしろ暗い underhanded; shady

warikirenai 割り切れない It looks all right on the surface, but *I'm not quite satisfied with it* (*I still have my doubts about it*).

イエスは答えて言われた、「神を信じなさい」.

まことに、あなたがたにつげます. だれでも、この山に向かって、『動いて、海にはいれ.』と言って、心の中で疑わず, ただ、自分の言ったとおりになると信じるなら、そのとおりになります. (マルコ 11 [22, 23])

44 GIRON 議論
DEBATE, DISCUSSION

benkai no yochi ga nai 弁解の余地がない there is no room for argument; there is no possible defense

dōdō meguri (da) 堂々巡り(だ) They kept *going round in circles* at the conference and couldn't reach a conclusion.

GIRON (suru) 議論(する) debate; discussion (debate; discuss)

~**de marumekomu** ～でまるめ込む confuse one with words; trip one up by logic

~**no yochi ga nai** ～の余地がない be beyond dispute; be indisputable

~**o tatakawasu** ～を戦わす engage in a battle of words; have a hot discussion

benron (suru) 弁論(する) debate; argument; pleading (argue the case)

gekiron (suru) 激論(する) heated argument (argue heatedly)

genron 言論 speech; discussion

gidai 議題 topic for discussion

giin 議員 member of an assembly

giketsu (suru) 議決(する) resolution; decision (resolve; decide)

gironzuki (da) 議論好き(だ) argumentative

hyōron 評論 editorial comment; critique; review

kaigi 会議 conference; meeting

kōkai tōron 公開討論 public debate

kōron (suru) 口論(する) dispute; quarrel (dispute [with]; argue)

kūron 空論 vain discussion

~ **ni hashiru** ～に走る use specious arguments; run around in circles

kyōgi (suru) 協議(する) deliberation; conference (deliberate; confer; hold a conference)

kyokuron (suru) 極論(する) extreme position (make a far-fetched argument)

kyokutan na riron 極端な理論 hypertheoretical argument

mizukakeron 水掛け論 futile argument

riron(teki) 理論(的) theory(theoretical)

rironzukeru 理論づける theorize; explain away

Ron yori shōko [P] 論より証拠 The proof of the pudding is in the eating [P].

ronbaku (suru) 論ばく(する) refutation (refute)

ronbun 論文 thesis; dissertation

ronchō 論調 tenor of argument

rondai 論題 subject of a theme

~ **o hazureta** ～をはずれた be beside the question; be irrelevant

rongi (suru) 論議(する) discussion (discuss)

rongichū 論議中 is being debated; is under discussion

ronjin o haru 論陣を張る argue; take a firm stand [for, against]

ronjiru 論じる argue; discuss

~ **kachi ga nai** ～価値がない be not worth discussing; be beneath arguing

~ **made mo nai** ～までもない needless to say...

ronpa (suru) 論破(する) refutation (refute)

ronpō 論法 logic; reasoning

ronri 論理 logic

~ **ni awanai** ～に合わない doesn't make sense; be illogical

ronriteki (da) 論理的(だ) logical

ronsen (suru) 論戦(する) battle of words (wrangle)

~ **o majieru** ～を交える engage in a heated argument

ronsha 論者 advocate

ronshi 論旨 point in question; point of an argument

~ **ga tsukamenai** ～がつかめない I *can't get the point of* his *argument.*

ronsō (suru) 論争(する) controversy (dispute)

~ **o makiokosu** ～を巻き起こす take issue with; cause a dispute

ronten 論点 point at issue

~ **ga bakuzen toshite iru** ～がばく然としている The *point of his argument is obscure.*

sōron (suru) 争論(する) argument; controversy (argue)

tōgi (suru) 討議(する) deliberation (deliberate; debate)

~ **o uchikiru** ～を打ち切る close a debate

tōron (suru) 討論(する) discussion (debate)

hanashiai (u) 話し合い(う) discussion (discuss; talk over together)

hiratai kotoba de ieba 平たい言葉で言えば to put it in simple words; speaking in plain language

hizazume dampan o suru ひざ詰め談

判をする press a demand; negotiate directly

iiarasoi (u) 言い争い(言い争う) dispute; quarrel (take issue with; have a battle of words)

iiharu 言い張る insist on

iikomeru 言いこめる talk one down; argue into silence

iwayuru いわゆる The *so-called* "leftists" failed to appear at the meeting.

jimon jitō suru 自問自答する answer one's own question

kikitadasu 聞きただす make sure [of]; ascertain

kōkaku awa o tobasu 口角あわを飛ばす When he got on that subject, he *argued vociferously* (*talked himself into a lather*).

kutte kakaru 食ってかかる say defiantly; talk back [to]; answer right back

mikaiketsu no mondai 未解決の問題 open question; be an unsettled problem

pinto ga hazureru ピントがはずれる be not pertinent; be irrelevant; be beside the point

RIKUTSU 理屈 reason; logic

  ~ ni awanai ~に合わない be unreasonable; be illogical; doesn't hold water

  ~ o iu ~を言う argue

  ~ o koneru ~をこねる argue for the sake of argument; put up an argument

  mottomo rashii rikutsu o tsukeru もっともらしい理屈をつける use subtle arguments; use plausible reasoning

  Muri ga tōreba, dōri ga hikkomu [P] 無理が通れば道理がひっこむ Extremism scares away reason.

  riro seizen to 理路整然と consistently; logically

sashi sematta mondai 差し迫った問題 the pressing issue; the burning question

sesshō (suru) 折衝(する) negotiation (negotiate)

settoku (suru) 説得(する) persuasion (persuade; convince)

  ~ ni tsutomeru ~に努める drive home one's point; try to persuade

SHINGI (suru) 審議(する) deliberation (deliberate; carefully discuss)

  keizoku shingi ni suru 継続審議にする carry the deliberation over into the next session

  shingichū (da) 審議中(だ) is under discussion; is being deliberated

shinpuku suru 信服(する) convince

shitsumon (suru) 質問(する) question (ask a question)

shuchō(suru) 主張(する) assertion; claim; allegation; insistence (assert; claim; allege; maintain; argue for)

sōdan (suru) 相談(する) talk; consultation (discuss; consult [with])

suji ga tatte inai 筋が立っていない be illogical; be contradictory

  sujimichi ga tōru 筋道が通る His *argument is logical.*

tazuneru 尋ねる put a question to [a person]

tonchinkan na henji o suru [C] とんちんかんな返事をする He was vague and *answered off the point* (*begged the question*).

yarikomeru やり込める talk (one) down; refute

yōten ni fureru 要点に触れる come to the point
⇨ 7

知者はどこにいるのですか. 学者はどこにいるのですか. この世の議論家はどこにいるのですか. 神は, この世の知恵を愚かなものにされたではありませんか.
(コリント I 1 ²⁰)

45 GISEI 犠牲 SACRIFICE

GISEI 犠牲 sacrifice

  [...o] ~ ni suru [...を] ~にする With this small budget you'll have to *sacrifice* beauty for durability in the house.

~ o harau ～ を払う His education didn't come easily; he *paid dearly* for it.

[...o] ~ toshite [...を] ～ として at the cost of; at the sacrifice of

hisō na gisei o harau 悲壮な犠牲を払う make a heroic sacrifice

jiko gisei 自己犠牲 self-sacrifice

giseiteki seishin 犠牲的精神 sacrificial spirit

hōshi (suru) 奉仕(する) service (serve)

ikenie [L] いけにえ animal sacrifice; expiatory offering

~ o sasageru ～をささげる offer an animal sacrifice; make a sacrifice on an altar

inochi o suteru 命を捨てる There is no greater love than this, that a man should *lay down his life* for his friends. (John 15 : 13)

ISSHIN o nagedasu 一身を投げ出す throw oneself into

~ o sasageru ～をささげる give up one's life [for]

kenshin (suru) 献身(する) devotion; dedication (devote oneself [to]; dedicate oneself [to])

kenshinteki (da) 献身的(だ) devoted; sacrificial

migawari ni naru 身代わりになる do something on behalf of another; stand as a substitute [for]

shimmei o nageutte (suru) 身命をなげうって(する) (do) at the risk of one's life

isshō o sasageru 一生をささげる Lincoln *devoted his life* to freeing the slaves.

kuimono ni suru 食い物にする Those parents *are exploiting* their child in the theatrical world.

mushō de teikyō suru 無償で提供する offer freely; offer gratuitously

sonaeru 供える offer up [food, etc.]

sonaemono 供え物 offering, votive offering

tsugunai (u) 償い(償う) restitution; redemption; expiation (make restitution; redeem; expiate)

tsumi no tsugunai (aganai) 罪の償い (あがない) expiation for sin; sacrifice for sin

そして自分から十字架の上で、私たちの罪をその身に負われました。それは、私たちが罪を離れ、義のために生きるためです。キリストの打ち傷のゆえに、あなたがたは、いやされたのです。（ペテロ I 2 ²⁴）

46   GOMAKASHI ごまかし
DECEPTION

azamuku 欺く deceive; delude

bake no kawa o hagasu 化けの皮をはがす By producing the evidence they were able to *rip off his mask* and show him up as a crook.

[...to iu] bimei no moto ni [...という]美名のもとに *Under the cloak of (masquerading as)* policemen, they entered the shop at night.

chakufuku suru 着服する The bank clerk *pocketed (embezzled)* funds for years before they caught him.

DAMASU だます trick; cheat

damashitoru だましとる The swindler *cheated* the old lady *out of* her savings.

damashiuchi だまし討ち surprise attack; sneak attack; foul play

yasu yasu to damasareru やすやすとだまされる My wife *was easily taken in* by the salesman and bought the useless machine.

[...no] furi o suru [...の]ふりをする Even though he was from a poor home, he *pretended to be (made out that he was)* from high society.

genkō fuitchi no hito 言行不一致の人

He's a *person who says one thing and does another.*

GISHŌ (suru) 偽証(する) perjury; false witness (perjure; bear false witness against)

    gisō (suru) 偽装(する) camouflage; disguise; sham (camouflage; disguise; be a sham)

    gizen 偽善 hypocrisy

      ~ o okonau ~ を行なう act insincerely; do [something] hypocritical

    itsuwari (ru) 偽り(偽る) lie; falsification (falsify; misrepresent)

    kyogi 虚偽 deception

    sagi 詐欺 fraud

GOMAKASHI (su) ごまかし(ごまかす) deception (deceive; cheat; fool)

    hito o gomakasu 人をごまかす fool a person; fool people

    jibun no kashitsu o gomakasu 自分の過失をごまかす He *cleverly covered up his own mistakes.*

    gomakashimono ごまかし物 What the dealer sold me turned out to be a *fake* (*phony*).

hyōri ga aru 表裏がある You can't believe what he says; he's *two-faced* (*a double-dealer*).

iikagen na koto o iu いいかげんな事を言う Be careful of that salesman; he always *talks irresponsibly.*

ikasama (da) [c] いかさま(だ) He turned out to be a *phony* (*bogus*) artist.

ikasamashi いかさま師 swindler

inchiki (da) [c] いんちき(だ) That ad is just a *come-on;* you don't get all they promise.

kakehiki かけ引き bargaining; haggling

    ~ no jōzu na hito ~ のじょうずな人 a good bargainer

[...no] kamen o kaburu [...の]仮面をかぶる He *puts on a front* that he is a rich man.

[hito o] katsugu [c] [人を]かつぐ That

real estate broker is clever at *leading people on* (*taking people for a ride; tricking people*).

kebyō o tsukau 仮病を使う feign sickness

kemu ni maku けむにまく With that high-sounding talk he *pulls the wool over* people's *eyes.*

kōkatsu (da) こうかつ(だ) craft; duplicity (crafty; sly; tricky; cunning)

KUCHI ga umai 口がうまい He *is a smooth talker,* so be careful.

    ~ o nugutte sumashite iru ~ をぬぐってすましている I saw him do it, but he *acts as if he hadn't done a thing.*

    kuchiguruma ni noseru [c] 口車に乗せる She *was talked into* (*was wheedled into*) selling her car at too low a price.

[hito ni] ippai kuwaseru [c] [人を]一杯食わせる He *pulled a fast one* on us and gave us an inferior product.

    ippai kuwasareru [c] 一杯食わされる He *was surely taken for a ride* by that crooked agent.

madowasu 惑わす mislead; lead astray

[hito o] marumekomu [人を]まるめ込む He *tricked* her *into* buying the land without seeing it.

ME ga kuramu 目がくらむ He *was dazzled* by the promise of money, and betrayed his country.

    ~ o kasumeru ~ をかすめる He was gambling at night *behind* his wife's *back.*

    ~ o kuramasu ~ をくらます With that gaudy show they are just *throwing dust in your eyes.*

mikake ni yoranai 見かけによらない You *can't judge* a book *by its cover.* A man *cannot be judged by appearances.*

    mikakedaoshi (da) 見かけ倒し(だ) deceptive appearance (showy)

    misekake (ru) 見せかけ(る) pretence (pretend)

neko o kaburu ねこをかぶる Little Johnny

was not himself acting so well mannered before our guests.

nisemono にせもの counterfeit

oku no te ga aru 奥の手がある We thought he was beaten, but he *had an ace in the hole* (*had something up his sleeve*).

  sono te ni wa noranai (sono te wa kuwanai) [C] その手には乗らない(その手は食わない) I *won't be fooled* (*won't be taken in*) by that scheme.

otoshiireru 落とし入れる trap ; ensnare

peten ni kakeru [C] ぺてんにかける He *cheated* (*played a trick on*) him and got title to the property.

  petenshi ぺてん師 swindler ; fraud

rimen kōsaku o suru 裏面工作をする There *was* much *maneuvering behind the scenes* at the political convention.

sagi (shi) 詐欺(師) fraud (impostor ; swindler ; counterfeiter)

shibai ni noru 芝居に乗る He *fell into the trap* (*was deluded*) and bought the bogus stock notes.

shirabakureru [C] しらばくれる He *acted dumb* before the questioners.

  shira o kiru しらを切る feign ignorance.

sode no shita o tsukau そでの下を使う He *bribed* (*bought off ; greased the palms of*) the customs officials to get his goods into the country.

sorazorashii そらぞらしい feigned ; empty

taburakasu たぶらかす cheat ; trick

tanuki neiri (suru) [C] たぬき寝入り、する、 I *feigned sleep* (*played possum*) while they were talking and heard everything.

teisai o tsukurou 体裁を繕う That girl *is* always *putting on airs*.

tsukaikomu 使い込む embezzle

[hito o] tsuru [人を]つる With his fast talk, he *will rope you in* [S] (*will get you hooked* [S] and you'll buy it.

umai shiru o suu [C] うまいしるを吸う He married the boss's daughter, so he's *got a good thing going* at the company.

ura o kaku 裏をかく He *outwitted* (*outguessed*) his opponent and won the contest.

uraguchi keiyaku 裏口契約 He made a *double contract* (*undercover agreement*) when he sold the land to avoid heavy taxes.

uso うそ lie ; falsification

  usotsuki うそつき liar ; prevaricator

wairo わいろ bribery

waraimagirasu 笑い紛らす He *smiled to cover up* his sorrow.

warudakumi 悪巧み evil design ; wiles

  warugashikoi 悪賢い wily ; crafty ; unscrupulous

  warujie 悪知恵 cunning ; guile ; craft

Yōtō o kakagete, kuniku o uru [P] 羊頭をかかげて狗肉を売る Cry wine and sell vinegar [P].

zōwai (suru) 贈賄(する) bribery (bribe)

zurui ずるい tricky ; sly ; foxy

⇨ 42

心はよろずの物よりも偽るもので, はなはだしく悪にそまっている. だれがこれを, よく知ることができようか. (エレミヤ書 17 ⁹)

47 GŌMAN ごうまん
ARROGANCE, PRIDE

bōjaku-bujin (da) 傍若無人(だ) insolent ; audacious

[...] buru [...]ぶる He goes around *putting on the airs of* a scholar when he hasn't even finished college yet.

  mottaiburu もったいぶる assume an air of importance

eragaru 偉がる boast ; be puffed up

fuson (da) 不そん(だ) arrogance (arrogant ; haughty)

GŌMAN ごうまん arrogance ; pride

  ~ na taido (o toru) ～な態度(をとる) proud attitude (act proudly)

  jiman (suru) 自慢(する) self-conceit ;

vainglory (pride oneself on; brag of; boast about)

kōman (da) 高慢(だ) arrogance; self-conceit (arrogant; conceited; proud) **~ ni furumau** ~ にふるまう He's *been on his high horse (been swaggering about)* ever since he got that degree.

manshin suru 慢心する be conceited; have a swelled head

hana ni kakeru 鼻にかける She's *obviously proud* of her good looks.

hanaiki ga arai 鼻息が荒い Since he's been promoted he has been quite *arrogant (imperious; snooty).*

hora o fuku ほらを吹く I can't stand him; he's always *blowing his own horn (talking big; boasting).*

hokoru 誇る boast [about]; be proud [of] **hokorigao de** 誇り顔で proudly; beaming with pride; triumphantly

ibaru いばる act proud; boast; be proud of oneself **kara ibari** からいばり empty boast; false pride

jibun no koto o fuichō suru 自分の事を吹聴する There he goes *singing his own praises (tooting his own horn)* again.

kaikaburu 買いかぶる over-rate; over-estimate one's ability

kuchi habattai koto o iu 口はばったい事を言う speak loftily; talk big

kyosei o haru 虚勢を張る Don't let him scare you; *he's* just *bluffing.*

makeoshimi o iu 負け惜しみを言う He said his arm was hurt, but he *was making excuses for losing.*

mie o haru 見えを張る She hasn't any money but wears those bright clothes *just for show.* **miebo** [C] 見え坊 He is just a *show-off.* **misebirakasu** 見せびらかす show off; make a show of

namaiki (da) 生意気(だ) presumptuous; cocky; cheeky; has a lot of gall

ōbō (da) 横暴(だ) domineering

ōhei (da) おうへい(だ) arrogant; haughty

ōburoshiki o hirogeru 大ぶろしきを広げる There he goes, *talking big (bragging)* in front of the boss again.

ogoru おごる be proud; be haughty

ōkina kao o suru 大きな顔をする Ever since being promoted, he's *been going around with his chest out.*

omoiagaru 思い上がる think too highly of; be arrogant

senetsu (da) せんえつ(だ) presumptuous **senetsunagara** せんえつながら This is forward of me, but...

shinzō da [C] しんぞうだ He surely *has a lot of nerve,* coming to the party without an invitation.

sondai (da) 尊大(だ) overbearing; arrogant; pompous

taigen sōgo suru 大言壮語する say boastful things

takaburu 高ぶる be puffed up; be arrogant; be haughty **takabisha ni** 高飛車に overbearingly; high-handedly

temaemiso na koto o iu [C] 手前みそな事を言う He isn't very well liked because he's so full of *self-admiration.*

tengu ni naru てんぐになる With just a little success he immediately *gets conceited (gets a big head).*

tetsumempi (da) 鉄面皮(だ) cheeky; brazen-faced

tokui ni naru 得意になる He *is happy with himself (is elated)* that he can play the piano so well.

tsuyogari o iu 強がりを言う He knew his illness was serious, but to us he *said it was nothing and made little of it.*

uchōten ni naru 有頂天になる become inflated with pride; take pride in

unubore (ru) うぬぼれ(る) self-conceit (be conceited; be vain)

~ **ga tsuyoi** ~ が強い be quite conceited
zūzūshii ずうずうしい impudent; shameless
  zūzūshiku mo...suru ずうずうしくも...す
  る He *had the face* (*had the nerve*) to
  ask for a higher salary than his boss.
⇨ **76**
同じように，若い人たちよ．長老たちに従いなさい．みな
互いに謙遜を身に着けなさい．神は高ぶる者に敵対し，
へりくだる者に恵みを与えられるからです．
(ペテロ I 5 ⁵)

48 GURETSU 愚劣
FOOLISHNESS, STUPIDITY

akimekura 明き盲 blind fool
asamashii ningen あさましい人間 base
person
BAKA (da) ばか(だ) fool; idiot; dunce
(foolish; outlandish)
  ~ **na mane o suru** ~ なまねをする He
  made a fool of himself (*played the
  fool*) at the party.
  ~ **ni suru** ~ にする make a fool of
  (one)
  ~ **ni tsukeru kusuri wa nai** [P]
  ~ につける薬はない You're wasting
  your time telling him; *there's no
  cure for a fool.*
  ~ **no hitotsu oboe** [P] ~ の一つ覚え
  A fool always harps on the same-
  thing.
  ~ **o iu** ~ を言う talk nonsense; talk
  through one's hat
  ~ **to hasami wa tsukaiyo** [P] ~ と
  はさみは使いよう Fools and scissors—
  it's all in the using.
  manzara baka demo nai まんざらば
  かでもない Well, for once he had a
  good idea; he's *not altogether a fool.*
bakabakashii ばかばかしい foolish;
ridiculous; absurd
bakageta koto o suru ばかげた事をする
do something foolish
bakarashii ばからしい absurd; silly

dekunobō でくの坊 buffoon; blockhead
GURETSU 愚劣 foolishness; stupidity
  gu ni mo tsukanai 愚にもつかない be too
  silly for words; be nonsense; be
  gibberish
    ~ **no kotchō** ~ の骨頂 height of folly;
    be very ridiculous
  gudon (da) [L] 愚鈍(だ) stupidity
  (stupid)
  gurō (suru) 愚弄(する) mockery (make
  fun of; ridicule)
  guron 愚論 foolish argument; nonsense
  oroka (da) 愚か(だ) foolishness (foolish;
  silly)
    ~ **nimo...suru** ~ にも...する Even
    though he couldn't swim very well,
    he *was foolish enough to* jump in
    the river.
  jōdan o tobasu 冗談を飛ばす crack a joke
  manuke [C] 間抜け He does the strangest
  things; he must *have a screw loose* (*must
  be off his rocker*).
  mukōmizu no hito 向こう見ずの人
  daredevil; devil-may-care person
  noroma [C] のろま slowpoke
  omedetai hito [C] おめでたい人 He always
  misses the point. What a *fat head!*
  shiryo no nai 思慮のない thoughtless; ill-
  advised; imprudent
  TARINAI 足りない slow; dull; not all
  there
    atama ga tarinai 頭が足りない The way
    he talks, I think he's *a little bit off*
    (he's *not quite all there*).
    doko ka tarinai tokoro ga aru どこか
    足りないところがある He's always doing
    crazy things like that; he must *have
    a nut loose somewhere.*
    nōmiso ga tarinai 脳みそが足りない be
    empty headed; be soft headed
  tohō mo nai 途方もない wild; ridiculous;
  preposterous
  usunoro [C] うすのろ You *half-wit!* Don't
  you ever catch on?

yota o tobasu よたを飛ばす talk rubbish; say silly things

⇨ **200**

自分の心を頼む者は愚である。知恵をもって歩む者は救を得る。(箴言 28 ²⁶)

49 HAIBOKU 敗北 DEFEAT

banji kyūsu 万事休す When he saw that they had all the evidence against him, he knew *his goose was cooked* (*he had had it*).

HAIBOKU 敗北 defeat

~ **o kissuru** ~ を喫する The regiment went out unprepared and were *brought down to defeat.*

~ **o maneku** ~ を招く court defeat

~ **o mitomeru** ~ を認める admit defeat; concede defeat

kaimetsuteki haiboku 壊滅的敗北 overwhelming defeat

haibokushugi 敗北主義 defeatism

haigun [L] 敗軍 defeated army; the vanquished

haiin 敗因 cause of defeat

haisen 敗戦 defeat; lost battle

haisenkoku 敗戦国 defeated nation

haisō (suru) 敗走(する) rout (be routed; take flight)

haitai (suru) 敗退(する) retreat (beat a retreat)

haizansha 敗残者 the defeated; the vanquished

kampai (suru) [L] 完敗(する) total defeat (suffer a complete defeat)

reihai (suru) 零敗(する) shutout game [baseball, etc.] (shut-out)

shippai (suru) 失敗(する) failure (fail; blunder; make a mistake)

taihai (suru) 大敗(する) great defeat (suffer a heavy defeat)

zampai (suru) 惨敗(する) complete defeat (be snowed under)

hekotareru [C] へこたれる I tried to reach the summit but finally *became exhausted* (*gave out*) and returned.

hetabaru [C] へたばる I tried to keep up the pace at work but finally *gave up* (*broke down*).

hōhō no tei de hikiageru ほうほうのていで引き揚げる Overwhelmed, the enemy troops *beat a hasty retreat* (*took to their heels and ran*).

kabuto o nugu かぶとを脱ぐ His ability at debating was so superior that I had to *acknowledge defeat.*

ki o nomareru 気をのまれる I *was overwhelmed* (*driven to the wall; overawed*) by his fast talk.

KŌFUKU (suru) 降服(する) surrender (surrender)

mujōken kōfuku 無条件降服 unconditional surrender

kōsan (suru) 降参(する) surrender (surrender)

kuppuku (suru) 屈服(する) submission (submit [to]; give in [to])

kussuru [L] 屈する give in [to]; yield [to]

mairu 参る give up; be beaten

makeru 負ける lose

moto no mokuami (da) 元のもくあみ(だ) He had made a small fortune but *lost all he gained* in the stock market crash.

nigegoshi ni naru 逃げ腰になる When I pointed out his inconsistency, he *backed down.*

oteage da [C] お手上げだ I don't know what else I can do; I *throw up my hands* (*throw in the sponge*).

shippo o maite nigeru しっぽを巻いて逃げる When Johnny saw the big boy come at him, he *turned tail and ran* (*put his tail between his legs and ran*).

shiro o akewatasu 城を明け渡す After being besieged many days, the defenders *surrendered their positions.*

teki o oiharau 敵を追い払う rout the enemy

~no te ni ochiiru ~の手に陥る fall into the hands of the enemy

todome o sasu とどめを刺す He *clinched the argument (gave the finishing blow)* with the new evidence.

tsubureru つぶれる collapse; go to pieces

uchinomesu 打ちのめす knock one flat; floor one

yabureru 破れる be defeated; be beaten; lose

uchiyaburu 打ち破る defeat one

yarareru やられる be defeated; be damaged; I've had it!

⇨ **52, 83**

悪に負けてはいけません. かえって, 善をもって悪に打ち勝ちなさい. (ローマ 12 ²¹)

50 HAJI 恥
EMBARRASSMENT, DISGRACE

ana ga attara hairitai 穴があったらはいりたい When the teacher caught me sleeping, I *felt like crawling into a hole (I could have dropped through the floor).*

asamashii あさましい shameful; base

atama ga agaranai 頭が上がらない I *feel small* around him; he knows too much about me.

batsu ga warui [C] ばつが悪い I *could hardly face* him after spoiling his party.

fumeiyo (da) 不名誉(だ) dishonor; shame (dishonorable; shameful)

furachi (da) ふらち(だ) insolent

futodoki (da) 不届き(だ) insolent; impudent

HAJI 恥 embarrassment; disgrace

　　~ mo gaibun mo nai ~も外聞もない feel no disgrace; know neither shame nor decency; be unconscious of the shame; be shameless

　　~ no uwanuri ni naru ~の上塗りになる If you say that to her now, it will be *adding insult to injury.*

~ o kaku ~をかく be put to shame; be disgraced; be taken down a peg

~ o kakaseru ~をかかせる bring shame on

~ o sarasu ~をさらす put one to open shame

~ o shinobu ~を忍ぶ bear the shame; swallow one's pride

~ o sosogu ~をそそぐ After that incident, he had to *live down the disgrace (clear his name)* in the town.

~ sarashi ~さらし disgrace; shame

~ shirazu (da) ~知らず(だ) shameless

Kiku wa ittoki no haji; kikanu wa matsudai no haji [P] 聞くは一時の恥, 聞かぬは末代の恥 To ask may be a moment's shame; not to ask may lead to lifelong disgrace.

Tabi no haji wa kakisute [P] 旅の恥はかき捨て Look at the way they're shoving on to that train! Just as they say, "*A traveler can do anything.*"

akahaji 赤恥 open shame; public disgrace

~ o kaku ~をかく be disgraced publicly; be put to open shame

hajiru 恥じる feel ashamed

　　hitome o hajiru 人目を恥じる Ever since being fired from his job, he *has been avoiding people.*

hazukashigaru 恥ずかしがる She *feels shy* around boys.

hazukashii 恥ずかしい I *am ashamed of* my poor English.

hazukashime はずかしめ shame; humiliation

kōgan muchi (da) [L] 厚顔無恥(だ) He was a *shameless and brazen-faced* man and lost many friends.

hanikamu はにかむ be shy; look ashamed

hikkomijian (da) 引っ込み思案(だ)

shyness; hesitation (hesitant; unenterprising)

KAO ga tatanai 顔が立たない When he
boasted about his marks and then failed
the exams, he *lost face* (*was humiliated*).

  ~ga tsubureru ~がつぶれる John *lost
face* (*was humiliated*) when the
small girl beat him at tennis.

  ~ni doro o nuru ~ にどろを塗る By
his conduct, he *brought dishonor to*
(*brought disgrace upon*) his father.

  ~o akarameru ~ を赤らめる get red
in the face; blush with shame

  awaseru kao ga nai 合わせる顔がない
I haven't paid my bill there and
I'm too ashamed to face them (I
cannot show my face to them).

  kaomake suru 顔負けする Her superb
performance tonight *put even me*, her
teacher, *to shame.*

  kaomuke ga dekinai 顔向けができな
い I'm *unable to face* the class after
that bungle.

katami no semai omoio (suru) 肩身の
狭い思いを(する) I *feel small* around all
those scholars.

kimari ga warui きまりが悪い I *felt
embarrassed* when he came into my
dirty room.

KUTSUJOKU 屈辱 disgrace; humiliation

  ~o ukeru ~ を受ける be humiliated

  bujoku (suru) 侮辱(する) insult;
indignity; affront (insult)

  chijoku 恥辱 insult; disgrace;
dishonor

  hikutsu ni naru 卑屈になる be
humiliated

  ojoku [L] 汚辱 disgrace

makka ni naru 真っ赤になる She *got red
all over* when they teased her.

MEMBOKU (memmoku) nai 面目ない
I *am ashamed of myself* for my actions
yesterday.

  ~o nakusu ~ をなくす lose face

omohayui 面はゆい He knew he didn't
deserve the ovation and *felt ashamed*
(*was loathe*) to face the audience.

sekimen suru 赤面する blush; be
embarrassed

taimen o kegasu 体面を汚す He
disgraced himself by such conduct.

tetsumempi (da) 鉄面皮(だ) shame-
lessness (shameless; brazen-faced;
bold; forward)

tsura no kawa ga atsui つらの皮が厚い
He *has a lot of gall* and doesn't mind
saying such things to anyone.

  ii tsura no kawa da! いいつらの皮だ!
Shame on you for saying that to
your teacher.

tsurayogoshi (da) [C] つらよごし(だ) He
has been *a disgrace* to his family.

misemono ni sareru 見せ物にされる He
was made a spectacle of (*was made an
example*) by the authorities for his
actions.

muchi (da) 無知(だ) shameless; impudent

naore 名折れ What he did was a *blot
upon his name* (*a discredit to himself*).

  ~ ni naru ~になる bring disgrace upon
oneself

sarashimono to naru さらし者となる be
exposed to the public; be brought into
disrepute

shikii ga takai 敷居が高い After causing
so much trouble there, I find it *hard to
call* (*hard to go back*) there.

teisai ga warui 体裁が悪い be unpresent-
able; look unseemly

zūzūshii ずうずうしい shameless; has a lot
of nerve

⇨ **98**

信仰の創始者であり,完成者であるイエスから目を離さ
ないでいなさい. イエスは, ご自分の前に置かれた喜びの
ゆえに, 恥をものとも思わずに十字架を忍び, 神の御座
の右に着座なされました. (ヘブル 12 ²)

51 HAJIME 初め
BEGINNING

ashi o fumiireru 足を踏み入れる I have never worked in that field, but I decided to *give it a try.*

bōtō 冒頭 the beginning; the opening

DAIICHI (da) 第一(だ) the first; number one

daiippo 第一歩 the first step; the start

~ **o fumidasu** ~を踏み出す Somebody had to *initiate the matter (take the first step),* so I decided to do it.

ichiban (da) 一番(だ) most; first; best

DEDASHI 出だし beginning; start

~ **ga warui (yoi)** ~が悪い(が良い) They *got off to a poor (good) start.*

furidashi 振り出し beginning; outset

~ **ni modoru** ~にもどる return to the starting point; make a fresh start

kakedashi jidai [C] 駆け出し時代 *When I was just getting started* at the job, I made many mistakes.

[...**o**] **kiridasu** [...を]切り出す I *broke the ice (broached the subject)* by telling a silly story.

shuppatsu (suru) 出発(する) starting (start; leave)

shusshinchi 出身地 birthplace

suberidashi すべり出し beginning; start

HAJIME 初め beginning; start (begin; start)

~ **kara** ~から from the beginning; from the outset

~ **no uchi wa** ~のうちは at first...

hajimari (ru) はじまり(はじまる) beginning; commencement ([something] begins; commences)

hatsu kaoawase 初顔合わせ first meeting

hatsu mimi (da) 初耳(だ) *That's the first I've heard of it; That's news to me!*

hatsuho 初穂 first fruits

hatsukoi 初恋 first love

hatsumono 初物 first fruits

saisho 最初 first; beginning

shodai 初代 first generation

shoho 初歩 beginning stage

shoki 初期 the first period

shoshinsha 初心者 beginner; novice

tehajime ni 手始めに in the beginning

tōsho (no) 当初(の) in the initial stage; in the beginning

uizan 初産 first childbirth

hajimeru はじめる begin; start

hakushi ni kaesu 白紙に返す Let's forget past problems and *start again with a clean slate.*

hibuta o kiru 火ぶたを切る The baseball season *commenced (was launched)* today at Meiji Park.

HOSSOKU (suru) 発足(する) initiation (initiate; inaugurate)

hakken (suru) 発見(する) discovery (discover)

hakkō (suru) 発行(する) publication

hassei (suru) 発生(する) genesis; generation; outbreak (be generated; break out)

Hitsuyō wa hatsumei no haha [P] 必要は発明の母 Necessity is the mother of invention [P].

hottan 発端 origin; start; outset

itoguchi 糸口 beginning; clue

~ **o miidasu** ~を見いだす He *found a clue* to the mystery by discovering their train tickets in the waste basket.

~ **to naru** ~となる Checking the names on the register *became the first step* in tracing them down.

KAIKAI (suru) 開会(する) opening; begin a meeting

kaibyaku irai [L] 開びゃく以来 from the dawn of history

kaikō ichiban [L] 開口一番 *At the very beginning of his speech* he mentioned the problem.

kaishi (suru) 開始(する) inauguration (inaugurate; commence)

kaitaku (suru) 開拓(する) pioneering (pioneer)

kaitakusha 開拓者 pioneer

kakkiteki 画期的 epoch-making

kizashi きざし first signs [of]

[...to iu] ~ **ga mieru** [...と言う] ~ が見える begin to show signs of

koto atarashiku 事新しく He gave the same old report *as if it were new.*

shinki maki naoshi ni suru 新規まき直しにする Next year I'm going to *turn over a new leaf (start over from scratch).*

mazu まず first of all; first; in the first place

me o dasu 芽を出す He was doing poorly, but now his *luck is picking up.*

minamoto 源 origin; source

motomoto 元々 from the outset; from the beginning

okori (ru) 起こり(起る) beginning; cause; source (happen; occur)

kigen 起源 origin; beginning

...**no kigen wa**...**ni aru** ...の起源は...にある Democratic principles *have* their *origin in* the Magna Charta and the Bible.

SAKI (da) 先(だ) first (first; ahead)

saisaki ga yoku さい先がよく They *made a good start* in the project, and it has been going well.

sakigake 先がけ They went into the jungle as *the advance party.*

senkusha 先駆者 forerunner

sente o utsu 先手を打つ Our rival company *struck first (beat us to the punch)* with a new product.

sutāto (suru) スタート(する) start (make a start)

tanjō (suru) 誕生(する) birth (be born)

tanjōbi 誕生日 birthday

tansho 端緒 the start; the beginning

TE o tsukeru 手をつける If you want to finish today, you had better *get going on it.*

chakushu suru 着手する start; set about [doing something]

tegakari 手掛かり the clue [to]

tehodoki o ukeru 手ほどきを受ける be initiated into; learn the ABC's [of]

torikakaru 取りかかる begin; set one's hand to

ubugoe o ageru [L] うぶ声を上げる Abe *first saw the light of day* in a little log cabin in Kentucky.

umidasu 産み出す bring forth; give birth to

はじめに神は天と地とを創造された. (創世記 1 ¹)

52 HAMETSU 破滅
DESTRUCTION, RUIN

ato o tatanai あとを絶たない Ever since that law was changed, there *has been no end of trouble.*

atokata mo nakunaru 跡形もなくなる there is no trace of anything left; nothing remains

BOTSURAKU (suru) 没落(する) fall; collapse; deterioration (fall into ruin; deteriorate; go into bankruptcy)

daraku (suru) 堕落(する) degradation; fall; degeneration (go bad; dissipate; degenerate)

reiraku (suru) 零落(する) lost social status (hit the bottom [financially])

dainashi ni naru だいなしになる Our picnic *was ruined (was spoiled)* by those rowdy drunks.

dame ni naru だめになる go bad; fall to pieces; fail; go on the rocks

danzetsu (suru) 断絶(する) extinction (become extinct; die off)

fuhai (suru) 腐敗す(る) decay; corruption (become corrupt)

[...**no**] **fukami ni hamaru** [...の]深みには
まる He *sank deeper and deeper* into debt.
HAMETSU 破滅 destruction; ruin

~ **ni otoshiireru** ~に落とし入れる
undermine; bring to ruin; consign
to destruction

~ **no soko ni ochikomu** ~の底に落
ち込む plunge into ruin

mi no hametsu o maneku 身の破
滅を招く Living the way he does,
he's only *inviting his own ruin*.

bokumetsu (suru) 撲滅(する) extermination [of pests, etc.] (exterminate)

daha (suru) 打破(する) breakdown
(overthrow)

hakai (suru) 破壊(する) destruction
(destroy)

hakairyoku 破壊力 destructive power

hakaiteki (da) 破壊的(だ) destructive

haki (suru) 破棄(する) breach [of];
abrogation (make a breach of;
abrogate; break off)

hasan (suru) 破産(する) bankruptcy;
failure (go bankrupt)

hason (suru) 破損(する) damage;
breakage (damage; break down)

hatan (suru) 破たん(する) failure;
rupture; bankruptcy (fail; be ruined)

~ **o kitasu** ~をきたす bring to ruin;
bring disaster upon

horobi (ru) 滅び(滅る) perdition
(perish; die; meet with destruction)

horobosu 滅ぼす overthrow; annihilate;
destroy

mi o horobosu 身を滅ぼす ruin
oneself

jimetsu (suru) 自滅(する) self-
destruction (ruin oneself)

~ **o maneku** ~を招く Drinking
heavily is *inviting one's own
destruction*.

kaimetsu (suru) 壊滅(する) destruction
(go to ruin; go to rack and ruin)

metsubō (suru) 滅亡(する) downfall;

collapse; destruction (fall; collapse)

shimetsu (suru) 死滅(する) extinction
(become extinct; die out)

zetsumetsu (suru) 絶滅(する) extermination (completely destroy; stamp
out; wipe out)

hidarimae ni naru [c] 左前になる The
bottom dropped out of the market and
he *is in financial straits* (*is going broke*).

kesu 消す blot out; erase; extinguish;
switch off

sugata ga kieru 姿が消える The *sight* of
men in kimono *has* almost *disappeared*
from the streets of Tokyo.

kōhai (suru) 荒廃(する) waste; ruin (be
laid waste; go to rack and ruin; go to
pot)

kowareru こわれる break; be broken; go to
pieces

buchikowasu ぶちこわす crush; smash;
knock the bottom out of

kowasu こわす break; destroy; shatter

kujo suru 駆除する exterminate

mechakucha ni suru めちゃくちゃにする
ruin; spoil; mess up

mizu no awa to naru 水のあわとなる
Overnight his efforts *went up in smoke*
(*came to nothing*).

mizukara boketsu o horu 自ら墓穴を
掘る *You'll be digging your own grave*
if you associate with those gangsters.

mu ni naru 無になる come to nothing; be
wasted; peter out

~ **ni suru** ~にする bring to naught

naki mono ni suru [L] なき者にする The
criminals vowed to *get rid of* (*do away
with*) him if he talked.

nigiritsubusu 握りつぶす crush; crumple;
squash

pechanko ni naru [c] ぺちゃんこになる The
house *was flattened* (*was crushed*) by the
earthquake.

shichi ni ochiiru 死地に陥る He *fell into
a terrible plight* (*landed in an awful fix*)

when the business failed.

seimei zaisan no sonshitsu 生命財産の
損失 loss of life and property

shōshitsu 焼失 destruction by fire

taeru 絶える cease to exist; die out; come
to an end

   tayasu 絶やす stamp out; exterminate;
root out

tōsan (suru) 倒産(する) bankruptcy (go
bankrupt)

zenkai 全壊 total ruin; complete
destruction
⇨ **49**

わたしは彼らに永遠のいのちを与えます. 彼らは決して滅
びることがなく, また, だれもわたしの手から彼らを奪い去
るようなことはありません. (ヨハネ 10 ²⁸)

53 HANTAI 反対
OPPOSITION

aiirenai 相いれない be contrary to; be at
odds [with]

   aihansuru 相反する Those two
concepts *are antithetical.*

atama o yoko ni furu 頭を横に振る When
I made the suggestion, he *shook his
head in disapproval (answered in the
negative).*

fusansei 不賛成 disapproval; disagreement

fushōchi 不承知 disagreement; disapproval; dissent; objection

gan to shite kikanai がんとして聞かない We
asked him to join our demonstration,
but he *would have nothing to do with it.*

gyaku (da) 逆(だ) contrariness (contrary;
opposite; inverse; reverse)

HANTAI (suru) 反対(する) opposition
(oppose)

   ~ iken o motsu ~意見を持つ have a
different opinion; be of a different
opinion

   ~ jimmon o suru ~尋問をする
cross-examine

~ o ukeru ~を受ける be opposed
[by]

~ tōhyō o suru ~投票をする He
voted against the new proposal.

mōretsu ni hantai suru ~猛烈に
反対する violently oppose; be dead
set against

hangyaku (suru) 反逆(する) revolt;
insurrection (rebel [against])

hankō (suru) 反抗(する) resistance;
opposition (resist; oppose)

hankōshin 反抗心 antagonistic spirit;
rebellious spirit

   ~ o motsu ~を持つ harbor antagonism; have animosity towards

hanron (suru) 反論(する) refutation;
rebuttal (refute)

hansuru 反する be opposed [to]; be
contrary to; be set against

hantaisetsu (ron) 反対説(反対論)
opposite view (opposite opinion)

hantaitō 反対党 the opposition party

seihantai (da) 正反対(だ) the exact
opposite (exactly opposite)

taihi 対比 opposition; contrast

taikō (suru) 対抗(する) confrontation
(confront; brave; oppose)

taisuru 対する face; confront

tekitai (suru) 敵対(する) hostility (be
opposed [to]; be hostile [toward]; be
at enmity [with])

   tekitai kōi 敵対行為 hostile act

hitei (suru) 否定(する) denial; negation
(deny; negate; contradict)

kao o shikameru 顔をしかめる He *frowned
upon* the idea.

   ii kao o shinai いい顔をしない He *didn't
look too happy* about our borrowing
his car.

ki ga susumanai 気が進まない I *cannot go
along with* the idea.

kinjiru 禁じる prohibit; forbid; ban

   kinshi (suru) 禁止(する) prohibition;
ban (prohibit; put a ban on)

kitsumon (suru) 詰問(する) cross-examination (cross-examine)

KOBAMU 拒む refuse; decline; turn down

kyohi(suru) 拒否(する) rejection (reject; turn down)

kyozetsu (suru) 拒絶(する) refusal; rejection (refuse; reject)

KOTOWARI (ru) 断わり(断わる) refusal (refuse; decline; nix)

　atama kara kotowaru 頭から断わる I asked the boss for a raise, but he *turned me down flat* (*turned me down cold*).

　kippari kotowaru きっぱり断わる refuse flatly; say it is out of the question

　muge ni kotowarenai むげに断われない He is a relative, so *I couldn't easily refuse* (*it was hard to say no*).

kuchigotae (suru) 口答え(する) retort (retort; answer back)

monoii o tsukeru 物言いをつける When Taiho was given the verdict, the judges immediately *protested* (*took exception to*) the decision.

nama henji o suru 生返事をする He *gave a half-hearted answer*, so perhaps he really doesn't want to go.

sakarau 逆らう go against; resist

iisakarau 言い逆らう answer back

shikametsura o suru しかめつらをする When we suggested this to him, he *frowned in disapproval.*

shirizokeru 退ける turn (one) down; refuse; turn (one) away; repel

shōfuku shikaneru 承服しかねる Because of their opposition to the bill, it will *be hard for them to fall into line* with the Democrats.

shōgai o daha suru 障害を打破する He tried to *break down the opposition.*

[...ni] somuku [...に]そむく turn against; run contrary to

tatetsuku たてつく be set against; be defiant

teikō(suru) 抵抗(する) resistance; defiance (resist; defy)

　~ o ukeru ~を受ける The Tories tried to amend the constitution and *met* immediate *resistance.*

teikōryoku 抵抗力 power of resistance

temukau 手向かう confront; offer resistance

yosetsuke nai 寄せつけない His cranky ways *keep people away* (*make him unapproachable*).

⇨ 185

あなたがたは、罪人たちのこのような反抗を忍ばれた方のことを考えなさい。それは、あなたがたの心が元気を失い、疲れ果ててしまわないためです。あなたがたはまだ、罪と戦って、血を流すまで抵抗したことがありません。(ヘブル 12 ³, ⁴)

54 HEIBON 平凡
COMMONPLACENESS

arifureta ありふれた common; commonplace; stock

　arikitari (da) ありきたり(だ) common; usual, customary; conventional; traditional

chimpu (da) 陳腐(だ) banality; commonplaceness; platitude (old-fashioned; out-of-date).

dare mo kare mo だれもかれも everybody; every Tom, Dick and Harry

futsū (da) 普通(だ) ordinary; average; regular; conventional

HEIBON (da) 平凡(だ) commonplaceness (ordinary; run-of-the-mill)

　~ na ningen ~な人間 an ordinary person

bonjin 凡人 ordinary person

bonyō (da) 凡庸(だ) mediocrity (mediocre; common)

heihei bonbon (da) 平々凡々(だ) mediocre; commonplace

heimin 平民 the common people; the rank and file

hikin na rei o ageru 卑近な例をあげる give familiar examples

ippan (da) 一般(だ) common; ordinary; general

ippon chōshi (da) 一本調子(だ) monotonous

kimarikitta 決まりきった regular; fixed; stereotyped

NAMI (da) 並み(だ) ordinary

   jūnin nami (da) 十人並み(だ) average; ordinary

   tsukinami no koto o iu 月並みの事を言う talk about ordinary things

nan no hentetsu mo nai なんの変哲もない nothing unusual; featureless; tasteless

NICHIJŌ 日常 everyday

   ~ seikatsu ~ 生活 daily life; everyday life

   ~ sahanji [L] ~ 茶飯事 In Tokyo, fatal traffic accidents are an *everyday occurrence*.

shominteki (da) 庶民的(だ) unsophisticated; common

taitei たいてい in most cases; generally; in the main; usually

tokushoku no nai 特色のない That part of the country *has no special characteristics (is featureless)* and is not so interesting to visit.

uzō muzō (da) [C] 有象無象(だ) common herd; rabble

yoku aru koto よくある事 Being able to read English without understanding it is *something we often see* these days.

zara ni aru ざらにある common.
互いに一つ心になり, 高ぶった思いを持たず, かえって身分の低い者に順応しなさい. 自分こそ知者だなどと思ってはいけません. (ローマ 12 ¹⁶)

55 HEIWA 平和 PEACE

ANJŪ (suru) 安住(する) peaceful existence (live peacefully)

   annei 安寧 public peace; well being

~ o tamotsu [L] ~ を保つ maintain peace

antai(da) 安泰(だ) tranquillity (tranquil)

kōan 公安 public peace and order

yasuraka (da) 安らか(だ) peacefulness (peaceful; tranquil)

   ~ na hi o okuru ~ な日を送る He retired and *is leading a tranquil life* in the country.

dōran o osameru 動乱を治める The police *put down the commotion (quelled the riot)*.

emman (da) 円満(だ) peacefulness; amicability (peaceful; amicable)

   ~ ni iku ~ に行く Those two seem *to get along well together*.

HEIWA 平和 peace

   ~ ni kurasu ~ に暮らす live in peace; dwell in peace

   ~ o aisuru ~ を愛する Let us strive to ...do all which may achieve and *cherish* a just and a lasting *peace* among ourselves and with all nations. (Lincoln)

   ~ o jochō suru ~ を助長する promote peace

   ~ o kaifuku suru ~ を回復する Our first goal is to *restore peace* in the war-torn country.

   ~ o kakuritsu suru ~ を確立する establish peace; achieve peace

   ~ o obiyakasu ~ を脅かす threaten the peace

   ~ o tamotsu ~ を保つ The President dispatched the National Guard to Alabama to *keep the peace*.

   ~ o yaburu ~ を破る The U.N. delegate warned that whoever *broke the peace* would be branded as an aggressor.

   ~ ronsha ~ 論者 pacifist; advocate of peace

   kōkyūteki heiwa 恒久的平和 permanent peace

sekaiteki no heiwa 世界的の平和 world peace

heiji 平時 time of peace

heion (da) 平穏(だ) serenity (serene)

～ buji ni kurasu ～ 無事に暮らす live in peace and quiet

heisei (da) 平静(だ) calmness; serenity (calm; serene)

  kokoro no heisei o tamotsu 心の平静を保つ He *remained calm (kept his presence of mind)* in the midst of the calamity.

heizen to 平然と calmly; with composure; coolly

heiwateki shudan 平和的手段 peaceful means

taihei 太平 perfect peace; tranquillity

  tenka taihei 天下太平 After six years of war, *peace reigned over the land* once more.

nakanaori suru 仲直りする After he apologized, the two factions *were reconciled (were restored to harmony)*.

nombiri shita kimochi のんびりした気持ち relaxed feeling; carefree feeling

odayaka (da) 穏やか(だ) mildness (mild; gentle; quiet)

shihō happō maruku osamaru 四方八方まるくおさまる After the big uproar in that department, *everything was peacefully settled.*

⇨ 4, 22, 156

その十字架の血によって平和をつくり，御子によって万物を，ご自分と和解させてくださったからです．地にあるものも天にあるものも，ただ御子によって和解させてくださったのです．（コロサイ 1 20)

56 HENKA 変化 CHANGE

fuchin 浮沈 ups and downs; vicissitudes

  ukishizumi no ōi 浮き沈みの多い many ups and downs; many vicissitudes

furui kara o nugisuteru 古いからを脱ぎ捨てる During the Meiji era, Japan *threw off the old garments* of feudalism.

HENKA (suru) 変化(する) change (change; make a change)

  ～ no nai ～ のない changeless; lacking in variety

  ～ no ōi ～ の多い full of change; full of variety

  ～ o shōjiru ～ を生じる effect a change; work a change

  ～ shiyasui ～ しやすい changeable

  gaikeiteki na henka 外形的な変化 outward change

  kyūgeki ni henka suru 急激に変化する change abruptly; fluctuate quickly; see a sudden change

  sesō no henka 世相の変化 changes of the times; changes in social conditions

aikawarazu 相変わらず as usual; as ever

gekihen (suru) 激変(する) sudden change; cataclysm (have an abrupt change)

hendō (suru) 変動(する) change; fluctuation (change; fluctuate)

  ～ o kitasu ～ をきたす bring about a change

  ～ o shōjiru ～ を生じる effect a change

  bukka no hendō 物価の変動 fluctuation in prices; price changes

henjiru [L] 変じる change into

henkaku 変革 revolutionary change; reform

henkei (suru) 変形(する) transformation; modification (transform; modify)

henkō (suru) 変更(する) modification; alteration (modify; alter)

  ～ o kuwaeru ～ を加える make alterations

  jūsho henkō (suru) 住所変更(する) change of address (change one's address)

hemmei de 変名で under a false

name; using an alias

henseiki 変声期 puberty

hensen (suru) 変遷(する) transition (shift)

henshoku (suru) 変色(する) change of color (change color; become discolored)

hensō (suru) 変装(する) disguise (masquerade)

hensoku 変則 irregularity; deviation

hentai 変態 abnormality; transformation

henten (suru) 変転(する) mutation (change)

~ **kiwamari nai** ~窮まりない endlessly changing; ever-shifting

hyōhen suru ひょう変する change abruptly; make an about-face

Kunshi wa hyōhen suru [P] 君子はひょう変する The wise are quick to adapt themselves to altered circumstances.

ippen suru 一変する make an abrupt change; make a complete change

mattaku ippen suru 全く一変する bring about a complete change

kaeru 変える change; alter

chōshi o kaeru 調子を変える He was all for the Socialists, but now he has *changed his tune.*

te no hira o kaesu yōni 手のひらを返すように After promising freedom, the government *made an about-face* and created a police state.

te o kaeru 手を変える He *changed his approach* at the office, and things have improved.

kaihen (suru) 改変(する) innovation (innovate)

kawariyasui 変わりやすい fickle; flighty; changeable; inconstant

kawaru 変わる vary; change

aku made mo kawaranai あくまでも変わらない He's *a dyed in the wool* Democrat.

eien ni kawaranai 永遠に変わらない eternally changeless

itsumo kawaranai いつも変わらない be always the same; be consistent

ki ga kawaru 気が変わる one's mood changes

Tokoro kawareba shina kawaru [P] 所変われば品変わる Different countries have different customs.

kyūhen (suru) 急変(する) abrupt change (change quickly)

kikō no kyūhen 気候の急変 sudden change in the weather

seihen 政変 change of government

sempen banka 千変万化 innumerable changes

taihen (da) たいへん(だ) exceeding; remarkable; awful; horrible

utsurikawari (ru) 移り変わり(移り変わる) changes (change; be transformed)

kisetsu no utsurikawari 季節の移り変わり seasonable changes; change of the seasons

shizen no utsurikawari 自然の移り変わり changes of nature

KAWARU 代る alternate

kawarugawaru かわるがわる by turns; alternately

~ **ni suru** ~にする Let's *take turns* driving the car.

kifuku ni tomu 起伏に富む If you take the train through Nagano Ken, you will see a beautiful, *ever-changing* landscape.

kirikaeru 切り替える switch; change

kōtai (suru) 交替(する) relief; change (relieve; alternate)

marude michigaeru yōni naru まるで見違えるようになる When I came back to Osaka after the war, it *had changed beyond recognition* (*didn't look like the same place*).

mujō (da) 無常(だ) transience; ephemera (transient; ephemeral)

muraki (**da**) むら気(だ) changeable person; fickle person

shūsei (**suru**) 修正(する) amendment; revision (amend; revise; modify)

  kaisei (**suru**) 改正(する) revision; amendment (revise; amend)

TENJIRU 転じる turn; shift; revolve

  hōkō tenkan o suru 方向転換をする change one's direction

  iten suru (**saseru**) 移転する(移転させる) shift; move (convert)

  kaiten (**suru**) 回転(する) revolution (revolve)

  kōten (**suru**) 好転(する) pick up; rally (change for the better)

  shinki itten suru 心機一転する Being traded to the Nankai Hawks *gave him a fresh start.*

  tenchi (**suru**) 転地(する) change of place; change of scenery (make a change of place)

  tenkan (**suru**) 転換(する) conversion; turn over (convert; switch over [to])

  tennin (**suru**) 転任(する) transfer of office (change one's post; be transferred [to])

すべての良い贈り物，また，すべての完全な賜物は上から来るのであって，光を造られた父から下るのです．父には移り変わりや，移り行く影はありません．(ヤコブ 1 ¹⁷)

57   HETSURAI へつらい
FLATTERY

aikyō o furimaku あいきょうを振りまく She's trying to get a boy friend; look at the way she *spreads her charm around.*

aisō no nai 愛想のない I don't like him; he's so *sour* (*unsociable*).

  ~ no yoi ~のよい sociable; affable; amiable

geigō (**suru**) 迎合(する) ingratiation; acceptance (accept uncritically; go along with; cater to)

happō bijin 八方美人 He's a *yes-man*

(*He's all things to all men*).

HETSURAI (**u**) へつらい(へつらう) flattery (flatter; butter up)

  Ue ni hetsurai, shita o anadoru [P] 上にへつらい，下を侮る Flatter superiors, despise inferiors

kangen de sasou 甘言で誘う He tried to *wheedle* me into buying it.

(**hito no**) **kanshin o kau** 人の歓心を買う You won't get very far in life if you try to *please everyone* (*patronize people*).

kaoiro o ukagau 顔色をうかがう He tries to get ahead by *playing up to* his superiors.

kigen o toru きげんを取る You'd better try to *get on* Dad's *good side* (*humor* Dad) before you ask him for a new suit.

kobiru こびる curry favor with; flatter

  kobihetsurau こびへつらう curry favor [with]; lay it on thick.

obekka おべっか flattery; soft soap

  ~ o tsukau ~を使う use flattery

ochōshimono お調子者 easily flattered person

odateru おだてる flatter

  odate ni noranai おだてに乗らない Flattery will get you nowhere.

omoneru おもねる fawn upon; ingratiate oneself [with]

OSEJI お世辞 compliment; flattery

  ~ no yoi hito ~のよい人 good flatterer

  kokoro ni mo nai oseji o iu 心にもないお世辞を言う give out insincere flattery; pay empty compliments

  miesuita oseji 見え透いたお世辞 outright flattery; obvious flattery

peko peko suru [C] ぺこぺこする He's always *kowtowing to* the boss.

toriiru 取り入る ingratiate oneself [with]; curry favor [with]

  umaku toriiru うまく取り入る They *took him for a ride* (*took him in*) at that real estate office.

tsuishō (**suru**) 追しょう(する) adulation;

flattery (adulate; flatter)
⇦ 42, 46
そのとなり人にへつらう者は，彼の足の前に綱を張る.
(箴言 29 ⁵)

58 HIHYŌ 批評 CRITICISM

ageashi o toru 揚げ足を取る The students *tripped up* the professor on his statements, and he became confused.

arasagashi あら捜し fault-finding
~ **o suru** ~ をする The boss *picked flaws in* (*found fault with*) our work.

HIHYŌ (suru) 批評(する) criticism (criticize)
~ **o abiseru** ~ を浴びせる heap criticism on
shinratsu na hihyō 辛らつな批評 severe criticism; scathing criticism
hikaku hihyō 比較批評 comparative criticism

akuhyō 悪評 bad reputation
~ **o tateru** ~ を立てる defame; speak ill of
~ **o ukeru** ~ を受ける receive unfavorable criticism

hihan (suru) 批判(する) criticism; critique (criticize)
~ **o kuwaeru** ~ を加える criticize
hihanteki (da) 批判的(だ) critical
hihyōka 批評家 critic; reviewer
himpyōkai 品評会 exhibition [flowers, vegetables, etc.]

hyōban 評判 reputation; popularity
~ **ga yoi** ~ が良い be popular
~ **ga warui** ~ が悪い unpopular
hyōka (suru) 評価(する) appraisal; evaluation (appraise; evaluate)
hyōron (suru) 評論(する) critical review (comment)
hyōronka 評論家 critic; commentator
jihyō 時評 comment on current events
kōhyō 好評 favorable criticism
~ **o hakusuru** ~ を博する That new

washing machine *is meeting with general favor* (*is meeting with approval*).
kokuhyō (suru) 酷評(する) severe criticism (castigate)
muhihan ni 無批判に uncritically
rompyō (suru) 論評(する) review (comment on)
shohyō 書評 book review
tekihyō (suru) 適評(する) apt criticism (offer fitting criticism)

jibun no koto o tana ni ageru 自分の事をたなにあげる He's *blind to his own faults.*
kokiorosu こきおろす The boss kept *running him down* (*picking him to pieces*) in front of the others.
tanaoroshi (suru) たなおろし(する) He was so conceited that I had to *take him down a peg.*
me ga takai 目が高い He *is a good critic* (*has a critical eye*).
ninki ga aru 人気がある He is *popular* with the students.
~ **ga nai** ~ がない be unpopular
⇨ 61
私にはやましいことは少しもありませんが，だからといって，それで無罪とされるのではありません．私をさばく方は主です．（コリント I 4 ⁴)

59 HIKARI 光 LIGHT

akari 明かり light; lamp
akarumi ni dasu 明るみに出す "…for he will *bring to light* what darkness hides and disclose men's inward motives." (I Cor. 4 ⁵)
~ **ni deru** ~ に出る come to light; be shown; be disclosed
akarusa 明るさ brightness
~ **o masu** ~ を増す increase the brightness
atataka na hizashi 暖かな日ざし The *warm rays of the sun streamed* in through my window.

DENKI 電気 electricity
　~ o kesu ~ を消す turn off the light
　~ o tsukeru ~ をつける turn on the light
dentō 電燈 electric light
kaichū dentō 懐中電燈 flashlight
hakuchū 白昼 broad daylight
HIKARI (ru) 光(る) light (shine)
　~ ga sasu ~ がさす light flashes; light shines
　~ ni sarasareru ~ にさらされる be exposed by the light; come under the searchlight [of]
　[...no] ~ ni terasareru [...の]~に 照らされる be illumined by; come under the searchlight of
　~ o ataeru ~ を与える give light; shed light on
　~ o hanatsu ~ を放つ emit light
　~ o hassuru ~ を発する send out light
　~ o kagayakasu ~ を輝かす shed light [on]
　~ o motomeru ~ を求める seek after light; search for the light
　~ o saegiru ~ をさえぎる eclipse; block the light
　hi no hikari 日の光 daylight
gekkō 月光 moonlight
hakkōtai 発光体 shining body; luminary
keikōtō けい光燈 fluorescent light
kōki 光輝 radiance; brightness
kōmyō 光明 bright light
kōnetsuhi 光熱費 light and heat expenses
kōsen 光線 beam of light; ray of light
kōtaku 光沢 brilliance; polish
kyakkō 脚光 floodlight
nikkō 日光 sunlight
kagaribi かがり火 beacon
KAGAYAKI (ku) 輝き(輝く) brightness; brilliance; shining (shine; sparkle; shimmer)
　hikari kagayaku 光り輝く shine brightly

kirabiyaka ni kagayaku きらびやかに 輝く glitter; shine brightly
mabayui hodo kagayaku まばゆいほど 輝く shine with dazzling brightness
keimō (suru) 啓もう(する) enlightenment (enlighten)
rōsoku ろうそく candle
tenka suru 点火する light a fire; make a fire
TERU 照る shine [the sun]
　terasu 照らす shine on; illuminate; lighten
　　kokoro o terasu 心を照らす ...until the day breaks and the morning star rises to *illuminate your minds.* (II Peter 1 ¹⁹)
tōdai 燈台 lighthouse
⇨ 142

イエスはまた彼らに語って言われた.「わたしは, 世の光 です. わたしに従う者は, 決してやみの中を歩むことがな く, いのちの光を持つのです.（ヨハネ 8 ¹²)

60 HIMITSU 秘密 SECRECY

abaku あばく divulge; disclose; reveal
angō 暗号 secret code
bakuro suru 暴露する expose; divulge; disclose
dare ni mo morasanai yōni だれにも漏 らさないように *Don't breathe a word to anyone* about our plans.
hara ni ichimotsu aru hito 腹に一物あ る人 He acts agreeable but is a *person with an axe to grind.*
HIMITSU 秘密 secrecy
　~ ga hisonde iru ~ が潜んでいる Don't take that statement at its face value; *there's a secret behind it.*
　~ gaikō ~ 外交 secret diplomacy
　~ kōshō ~ 交渉 secret negotiations
　~ ni fusete oku ~ に伏せておく We've decided to *keep it a secret (keep it under our hats).*

~ ni suru hitsuyō ga nai ~にする必要がない *There's no need to keep it a secret.*

~ o akasu ~を明かす expose the secret

~ o bakuro suru [C] ~を暴露する expose the secret; spill the beans

~ o chikau ~を誓う After he told us his plans, we all *swore secrecy* and left the room.

~ o mamoru ~を守る keep a secret

~ o shiru ~を知る discover a secret; find out the secret

~ o toku ~を解く solve the riddle; unravel the mystery

~ tantei ~探偵 secret agent

kōzen no himitsu 公然の秘密 open secret

gokuhi (da) 極秘(だ) strict secret (top secret)

gokuhiri ni 極秘裏に with strict secrecy

hiketsu 秘けつ key; secret [to]

hisoka ni ひそかに in secret; privately; stealthily

hizō (suru) 秘蔵(する) treasuring; hoarding (hiding articles)

kimitsu (da) 機密(だ) secrecy (secret; confidential)

~ shorui ~書類 confidential document

mikkai 密会 secret meeting

misshi 密使 secret errand

mittei 密偵 secret agent

naimitsu (da) 内密(だ) confidence (off the record; confidentially)

shimpi (da) 神秘(だ) mystery (mysterious)

hiso hiso to hanasu ひそひそと話す They *are talking so that no one can overhear*

hisomu 潜む lurk; lie behind

hitobarai o suru 人払いをする He *cleared the room of everyone* and talked to me in private.

hitome o shinonde...suru 人目を忍んで...する Nehemiah surveyed the walls of Jerusalem *out of sight of everyone (in secret).*

[...o] honomekasu [...を]ほのめかす She *hinted at (gave me a clue to)* the secret.

imbō o takuramu 陰謀をたくらむ plot in secret; conspire

kakumau かくまう shelter; harbor; screen

kakureru 隠れる take cover; hide; be concealed

kakurete...suru 隠れて...する The things they *do in secret* it would be shameful even to mention. (Ephesians 5 : 12)

kakusu 隠す cover; conceal; hide

koso koso to こそこそと secretly; sneakily

koso koso yaru こそこそやる do clandestinely

kossori to こっそりと secretly; on the sly

me o nusunde...suru 目を盗んで...する He *did* it *behind her back (did* it *on the sly).*

mimiuchi suru 耳打ちする whisper privately; put a bug in one's ear

NAISHO ないしょ secret; private matter

~ ni suru ~にする keep [it] a secret; keep [it] on the QT

naibukōsaku 内部工作 party intrigues

naihō (suru) 内報(する) secret information; unofficial report; tip-off (give a tip; tip off)

nainai (da) 内々(だ) secret; confidential

~ ni suru ~にする Please *keep the matter confidential (keep it mum).*

naishobanashi o suru ないしょ話をする have a private talk; have a tête-à-tête

uchimaku 内幕 It took me a long time to discover the *inner workings* of the organization.

uchiwa no kekkon 内輪の結婚 private marriage

okugi 奥義 the secrets of; the mysteries of [an art; a culture; etc.]

sempuku (suru) 潜伏(する) hiding (conceal oneself; be in hiding; lurk)

senzai (suru) 潜在(する) latency (lie dormant; be latent)

suppanuku [c] すっぱ抜く uncover; bring out into the open; expose

supai スパイ spy

tokumei (da) 匿名(だ) anonymity (anonymous)

uraguchi kara 裏口から He got into college *through the back door* (*by unfair means*).

yami ni hōmuru やみに葬る The politician wanted to *hush up* (*cover up*) the affair.

⇨ 204

隠れているもので，あらわにならぬものはなく，秘密にされているもので，知られず，また現われないものはありません．(ルカ 8 ¹⁷)

61 HINAN 非難
CENSURE, CRITICISM

abura o shiborareru [c] 油をしぼられる I was *called on the carpet* (*taken to task*).

ashizama ni iu あしざまに言う speak evil of

atama gonashi ni iu 頭ごなしに言う She *read him the riot act* (*ranted and raved at him*) for failing to call her.

dokuzuku 毒づく speak bitterly against

gamigami iu がみがみ言う He *spoke crossly* (*spoke in a snarly way*) to her about the problem.

hometa hanashi de wa nai ほめた話ではない *There is nothing admirable about* his actions. (His actions *deserve criticism*.)

HINAN (suru) 非難(する) censure; criticism; rebuke (censure; criticize; rebuke)

~ gōgō ~ ごうごう loud complaints; hisses and boos; catcalls

~ kōgeki o kuwaeru ~ 攻撃を加える The newspapers *made critical attacks* on Lincoln.

~ no koe ga agaru ~ の声があがる After the Tsurumi train disaster, the *voice of censure was raised* against the National Railways.

~ no mato to naru ~ の的となる become the target of criticism

~ sarezu ni ~ されずに without reproach

surudoi hinan するどい非難 sharp rebuke

tsūretsu ni hinan suru 痛烈に非難する rebuke one sharply

kechi o tsukeru けちをつける be hypercritical; pick flaws [in]

kibishii きびしい overly critical; censorious

kōgeki (suru) 攻撃(する) attack (denounce)

kogoto 小言 rebuke; scolding

~ o iu ~ を言う scold; bawl out

kokiorosu こきおろす She *is* always *running* him *down*.

kokuhyō (suru) 酷評(する) scathing criticism (castigate; be hard on; sail into [one])

me ni kado o tateru 目にかどをたてる She *scowled at* her son, who was acting up in front of the company.

najiru なじる rebuke

SHIKARU しかる scold; find fault [with]; rake one over the coals

sanzan shikarareru さんざんしかられる I really *got bawled out* for that mistake.

shikaritobasu しかり飛ばす She *gave* her child a *piece of her mind* for messing up the house.

SEMERU 責める ostracize; attack; reproach

hi o semeru 非を責める The publisher *took* the editor *to task* for the many blunders found in the book.

kibishiku semeru きびしく責める pull one up sharply

soshiri (ru) そしり(そしる) censure; blame (censure; disparage)

~o maneku ~を招く He *brought reproach upon himself* for accepting the bribe.

togame (ru) とがめ(る) fault-finding (find fault [with]; rebuke)

tsumahajiki sareru つまはじきされる Because of his actions, he *is shunned* (*is ostracized*) by the whole village.

tsumi o nasuritsukeru 罪をなすりつける He was at fault, but he *laid the blame on* others.

urusai うるさい overly critical; exacting

yakamashii やかましい hypercritical; noisy about

⇨ 58

主も，あなたがたを，私たちの主イエス・キリストの日に責められるところのない者として，最後まで堅く保ってくださいます．（コリント I 1 ⁸）

62 HINEKURE ひねくれ PERVERSENESS

amanojaku (da) あまのじゃく(だ) He's *a cross-grained person.*

futekusareru [C] ふてくされる What's the matter with him today? He*'s so sulky* (he*'s so sullen*).

hikutsu (da) 卑屈(だ) servile; sniveling
~ na konjō ~な根性 servile spirit
~ ni naru ~になる become sneaky

HINEKURE (ru) ひねくれ (ひねくれる) perverseness (be perverted; be warped)
hinekureta seishitsu ひねくれた性質 twisted nature; warped nature

ijikeru いじける be warped; be twisted [in disposition]
ijiketa taido いじけた態度 warped attitude

ijiwarui 意地悪い mean; malicious
ijiwaru o iu 意地悪を言う He is always *saying spiteful things* (*saying mean things*) to me.

jōki o issuru 常軌を逸する His actions *have been abnormal* (He has been *behav-*

ing strangely) ever since he joined that fanatical sect.

kojitsuke (ru) こじつけ (こじつける) forced meaning (distort the meaning)
jijitsu o kojitsukeru 事実をこじつける distort the facts; twist the facts

kokoro ga nejikeru 心がねじける His *mind has been warped* by reading that literature.
nejiketa seishitsu ねじけた性質 twisted nature

konjō no warui 根性の悪い ill-natured; perverse

MAGARU 曲がる become twisted; become warped
tsumuji o mageru つむじを曲げる get cranky; be out of sorts; get cross
hesomagari [C] へそ曲がり She just doesn't play right with the other children; she's quite *difficult* (*stubborn; twisted*).
kyokkai suru 曲解する distort the meaning; misinterpret
waikyoku [L] 歪曲 perversion
te ni oenai hito 手に負えない人 I don't know what to do; he's an *uncontrollable person.*
yakkai mono やっかいもの nuisance; [a person] hard to get along with

…あなたがたが，非難されるところのない 純真な 者となり，また，曲がった邪悪な世代の中にあって傷のない神の子どもとなり．…（ピリピ 2 ¹⁵）

63 HINIKU 皮肉 SARCASM

atekosuri (ru) 当てこすり(当てこする) insinuation; innuendo (make a sarcastic remark)
atetsukeru 当てつける insinuate; rub it in

fūshi (suru) 風刺(する) sarcasm; satire; irony (satirize)
~ bungaku ~文学 satire
fūshiteki (da) 風刺的(だ) satirical;

ironical; sardonic
HINIKU 皮肉 sarcasm
- **~ na bishō o ukabete** [L] ~ な微笑 を浮かべて He answered us *with a sarcastic smile.*
- **~ ni kikoeru** ~ に聞こえる Your remark *sounds like sarcasm* to me.
- **~ no fukumareta oseji** ~ の含まれ たお世辞 Saying my speech was nice and long was a *left-handed compliment.*
- **~ ni mo** ~ にも *Ironically enough,* he ended up marrying the girl he disliked the most.
- **~ o iu** ~ を言う be sarcastic; talk sarcastically
- **~ o majiete** ~ を交じえて half sarcastically; flippantly
- **~ tappuri ni iu** ~ たっぷりに言う He *said something dripping with sarcasm; said something really ironic.*
kokkei na hiniku こっけいな皮肉 humorous sarcasm
tekibishii hiniku 手きびしい皮肉 cutting sarcasm
tsūretsu na hiniku 痛烈な皮肉 cutting sarcasm
hinikkuta mono 皮肉った者 something full of satire
hinikuya 皮肉屋 cynic; skeptic
itai tokoro o tsuku 痛い所を突く You *hit where it hurts* (*hit my weak spot*) when you mentioned tardiness.
iyami いやみ sarcastic remarks
- **~ o iu** ~ を言う Whenever Lincoln was humorous, Stanton would *say something disagreeable.*
- **~ tappuri no** ~ たっぷりの sarcastic; disagreeable
kuchi ga warui 口が悪い sharp tongued; flippant; sarcastic
seserawarau せせら笑う jeer [at]; laugh at one in scorn
shinratsu ni iu しんらつに言う make a stinging remark; make scathing statements
⇨ **61**

悪いことばを、いっさい口から出してはいけません．ただ，必要なとき，人の徳を養うのに役立つことばを話し，聞く人に恵みを与えなさい．（エペソ 4²⁹）

64 HINKON 貧困 POVERTY

fuji no yōi o suru 不時の用意をする You'd better *save for a rainy day.*
hi no kuruma (da) 火の車(だ) He's out of work and *living from hand to mouth.*
HINKON 貧困 poverty
- **~ ni ochiiru** ~ に陥る be reduced to poverty
bimbō 貧乏 poverty (poor)
- **~ hima nashi** [P] ~ 暇なし I'm busy all the time. As they say, "*The poor must always keep at it.*"
Kasegu ni oitsuku bimbō nashi [P] かせぐに追いつく貧乏なし A hard worker will never know poverty.
bimbōgurashi 貧乏暮らし poor circumstances
bimbōkusai 貧乏くさい His clothes *look poor* (*are seamy*).
bimbōnin 貧乏人 the poor; poor person
bimbōsho 貧乏性 [a person] born to be poor
himmin 貧民 the poor; the needy
- **~ kutsu** ~ くつ slums
himpu 貧富 wealth and poverty
Hin sureba donsuru [P] 貧すれば鈍する Poverty makes one dull.
hinjaku (da) 貧弱(だ) scanty; poor-looking; cheap-looking; shabby
- **~ na naiyō** ~ な内容 poor content
hinkonsha 貧困者 the poor; the needy
hinku 貧苦 straitened circumstances
- **~ ni nayamu** に悩む struggle against poverty; fight to keep the wolf from the door

~ **no betsu naku** ～ の別なく rich and poor alike

hinsō (**da**) 貧相(だ) poor-looking; impoverished

komaru 困る be distressed; be hard up

kane ni komaru 金に困る be hard up; be broke

konku 困苦 privation; hardship

~**ni nareru** ～に慣れる become used to hardships

~ **ni taeru** ～ に堪える She has learned to *put up with hardships and poverty.*

~ **o nameru** [L] ～ をなめる He has *tasted hardship;* you can count on him to endure anything.

konkyū (**suru**) 困窮(する) destitution (be reduced to poverty)

mazushii 貧しい poor; in need

seihin [L] 清貧 honest poverty

~ **ni amanjiru** [L] ～ に甘んじる He avoided corruption, *content to live in honest poverty.*

Sekihin arau ga gotoshi [L] 赤貧洗うがごとし That old lady *is as poor as a church mouse.*

hodokoshi (**su**) 施し(施す) benevolence; charity (bestow [upon]; grant [to])

hodokoshi o kou 施しを請う beg; ask for charity

ichimon nashi de 一文なしで I came to Tokyo *penniless (flat broke).*

KETSUBŌ (**suru**) 欠乏(する) lack (lack; be in want)

~ **o tsugeru** [L] ～ を告げる cause a shortage

jinzai no ketsubō 人材の欠乏 dearth of talent

kyūbō 窮乏 want

toboshii 乏しい scarce; short; scanty

kojiki konjō こじき根性 begging attitude

kubi ga mawaranai [C] 首が回らない When the business failed, he *was in dire financial straits (was up to his neck in debt).*

KURASHI ga tatanai 暮らしが立たない In his early days as a lawyer, Lincoln *couldn't make ends meet (couldn't make a living).*

hosoboso to kurasu 細々と暮らす Ever since her husband died, she *has barely eked out a living (has lived in humble circumstances).*

sono higurashi その日暮らし The newlyweds *were living from hand to mouth.*

kurushii seikatsu o suru 苦しい生活をする lead a hard life

misuborashii みすぼらしい seedy; shabby

~ **fukusō** (**minari**) ～ 服装(みなり) shabby dress; down-at-the-heels look

ochibureru 落ちぶれる be ruined; be reduced to poverty

reiraku suru 零落する be ruined [financially]; hit the bottom; see bad days

rotō ni mayou 路頭に迷う After the father left them, the family *was rendered homeless (was put out in the cold; was cast adrift).*

saimin gai 細民街 slum areas

shayōzoku 斜陽族 the fallen aristocracy; the has-beens

teippai no seikatsu o suru 手一杯の生活をする Young Abe worked at several jobs but *could barely keep body and soul together (could barely make a living).*

Zashite kuraeba, taizan mo munashi [P] 座して食らえば、大山もむなし Idleness can squander a fortune.

正しくあゆむ 貧しいものは、曲った道を歩む富める者にまさる. (箴言 28 ⁶)

65 HŌFU 豊富 ABUNDANCE

afureru あふれる be overflowing; be affluent

AMARI (**ru**) 余り(余る) remainder; leftovers (be leftover; be in excess)

ariamaru あり余る be enough and to spare

yobun (da) 余分(だ) superfluous

yokei (da) 余計(だ) abundance; excess (abundant; excess; unnecessary)

anraku na seikatsu o suru 安楽な生活をする live an easy life; be on easy street

hana o sakaseru 花を咲かせる He *has been in his glory* ever since the project was a success.

hanayaka (da) はなやか(だ) colorful; abundant

HŌFU (da) 豊富(だ) abundance (abundant; affluent)

~ **na keiken (chishiki, naiyo)** ~ な 経験(知識，内容) wide experience (wide knowledge; full of content)

~ **ni suru** ~ にする enrich

fuyū kaikyū 富裕階級 the rich; the wealthy; the well-off

hōnen 豊年 abundant year; year of a good harvest

hōryō 豊漁 big catch of fish

hōsaku 豊作 bumper crop

tomi (mu) [L] 富(富む) riches; fortune (grow rich; be rich [in])

kyoman no tomi o kizuku [L] 巨万の富を築く He *amassed a fortune* in stocks.

yutaka (da) 豊か(だ) abundance (abundant; plentiful)

~ **ni kurasu** ~ に暮らす live in luxury; live in clover

kizoku no umare 貴族の生まれ He was *born with a silver spoon in his mouth.*

michitariru 満ち足りる have enough and to spare; be more than enough; be replete with

nani fusoku naku kurasu 何不足なく 暮らす lack nothing in life; have everything one wants

mujinzō (da) 無尽蔵(だ) inexhaustible; without measure

ogoru おごる be extravagant; live in luxury

omou zombun ni 思う存分に to one's heart's content; to the full

SAKAERU 栄える be prosperous; flourish

eiga 栄華 prosperity; opulence

~ **o kiwameru** ~ を窮める live in splendor

eiyōeiga ni kurasu 栄よう栄華に暮らす Ever since they inherited that fortune, they *have been living it up* (*they have been living high*).

sankai no chimmi 山海の珍味 all sorts of delicacies

shindai o kuitsubusu 身代を食いつぶす He *squandered his inheritance* within a few months.

shokushō (suru) 食傷(する) surfeit; gluttony (be satiated with)

yūfuku (da) 裕福(だ) well-to-do; well-fixed; well-off; well-heeled

zaisan o motte iru 財産を持っている be wealthy; have means

~ **o tsukaihatasu** ~ を使い果たす squander a fortune; use up an estate

zeitaku (da) ぜいたく(だ) luxury (luxurious; extravagant)

~ **ni kurasu** ~ に暮らす live a life of luxury

~ **ni tsukau** ~ に使う use lavishly; squander

⇨ **138**

この世で富んでいる人たちに命じなさい。高ぶらないように。また、たよりにならない富に望みを置かないように。むしろ、私たちすべての物を豊かに与えて楽しませてくださる神に望みを置くように。(テモテ I 6 ¹⁷)

66 HŌSHŌ 報奨
REWARD, COMPENSATION

chingin 賃金 pay; wages

~ **o harau** ~ を払う pay wages; pay a salary

henrei suru 返礼する give a present in return; return the honor

homeru ほめる praise; commend
HŌSHŌ 報奨 reward; commendation
  hōbi ほうび reward; prize
    ~ o ataeru ~ を与える give a prize
    ~ o morau ~ をもらう be rewarded; get a prize
    ~ to shite ~ として We want to give you this book *in reward for* your faithful attendance.
  hōshū 報酬 prize; reward
    ~ o dasu ~ を出す reward; compensate [one for his services]
    ~ nashi de ~ なしで They want to work *without pay* (*without remuneration*).
    ~ o ukeru ~ を受ける If a man's building stands, he will *be rewarded*. (I Corinthians 3 : 15)
  ittōshō o toru 一等賞を取る take first place; win first prize
  kenshōkin 懸賞金 prize money; reward
  mukui (ru) 報い(る) reward (reward; pay back; render [to])
    ~ o ukeru ~ を受ける get one's reward; have one's reward
    ~ toshite ~ として He cheated other people, so this loss was simply *getting what was coming to* him.
  on ni mukuiru 恩に報いる return a favor; repay one for one's kindness
  tōzen no mukui 当然の報い Most felt the killer *got what he deserved*.
  onshō 恩賞 reward; prize
  shō 賞 prize
    [...ni] sōtō suru shō (batsu) o ataeru [...に]相当する賞(罰)を与える They *gave* him his *just desserts* for the work he did. (The judge *meted out justice that* fit the crime.)
  shōbatsu 賞罰 praise and blame; desserts
  shōhin 賞品 prize [trophy, etc.]
  shōkin 賞金 prize-money
  shōsan (suru) 賞賛(する) admiration

(admire; praise)
shōyo 賞与 bonus
shōyokin 賞与金 bonus money
ii kimi da! [C] いい気味だ! It serves you right!
jigō-jitoku (da) 自業自得(だ) As one sows, so one reaps. You have only yourself to blame.
shiharai (u) 支払い(支払う) payment (pay; make payment)
sono kawari ni... その代わりに... in return for; as compensation for; to make up for
suisen (suru) 推薦(する) recommendation (recommend)
suishō (suru) 推奨(する) commendation (commend)

今からは，義の栄冠が私のために用意されているだけです．かの日には，正しい審判者である主が，それを私に授けてくださるのです．私だけでなく，主の現われを慕っている者には，だれでも授けてくださるのです．
(テモテ II 4 [8])

67 IGAI 意外
UNEXPECTEDNESS

angai (da) 案外(だ) contrary to expectation
aita kuchi ga fusagaranai あいた口がふさがらない I *was dumbfounded* (*was flabbergasted*) when I saw him jump from the roof.
akke ni torareru あっけに取られる be taken aback; be amazed; be bowled over
akireru あきれる be surprised
ari sō mo nai ありそうもない It is an *unlikely* (*incredible*) story.
ashimoto kara tori ga tatsu yōni 足もとから鳥が立つように The news that the owner had sold our rented house came *like a bolt from the blue* (*as a complete shock*).
ayashimu 怪しむ wonder at; be surprised; be perplexed

bikkuri suru びっくりする be surprised

dashinuke ni 出し抜けに all of a sudden

dokitto suru どきっとする I *gave a start* when he knocked at the door.

furyo (no) 不慮(の) unforeseen; unexpected
~ **no sainan** ~の災難 unexpected disaster

FUSHIGI (da) 不思議(だ) wonder (strange)
~ **de naranai** ~でならない I *can't account for* his leaving that wonderful job.
~ **ni omou** ~に思う I *think it strange* that he left so quickly.

omoi mo yoranai 思いも寄らない His getting sick *was totally unlooked for* (*was least expected*).
omoi no hoka 思いのほか unanticipated

omoigake naku 思いがけなく unexpectedly; accidentally; by chance

IGAI (da) 意外(だ) unexpectedness (unexpected)
~ **ni hayaku** に早く He came *sooner than I expected.*
~ **ni omou** ~に思う think it strange; think it odd
Kore wa igai da! これは意外だ This is a surprise!

fui (da) 不意(だ) unexpectedly
~ **ni osou** ~に襲う suddenly overtake
~ **o utsu** ~を打つ take one by surprise; catch one napping
fuiuchi o kurau 不意打ちをくらう He came suddenly and I *was caught off guard* (*caught unprepared*).

ihyō ni deru 意表に出る He took us by surprise (*jumped the gun on us*) and announced the new project.

ikinari いきなり suddenly; abruptly

itsu no ma ni ka いつの間にか *Before I knew it,* the boy had become a man.

kimo o tsubusu 肝をつぶす I *was fright-*

ened out of my wits by that big dog.

koto no hoka ことのほか *Contrary to what I had expected,* he was turned down at the job.

kyū (da) 急(だ) suddenness (suddenly)

maebure naku 前触れなく *Without warning* they came and demanded payment.

nemimi ni mizu (da) 寝耳に水(だ) It was a *great shock* to learn that he secretly married my fiancee.

niwaka ni にわかに suddenly

odoroku 驚く be amazed; be astonished
odorokasu 驚かす surprise; bowl one over

seiten no hekireki 青天のへきれき The young man's death *came as a complete surprise* to us.

sukkari menkurau すっかり面くらう I *was flabbergasted* (*was nonplussed*) when I bumped into the boss at the ball game because I had taken sick leave that day.

toki no hazumi de 時のはずみで He did it *on the spur of the moment* (*on a sudden impulse*).

TOTSUZEN (da) 突然(だ) all at once; out of the blue
~ **no koto de** ~の事で This *is too sudden;* I can't make a decision.

toppatsu jiken (jiko) 突発事件(事故) sudden event (accident)

toppatsuteki ni 突発的に all of a sudden; unexpectedly

ura o kaku [C] 裏をかく They *outwitted us* and produced their product first.

yabu hebi ni naru やぶへびになる *That's the thanks I get!* (*Did I get a slap in the face!*) I tried to help and they sued me.

yabu kara bō ni やぶから棒に He seemed to be enjoying his work at the office, so his resignation came as *a bolt from the blue.*

yoki shinai 予期しない We *did not anticipate* his action.

yosōgai (da) 予想外 (だ) unforeseen; beyond expectation
⇨ 136

主の日が夜中の盗人のように来るということは, あなたがた自身がよく承知しているからです。
しかし, 兄弟たち。あなたがたは暗やみの中にはいないのですから, その日が, 盗人のようにあなたがたを襲うことはありません。(テサロニケ I 5 ², ⁴)

68 IGEN 威厳 DIGNITY

atama ga sagaru 頭が下がる *I am quite impressed with him* (*I give him the credit*); he sacrificed much for the poor.

chomei (da) 著名 (だ) prominence (prominent; eminent; celebrated)

daijinbutsu 大人物 great figure

dōdō to shita 堂々とした imposing; commanding

erai 偉い great; grand

fūsai ga agaranai 風彩が上がらない *There is no dignity about* his slovenly mannerisms.

HAKU ga tsuku はくがつく gain prestige
~ **o tsukeru** ~をつける The honorary degree *added prestige* to the professor.

HIN'I 品位 dignity; grace
~ **o otosu** ~を落とす degrade oneself; lose one's dignity
~ **o takameru** ~を高める refine; dignify; ennoble
~ **o tamotsu** ~を保つ bear oneself honorably; keep one's dignity
kihin ga aru 気品がある have dignity; be dignified

idai (da) 偉大 (だ) greatness (great; grand)

IGEN 威厳 dignity
~ **ni kakawaru** ~にかかわる beneath one's dignity
~ **no aru** ~のある dignified
genshuku (da) 厳粛 (だ) solemnity (solemn; grave)
iatsuteki taido 威圧的態度 overbearing attitude

igi o tadasu 威儀をただす He rose to greet us *in a dignified manner.*

ikō 威光 power; authority; influence

ishin 威信 dignity; prestige

sōgon (da) 壮厳 (だ) magnificence (magnificent; sublime; solemn)

songen 尊厳 dignity; majesty

ikameshii いかめしい solemn; august
~ **katagaki** ~肩書き high-sounding title

kanroku 貫録 weight; dignity

kedakai 気高い noble; lofty; exalted

kibishisa きびしさ sternness; strictness

kō o tateru 功を立てる Horie *distinguished himself* by sailing across the Pacific alone.

kōei aru 光栄ある glorious; honored
~ **ni omou** ~に思う I *feel honored* to be able to address you this evening.
~ **ni yokusuru** ~に浴する have the honor of

koken ni kakawaru こけんにかかわる It would *be beneath him* (*be beneath his dignity*) to go uninvited.

mibun no takai 身分の高い distinguished; noble; aristocratic

ogosoka (da) おごそか (だ) solemnity (grave; solemn; august)

omodatta 重立った leading; chief

otoko o sageru 男を下げる He *discredited himself* by acting in that cowardly way.

SONKEI (suru) 尊敬 (する) respect (respect; look up to; esteem; honor)
~ **o ukeru** ~を受ける win respect; command respect; earn respect
keii o hyōsuru 敬意を表する He *deferred to* the professor, asking him to speak first.
sonchō (suru) 尊重 (する) respect (respect; esteem)
sondaisa 尊大さ air of importance
tattobu (tōtobu) 尊ぶ (とうとぶ) value highly; esteem one highly

tattoi (tōtoi) 尊い(とうとい) noble; exalted

uyamau 敬う respect; honor; esteem ⇨ 136

誉と，威厳とはそのみ前にあり，力と，うるわしさとはその聖所にある．(詩篇 96 ⁶)

69 IKARI 怒り
ANGER, WRATH

bakuhatsu suru 爆発する When they came in late, the boss's *anger flared up* (the boss *burst into anger*) (the boss *hit the ceiling*).

donaru どなる shout at

FUNGAI (suru) 憤慨(する) indignation; resentment (be indignant; resent)
   ~ ni taenai ~に耐えない They *feel burning resentment* (*are up in arms*) at the city for their failure to prevent this accident.

fumman 憤まん resentment; indignation

fungeki (suru) 憤激(する) rage; passion (become enraged; fall into a passion)

gekido (suru) 激怒(する) violent anger (be infuriated)

gekkō (suru) 激高(する) excitement; rage; fury (get worked up; become enraged; become infuriated)

gifun 義憤 righteous indignation

hifun-kōgai (suru) 悲憤慷慨(する) indignation (be indignant; deplore)

gaman dekinai がまんできない I *can't stand it* any longer.

HARA ga tatsu 腹が立つ When they mentioned his poor English, he *got mad* (*got stirred up*).
   ~ o tateru ~を立てる get angry; get one's dander up; get sore

haradachi magire ni 腹立ちまぎれに *In a fit of anger* he punched him in the nose.

haradatashii 腹立たしい provoking; exasperating

mukappara o tateru むかっ腹を立てる fly into a rage

rippuku (suru) 立腹(する) anger (lose one's temper; get sore)

IKARI (ru) 怒り(怒る) anger; wrath (get angry)
   ~ o maneku ~を招く He *incurred the wrath of* the other employees when he fired her.
   hageshii ikari ni karareru 激しい怒りにかられる give vent to anger; boil over with rage

doki 怒気 rage; anger; fury
   ~ o fukunde ~を含んで *With ire* (*Angrily*) he demanded immediate payment of the bill.

okoridasu おこりだす fly into a rage; fly off the handle

okorippoi おこりっぽい hot-tempered; touchy

okoru おこる get angry; get mad
   aosuji o tatete okoru 青筋を立てておこる His *blood boiled over* when he saw the man mistreating the child.
   kankan ni natte okoru かんかんになっておこる throw a fit; storm at one
   makka ni natte okoru 真赤になっておこる He *saw red* when they ran down his school.
   medama no tobideru hodo okorareru 目玉の飛び出るほどおこられる I *got a good scolding* (*was raked over the coals*) for coming in late last night.

ikkatsu (suru) 一かつ(する) shouting (thunder at; shout at one)
   ~ kurawasu ~食らわす He *shouted at me in anger* (*roared at me in anger*).

ikidōri (ru) 憤り(憤る) wrath; indignation (be indignant)
   ~ o kanjiru ~を感じる be roused to anger; be exasperated

ikimaku いきまく fume at; be enraged

ikiritatsu いきり立つ get angry; get ruffled

kan ni sawaru かんにさわる The remark *touched his sore spot* and he got mad.

kanjō o gai suru 感情を害する By saying you were not interested in their art work, you *hurt their feelings*.

Kannin-bukuro no o ga kireru [P] 勘忍袋の緒が切れる The boss kept warning him about tardiness, so when he came late this morning, *it was the straw that broke the camel's back* (*his patience ran out; that did it*).

katto natte かっとなって in a sudden fit of anger

kentsuku o kuwaseru [C] 剣突くを食わせる He *angrily rebuked* the careless boy.

ki ni sawaru koto o iu 気にさわることを言う You *said something that got a rise out of* her.

[...**no**] **ki o sokoneru** [...の]気をそこねる goad one into anger

kutte kakaru [C] 食ってかかる I mentioned her untidy hair and she *flared up at* me.

mushakusha suru むしゃくしゃする get irritated; be fretful

ōmedama o kuu 大目玉を食う The boy *was given a good scolding* (*really caught it*) for going swimming alone.

SHAKU ni sawaru しゃくにさわる When she talks like that I *get peeved at* her.

kanshaku o okosu かんしゃくを起こす *In a fit of rage* he said all kinds of wild things.

kanshakudama o haretsu saseru かんしゃく玉を破裂させる He kept complaining about the food day after day until finally today the cook *exploded* (*blew his stack*).

shikaritobasu しかり飛ばす She *thoroughly scolded him* for playing hookey from school.

uppun o harasu うっぷんを晴らす He *vented his anger against* us by telling

everything to the boss.

...不義をもって真理をはばんでいる人々のあらゆる不敬虔と不正に対して、神の怒りが天から啓示されている... (ローマ 1 ¹⁸)

70 IKEN 意見 OPINION

ankēto アンケート questionnaire

~ **o toru** ~を取る take a poll; take a census

IKEN 意見 opinion

~ **ga awanai** ~が合わない We *don't see eye-to-eye* on politics.

~ **ni hiraki ga aru** ~に開きがある Regarding this problem, *there are divergent opinions* among us.

~ **o iu (noberu)** ~を言う(述べる) give one's opinion; speak one's piece

~ **o kikiireru** ~を聞き入れる take advice; give ear to

~ **o kimeru** ~を決める form an opinion

~ **o koshu suru** ~を固守する He *sticks to his opinion*.

~ **ga kuichigau** ~が食い違う have conflicting views [on]; have different views

dokuzenteki na iken 独善的な意見 dogmatic opinion

jibun no iken o iifurasu 自分の意見を言いふらす He never misses a chance to *broadcast his opinions* (*advertise his views*) on politics.

kenkai 見解 opinion; version

~ **no sōi** ~の相違 difference in opinion; difference in interpretation

~ **o koto ni suru** ~を異にする have a different view

takken 卓見 good idea; foresight

teiken 定見 settled conviction; considered opinion

~ **ga nai** ~がない I *have no fixed opinion about* the matter.

IRON 異論 different opinion

~ **ga nai** ～がない I *am of the same
mind as* she in the matter.

~ **o sashihasamu** ～をさしはさむ put
in an opposing view

~ **o tonaeru** ～を唱える offer a
dissenting voice

igi 異議 protest; objection; dissent

~ **naku** ～なく with no objections;
unanimously

iken 異見 divergent view; different
idea

jiron 持論 pet theory

~ **o magenai** ～を曲げない stick to
one's opinion

seron 世論 public opinion

shōron (suru) 詳論(する) detailed
explanation (dwell on)

ippan no setsu 一般の説 general view

jisetsu 自説 one's personal opinion

~ **o tateru** ～を立てる form one's
opinion

jukuryo no ue 熟慮のうえ after serious
consideration

shoshin o jikkō suru 所信を実行する
carry out one's convictions

daitan ni shoshin o noberu 大胆に所
信を述べる courageously give one's
opinion; have the boldness to speak
up

SHUCHŌ (suru) 主張(する) stress; claim;
emphasis (emphasize)

~ **o mageru** ～を曲げる He *conceded
a point* and the motion carried.

~ **o tōsu** ～を通す He *pushed his claim
through* during the meeting.

shugi 主義 principle; policy

~ **toshite** ～として on principle; as a
matter of principle

takaku hyōka suru 高く評価する They
hold his art works *in high regard.*

⇒ **73, 86**

主のはかりごとはとこしえに立ち，
そのみこころの思いは世々に立つ．(詩篇 **33** ¹¹)

71　INORI 祈り PRAYER

INORI (ru) 祈り(祈る) prayer (pray)

~ **ga kanau** ～がかなう prayer is
heard; prayer is answered

~ **ga wakideru** ～がわき出る prayer is
made spontaneously

~ **no funiki** ～のふんい気 atmosphere
of prayer

~ **o sasageru (ageru)** ～をささげる(上
げる) offer up a prayer; say a prayer

~ **o suru** ～をする pray

hitasura (hitoe ni) inoru ひたすら(ひ
とえに)祈る pray diligently; pray
from the heart

hizamazuite inoru ひざまずいて祈る
I *kneel in prayer* to the Father,
from whom every family in heaven
and earth takes its name.
(Ephesians 3 : 14)

isshin komete inoru 一心込めて祈る
pray with heart and soul

Kami ni inoru 神に祈る pray to God

tayumazu inoru たゆまず祈る pray
untiringly

tsutsushinde inoru 慎んで祈る pray
reverently

inorimotomeru 祈り求める pray for

kitō (suru) 祈禱(する) prayer (pray)

kitōkai 祈禱会 prayer meeting

kitōsho 祈禱書 prayer book

mokutō (suru) 黙禱(する) silent prayer
(pray silently)

NEGAI (u) 願い(願う) wish; desire (wish
[for]; desire; ask [for])

~ **o kanaeru** ～をかなえる The judge
granted the prisoner's *request,*
allowing his mother to visit him.

kokoro kara no negai 心からの願い
" Brothers, my *deepest desire* and
my prayer to God is for their salvation." (Romans 10:1)

onegai mōshiagemasu お願い申し
上げます I *earnestly ask* (I *humbly*

implore) that you grant me this request.

kigan (suru) 祈願(する) prayer; supplication (pray; make supplication)

koinegau こいねがう beg; implore

kongan (suru) 懇願(する) entreaty (entreat)

tangan (suru) 嘆願(する) entreaty (entreat; supplicate)

祈るとき, 異邦人のように同じことばを, ただくり返してはいけません. 彼らはことば数が多ければ聞かれると思っているのです. だから, 彼らのまねをしてはいけません. あなたがたの父なる神は, あなたがたがお願いする先に, あなたがたに必要なものを知っておられるからです.
(マタイ 6 ⁷, ⁸)

72 INSHŌ 印象
IMPRESSION

atama ni kobiritsuku 頭にこびりつく I *can't get out of my mind* what I saw last night. (What I saw last night *still sticks in my mind*.)

honemi ni shimiru 骨身にしみる I *feel* what he said on his deathbed *in the depths of my being*. (What he said on his deathbed *really came home to me*.)

INSHŌ 印象 impression

   ~ o fukameru ~ を深める Lincoln's use of homey illustrations *deepened the impression* he made on his audiences.

   ~ o nokosu ~ を残す leave one's mark on; leave an impression on one.

   daiichi inshō 第一印象 first impression

   me ni ataeru inshō 目に与える印象 fresh impression; vivid impression

   me no sameru yōna inshō 目のさめるような印象 striking impression; vivid impression

   mimi ni ataeru inshō 耳に与える印象 auditory impression

   namanamashii inshō なまなましい印

象 graphic impression; fresh impression; vivid impression

tsuyoi inshō o ukeru 強い印象を受ける be deeply impressed [by]

warui inshō o ataeru 悪い印象を与える make a poor impression

wasuregatai inshō o ataeru 忘れがたい印象を与える He *made an unforgettable impression on* me.

yoi inshō o ataeru 良い印象を与える The visiting official *made a good impression* on everyone.

inshōteki (da) 印象的(だ) impressive

inshōzukeru 印象づける impress one

KAMMEI (suru) 感銘(する) impression (impress one; make an impression on one)

kanjusei 感受性 impressionability

   ~ no tsuyoi ~ の強い impressionable; susceptible

kōkan o ataeru 好感を与える impress one favorably

kioku kara kienai 記憶から消えない His words *will live in my memory forever.*

kizamu 刻む inscribe; impress; engrave

meiki suru 銘記する take [it] to heart

KOKORO ni kizamikomu 心に刻み込む write indelibly upon one's heart; engrave upon one's heart

   ~ni kuiiru ~ に食い入る invade one's thinking; prey on one's mind

   ~ni shimiru ~ にしみる sink into one's heart; be steeped in

   ~ni yakitsukeru ~ に焼きつける leave an indelible impression; burn upon one's heart

   ~o eguru yōna omoi ~ をえぐるような思い heart-rending experience

   ~ o toraeru ~ を捕える Our *hearts were captivated* by that beautiful singer.

mimi no soko ni nokoru 耳の底に残る The sound of those pitiful screams *keeps ringing in my ears.*

⇨ 33, 113

あなたがたが 私たちの奉仕によるキリストの 手紙であり, 墨によってではなく, 生ける神の御霊によって書かれ, 石の板にではなく, 人の心の板に書かれたものであることが明らかだからです. (コリント II 3 ⁸)

73 ISHI 意志 [心理学]・意志 [法令] WILL

ISHI 意志 will
- **~ hakujaku (da)** ~ 薄弱(だ) He is a *weak-willed* man.
- **~ dōri ni suru** ~ どおりにする In this company, you have to *do exactly as* the boss *wants*.
- **~ ga tsūjiru** ~ が通じる The *wishes* of the principal *are well understood* by the studen:s.
- **~ no chikara** ~ の力 will-power
- **~ no tsuyoi (yowai)** ~ の 強い (弱い) strong-willed (weak-willed)
- **jiyū ishi de** 自由意志で He did it *of his own free will* (*of his own volition*).
- **fuhon'i nagara** 不本意ながら I consented *against my will* to their going.
- **i ni hansuru** 意に反する be against one's wishes
  - **~ ni kanau** ~ にかなう The plan *is agreeable to* him.
  - **~ no mama ni naru** ~ のままになる He wants everyone to *do just as he wants* (*be at his beck and call*).
- **ikō** 意向 intention; inclination
  - **~ o saguru** ~ を探る Party members came to *sound out* Lincoln's *intentions* in the slavery issue.
  - **~ o tashikameru** ~ を確かめる You'd better *ascertain his feelings* (*make sure of his intentions*) before you proceed.
- **ishi** 意思 intention; purpose
- **ito (suru)** 意図(する) intention; aim (intend; aim at)

- **~ o motsu** ~ を持つ have an ulterior motive
- **iyoku ga waku** 意欲がわく Unless *desire* for free elections *springs from* the people, democracy will fail.
- **koi ni** 故意に willfully; intentionally; purposely; on purpose
- **kokorozashi** 志 will; aim; ambition; determination
  - **~ o tateru** ~ を立てる aspire after; set a goal in life
  - **~ o togeru** ~ を遂げる achieve one's goal
  - **~ o tsugu** ~ を継ぐ He *carried out* his father's *ambition* to expand the company.
  - **koto kokorozashi to chigau** こと志と違う The whole undertaking *proved contrary to my expectations* (*went wrong*).
- **kokumin no sōi** 国民の総意 the national will
- **shin'i** 真意 one's true motive; one's real intention
- **zuii ni** 随意に at one's discretion; voluntarily; freely
- **jibun katte ni suru** 自分かってにする do as one pleases; have one's own way
- **kimama ni suru** 気ままにする do as one pleases
  - **ki no muku mama** 気の向くまま I walked along the banks of the Naguri River *wherever fancy led me*.
- **kokoro** 心 will; mind; heart
  - **~ narazu mo** ~ ならずも He went ahead *even against my will*.
- **mune** 旨 will; heart
- **omou mama ni suru** 思うままにする The boss told us to *do as we wanted* and not bother him with details.
- **oshi no tsuyoi hito** [c] 押しの強い人 He gets things done because *he's a pusher* (*he's a driver*).
  - **shugi o oshitōsu** 主義を押し通す insist.

on one's principle; stick to one's belief to the end

wagamama ga tsunoru わがままがつのる That spoiled boy *is becoming more and more self-willed* (*is getting out of hand*).

~ ni furumau ～にふるまう behave willfully

waza to わざと purposely; on purpose ⇨ **121, 145**

わたしに向かって、『主よ，主よ』と言う者がみな天の御国にはいるのではなく、天におられるわたしの父のみこころを行なう者がはいるのです。（マタイ 7 ²¹）

74 ITCHI 一致
AGREEMENT, CONCORD

aizuchi o utsu 相づちを打つ He always *falls in with* everything the boss says.

atama o tate ni furu 頭を縦に振る They *consented* (*nodded affirmatively*) to his proposal.

AU 合う agree; fit in with; meet

chōshi o awaseru [C] 調子を合わせる Now he is *singing the same tune* as the boss.

kokoro o awaseru 心を合わせる have the same turn of mind; feel alike

pittari au ぴったり合う just fits; goes well with

fugō suru 符合する completely agree [with]; be consistent with

ikitōgō suru 意気投合する have the same turn of mind; see eye-to-eye [on things]

kataku musubiatte iru 堅く結び合っている be closely knit together; be firmly bound together

oriai o tsukeru 折り合いをつける They finally *came to an understanding over* (*settled on; came to an agreement on*) the issue.

wagō (suru) 和合(する) harmony; unity (be in harmony with; be united with)

DŌI (suru) 同意(する) agreement; consent

(agree with; consent to)

ichi mo ni mo naku dōi suru 一も二もなく同意する When I suggested the plan they all *fully agreed* to it.

dōkan 同感 identical feelings

dōshi 同志 of the same mind; like-minded [person]; kindred spirit

ichidō 一同 all; all concerned

iku dōon ni 異口同音に with one voice; with one accord

onaji omoi o idaku 同じ思いをいだく be of the same mind; be of one mind

ITCHI (suru) 一致(する) agreement; concord (agree with)

~ kyōryoku suru ～協力する work together; join forces [with]

~ shite ～して unitedly

~ ten ～点 points of agreement

manjō itchi de 満場一致で They *unanimously* approved the new plan.

fuitchi (da) 不一致(だ) disunity (disunited)

gatchi (suru) 合致(する) agreement (be in agreement [with])

hitotsu ni naru 一つになる become one with; be at one with

~ kokoro ni naru ～心になる They *became one in spirit* as they worked together.

ittai 一体 one body

~ to naru ～となる become as one; become united

izon naku 異存なく without objection

kessoku (suru) 結束(する) union; rapprochement (unite)

koe o soroete 声をそろえて in unison; with one voice

kyōmei (suru) 共鳴(する) accord (be in accord)

kyōtei ga seiritsu suru 協定が成立する come to an agreement

naka yoku 仲よく harmoniously

SANDŌ (suru) 賛同(する) support; approval (support; approve)

sanjo (suru) 賛助(する) backing; support (back; support)

sansei (suru) 賛成(する) approval; consent (approve; consent to)

wakai (suru) 和解(する) reconciliation (be reconciled)

　~ o ukeru ~ を受ける …When we were God's enemies, we *were reconciled* to Him through the death of His Son. (Romans 5: 10)

⇨ **22, 55, 165**

見よ，兄弟が和合して共におるのはいかに麗しく楽しいことであろう．(詩篇 133 ¹)

75 JIKAN 時間 TIME

aketemo kuretemo 明けても暮れても day in, day out; at all times; time and time again

ato あと after; later; subsequent

　igo 以後 after

dandan だんだん gradually; little by little

dondon どんどん rapidly

genzai (wa) 現在(は) the present (at present)

han de oshita yōni 判で押したように He shows up *punctually* every morning at 9:00 o'clock (*sharp; on the dot*).

hayame ni 早めに ahead of time

hima 暇 leisure time; free time; time to spare

IKKOKU o arasou 一刻を争う *There is not a moment to lose* in solving this problem.

　　~ mo yūyo dekinai ~ も猶予できない can't waste any time; have no time to spare

　　~ senkin [P] ~ 千金 Time is precious.

chikoku (suru) 遅刻(する) tardiness (be tardy; be late)

jiji kokkoku 時々刻々 from one minute to the next

jikoku 時刻 time of day; hour

teikoku 定刻 the fixed time

IMA 今 now; presently

　~ no tokoro ~ のところ for the present; for the time being; just now

　tatta ima たった今 just now; just this instant

imagoro 今ごろ at about this time

imasara 今さら after so long a time; now; when it is this late

kondo 今度 this time; next time

konkai 今回 this time

konnichi 今日 today

konoaida この間 the other day

konogoro このごろ lately; of late

tadaima ただいま just now

Itchō isseki ni…nai [P] 一朝一夕に…ない Yes, we must build better roads in Tokyo, but *it can't be done overnight* (*Rome wasn't built in a day*).

ittan 一たん once

ITSU いつ when

　~ demo ~ でも at all times; always; all the time

　~ made ~ まで how long; until when

itsuka いつか sometime

itsumo いつも anytime

iyoiyo いよいよ at last; finally; at long last

izure いずれ some day; sometime

JIKAN 時間 time

　~ dōri (da) ~ どおり(だ) on time; right on the dot

　~ ga kakaru ~ がかかる *It takes time* to do that job.

　~ ga nai ~ がない have no time [for]

　~ ga semaru ~ が迫る *Time is closing in on us;* we had better finish quickly.

　~ ga tatsu ~ がたつ time passes

　~ genshu ~ 厳守 punctuality

　~ ni shibarareru ~ に縛られる I'm *pressed for time* today.

　~ no kannen ga nai ~ の観念がない He *has no sense of time;* you can't tell when he'll come.

~ no mondai (da) ~ の問題(だ) He is gravely ill; *it's just a matter of time.*

~ o kakeru ~ をかける You'll have to *put time into* the job to do it right.

~ o mamoru ~ を守る Please *be punctual.*

~ o moteamasu ~ をもてあます Let's go for a walk; I *have time on my hands.*

~ o seigen suru ~ を制限する limit the time; put time restrictions on

~ o sugosu (tsuiyasu) ~ を過ごす(費やす) spend time [on]; take time; pass the time

~ o tsubusu ~ をつぶす kill time

~ o yūkō ni tsukau ~ を有効に使う He *made good use of his time.*

eigyō jikan 営業時間 business hours

giri giri no jikan ni ぎりぎりの時間に We made it *at the last moment* (*just under the wire*).

jugyō jikan 授業時間 class hours

kichō na jikan 貴重な時間 He wasted *precious time* on it.

seikaku na jikan 正確な時間 the exact time; the correct time

shimekiri jikan 締め切り時間 the closing hour

shitsumu jikan 執務時間 business hours

shoyō jikan 所要時間 required time

yakusoku no jikan 約束の時間 the appointed time; the time promised

chūkan (hiruma) 昼間(ひるま) the daytime

dōji ni 同時に simultaneously

ichiji (no) 一時(の) temporarily; for the time being

jibun 時分 time; season

jidai sakugo (da) 時代錯誤(だ) old fashioned; out of date; archaic

jigen 時限 time limit

jihō 時報 time signal

jikangai ni hataraku 時間外に働く work after hours; work overtime

jikanhyō (jikanwari) 時間表(時間割) schedule; time table

jikankyū 時間給 hourly wage; pay by the hour

jikanreikō 時間励行 promptness; carefulness about appointments

jisei 時勢 the times; the age

jisetsu 時節 times

jisoku 時速 speed [per hour]

katatoki mo 片時も He can't be away from her *even for a moment.*

nanji 何時 when; what time

shunkan 瞬時 instant; moment

tema ga kakaru 手間がかかる requires time and energy

~ o toru ~ をとる He *took the time to* fix it.

tōji 当時 that period; at that time

tokei 時計 watch; clock

~ ga okureru ~ が遅れる My watch *is losing time* (*is slow*).

~ ga susumu ~ が進む My watch *is gaining* (*is fast*).

toki 時 time

~ ga tatsu ni tsurete ~ がたつにつれて as time went on; as time passed

~ no nagare ni shitagatte ~ の流れに従って with the passing of time

~ o kasegu ~ をかせぐ Our team had a good lead, so at the end of the game they *just used up the time* (*stalled for time; ran out the clock*).

~ o utsusazu ~ を移さず without delay; immediately

~ wa kane nari [P] ~ は金なり Time is money [P].

tokidoki 時々 occasionally; now and then; every so often

kako 過去 the past

katsute かつて formerly; once

KIGEN 期限 time limit; deadline

~ ga kireru ~ が切れる the term expires

~ **ga semaru** ~ が迫る the deadline approaches

~ **ni naru** ~ になる Tomorrow *it will fall due (will be the deadline)*.

kikan 期間 term; period

JŌJUN 上旬 the first part of the month [the first ten days]

chūjun 中旬 the middle of the month [the middle ten days]

gejun 下旬 the last of the month [the last ten days]

Kōin ya no gotoshi [P] 光陰矢のごとし Time flies like an arrow. Tempus fugit.

mada まだ not yet; still

imada いまだ as yet; yet

mae 前 before

izen 以前 before

zengo (no) 前後(の) before or after; around that time

maniau 間にあう be in time

metta ni めったに rarely; seldom; once in a blue moon

mirai 未来 future; time to come

shōrai 将来 future; in the future

mokka 目下 for the present

~ **no tokoro** ~のところ for the time being; for the present time

mukashi 昔 of old; in times past

~ **mukashi** ~昔 once upon a time

ōmukashi kara 大昔から from time immemorial

nengara nenjū 年がら年じゅう always; incessantly; constantly

okureru 遅れる be late

teokure ni naru 手遅れになる We rushed the injured man to the hospital, but we *were too late (were not in time)*.

oriori おりおり now and then; from time to time; occasionally

saigetsu [L] 歳月 years and months

~ **hito o matazu** [P] ~人を待たず Time waits for no man [P].

sakki さっき a little while ago

shibaraku deshita! しばらくでした! It's been a long time since I've seen you.

~ **shite kara** してから after a while

shidai ni 次第に gradually

SHIJŪ 始終 He worked *continuously* (*from start to finish*) on the project.

shotchū しょっちゅう Accidents are happening there *all the time*.

shūshi 終始 He told the story *from start to finish*.

sono uchi ni そのうちに before long; in the course of time

sude ni すでに previously; already

sugu ni すぐに right away; at once; immediately

tabigoto ni たびごとに *Every time* I go there they do something different.

tama ni たまに every now and then

tōbun no aida 当分の間 I expect to be in Japan *for some time*.

toriaezu とりあえず That will do *for the time being*.

tsuki tarazu 月足らず premature [birth]; before time; ahead of time

tsune ni 常に always; all the time

yagate やがて in the course of time; some time later

yōyaku ようやく finally; at last

yūshi irai 有史以来 since the dawn of history

神は言われます.
「わたしは、恵みの時にあなたに答え、救いの日にあなたを助けた.」
確かに、今は恵みの時、今は救いの日です.
(コリント II 6 ²)

76 JIKO 自己 EGO, EGOISM

dada o koneru [C] だだをこねる When I told her to stop playing, she just stood there and *sulked* (*stamped her feet*).

dasanteki (da) 打算的(だ) calculating; mercenary

dokuzen ni ochiiru 独善に陥る It is

sometimes easy to *slip into self-complacency*.

dokuzenteki (da) 独善的(だ) self-complacent; self-righteous

gotsugō shugi (no hito) ご合都主義(の人) opportunism (opportunist)

hansei (suru) 反省(する) self-examination (examine oneself)

~ **o semaru** ~ を迫る In his frequent letters Lincoln *pressed* McClellan *to examine himself* on his command of the army.

hito o oshinokeru 人を押しのける He climbed the ladder of success but *stepped on people* (*shoved others aside; elbowed others*) along the way.

hitoriyogari (da) ひとりよがり(だ) self-complacency (self-complacent)

hiyorimishugisha ひより見主義者 opportunist

hoshii mama ni suru ほしいままにする do as one pleases

iji kitanai 意地きたない He *is a greedy* person.

JIKO 自己 ego; egoism

~ **chūshin (da)** 中心(だ) self-centered; egocentric

~ **giman** ~ 欺まん self-deception

~ **hansei** ~ 反省 introspection

~ **hihan** ~ 批判 self-criticism

~ **hon'i** ~ 本意 egotism; self-centeredness

~ **manzoku** ~ 満足 self-satisfaction

~ **o takaku hyōka suru** ~ を高く評価する He *rates himself too highly*.

~ **o semeru** ~ を責める reproach oneself

~ **senden** ~ 宣伝 self-advertisement

~ **shōkai** ~ 紹介 self-introduction

jibun 自分 oneself

~ **jishin** ~ 自身 one's own self; one's very self

~ **katte na furumai** ~ かってなふるまい selfish behavior

~ **o hige suru** ~ を卑下する deprecate oneself; belittle oneself

jichō suru 自重する You have a future ahead so *watch out for yourself* (*take good care of yourself*).

jifu (suru) 自負(する) conceit (be conceited)

jiga 自我 the self; the ego

~ **jisan (suru)** ~ 自賛(する) self-praise (blow one's own horn)

jisei (suru) 自省(する) self-examination; introspection (examine oneself)

~ **o unagasu** ~ を促す cause one to examine himself

jisei (suru) 自制(する) self-control (control oneself)

jiseki (suru) 自責(する) self-accusation (reproach oneself)

~ **no nen ni taenai** ~ の念にたえない He *is conscience-stricken* over hitting the little girl.

jishin 自信 confidence; self-confidence

jishō (suru) 自称(する) He *is a self-styled* (*professes to be an*) artist.

jisonshin 自尊心 self-esteem; self-respect

~ **ga tsuyoi** ~ が強い have great self-respect

~ **o kizutsukeru** ~ を傷つける You *hurt his pride* when you told him he couldn't sing well.

~ **o ushinau** ~ を失う lose one's self-respect

Onore no hossezaru tokoro o hito ni hodokosu nakare [P] おのれの欲せざるところを人に施すなかれ Do unto others as you would have them do unto you [P].

rikoshugi 利己主義 egoism; selfishness

rikoteki (da) 利己的(だ) egoistic; selfish

kaerimiru 省みる examine oneself

kanjōdakai hito 勘定高い人 mercenary person

KATTE (da) かって(だ) selfish

~ kimama (da) ~ 気まま(だ) self-seeking; egotistic

~ na koto o iu ~ な事を言う say selfish things; say what one pleases

~ ni suru ~ にする do as one pleases

temaegatte (da) 手前がって(だ) self-seeking; egotistic

kimama (da) 気まま(だ) self-willed; capricious

  kigurai ga takai 気位が高い She comes from a wealthy family and *is proud of it (is snobbish; is stuck up)*.

kojinteki (da) 個人的(だ) individual; personal

kōriteki (da) 功利的(だ) calculating; pragmatic; utilitarian

makezugirai (da) 負けずぎらい(だ) unyielding; relentless

mi no hodo o shiranai 身のほどを知らない He is trying to write a book on the subject, but he *doesn't know his own limitations.*

mizukara [L] 自ら oneself

mushi no ii yōkyū [C] 虫のいい要求 *This is a selfish request*, but would you let me read that book before you do?

tanin no koto o kōryo shinai 他人のことを考慮しない He *has no consideration for others.*

temaemiso o naraberu 手前みそを並べる There he goes *singing his own praises (blowing his own horn)* again.

tsun to torisumasu つんと取り澄ます She dresses in the finest clothes and at parties *acts smug (is haughty; is standoffish).*

uchōten ni naru 有頂天になる He *walked on air (was carried away)* when he got that promotion.

unubore (ru) うぬぼれ(る) conceit (be conceited; be vain)

WAGAMAMA (da) わがまま(だ) willfulness (willful; individualistic)

  ga o haru 我を張る They tried to reason

with him but he *asserted himself* and refused to listen.

gaden insui 我田引水 He's just *feathering his own nest (looking after number one).*

shiri o hakaru 私利を図る He *was counting on personal gain (had a selfish motive)* when he joined the Red Cross.

  ~ o musaboru ~ をむさぼる hope for personal gain

  ~ shiyoku ~ 私欲 self-interest; personal ambitions

shishin o hasamu 私心をはさむ Most people who came offering their services to Lincoln *had some axe to grind.*

wagamonogao ni わがもの顔に He walks around here *as if he owned the place (in a lordly manner).*

waregachi (da) われがち(だ) Grab a seat when the doors open; *it's everyone for himself.*

⇨ 77, 208

「...だれでもわたしについて来たいと思うなら，自分を捨て，日々十字架を負い，そしてわたしについてきなさい。(ルカ 9 ²³)

77 JINKAKU 人格
CHARACTER, PERSONALITY

akeppanashi (da) あけっぱなし(だ) open natured; open hearted; frank

[ningen no] deki ga chigau [人間の]できが違う You can see from the thoroughness of his work that he *is of a different caliber.*

futoku no itasu tokoro desu! 不徳のいたすところです *Due to my own inadequacy (Due to my own limitations)* the plan has failed.

GARA de wa nai 柄ではない It *was out of character* for him to speak so rudely to the teacher.

  ~ ga warui ~ が悪い He *is an ill-bred*

person (*is a person of bad upbringing*).

~ **ni nai** ～にない Such actions *are unlike* (*are unbecoming to*) him.

hitogara 人柄 personality

~ **no yoi** ～の良い has a good personality; is good natured

hito kado no ningen ひとかどの人間 If you want to *amount to something* (*be someone*) you will have to study.

honshin 本心 one's true self

jigane ga deru 地金が出る You can *see* his *true colors* by the way he uses people for his own ends.

JIKO 自己 self

~ **o ikasu** ～を生かす make the most of oneself; find oneself

~ **o kizukiageru** ～を築き上げる develop an integrated personality

~ **o takameru** ～を高める He broadcasts his accomplishments to *build himself up* before people.

JINKAKU 人格 character; personality

~ **keisei** ～形成 character development

~ **no kōshō na hito** ～の高尚な人 person of noble character

fūkaku 風格 personality; presence; appearance

hitozukuri 人づくり character building

jimbutsu 人物 personality; person

~ **hon'i ni suru** ～本位にする When hiring new employees, most firms *lay emphasis on personal character*.

jimpin 人品 personal appearance; bearing

kijin 奇人 eccentric person; a character; individualist

kado no toreta hito かどの取れた人 person with a well-rounded personality; well-adjusted person

kakegae no nai hito かけがえのない人 irreplaceable person; indispensable person

shikkari shita hito しっかりした人 man of character

katagi かたぎ turn of mind; character; spirit

kidate 気立て disposition; temperament

kishitsu 気質 nature; temper

kojin (teki da) 個人 (的だ) individual; person (individual; personal)

~ **sonchō** 個人尊重 respect for the individual

kōketsu (da) 高潔 (だ) [of] noble character

mekki ga hageru [C] めっきがはげる one's true colors are shown

mizukara [L] 自ら oneself; personally; of one's own accord

SEISHITSU 性質 temperament; nature; quality; character

~ **no yoi (warui)** ～の良い (悪い) be of good (bad) character

kachiki na seishitsu 勝ち気な性質 a nature that hates to lose; [person] determined to win

gaikōsei 外向性 extrovert

hinsei 品性 character

honshō 本性 one's true character

~ **o arawasu** ～を現わす In the last war men *revealed their true natures* by the cruelties they inflicted on their fellow men.

kishō 気性 disposition; nature

~ **no tsuyoi** ～の強い person of strong character

take o watta yōna kishō 竹を割ったような気性 straight-forward character

kosei 個性 individuality

~ **o ikasu** ～を生かす make the most of one's personality; develop one's personality

minzokusei 民族性 national character

naikōsei 内向性 introvert

seikaku 性格 character; disposition; idiosyncrasy

~ **ga nijimideru** ～がにじみ出る A man's *character is revealed* in his deeds.
shō ni awanai 性に合わない go against one's grain; rub one the wrong way
shōbun 性分 natural endowment; constitution
toku no takai 徳の高い be virtuous
~ **o migaku** ～をみがく refine one's character
TOKUCHŌ 特徴 distinctive characteristic
tokusei 特性 special trait; distinctive trait
tokushitsu 特質 essential quality
UMARETSUKI (da) 生まれつき (だ) disposition; nature (by nature)
motte umareta 持って生まれた inherent
seirai(no) 生来 (の) by nature; natural; from birth
umarenagara(no) 生まれながら (の) He is *a born* pianist.
⇨ **76**
それ ばかりではなく，患難さえも喜んでいます．それは，患難が忍耐を生み出し，忍耐が練られた品性を生み出し，練られた品性が希望を生み出すと知っているからです．(ローマ 5 ³, ⁴)

78 JINSEI 人生
LIFE'S COURSE

JINSEI 人生 life; life's course
~ **kōro** ～航路 path of life; course of life
~ **no hakanasa o ajiwau** ～のはかなさを味わう experience the vanity of life; experience the transiency of life
~ **no kairaku** ～の快楽 pleasure of life; life's pleasures
~ **no kiro ni tatsu** ～の岐路に立つ Now that you *are standing at the crossroads* of life, you must make a decision.

~ **no owari** ～の終わり end of the road
~ **no ukishizumi** ～の浮き沈み ups and downs of life; vicissitudes of life
~ **o hikan suru** ～を悲観する be pessimistic about life
~ **o rakkan suru** ～を楽観する be optimistic about life
atarashii jinsei no shuppatsu o suru 新しい人生の出発をする make a fresh start in life
futoku mijikaku ikiru 太く短く生きる He *is living it up* now and doesn't seem concerned about the future.
hansei 半生 half of one's life
isshō 一生 one's life; lifetime
~ **o sasageru** ～をささげる Dr. Hepburn *devoted his life* to presenting the Bible to the Japanese people.
suki o kiwameta isshō 数寄を窮めた一生 As clerk, boatman, postmaster, surveyor, lawyer, and politician, Lincoln lived an *extremely varied life.*
jinseikan o motsu 人生観を持つ hold a [certain] view of life
shōgai 生涯 one's whole life
jumyō 寿命 life span
me no kuroi uchi wa 目の黒いうちは As *long as I live,* you can count on me to take care of mother.
minouebanashi 身の上話 one's life story
udatsu ga agaranai うだつが上がらない Without an education one *cannot get along in life.*
ushinawareta seishun 失われた青春 one's lost youth
YO no naka o wataru 世の中を渡る Without ethical principles you will find it difficult *making your way through life.*
~ **no naka wa sechigarai** ～の中はせちがらい [P] What a hard world to live in! It's a cruel world!
~ **o amaku miru** ～を甘く見る He *is*

looking at life through rose-colored glasses and will soon be disappointed.

seken shirazu 世間知らず know nothing of life; be naive

shusse suru (risshin suru) 出世する (立身する) succeed in life; make one's mark in the world

ukiyo (no) 浮き世 (の) this transitory world (worldly; mundane)

yowatari 世渡り going through life

  ~ **ga jōzu** ~ がじょうず He *knows how to get along in the world.*

  ~ **no michi** ~ の道 He learned *the art of living* (*how to get along*) pretty quickly after graduation.

⇨ 168, 170

あなたがたには、あすのことはわからないのです。あなたがたのいのちは、いったいどのようなものですか。あなたがたは、しばらくの間現われて、それから消えてしまう霧にすぎません。(ヤコブ 4 ¹⁴)

79 JIYŪ 自由
FREEDOM, LIBERTY

HANASU 放す set one free; release; let one go

hōnin (suru) 放任 (する) non-interference (allow one to do as he pleases)

hōninshugi 放任主義 non-interference policy; laissez faire

shakuhō (suru) 釈放 (する) release; liberty (release; set at liberty)

hane o nobasu 羽根を伸ばす After work I went to Hakone to *take it easy.*

iyaku (suru) 意訳 (する) free translation (translate freely)

JIYŪ 自由 freedom; liberty

  ~ **ga kikanai** ~ がきかない One's *freedom is curtailed* by all those rules.

  ~ **ishi de** ~ 意志で of one's own free will

  ~ **kōdō** ~ 行動 freedom of action; a free hand

  ~ **kyōsō** ~ 競争 free competition

  ~ **ni furumau** ~ にふるまう act freely; do as one pleases

  ~ **ni hanaseru** ~ に話せる He *can speak freely* in Japanese.

  ~ **ni katsuyaku suru** ~ に活躍する I'm sure you can *work freely* (*have a free hand*) in that department.

  [...**no**] ~ **ni naranai** [...の] ~ にならない That particular problem *is beyond my province* (*is beyond my control*).

  ~ **ni suru** ~ にする free one; set one free

  ~ **no mi ni naru** ~ の身になる become free; become a free man

  ~ **o ataeru** ~ を与える grant liberty [to]

  ~ **o esaseru** ~ を得させる " You shall know the truth, and the truth shall *make you free.*" (John 8 : 32)

  ~ **o sokubaku suru** ~ を束縛する restrain freedom; restrict liberty

  ~ **o ushinau** ~ を失う The President warned that men *lose* their *freedom* only when they refuse to fight for it.

  ~ **sentaku** 選択 free choice; elective

  ~ **shisō** 思想 free thought; liberal ideas

  ~ **shugi** 主義 liberalism

dōzo gojiyū ni! どうぞご自由に Please help yourself. Please feel free to do as you like.

fujiyū (da) 不自由 (だ) handicapped; constrained; limited; inhibited

jiyūjizai ni hanasu 自由自在に話す He *speaks* English *freely* (*has full command of* English).

katte ni shinasai かってにしなさい Do as you please! Have your own way!

kimama ni makasete oku 気ままに任せておく He *let* the children *get away with anything.*

nan no samatage mo nai なんの妨げもない have no obstacles whatsoever

nin'i (da) 任意 (だ) option (optional)

omou zonbun (ni) 思う存分 (に) to one's heart's content; to the full

    omoi dōri ni saseru 思いどおりにさせる *Leave* it *up to* him!

te ga aku 手があく I *am free* to help you now.

ugoki ga torenai 動きがとれない Until the debt is paid, I'm not able to *operate freely* in the new venture.

⇨ 27

私はだれに対しても自由ですが，より多くの人を獲得するために，すべての人の奴隷となりました。

(コリント I 9 ¹⁹)

80 JUNBI 準備
PREPARATION

JUNBI 準備 preparation

    ~ kikan ~ 期間 preparatory period

    ~ o kanzen ni totonoeru ~ を完全にととのえる thoroughly prepare [for]

    shūtō na junbi 周到な準備 thorough preparedness; careful preparation

bihin 備品 fixtures; furnishings

sonaeru 備える provide; furnish; prepare for

    man'ichi no toki ni sonaeru 万一の時に備える prepare for an emergency; save for a rainy day

sonaetsuke 備え付け provision; equipment

sonawaru 備わる be furnished with

kakugo (suru) 覚悟 (する) preparedness; readiness (resolve)

    ~ o kimeru ~ を決める It was a dangerous mission, but he *was resolved* (*was determined; was bound and determined*) to go through with it.

kokorogamae ga dekite iru 心構えができている The coach made sure the team *was mentally prepared* for the game.

maemotte 前もって in advance; beforehand

ozendate o suru おぜん立てをする The ambassador went in advance to *set up* (*lay the groundwork for*) the meeting of both presidents.

seiri (suru) 整理 (する) arrangement; order (arrange; put in order)

seiton (suru) せいとん (する) order (put things in good order)

shitagoshirae o suru 下ごしらえをする We must *make basic preparations* for the conference.

    shitaji o tsukuru 下地を作る They *are now laying the groundwork* for constructing a new highway.

shitaku (suru) したく (する) preparations; arrangements (prepare; arrange)

takuwaeru 貯える lay aside; save; lay in stock

tehazu o totonoeru 手はずをととのえる He has *made* all necessary *arrangements for* our meeting today.

    temawashi ga yoi 手回しがよい *Good forethought* went into that excursion to Nikko.

    tetsuzuki o toru 手続きをとる take steps; go through the necessary procedures [for]

uchiawase (ru) 打ち合わせ (打ち合わせる) arrangement (arrange [the hour])

yōi (suru) 用意 (する) preparation (prepare)

    ~ bantan totonoeru ~ ばんたん整える make everything ready; make full preparations [for]

...目が見たことのないもの，耳が聞いたことのないもの，そして，人の心に思い浮かんだことのないもの。神を愛する者のために，神の備えてくださったものは，みなそうである。(コリント I 2 ⁹)

81 JŪYŌSEI 重要性
IMPORTANCE

chūshin 中心 central part; center; crux; core; heart

DAIJI (da) 大事 (だ) importance (important; serious)

  ~ ni suru ~ にする set great value on; cherish

  yuyushii daiji ゆゆしい大事 matter of grave concern

ōdatemono (ōmono) 大立て者 (大物) leading figure; VIP

erasō ni furumau 偉そうにふるまう He *carries himself with an air of importance.*

ippun ichibyō o arasou mondai 一分一秒を争う問題 I *would appreciate your help; this is a matter that needs immediate attention.*

JŪYŌSEI 重要性 importance

jūdai (da) 重大 (だ) weighty; important; grave; serious

jūshi (suru) 重視 (する) lay importance on

jūten 重点 important point; emphasis

jūyaku 重役 director; important responsibilities

jūyō (da) 重要 (だ) important; valuable

  ~ na chii o shimeru ~ な地位を占める Japan *now occupies an important position* in the free world.

  mottomo jūyō na koto 最も重要な事 matter of paramount importance

jūyōshi suru 重要視する regard as important

kichō (da) 貴重 (だ) valuable; priceless; costly

omo (da) おも (だ) principal; main

omodatta 重立った conspicuous; leading; outstanding

omoi 重い heavy

[...ni] omoki o oku [...に] 重きをおく The President *placed heavy importance on* (*took great stock in*) the general's opinions.

shuyō (da) 主要 (だ) leading; chief; main; important

  ~ na jinbutsu ~ な人物 Captain Fuchida *played an important role* in the Pearl Harbor attack.

kakegae no nai hito かけがえのない人 When asked to dismiss Grant, Lincoln replied, " *I can't spare that man;* he fights."

kanjin (da) かんじん (だ) vital; essential

  ~ kaname no ~ かなめの The quarterback is *the crucial man* on a football team.

karugarushiku toriatsukau 軽々しく取り扱う I was concerned about it, but he *played it down* (*treated it lightly*).

ketteiteki na yakuwari o enjiru 決定的な役割を演じる He *will play a decisive role* in the coming election.

kyūsho o hazureta 急所をはずれた The bullet *missed any vital part* of his body.

mottaiburu もったいぶる assume an air of importance; put on airs

  mottai o tsukeru もったいをつける He *made much of* (*attached importance to*) his own report, but there was nothing to it.

ni no tsugi 二の次 of secondary importance

orekireki [C] お歴々 dignitaries; VIPs; big shots

Se ni hara wa kaerarenu [P] 背に腹はかえられぬ Must is master.

shikatsu (seishi no) mondai 死活 (生死の) 問題 They regard their independence as a *matter of life and death.*

shinu ka ikiru ka no setogiwa 死ぬか生きるかのせとぎわ As the fleet sailed past Midway Island, Admiral Nagumo realized Japan was *standing on the brink of life or death.*

taisetsu (da) たいせつ (だ) important; cherished

toru ni tarinai 取るに足りない I am on the

council, but what I actually do *is of no importance (is insignificant).*

yūryoku (da) 有力 (だ) influential; important; strong; reliable

yūsenteki ni toriatsukau 優先的に取り扱う We had better *give priority* to this problem.

⇨ **82**

わたしは一つの事を主に願った. わたしはそれを求める. わたしの生きるかぎり，主の家に住んで，主のうるわしきを見，その宮で尋ねきわめることを.
(詩篇 **27** ⁴)

82 KACHI 価値 VALUE

[...no] **arigatami o kanjiru** [...の] ありがたみを感じる It was only after I had grown up that I began to *feel an appreciation* for my parents.

Asu no hyaku yori kyō no gojū [P] あすの百よりきょうの五十 A bird in the hand is worth two in the bush [P].

Buta ni shinju [P] 豚に真珠 Do not give dogs what is holy; do not feed your *pearls to pigs.* (Matthew 7: 6)

hakari ni kakerareru はかりにかけられる value [something]; be weighed on the scales

hashi ni mo bō ni mo kakaranai はしにも棒にもかからない No matter how much I tried to help him, he got into trouble again. He's *hopeless (beyond help).*

horidashi mono o suru 掘り出し物をする make a good find; find a real bargain

ikigai ga aru 生きがいがある If you have a worthwhile goal, you will *find life worth living.*

KACHI 価値 value

~ **no aru** ~ のある valuable

keizaiteki kachi 経済的価値 economic value

kiku kachi ga aru 聞く価値がある be worth listening to

senden kachi 宣伝価値 propaganda value

sukoshi no kachi mo nai 少しの価値もない be good for nothing; be not worth a cent

atai 価 price; cost

[...**ni**] **atai suru** (...に) 価する be worthy of; merit; be deserving

bukka 物価 (commodity) prices

~ **ga geraku suru** ~ が下落する prices drop

daika 代価 price; cost

hyōka (suru) 評価 (する) evaluation (value)

kakaku 価格 value; cost; worth

kōka (da) 高価 (だ) high-priced; expensive

mukachi (da) 無価値 (だ) worthless; valueless

ne o tsukeru 値をつける estimate; set a price on

nedan 値段 price; marked price

~ **o mitsumoru** ~ を見積もる appraise; estimate the cost

neuchi 値打ち value; worth

~ **ga nai** ~ がない That old car is *valueless (is not worth beans).*

~ **ga sagaru** ~ が下がる decline in value; depreciate

saihyōka (suru) 再評価 (する) re-evaluation (re-evaluate)

shinka 真価 true worth

~ **o hakki suru** ~ を発揮する In the Giants-Lions series Nagashima *showed his true mettle.*

kaikaburu 買いかぶる overestimate; pay too much for

Kusatte mo tai [P] 腐ってもたい I know it's old, but a *Rolls-Royce is still a Rolls-Royce.*

manzara suteta mono de mo nai まんざら捨てたものでもない Some ridiculed the iron-clad ship *Monitor,* but Lincoln felt it *was worthy of some notice (was not wholly without value).*

mitsumori (ru) 見積もり (見積もる) estimate (estimate; make an estimate)

[...ni] omoki o oku [...に] 重きを置く The Soviets *attach much importance to* the communization of Cuba.

kichō (da) 貴重 (だ) valuable; precious

origamitsuki (da) 折り紙つき (だ) certified; guaranteed

satei (suru) 査定 (する) appraisal (place a value on)

shiyō massetsu 枝葉末節 minor details; insignificant part

sōba 相場 the going price; market price

[...ni] sōtō suru [...に] 相当する corresponds to; be equal in value to

taka no shireta たかの知れた trifling; trivial; insignificant

sontoku 損得 profit and loss

torie とりえ worth; merit

~ no nai ~のない be worthless; be good for nothing

tōtoi (tattoi) 尊い (たっとい) precious; valuable

yarigai ga aru やりがいがある be worthwhile doing

Yasumono kai no zeni ushinai [P] 安物買いのぜに失い Penny wise and pound foolish [P].

⇨ 81

あなたがたは, 代価を払って買い取られたのです。ですから自分のからだをもって, 神の栄光を現わしなさい。(コリント I 6 ²⁰)

83 KAIHI 回避 EVASION

dassō (suru) 脱走 (する) escape; flight (escape; flee; break loose; get away)

enkyoku ni iu 婉曲に言う talk in a round-about way

gedatsu (suru) 解脱 (する) (Buddhist) emancipation (be emancipated; escape; opt out)

gen o sayū ni suru 言を左右にする He *beat around the bush* and didn't come to the point.

hōkaburi o suru [C] ほおかぶりをする Whenever we mention the debt, he *avoids the issue* (*buries his head in the sand*).

KAIHI (suru) 回避 (する) evasion (evade)

hinan (suru) 避難 (する) refuge; shelter (take refuge; escape from danger)

hinanjo 避難所 shelter; refuge; covert

kihi suru 忌避する shirk; dodge; evade

sakeru 避ける avoid; steer clear of; give [something] a wide berth

tōhi (suru) 逃避 (する) escape; flight; evasion (escape; flee; evade)

hisomu 潜む be in hiding; hide out

jibun no koto o tana ni ageru 自分のことをたなにあげる He criticizes others but *is unmindful of his own shortcomings* (*sidesteps his own faults*).

kakeochi o suru かけ落ちをする elope

kōjitsu 口実 excuse; pretext

~ o tsukeru ~をつける make an excuse; offer a pretext

kumogakure suru 雲隠れする After the news got out about him, he *made himself scarce* for a few months.

mi o kakusu 身を隠す hide; escape; fly the coop

manukareru 免れる avoid; escape [from]; flee

NIGERU 逃げる escape; run away; get away

hōhō no tei de nigeru ほうほうのていで逃げる When he saw the police, the thief *took to his heels and got away*.

ichimokusan ni nigeru いちもくさんに逃げる run for one's life

kosokoso nigeru こそこそ逃げる sneak off; slink away

kumo o kasumi to nigeru 雲をかすみと逃げる The assailant slashed him with a knife then *vanished into thin air* (*fled with the wind*).

shippo o maite nigeru しっぽを巻いて逃げる Seeing the big boy come at him, Johnny *ran away with his tail between his legs.*

iinogare (ru) 言いのがれ(言いのがれる) evasion; excuse (evade the issue; make an excuse)

nigeba o ushinau 逃げ場を失う In the roaring flames he *lost his avenue of escape* and had to jump from the window.

nigedasu 逃げ出す escape [from prison]; sidestep [a problem]

nigegoshi ni naru [C] 逃げ腰になる In the face of their clinching arguments he *took an evasive attitude.* When challenged by that boy, the bully *took to his heels* and ran.

nigeguchi 逃げ口 escape hatch; loophole

nigemawaru 逃げ回る run away trying to escape

nigemichi 逃げ道 way of escape

nogareru のがれる escape; flee; run away
   ichiji nogare no iiwake 一時のがれの言いわけ excuse for the moment; temporary alibi

nukedasu 抜け出す steal out [of a house]; avoid [people]; duck out
   iinukeru 言い抜ける talk oneself out of [a difficulty]; get around [a problem]; wiggle out of

shirizoku 退く withdraw from

tōzakaru 遠ざかる keep away from; keep one's distance [from]
   keien suru 敬遠する keep one at a respectful distance; keep one at arm's length

yokeru よける keep aloof [from]; shun; avoid
⇨ 49

あなたがたの会った試練はみな人の知らないようなものではありません。神は真実な方ですから、あなたがたを耐えることのできないような試練に会わせるようなことはなさいま

せん。むしろ、耐えることのできるように、試練とともに、脱出の道も備えてくださいます。（コリント I 10 ¹³）

84 KAIKETSU 解決
SOLUTION

chōtei (suru) 調停(する) arbitration (arbitrate)

dakai saku o kōjiru 打開策を講じる They were at an impasse over the issue, but finally they *broke the deadlock (found a solution).*

harainokeru 払いのける They *got rid of (disposed of)* the little details and went to work on the main issue.

[...no] kagi o nigiru [...の]がぎを握る He *holds the key to (has the solution to)* the problem.

KAIKETSU (suru) 解決(する) solution (solve)
   ~ ga tsuku ~ がつく be solved; come to a solution
   ~ no medo ~ のめど prospects for a solution
   jibun de kaiketsu suru 自分で解決する I'm too busy; you'll have to *see to it yourself (take care of it yourself).*
   katateochi no kaiketsu 片手落ちの解決 one-sided solution; unfair solution
   manzoku na kaiketsu o motarasu 満足な解決をもたらす This suggestion *will bring about a satisfactory solution.*
   ombin ni kaiketsu suru 穏便に解決する They *brought* the problem *to a peaceful settlement* without going to court.
   zanteiteki kaiketsu 暫定的解決 temporary solution
   kaiketsuhō 解決法 means of solving [a problem]

kaiketsusaku 解決策 means of settlement

kaitō (suru) 解答(する) solution to a problem; answer to a question (solve a problem; answer a question)

ketchaku (suru) 決着(する) conclusion; end (conclude; end; settle)
~ **o tsukeru** ～をつける solve [a problem]; reach a conclusion

kettei (suru) 決定(する) settlement; decision (settle; decide)

mikaiketsu (da) 未解決(だ) unsolved; pending; in the air

KETSURON 結論 conclusion
~ **ga denai** ～が出ない We *haven't reached any conclusion yet*, so I can't give you an answer.
~ **ni michibiku** ～に導く bring about a conclusion
~ **o dasu** ～を出す draw a conclusion
~ **o isogu** ～を急ぐ hasten on to a conclusion
~ **o saki ni suru** ～を先にする I might as well *state our conclusion at the outset*. We have rejected your offer.
~ **to shite** ～として After all that discussion, the *conclusion is* (*the long and short of it is*) that we cannot go ahead.
kō iu ketsuron ni naru こういう結論になる it comes to this conclusion; it boils down to this
[...**no] kekka o umu** [...の]結果を生む This procedure *will bring about* (*yield*) a bigger and better product.

kekkyoku 結局 after all; finally

kiri ga nai きりがない Once you start doubting people, *there's no end to it* (*it becomes endless*).

maruku osamaru まるくおさまる The matter *was settled amicably* (*was ironed out smoothly*).

osamari ga tsukanai おさまりがつかない be unsettled; can't come to a conclusion

MATOMARI (ru) まとまり(まとまる) completion; settlement (be settled; be arranged)
~ **ga tsuku** ～がつく be settled; a conclusion is reached
~ **no nai hanashi** ～のない話 He touched on many matters, but it *was* really *inconclusive talk*.
hanashi ga matomaru 話がまとまる After much haggling over the price, finally an *agreement was reached*.
matomeru まとめる settle; complete

rachi ga akanai らちがあかない The meeting was opened yesterday, but the negotiators *can't get together* (*don't see eye-to-eye; are making no headway*).

shimatsu ga warui 始末が悪い be difficult to deal with; be hard to wind up
~ **ni oenai** ～におえない By his adamant stand one negotiator made the problem *unmanageable* (*impossible*).

tsumari つまり in short; in a word

waridasu 割り出す infer; deduce [from]

yahari (yappari) やはり(やっぱり) when all is said and done

yō suru ni 要するに in short
⇒ 107, 159

事の帰する所は、すべて言われた. すなわち、神を恐れ、その命令を守れ. これはすべての人の本分である.
(伝道の書 12 ¹⁸)

85 KAKKI 活気 VIGOR

ashi ga karui 足が軽い be lightfooted; [with] a high step

binshō (da) 敏しょう(だ) quickness; alacrity (quick; alert)

hatsuratsu to shita はつらつとした fresh; lively; vigorous

HIRŌ 疲労 exhaustion; fatigue
~ **kompai** ～困ぱい be completely exhausted; be all tired out
tsukareru 疲れる be tired
kutakuta ni tsukareru [C] くたくたに

疲れる After that tennis game I'm *completely worn out* (*bushed*).

KAKKI 活気 vigor

~ **ga aru** ~がある be brisk; be animated; be lively; show activity

binkatsu (da) 敏活(だ) promptitude; alacrity (prompt; quick)

fukeiki (da) 不景気(だ) depression; business slack; bad times; recession (slow)

~ **na kao o suru** ~な顔をする The boss *looks out of sorts* (*looks depressed*) today.

genki 元気 vigor; vitality (peppy; vigorous; vital)

~ **ippai (ni)** ~いっぱい(に) be full of energy; [with] boundless energy

~ **ōsei (ni)** ~おう盛(に) with great vigor

kara genki から元気 bluff; show of courage

genkizukeru 元気づける energize; brace up

ikigomi 意気込み enthusiasm

ikiiki to shita 生き生きとした lively; full of life

kaikatsu (da) 快活(だ) animated; active; cheerful

kakkizukeru 活気づける invigorate; enliven

kakkyō 活況 activity

kappatsu (da) 活発(だ) activity; aggressiveness (active; aggressive; energetic; vigorous)

katsudō (suru) 活動(する) activity (be active; lead an active life)

katsudōryoku 活動力 vitality; activity

katsuryoku 活力 vigor; vitality

keiki ga yoku nai 景気がよくない *Business is bad.* *Things are slow* everywhere. The *bottom has dropped out of the market.*

~ **o tsukeru** ~をつける enliven; make things hum

ki ga nuketa yōna yōsu 気が抜けたようなようす After losing the race, he looked dejected for days.

ki o haku 気をはく He *displayed real vigor* in the tennis match.

kinori shinai 気乗りしない I suggested we go skiing, but he *had no enthusiasm for* (*was disinterested in*) it.

kiryoku 気力 spirit; vigor

~ **ga nai** ~がない lack spirit; be spiritless

~ **ga otoroeru** ~が衰える Without ever-widening goals, men *lose their vigor* (*lose their spirit*).

~ **no aru** ~のある be energetic; be full of vigor

kisei o ageru 気勢を上げる The Waseda team *had their spirits buoyed up* (*had their spirits raised up*) by the pep rally.

mukiryoku (da) 無気力(だ) dull spirit (lethargic)

seiki 生気 vitality; spark of life

~ **no nai** ~のない lifeless

kakushaku to shite iru かくしゃくとしている The old man who crossed the Pacific alone on a raft *is still very energetic* (*is still hale and hearty*).

kōdōteki (da) 行動的(だ) lively; active

komame ni hataraku 小まめに働く He *worked like a beaver* and finished a week early.

kutabireru くたびれる be tired out; be worn out; be dead-tired

namanurui なまぬるい He *is lukewarm* about everything.

pin pin shite iru [c] ぴんぴんしている He just had an operation but he *is full of pep* (*is alive and kicking*).

seiryoku 精力 vigor; energy

seiryokuteki (da) 精力的(だ) energetic; aggressive

sekkyokuteki (da) 積極的(だ) aggressive; positive; progressive

shōkyokuteki (da) 消極的(だ) unaggressive; negative; conservative
subayai すばやい quick; nimble; agile
tabō (da) 多忙(だ) *I'm busy as a beaver* (*Things are hectic around here*) trying to get ready for the party.
tairyoku 体力 physical energy; vitality
tekipaki to てきぱきと briskly; promptly
undō (suru) 運動(する) motion; exercise (exercise)
  ~ o okosu ~を起こす The students *launched a crusade* (*started a movement*) to abolish the security pact.
⇨ 13
わたしは，あなたの行ないを知っている．あなたは，冷たくもなく，熱くもない．わたしはむしろ，あなたが冷たいか，熱いかであってほしい．
このように，あなたはなまぬるく，熱くも冷たくもないので，わたしの口からあなたを吐き出そう．（黙示録 3 ¹⁵,¹⁶）

86 KAKUSHIN 確信
ASSURANCE

chikarazuyoi 力強い emboldened
gutaiteki (da) 具体的(だ) concrete
HOSHŌ (suru) 保証(する) guarantee; certainty; warranty; (guarantee; certify; be warranted)
  hoshōtsuki (da) 保証つき(だ) guaranteed; warranted
  shōko 証拠 proof
    ~ o motomeru ~を求める seek proof
  shōmei (suru) 証明(する) testimony; evidence; proof (testify; give evidence; prove)
jijitsu o utagawanai 事実を疑わない *There is no question about the fact that* he did exactly as he said.
KAKUSHIN (suru) 確信(する) assurance; confidence (be assured [that]; be convinced [that]; feel certain [that])
  ~ ga guratsuku ~がぐらつく one's confidence wavers; confidence is shaken

  ~ ni michite ~ に満ちて He went into the contest *full of confidence.*
  ~ o motte ~をもって I say *with confidence* that you should have no fears concerning the outcome of this venture.
futashika (da) 不確か(だ) uncertain
jishin 自信 confidence
  ~ ga aru ~ がある have confidence
  ~ mamman (da) ~ 満々(だ) Before the election, both candidates seemed to *be full of confidence.*
  ~ o eru ~を得る gain confidence
  ~ o kaku ~を欠く lack confidence
  ~ o ushinau ~を失う After the accident John *lost confidence* in his own driving ability.
kakuho (suru) 確保(する) certainty; security (make certain; make secure)
kakujitsu (da) 確実(だ) reliability; certainty (reliable; certain; sure)
kakunin (suru) 確認(する) confirmation (confirm; certify)
kakuritsu (suru) 確立(する) establishment (establish; build up)
kakushō 確証 confirmation; conclusive evidence
  ~ o nigiru ~をにぎる secure positive evidence
  ~ o shimesu ~を示す give assurance; show conclusive evidence
kakutei (suru) 確定(する) decision (be established)
shoshin o magenai 所信を曲げない be unyielding in one's convictions; refuse to give up one's principles
tashika (da) 確か(だ) sure; certain (surely; certainly)
tashikameru 確かめる make sure [of]; confirm; ascertain
kanarazu 必ず without fail; certainly
kesshite 決して not at all; by no means
ki ga susumanai 気がすすまない The weather looks bad; *I feel uneasy about* going (*I'm reluctant to* go).

kiso (teki da) 基礎(的だ) foundation; ground (foundational; basic)

machigai naku まちがいなく I will be there *without fail.*

mattaku 全く completely; quite; entirely

mottomo (da) もっとも(だ) reasonable; justifiable; understandable

mochiron (muron) もちろん (むろん) of course; naturally; needless to say

nen niwa nen o ireru 念には念を入れる They *made doubly sure* about all the arrangements.

shikkari しっかり firmly; strongly; decidedly

~ shita ~ した solid; firm; secure; reliable

shugi ni kodawaru 主義にこだわる They tried to convince him, but he *stuck to his colors.*

taikoban o osu 太鼓判を押す If it's he, I'll *give my full endorsement.*

ukeau 請け合う assure; vouch for; guarantee

yahari (yappari) やはり(やっぱり) after all; as expected; still

YAKUSOKU (suru) 約束(する) promise; appointment(promise; make a promise; make an appointment)

~ o mamoru ~ を守る You can count on him to *keep his promise (stick to his promise).*

~ o yaburu ~ をやぶる break a promise; break one's word; make a breach of contract

zettai(da) 絶対(だ) absolutely; positively; unequivocally

⇨ 175, 177 -

愛する者たち．もし自分の心に責められなければ，大胆に神の御前に出ることができ，
また求めるものは何でも神からいただくことができます。なぜなら，私たちが神の命令を守り，神に喜ばれることを行なっているからです。(ヨハネ I 3 ²¹, ²²)

87 KANASHIMI 悲しみ
SORROW

AWARE (da) 哀れ(だ) pity (pitiable; pathetic)

~ o moyoosu ~ を催す Seeing the crippled children, he *was moved to pity* and offered to help.

aishū 哀愁 sadness

aitō 哀悼 grief; mourning; sorrow

~ no i o arawasu ~ の意を表わす He *expressed his condolences* to the parents of the dead child.

danchō no omoi ga suru 断腸の思いがする I *was torn with grief* when I heard the news of her death.

FUKŌ 不幸 misfortune; unhappiness

~ o maneku ~ を招く He *is courting disaster* by going around with those Shinjuku hoods.

~ o nageku ~ を嘆く She *grieved over her misfortune* for days.

isshō no fukō 一生の不幸 life-long misfortune

KANASHIMI (mu) 悲しみ(悲しむ) sorrow; (feel sad; feel sorrowful)

~ ni shizumu ~ に沈む be lost in sorrow; be overwhelmed with sorrow

~ ni taeru ~ に堪える bear the sorrow

~ o yawarageru ~ を和らげる lessen the sorrow; alleviate one's sorrow

hiai 悲哀 misery; grief; pathos

~ o kanjiru ~ を感じる feel pathetic; feel sad

gemmetsu no hiai 幻滅の悲哀 sad disillusionment

higeki 悲劇 tragedy

higekiteki (da) 悲劇的(だ) tragic

hihō 悲報 sad news; bad news

hikan 悲観 pessimism

himei o ageru 悲鳴をあげる give a shriek

hisan(da) 悲惨(だ) miserable; wretched

hitan 悲嘆 grief; sorrow

~ ni kureru ~ にくれる She *was overcome with grief* at the death of her son.
hitsū 悲痛 pathos
kanashii 悲しい sad
kanashisa no amari 悲しさのあまり *In bitter grief* over the death of little Willie, Mrs. Lincoln refused to see anyone for days.
KOKORO no naka de naku 心の中で泣く When he heard the news, he showed no visible grief but *cried inside*.
  ~ o itameru ~ を痛める be distressed; be grieved at heart
shintsū 心痛 heartache
shōshin 傷心 heartbreak; distress; grief
me mo aterarenai arisama 目もあてられないありさま Before us was the *unbearable sight* of wounded men lying in the rain.
mijime (da) みじめ(だ) wretched; miserable
MUNE no harisakeru yōna omoi 胸の張り裂けるような思い Losing children like that was *heart-rending sorrow* I shall never forget.
  ~ no itami ~ の痛み heartache
  ~ o shimetsukerareru omoi ~ を締めつけられる思い Seeing those suffering children was a *heart-rending experience*.
Naki tsura ni hachi [P] 泣きつらにはち I lost my job; then *to make matters worse* my wife came down sick.
namida no tane 涙の種 Friction with her mother-in-law is a *source of sorrow* in the home.
namidagumashii kimochi 涙ぐましい気持ち pathetic feeling
nasake nai 情けない be pitiful; be miserable
saigai ni au 災害に会う meet with disaster
tonda sainan とんだ災難 sudden dis-

aster; unexpected misfortune
setsunai omoi o suru せつない思いをする Ever since he broke up with his sweetheart, he's been *eating his heart out*.
tabemono ga nodo o toranai 食べ物がのどを通らない The children are lost, and I'm so worried I *can't eat*.
ukime o miru うきめを見る go through a bitter experience
urei 憂い grief; distress
⇨ **148, 150**
神のみこころに添った悲しみは，悔いのない，救いに至る悔い改めを生じさせますが，世の悲しみは死をもたらします．(コリント II 7 ¹⁰)

88 KANGEKI 感激
INSPIRATION, IMPULSE

dageki 打撃 blow
  ~ o ataeru ~ を与える deal a blow
  ~ o ukeru ~ を受ける He *received a setback* (*was dealt a blow*) when his stocks fell in value.
KANGEKI (suru) 感激(する) inspiration; impulse
  ~ ni hitaru ~ に浸る be filled with emotion; be deeply touched
  ~ no namida ga hō o tsutawaru ~ の涙がほおをつたわる *Tears of deep emotion flowed down his cheeks* when he heard the news of victory.
gekirei (suru) 激励(する) encouragement; stimulation (encourage; stimulate)
kan 感 feeling
  ~ kiwamaru ~ 窮まる be filled with emotion; be deeply moved [by]
  ~ ni taenai ~ に堪えない be filled with uncontrollable emotion
kandō (suru) 感動(する) impression; inspiration (be impressed; be inspired)
kangai muryō (da) 感慨無量(だ) I *was*

deeply moved when I visited the Lincoln Memorial in Washington, D.C.

kankyū suru 感泣する be moved to tears; be touched

kammei (suru) 感銘(する) impression (make an impression)

~ **ga usui** ～が薄い He spoke loud and long but *made little impression* on us.

~ **o ataeru** ～を与える The story of his exploits *inspired* (*made an impression upon*) me.

~ **o ukeru** ～を受ける I *was inspired* as I read Milton's *Paradise Lost.*

kanshin (suru) 感心(する) admiration (admire; be impressed [with])

kyōkan o yobu 共感を呼ぶ The audience *evinced a feeling of admiration* when they heard of Dr. Carlson's martyrdom in Africa.

reikan 霊感 inspiration

kobu (suru) 鼓舞(する) incitement; stimulation (incite; stimulate)

shiki o kobu suru 士気を鼓舞する Lincoln visited the front lines to *bolster the morale* of the troops.

KOKORO ni fureru 心に触れる His pathetic plea *touched our hearts.*

~ **ni meiki suru** ～に銘記する be imprinted on one's mind

~ **o ugokasu** ～を動かす move one's heart; stir one's heart

~ **o utsu** ～を打つ strike the cords of one's heart

MUNE ga dokidoki suru 胸がどきどきする As I stood ready to ski down that slope, my *heart skipped a beat or two* (*my heart was pounding*).

~ **ga ippai ni naru** ～がいっぱいになる At the news of her husband's death, she *became choked with emotion.*

~ **ga tsumaru** ～がつまる I *choked up* when I saw him lying helpless on the hospital bed.

~ **ga utareru** ～が打たれる be deeply moved

~ **ni komiagete kuru** ～にこみあげてくる swell up in one's heart

~ **ni semaru** ～に迫る be overwhelmed [by]

namida o sasou 涙を誘う move one to tears

namidagumashii kōkei 涙ぐましい光景 tearful scene; moving scene

SHŌDŌ 衝動 impulse

~ **ni karareru** ～にかられる He *was carried away by an impulse* to jump into the waterfall.

shōgeki 衝撃 impact; shock

~ **o ataeru** ～を与える The news of the mine explosion *shocked* (*floored*) the officials.

sukoshi mo dōjinai 少しも動じない He *was not influenced at all* (*was not moved a bit*) by their threats.

shokku o ukeru ショックを受ける We *were shocked* (*were stunned*) by the news of his death.

tokimeki ときめき palpitation; throb

uchōten ni naru 有頂天になる He *has been in ecstasy* (*has been walking on clouds*) ever since he won that English contest.

⇨ 33, 72, 89, 90

それには何よりも次のことを知っていなければいけません. すなわち, 聖書の預言はみな, 人の私的解釈を施してはならない, ということです. なぜなら, 預言は決して人間の意志によってもたらされたのではなく, 聖霊に動かされた人たちが, 神からのことばを語ったのだからです. (ペテロ II 1 [20], [21])

89 KANJŌ 感情 EMOTION

KANJŌ 感情 emotion

~ **ga moeagaru** ～が燃え上がる emotions flare up; get passionate over

~ **ga takamaru** ～が高まる become excited

~ **ni hashiru** ～に走る He *gave way*

to *his feelings* (*gave vent to his feelings*) and said some wild things.

~ **ni makeru** ~ に負ける The judge should have sentenced her severely, but his *feelings entered into it* (he *let emotions get the better of him*).

~ **no hageshii hito** ~の激しい人 excitable person; person of violent emotions

~ **o gaisuru** ~を害する You *hurt his feelings* with those critical remarks.

~ **o kakusu** ~を隠す hide one's feelings; keep a straight face; be a poker-face

~ **o kakitateru** ~をかき立てる stir up one's emotions; arouse sentiment

~ **o kao ni arawasu** ~を顔に表わす betray one's feelings; show one's feelings

~ **o komete** ~を込めて with feeling

~ **o osaeru** ~を押える suppress one's feelings; control one's feelings

akkanjō o idaku 悪感情をいだく *There is bad blood* (*There is ill-feeling*) between the two political rivals.

gekijō 激情 strong emotion

jikkan 実感 actual feeling; realization

~ **ga deru** ~が出る His powers of description were so forceful that we *felt as if we were really there.*

jō 情 emotion

~ **ni moroi** ~にもろい Don't mention that sad event to her; she *is very emotional* (*is easily upset*).

~ **ni uttaeru** ~に訴える appeal to the emotions

jōcho 情緒 sentiment; mood

~ **ga nai** ~がない lack feeling; be dispassionate

jōchō 情調 feeling

shiteki jōchō 詩的情調 poetical mood

kanjiyasui 感じやすい be sensitive; be emotional

kanjusei 感受性 sensibility; susceptibility

~ **ga tsuyoi** ~が強い Be careful how you talk in front of that boy; *he's very sensitive* (he's *quite impressionable*).

kanshō 感傷 sentimentality

[...**to iu**] **ki ga okoru** [...という] 気がおこる It was such a nice day that I *felt like* going to the mountains.

[...**suru**] **ki ni naru** [...する] 気になる I *feel inclined to* return her the money since she is dissatisfied.

kidoairaku 喜怒哀楽 One must taste the *joys and sorrows* of life to understand it.

komayaka (da) こまやか(だ) delicate

muki ni naru むきになる He was offended at my remark because he *took it seriously.*

⇨ **88, 90, 111**

それは，私たちがもはや，子どもではなくて，人の悪巧みや，人を欺く悪賢い策略により，教えの風に吹き回されたり，波にもてあそばれたりすることがなく，むしろ，愛をもって真理を語り，あらゆる点において成長し，かしらなるキリストに達することができるためなのです。
(エペソ 4 ¹⁴, ¹⁵)

90 KANKAKU 感覚 SENSATION, SENSE

atama ni kuru [C] 頭にくる Don't mention his poor Japanese; *he's very touchy about it.*

bimyō (da) 微妙(だ) delicateness (delicate)

gan to mune ni kotaeru がんと胸にこたえる Seeing all the wounded soldiers coming back from battle *made a profound impression on* (*made a striking impression on*) Lincoln.

gokan 五官 the five senses

Hyakubun wa ikken ni shikazu [P] 百聞は一見にしかず Seeing is believing [P].

kan ga ataru 勘が当たる I had a feeling he might not come, and my *hunch proved right.*

  ~ ga ii (warui) ~が良い(が悪い) have quick perception (have slow perception)

KANKAKU 感覚 sensation; sense

  ~ ga mahi suru ~がまひする After sitting so long, my leg *is asleep* (*is numb*). His finger *was anesthetized* before the operation.

  ~ ni uttaeru ~に訴える appeal to the senses

  ~ o shigeki suru ~を刺激する stimulate

  ~ o ushinau ~を失う be dead to all feeling; become past feeling

  biteki kankaku 美的感覚 aesthetic sense

  binkan (da) 敏感(だ) sensitive

  donkan (da) 鈍感(だ) dull; insensitive

  [...no] kanji ga suru [...の]感じがする feel as if; have a [strange, etc.] feeling

  yoi (warui) kanji o ataeru 良い(悪い)感じを与える He *made a favorable* (*unfavorable*) *impression on* his audience He *impressed* his audience *favorably* (*unfavorably*).

  tsūkan suru 痛感する He *feels* the problem *to his bones* (*feels* the problem *deeply*).

[...ni] ki ga tsuku [...に]気がつく I *noticed that* he made a mistake as he was speaking.

  kimochi 気持ち feeling

kokoro o toraeru 心を捕える Kennedy *captivated the hearts* of the people.

mi ni shimiru 身にしみる Lincoln's words, " Do not I destroy my enemies when I love them? " were *felt deeply* by her.

  honemi ni kotaeru 骨身にこたえる His stern remarks really *came home to me.*

mimizatoi 耳ざとい That child *has sharp*

ears; be careful of what you say!

SHINKEI 神経 nerves

  ~ ni sawaru ~にさわる That jangling music *gets on my nerves.*

  ~ no surudoi ~の鋭い He is a person who *is always on his toes.*

  ~ o togarasu ~をとがらす *Our nerves were kept on edge* waiting for the news of his recovery.

  ~ o tsukau ~を使う Our coach always *gets fidgety* (*gets nervous*) before a game.

shōdō 衝動 impulse

ware ni kaeru 我に帰る recover one's senses; come to oneself

  ~ o wasureru ~を忘れる forget oneself; be enraptured by

⇨ **72, 88, 89**

初めからあったもの，私たちが聞いたもの，目で見たもの，じっと見，また手でさわったもの，すなわち，いのちのことばについて。（ヨハネ I 1 ¹）

91 KANKEI 関係
RELATIONSHIP

aidagara 間がら relationship

  tsuzukigara 続きがら lineal relationship

aka no tanin 赤の他人 complete stranger; total stranger

chokketsu (suru) 直結(する) direct connection (connect directly with)

EN 縁 connection, affinity

  ~ ga nai ~がない He hoped to marry her, but it didn't work out. It just *wasn't meant to be* (*wasn't in the cards*).

  ~ ga tōi (chikai) が遠い(近い) a stranger to; distantly related (closely related; akin)

  Kane no kireme ga en no kireme. [P] 金の切れ目が縁の切れ目 Out of money, out of friends.

endōi 縁遠い She is old and has *little chance of marriage.*

entsuzuki 縁続き relationship; a relative

innen 因縁 relationship with a previous existence

fukabun (da) 不可分(だ) inseparable

[...ni] fureru [...に]触れる touch upon

fukairi suru 深入りする be engrossed in; get entangled in

himotsuki (no) ひもつき(の) with strings attached; puppet

kaiko (suru) 解雇(する) dismissal (fire)

kakariai かかりあい involvement

kakawari (ru) かかわり(かかわる) connection; relation; link (concern; have to do with)

kandō (suru) 勘当(する) disinheritance (disinherit)

KANKEI 関係 relationship
> ~ **ga aru** ~がある be related [to]; have something to do with
> ~ **naku** ~なく regardless of
> **[...to wa]** ~ **ga nai** [...とは]~がない I *have nothing to do with* that business.
> **[...to]** ~ **o musubu** [...と] ~を結ぶ establish relations with; form (establish) a connection with
> **[...to]** ~ **o tatsu** [...と] ~を絶つ break relations with; sever connections with; be through with
> **hyōri ittai no kankei** 表裏一体の関係 There is a *very intimate relationship* (*an indissoluble relationship*) between the two parties.
> **kitte mo kirenai kankei** 切っても切れない関係 an inseparable relation
> **missetsu na kankei** 密接な関係 close relation; close connection
> **[...no] mondai ni kankei ga aru** [...の]問題に関係がある It *is relevant to* that problem.
> **sōgo kankei** 相互関係 mutual relationship
> **taijin kankei** 対人関係 human relationships

kankeisha 関係者 person concerned

kanren (suru) 関連(する) reference; relationship; association (be related to)

kansuru 関する be related to; concern

mukankei (da) 無関係(だ) unrelated; unconcerned
> **[...to wa] mukankei ni** [...とは]無関係に regardless of; independently of

kanshō (suru) 干渉(する) interference; meddling (interfere; meddle)

ketsuzoku 血族 relation by blood [or marriage]

kinkō 均衡 balance; equilibrium

kōshō (suru) 交渉(する) negotiation (negotiate)
> **kōsai (suru)** 交際(する) association (associate with; keep company with)

kubi ni suru [C] 首にする The boss *fired* him for his ineptness on the job.

kuchidashi o suru 口出しをする butt in; horn in [on] [a person, a conversation]

makizoe o kuu 巻き添えを食う get involved involuntarily
> **makikomareru** 巻き込まれる get involved in; be embroiled in

miuchi 身内 close relation; relative

mizo みぞ gulf; gap
> ~ **ga dekiru** みぞができる When Lincoln was elected, a *deep gulf was formed* between North and South.

mizu irazu de 水いらずで Let's eat *just by ourselves* (*alone*) tonight.

mongaikan 門外漢 outsider

nakama to naru 仲間となる keep company with; become partners with

renraku ga tsuku 連絡がつく be able to contact; be connected

ryōhō 両方 both; both parties

Sawaranu kami ni tatari nashi. [P] さわらぬ神にたたりなし Let sleeping dogs lie [P].

SHINRUI 親類 relation; relative; kin

shinseki 親せき relation; relative; kin
shinzoku 親族 relation; relative; kin
SŌGO 相互 mutual
    aiirenai 相いれない be incompatible [with]; be out of harmony [with]
    aite 相手 one's opponent; the other person; one's companion
    ichimyaku aitsūjiru tokoro ga aru 一脈相通じるところがある They differ in background and profession, but *there is some common ground between them.*
    sōtaiteki (da) 相対的(だ) relative; correlative
    ~**shinri** 真理 relative truth
TE ga haitte iru 手がはいっている have a hand in [a matter]
    ~**o dasu** を出す meddle with; put one's finger in the pie
    ~**o hiku** を引く withdraw from; wash one's hands of
tomo ni suru 共にする do together; do cooperatively
tomonau 伴う accompany; go hand-in-hand
[...ni] tsuite [...に]ついて about; concerning
tsukimatou つきまとう follow persistently; pursue; shadow
[...ni] tsunagari ga aru [...に]つながりがある be bound up with; be closely connected [with]
yokei na osewa da! よけいなお世話だ Mind your own business! It's none of your business!
yokoyari o ireru 横やりを入れる Just as we were going ahead with the project, that engineer *threw a spanner in the works* with a counter plan.
yukari ゆかり affinity; acquaintance; connection
yukigakari jō 行きがかり上 *By force of circumstances* we had to abandon those plans.

そのころのあなたがたは，キリストから離れ，イスラエルの国から除外され，約束の契約については他国人であり，この世にあって望みもなく，神もない人たちでした．（エペソ 2 [12]）

92 KANSATSU 観察
OBSERVATION

chūshi (suru) 注視(する) note with care
KANSATSU (suru) 観察(する) observation (observe)
    kankō (ryokō) 観光(旅行) sight-seeing (sight-seeing trip)
    kanran (seki) 観覧(席) viewing (grandstand seat; bleachers)
    kansatsuryoku 観察力 power of observation
    kanshi suru 監視する keep under observation; keep watch over
    yōgisha o kanshi suru 容疑者を監視する The F. B. I. *are keeping* the suspicious characters *under surveillance.*
    kansoku (suru) 観測(する) observation; survey (survey; make a survey)
    kanten 観点 viewpoint
    shisatsu (suru) 視察(する) inspection (inspect)
    ~**ryokō** 旅行 inspection trip
KENSA (suru) 検査(する) inspection; test (inspect; test)
    shinsa (suru) 審査(する) investigation; judge (investigate; judge)
koshi tantan to shite 虎視たんたんとして *With a vigilant eye* the guards kept watch over the prisoners.
ME ga todokanai 目が届かない One person alone *cannot keep an eye on* all those children in the pool.
    ~**ni tomaru** ~にとまる Standing on the deck of the ship, I *caught sight* of a large whale.
    ~**ni tsuku** ~につく comes into view
    ~**o samasu** ~をさます You must *be alert* at all times when on duty.

~ o tōsu ～を通す I *scanned* (*looked over*) the newspaper but failed to notice your article.

~ o tsukeru ～をつける The police *are keeping an eye on* all members of the gang.

u no me taka no me de うの目たかの目で *With longing eyes* (*With wistful eyes*) he kept looking at the coveted prize. *With eagle eyes* he kept looking for the missing jewels.

chūmoku (suru) 注目(する) attention (attend to; notice)

~ o hiku ～を引く The Olympic Games *attracted the attention* of the whole world.

~ subeki ～すべき be noteworthy

ichimokuryōzen 一目りょうぜん *You can tell at a glance* that the building was poorly built.

medatsu 目立つ stand out

MIRU 見る see; look

ana no aku hodo miru 穴のあくほど見る She *gaped at* (*stared right through*) me.

jiro jiro miru じろじろ見る look one over; stare at

mita tokoro dewa 見たところでは *From what I see* here, you are in need of help.

ōme ni miru 大目に見る Many boys were climbing over the fence into the ball game, but the guards *overlooked* (*shut their eyes to*) it.

tsukuzuku miru つくづく見る look closely [at]

kembutsu (suru) 見物(する) sightseeing (sight-see)

takami no kembutsu o suru 高見の見物をする There was an awful fight in the station, but everyone *looked on impassively*.

miharashi ga yoi 見晴らしがよい From the top of the peak you *have a good view* of the whole valley.

miharu 見張る look out; watch

mimamoru 見守る guard; watch closely

mimawasu 見回す look around; survey

atari o mimawasu あたりを見回す look around

mitōshi ga yoi 見通しがよい The *prospects* of that business *are good*.

mitōsu 見通す see through; see into; look ahead (into the future)

mitsumeru 見詰める stare at; gaze at

shigeshige to mitsumeru しげしげと見詰める scrutinize; look fixedly at; stare hard at

miwatasu kagiri 見渡すかぎり as far as one can see; as far as the eye can see

hitome de miwatasu 一目で見渡す He *took in* the whole panorama *at a glance*.

NAGAME (ru) ながめ(ながめる) view (view; gaze; watch)

bonyari nagameru ぼんやりながめる stare blankly [at]

kuiiru yōni nagameru 食い入るようにながめる stare right through; keep one's eyes peeled [for]

sensaku (suru) せんさく(する) search; probe; investigation (search; probe; investigate)

shiraberu 調べる check; check up [on]; investigate; examine

⇨ 30

地の果てなるもろもろの人よ，わたしを仰ぎのぞめ，そうすれば救われる．わたしは神であってほかに神はないからだ．(イザヤ書 45 ²²)

93 KANSEI 完成 COMPLETION

ban'irō naku 万遺漏なく without omission; thoroughly

banzen o kisuru tame 万全を期するため *To achieve perfection* in flight the space capsule was checked and rechecked many times.

chaku chaku to susumu 着々と進む We are *steadily advancing* in the project.

chanto ちゃんと perfectly; exactly

chitsujo seizen to 秩序整然と in perfect order; in apple pie order

chūto hampa (da) 中途半ば(だ) I can't employ him; he does everything in a *half-way* manner.

DEKIAGARU でき上がる be finished; be completed

  hito ga dekite iru 人ができている He has *a well-rounded personality.*

  shiage (ru) 仕上げ(仕上げる) finishing (finish; wind up)

  tsukuriageru 作り上げる complete

dō ni ka kogitsukeru どうにかこぎつける We had a lot of trouble with the project but managed to *get by somehow.*

hatasu 果たす fulfill; carry out

hi no uchidokoro ga nai 非の打ち所がない The job he has done *is above reproach (is flawless).*

itareri tsukuseri (da) 至れり尽くせり(だ) *There was nothing left to be desired* in the preparations for the banquet.

KANSEI (suru) 完成(する) completion (complete)

  ~ ni chikai ~に近い They said that the building *is near completion.*

  jiko kansei o mezasu 自己完成を目ざす aim at personal perfection; advance toward maturity

  migoto ni kansei suru 見事に完成する He *made a splendid job of* it.

jōju (suru) 成就(する) fulfillment (be fulfilled; be accomplished)

kambi shita 完備した fully equipped; complete

kanketsu(suru) 完結(する) termination; completion (be terminated; be completed)

kampeki 完ぺき perfection; flawlessness

  ~ o kisuru ~を期する aim at perfection

kanryō (suru) 完了(する) completion (complete; finish; conclude)

kanzen (da) 完全(だ) perfectness (perfect)

  ~ muketsu (da) ~無欠(だ) perfect; faultless

  ~ na hitosoroi ~な一そろい complete set [of books, etc.]

  ~ ni suru ~にする make perfect; perfect

  ~ no iki ni tassuru ~の域に達する perfection is achieved; attain perfection

naritatsu 成り立つ be realized

nashitogeru 成し遂げる accomplish; carry out; achieve

rakusei (suru) 落成(する) completion (finish up) [a building, etc.]

seijuku (suru) 成熟(する) ripeness; maturity (get ripe; grow mature)

seiritsu (suru) 成立(する) materialization (be materialized; be effected; be realized)

matomari ga tsuku まとまりがつく All the affairs of the conference *were wound up,* and we went home.

mattō suru 全うする complete; bring to perfection

mattaku 全く completely; truly

mehana ga tsuku 目鼻がつく The plans for the expedition *are taking shape.*

mizu mo morasanu 水も漏らさぬ The police spread a *tight (escape-proof)* dragnet to trap the criminal.

mono ni suru ものにする He's decided to really *make something of (perfect)* his English knowledge.

seikaku (da) 正確(だ) exactness (exact)

  seitō (da) 正当(だ) orthodox; traditional

sotsu ga nai そつがない He is one of those people who does everything *just so (neatly).*

sotsugyō (suru) 卒業(する) graduation; completion of a course (graduate)

tassuru 達する reach; arrive at

tatsujin 達人 accomplished person

[...ni] tessuru [...に] 徹する follow through; go through [with]

todokōri naku sumu 滞りなく済む The welcoming party for Smith *went off without a hitch.*

yukitodoku 行き届く be thorough; be scrupulous

⇨ 159

だから，あなたがたは，天の父が完全なように，完全であ りなさい。(マタイ 5 ⁴⁸)

94 KANSHA 感謝
GRATITUDE, APPRECIATION

ARIGATAI ありがたい be thankful

arigata meiwaku ありがた迷惑 annoying politeness; politeness to a fault

goshinsetsu ni arigatō gozaimasu ご親切にありがとうございます That's very kind of you. I appreciate your kindness.

KANSHA (suru) 感謝(する) gratitude; appreciation (be thankful; appreciate)

~ ni atai suru ~ に値する be worthy of one's appreciation; be deserving of one's thanks

~ ni taenai ~ に絶えない I *cannot express my deep thanks* to you.

~ no i o hyōsuru ~ の意を表する express appreciation; express one's feeling of gratitude

~ no kimochi ~ の気持ち feeling of thanksgiving

~ no kotoba mo arimasen ~ の言葉もありません *There are no words to express my thanks* to you.

~ no nen o ushinau ~ の念を失う become ungracious; become an ingrate

~ no shirushi to shite ~ の印として *As a token of his gratitude* Lincoln promoted the wounded lieutenant.

~ o sasageru ~ をささげる offer thanks

~ shite ~ して *With thanks*, I accept your invitation.

kokoro kara kansha suru 心から感謝する *I thank you from the bottom of my heart.*

kanshajō 感謝状 letter of thanks; letter of appreciation

kanshasai 感謝祭 Thanksgiving Day

shai 謝意 appreciation; thanks; gratitude

~ o hyōshite ~ を表して expressing one's thanks; as a token of one's appreciation

sharei 謝礼 remuneration; thanks

shasuru 謝する express one's appreciation

kōi o shasuru 厚意を謝する *Thanks for your kindness* in getting him that job.

okage sama de おかげさまで Thanks to you!

ON 恩 indebtedness; obligation; favor

~ ni kiseru ~ に着せる make one feel obligated

~ o kanjiru ~ を感じる feel obligated [to]; feel appreciation [for]

~ shirazu (da) ~ 知らず(だ) ingratitude (an ingrate; an ungrateful person)

hōon 報恩 gratitude

onkei 恩恵 gratitude; benefit; obligation

orei お礼 thanks; gift of thanks

atsuku orei mōshiagemasu 厚くお礼申し上げます I want to *give my heartfelt thanks* to all of you for your help.

rei o noberu 礼を述べる express one's thanks; express appreciation [for]

⇨ 160

われらは感謝をもって，み前に行き，主にむかい，さんび

の歌をもって，喜ばしい声をあげよう．(詩篇 95 ²)

95　KANSHIN 関心
INTEREST

endōi 縁遠い His *interests are far removed from* classical music. He *is in a different world* as far as classical music is concerned.

KANSHIN 関心 interest; concern; appreciation

   ~ ga usuragu ～が薄らぐ interest drops off; interest wanes

   ~ o hiku ～をひく He *has captured our interest* with his fascinating explanations of astronomy.

   ~ o idakaseru ～をいだかせる The space pictures of Mars *have created interest* among scientists about the possibilities of exploring other planets.

   ~ o motsu ～を持つ be interested [in]; be keen about

  kokoro o hikareru 心をひかれる be enthralled by; be captivated by; be enraptured by

   ~ ni kakeru ～にかける Abe couldn't enjoy the White House festivities, for he *was concerned about* little Willie's fever.

KI ga aru 気がある have an interest in; go in for

   ~ ga susumanai ～が進まない be reluctant [to]; be not very interested [in]; be unwilling [to]

   ~ ni iru ～に入る strike one's fancy; be attracted to; take a liking to

  kinori ga shinai 気乗りがしない I suggested that we go for a picnic, but he *was unwilling* (*was disinclined*) to go with us.

  noriki (da) 乗り気(だ) willingness; interest (willing; interested)

~ ni naru ～になる He was opposed at first, but lately he *has been warming up to* (*has taken an interest in*) the idea.

kikimimi o tateru 聞き耳を立てる prick up one's ears; try to catch what is being said

KONOMI (mu) 好み(好む) liking; fancy (like; take a fancy to)

   ~ ni awanai ～にあわない Golf just *doesn't suit my fancy* (*doesn't appeal to me*).

Heta no yokozuki [P] へたの横好き A Jack of all trades and master of none.

kōkishin 好奇心 curiosity; inquisitiveness

monozuki (da) 物好き(だ) fancifulness; whim (fanciful; whimsical)

   ~ na hito ～な人 curious person; oddball

suki (da) 好き(だ) liking; fondness (like; be fond of)

koru こる be crazy about

KYŌMI 興味 interest

   ~ ga aru ～がある have an interest in; be interested in

   ~ ga wakanai ～がわかない have no interest in; [it] does not interest one

   ~ hon'i (da) ～本位(だ) He wrote up the article *just to entertain* the readers (*just for human interest*).

   ~ o hiku ～を引く draw out one's interest [in]

   ~ o sosoru ～をそそる arouse one's interest

  amari kyōmi ga nai あまり興味がない I'*m not particularly interested in* baseball.

aji ga aru 味がある I don't know why, but I *have a liking for* that old Japanese block print.

   ~ ga nai ～がない To me, playing cards *is* an *insipid* pastime. I'm *just not interested* in playing cards.

kankyō 感興 interest; fun

~ **ga waku** ~ がわく become interested [in]; warm up to

~ **o sasou** ~ をさそう stimulate one's interest [in]

~ **o sogu** ~ をそぐ Too many commercials tend to *dampen one's interest* in the program.

kyō 興 amusement; fun; interest

~ **ni notte** ~ にのって To *join in the fun* he played the piano for us.

ichidan to kyō o soeru 一段と興を添える To *add further interest to* the program he sang for us.

kyōmibukai 興味深い be of great interest; be very amusing

kyōzameru 興ざめる His *enthusiasm* for chess *has flagged.* He *has cooled off on* chess.

shumi 趣味 hobby; taste; interest

miryoku o kanjiru 魅力を感じる be charmed by; feel an attraction for

monomidakai hito 物見高い人 novelty hunter; curiosity seeker

muga muchū ni naru 無我夢中になる In his enthusiasm for Zen art, he has *forgotten himself* and spends hours searching for paintings.

netchū shite 熱中して with absorbing interest

ukimi o yatsusu うき身をやつす I'm worried about him; he's *spending all his time and energy on* mahjong.

⇨ 1, 23

あなたがたは、地上のものを思わず、天にあるものを思いなさい。 (コロサイ 3²)

96 KANTAN 簡単
SIMPLICITY

asameshi mae (da) [c] 朝飯前(だ) There's nothing to it. It's a cinch.

assari to あっさりと briefly; simply

heii (da) 平易(だ) easy; plain

hito tamari mo naku ひとたまりもなく The flood waters rushed into Nagoya and *with one sweep* washed away everything in their path.

kaitsumamu かいつまむ summarize; sum up

kaitsumande ieba かいつまんで言えば in short; to make a long story short

KANTAN (da) 簡単(だ) simplicity (simple)

kan'i (da) 簡易(だ) easy; plain

kan'ika (suru) 簡易化(する) simplification (simple)

kanketsu (da) 簡潔(だ) brief

kanketsu de yō o ete iru 簡潔で要を得ている His report was *simple yet to the point.*

kammei (da) 簡明(だ) conciseness (concise)

kansoka (suru) 簡素化(する) simplification (simplify)

tanjun (da) 単純(だ) plain; simple; simple-minded

karuku katazukeru 軽くかたづける They *easily disposed of* the problem. They *made short shrift* of his suggestion.

kidoranai 気どらない unaffected

mujaki (da) 無邪気(だ) simple; naive; innocent

ochanoko saisai [c] おちゃのこさいさい I don't mind doing it; that job *is easy (is mere child's play; is a snap).*

oisore to wa ikanai おいそれとはいかない I know you are in a rush, but this work *cannot be done in a hurry (cannot be done at a moment's notice).*

ōzappa (da) 大ざっぱ(だ) rough

tampaku (da) 淡白(だ) simple; candid; frank; open

TAYASUI たやすい easy

Anzuru yori umu ga yasui [P] 案ずるより産むがやすい All things are difficult before they are tried.

yasu yasu to やすやすと quite easily
tettoribayaku ieba 手っ取り早く言えば quickly coming to the point
wake nai わけない [there's] nothing to it; it's a snap
yasashii やさしい simple; easy
yōi (da) 容易(だ) easy
zōsa nai 造作ない simple; easy
⇨ 142, 161

しかし、へびが悪巧みによってエバを欺いたように，万一にもあなたがたの思いが汚されて，キリストに対する真実と貞潔を失うことがあってはと，私は心配しています。(コリント II 11 ³)

97 KANYŌ 寛容 TOLERANCE, MAGNANIMITY

doryō 度量 bigness; magnanimity
　~ no aru hito ~のある人 He is a *bighearted person.*
garyō 雅量 generosity
hara ga ōkii (futoi) 腹が大きい(太い) He won't be offended at your criticism; he's too *big* for that.
kannin (suru) 堪忍(する) patience (forgive; forbear; overlook)
　Naranu kannin suru ga kannin [P] ならぬ堪忍するが堪忍 Forgiving the unforgivable is true forgiveness.
KANYŌ 寛容 tolerance; magnanimity
　kandai (da) 寛大(だ) broad-minded; magnanimous; liberal
　　~ na kokoro ~な心 large heart; broad mind
　　~ ni toriatsukau ~に取り扱う Lee surrendered his forces to Grant, for he knew Lincoln would *treat them tolerantly.*
yōsha suru 容赦する use leniency
ki ga ōkiku naru 気が大きくなる Most of us *start feeling big* the minute we get money in our pockets.

kimae no ii 気前のいい He's tightfisted in business but *liberal* (*generous*) with his children.
kodawaranai こだわらない He *is not particular about* what grades he gets. He *is not upset* over his low grades.
[...ni] kōdei shinai [...に]こうでいしない Lincoln *was not a stickler for details* (*was not concerned over trifles*).
minogasu 見のがす overlook
ōme ni miru 大目に見る look the other way; overlook
ōraka (da) おおらか(だ) broad-minded
　~ na kokoro ~な心 bighearted
oshimi naku hodokosu 惜しみなく施す ... From the depths of their poverty they have *shown themselves lavishly openhanded.* (II Corinthians 8 : 2)
ōyō (da) おうよう(だ) liberal; generous
⇨ 141, 216

私はこう考えます。少しだけまく者は，少しだけ刈り取り，豊かにまく者は，豊かに刈り取ります。ひとりひとり，いやいやながらでなく，しいられてでもなく，心で決めたとおりにしなさい。神は喜んで与える人を愛してくださいます。(コリント II 9 ⁶'⁷)

98 KAO 顔 FACE

bibō 美ぼう good looks; pretty (handsome) face; physical attractiveness
bishō o ukabete 微笑を浮かべて with a smile on one's face; with a smiling face
hyōjō 表情 expression; look; visage
KAO 顔 face
　~ ga tatanai ~が立たない lose face; cannot face
　~ ni arawasu ~に表わす When I told him his mother was seriously ill, he was shocked and *showed it on his face* (*betrayed his feelings*).
　~ o dasu ~を出す show up; show one's face; appear
　~ o hokorobasu ~をほころばす break

into a smile; have a beaming face

~o naosu ~を直す She is *making herself up* (*prettying herself up*) before the party.

~o oboete iru ~を覚えている I *remember his face*, but I've forgotten his name.

~o shikameru ~をしかめる wrinkle one's face; grimace in pain

~o shitte iru ~を知っている know a person by sight

~o tateru ~を立てる save [a person's] face; back [someone] up

~o tsubusu ~をつぶす disgrace (a person)

~o yogosu ~をよごす defame; disgrace (a person)

akarui kao 明るい顔 bright face

aratamatta kao 改まった顔 serious face; solemn face

harebare to shita kao 晴れ晴れとした顔 bright face; cheerful look

haritsumeta kao 張り詰めた顔 strained look; tense face; drawn expression

iya na kao o suru いやな顔をする look hurt; look displeased; look dead serious

majime kusatta kao o suru まじめくさった顔をする look dead serious

matomo ni hito no kao o minaide まともに人の顔を見ないで without looking one directly in the face

mono hoshi sō na kao 物欲しそうな顔 an eager look [on his face]; a wistful look; a longing look

satotta yō na kao 悟ったような顔 a " know-it-all " look

shiran kao (furi) o suru 知らん顔(ふり)をする feign ignorance; pretend to know nothing

dōgan 童顔 child's face; boyish face; youthful face

egao 笑顔 smiling face

gammen 顔面 face

hitomachigao 人待ち顔 When I saw him in front of the station, he *looked as if he were waiting for someone.*

kaobure ga kawaru 顔ぶれが変わる Everytime I go in that store they have *new faces there* (*new personnel*).

kaodachi 顔だち facial features

kaodashi suru 顔出しする put in an appearance; show up

kaoiro 顔色 complexion; color; humor

~ga kawaru ~が変わる turn pale

~o kaeru ~を変える change color

~o ukagau ~をうかがう Before you ask for a raise, you'd better *see what mood he's in.*

~o yomu ~を読む know what humor one is in; read another's face

kaokatachi 顔かたち looks; countenance

kao mishiri 顔見知り know one by sight

kaotsuki 顔つき countenance; physiognomy

osanagao 幼顔 looks one had when a child

yokogao 横顔 profile

kiryō 器量 looks; personal appearance

mehanadachi 目鼻立ち features; looks

MEN to mukatte 面と向かって Talk to him *face to face*, not behind his back.

mentsu o tateru めんつを立てる save one's face

menzen de 面前で right in one's face

shikamettsura しかめっつら wry face; grimace

taimen suru 対面する interview; confrontation (face each other; have an interview)

tsura [C] つら surface; skin; face

tsuragamae [C] つらがまえ looks

dōmō na tsuragamae どうもうなつらがまえ a ferocious look

misekake o yoku suru [C] 見せかけをよく
する put up a good front
muki o kaeru 向きを変える turn around;
change direction of one's sight
utsubuse ni naru うつ伏せになる put one's
face down [on a desk, etc.]
主を仰ぎ見て、光を得よ. そうすれば、あなたがたは、恥じ
て顔を赤くすることはない. (詩篇 34 ⁵)

99 KEIBETSU 軽べつ
CONTEMPT

aite ni shinai 相手にしない He's so unreliable I've decided to *have nothing more
to do with* him.
anadoru 侮る scorn; despise
azakeri (ru) あざけり(あざける) taunt;
mocking (taunt; mock; ridicule)
azawarai あざ笑い derision; sneer
(deride; sneer at; laugh at)
  isshō ni fusuru 一笑に付する The boss
  scoffed at my idea of setting up a
  factory in Brazil. The boss *dismissed*
  my idea of setting up a factory in
  Brazil *with a laugh.*
  seserawarau せせら笑う sneer at; laugh
  scornfully
besshi suru 蔑視する hold in contempt;
hold lightly
BUJOKU (suru) 侮辱(する) insult; contempt (insult; slight)
  chijoku 恥辱 disgrace; dishonor
  kutsujoku 屈辱 shame; humiliation
doko no uma no hone ka wakaranai
[C] どこの馬の骨かわからない You'd better
check up on him because I *don't know
anything about him.*
dokuzuku 毒づく say bitter things; hurl
abuse at
dorei atsukai ni sareru 奴隷扱いにされる
At that restaurant the waitresses *are
treated like slaves.*
genkanbarai o kuu [C] 玄関払いを食う

The salesman *was turned away at the
door.* When I went to see my old friend,
I *was brushed off (was snubbed).*
hige suru 卑下する degrade; debase
hito o fuminijiru 人を踏みにじる Stanton
was prone to *run roughshod over people,*
but Lincoln patiently listened to their
requests.
[hito o] kutta taido [人を] 食った態度
He talked to us with a *contemptuous
attitude.*
iikagen ni ashirau いいかげんにあしらう
treat one contemptuously; treat one
like dirt
KEIBETSU (suru) 軽べつ(する) contempt;
(scorn; treat contemptuously)
  ~ no nen o idaku [L] ～の念をいだく
  have scorn for
  keishi suru 軽視する treat lightly; make
  little of; hold cheap
kenasu けなす degrade; downgrade
MISAGERU 見下げる sell short; look
down on
  misagehateta 見下げはてた contemptible; despicable
  mikubiru 見くびる make light of; hold
  cheap; look down on
  mikudasu 見くだす consider inferior;
  despise
  ichidan shita ni miru 一段下に見る He
  considers those people *beneath* him.
  shiroi me de miru 白い目で見る When
  the new girl walked into the class,
  the other girls *shunned her (looked at
  her with critical eyes).*
mokusatsu suru 黙殺する When I made
the suggestion, they *treated* it *with
silent contempt.*
nonoshiru ののしる hurl abuses at; speak
ill of
sagesumu さげすむ look down on; despise
⇨ **11**
そのようなことをしている人々をさばきながら，自分で同
じことをしている人よ．あなたは，自分は神のさばきを免

れるのだとでも思っているのですか.
それとも，神の慈愛があなたを悔い改めに 導くことも知
らないで，その豊かな慈愛と忍耐と寛容とを軽んじてい
るのですか. (ローマ 2 ³, ⁴)

100 KEIKEN 経験
EXPERIENCE

ajiwau 味わう taste; experience; meet with

bakazu o fumu [C] 場数を踏む He *gained a lot of actual experience* in the Peace Corps.

benkyō ni naru 勉強になる will profit by; will get something out of

hi ga asai 日が浅い He *hasn't been at* this kind of work *long*.

hidoi me ni au ひどい目に会う Lost in the mountains, they *went through* many *trying experiences*.

jinsei 人生 life's course

jitchi 実地 practice; actuality

~ **o fumu** ~を踏む actually experience; get practical experience

jukurensha 熟練者 expert; skilled worker

rōren (da) 老練(だ) veteran; experienced

kakedashi 駆け出し a beginner; a novice

KEIKEN 経験 experience

[...**ni**] ~ **ga aru** [...に] ~がある Lincoln *had* some *experience in* clerking, farming, and surveying.

~ **ni motozuku** ~にもとづく Abe's sympathy for the common soldier was *based upon* his own *experience* in the Indian wars.

~ **ni toboshii** ~に乏しい Lincoln *lacked experience* in financial matters and left that up to Chase.

~ **no aru** ~のある experienced; skilled

~ **o ikasu** ~を生かす make use of one's experience

~ **o tsumu** ~を積む accumulate experience; become an expert [in]

naganen no keiken 長年の経験 long years of experience

keikendan 経験談 one's experience

keikensha 経験者 man of experience; an old hand [at]

keireki 経歴 one's past history

iro iro no keireki no aru hito いろいろの経歴のある人 man of varied experience

taiken (suru) 体験(する) experience (experience; go through)

kokoroeru 心得る get to know the ropes

korigori suru [C] こりごりする I *learned the hard way* that you can't depend on him.

kusuri ni naru 薬になる He was getting overconfident, so perhaps failure will *be good medicine* for him.

[...**ni**] **kuwashii** [...に] 詳しい be familiar with; be well-informed on; be an authority on

[...**ga**] **mi ni shimiru** [...が]身にしみる experience deeply

nariagari mono 成り上がり者 He's just *an upstart* (*flash in the pan*) who happened to hit the stock market right.

nareru 慣れる get used to; grow accustomed to.

[...**ni**] **nenki o irete iru** [...に]年期を入れている That carpenter has *had many years' experience in* his work.

toshi no kō 年の功 the wisdom of age

[...**no**] **omoi o suru** [...の]思いをする experience

rirekisho 履歴書 personal history

seken shirazu (da) 世間知らず(だ) He treats people discourteously because he *is ignorant of life*.

shimmai 新まい beginner; greenhorn; novice; new hand; tenderfoot

taitoku (suru) 体得(する) master (learn from experience)

yatte miru やってみる try one's hand at; give [it] a try

主の恵みふかきことを味わい知れ，
主に寄り頼む人はさいわいである．（詩篇 34⁸）

101　KEISHIKI 形式
FORMALITY

aratamaru 改まる stand on ceremony; be formal

eri [igi] o tadasu えり(威儀)をただす When the President came into the room, we *all stiffened up* and became formal.

gaikan 外観 outward show; external appearance

ikameshii いかめしい rigid; unbending

jimuteki (da) 事務的(だ) business-like

kamishimo o tsukeru かみしもをつける Don't *act like a stuffed shirt* at the party tonight.

KATA ni hamatta 型にはまった The speaker gave a *cut and dried (conventional)* talk that was too long.

　~ o yaburu ~ を破る depart from formality; break from the traditional; be unconventional

katagurushii 堅苦しい formal; stiff

KEISHIKI 形式 formality

　~ ni kodawaru ~ にこだわる be particular about formality; stick to form

　~ ni nagareru ~ に流れる become merely formal

　~ nuki ni ~ 抜きに skipping formalities

gaikei 外形 external; external form

gishiki 儀式 ceremony; ritual

　~ o okonau ~ を行なう conduct a ceremony

gishikibaru 儀式張る stand on ceremony; be ceremonious

hikōshiki (da) 非公式(だ) unofficial; informal; casual

kakushikibatta 格式張った formal

keishikishugi 形式主義 formalism

keishikiteki (da) 形式的(だ) formal

kōshiki (no) 公式(の) formal; official

seishiki (no) 正式(の) formally; with due formality

　~ no tetsuzuki ~ の手続き formal procedure

shiki o ageru 式をあげる hold a ceremony

kichōmen (da) きちょうめん(だ) punctual; methodical

kudaketa mono no iikata o suru くだけた物の言い方をする Lincoln *used a simple way of speaking* that was understandable to the man in the street.

KYOREI 虚礼 empty formality

　~ ni ochiiru ~ に陥る slip into empty formalism

bureikō de iku 無礼講で行く Speak out frankly to anyone here. Tonight we're *skipping ceremony (abandoning formalities)*.

gireiteki hōmon 儀礼的訪問 courtesy visit

mie o haru みえを張る show off; be pretentious; be ostentatious

ozanari お座なり mere formality; commonplace

　~ no yarikata de ~ のやり方で in a conventional way

tanin gyōgi 他人行儀 formality

teisai o tsukurou 体裁をつくろう He really doesn't belong in that society—he's just *keeping up appearances (putting on airs)*.

tōri ippen no aisatsu 通りいっぺんのあいさつ casual greeting; perfunctory greeting

yosoyososhii よそよそしい formal; standoffish; unconcerned; withdrawn; aloof ⇨ **160, 180**

しかし主はサムエルに言われた，顔かたちや身のたけを見てはならない．わたしはすでにその人を捨てた．わたしが見るところは人とは異なる．人は外の顔かたちを見，主は心を見る．（サムエル記上 16⁷）

102 KEISOTSU 軽卒
THOUGHTLESSNESS

asahaka (da) あさはか(だ) frivolous; shallow; flippant

ato saki mizu ni あと先見ずに without forethought; not thinking ahead

Baka no hitotsu oboe [P] ばかの一つ覚え *A fool sticks to the one thing he has learned*, so forgive me for quoting Shakespeare again.

chi no meguri ga warui [C] 血のめぐりが悪い Don't expect him to catch on; he's quite *thick-headed* (*fatheaded; obtuse*).

chie no tarinai (hito) 知恵の足りない(人) [one] lacking in wisdom

fukinshin (da) 不謹慎(だ) indiscretion (indiscreet)

    ~ nimo...suru ~ にも...する He *had the indiscretion to* use foul language in front of our guests.

fumbetsu no nai hito 分別のない人 an indiscreet person

KEISOTSU 軽率 thoughtlessness

    ~ ni shite wa naranai ~ にしてはならない Don't do anything rash. Don't go off half-cocked.

    ~ ni yakusoku suru ~ に約束する make a rash promise

karugarushiku 軽々しく lightly; rashly

karuhazumi na koto o suru 軽はずみなことをする Those young people *did a very thoughtless thing*—going up that mountain without sweaters.

keihaku (da) 軽薄(だ) frivolity (frivolous; flippant)

kikiwake ga nai 聞き分けがない That child *is very headstrong* and will not listen to a thing you say.

mōmoku 盲目 blindness

mucha (da) むちゃ(だ) reckless; heedless

muchi (da) 無知(だ) ignorant; stupid

mufumbetsu (da) 無分別(だ) indiscreet; imprudent

    ~ nimo...suru ~ にも...する be thoughtless enough to...

muteppō (da) 無鉄砲(だ) rash; reckless; (devil-may-care)

    ~ na koto o suru ~ なことをする do something reckless

seken o minai 世間を見ない be blind to reality; be unrealistic

shiryo o kaku 思慮を欠く lack common sense; lack prudence

yarisugiru やり過ぎる run [something] into the ground

yukisugi (ru) 行き過ぎ(行き過ぎる) overdoing (overdo; carry [a matter] too far) ⇨ **48, 187**

あなたがたの中に知恵の欠けた人がいるなら，その人は，だれにでも惜しげなく，とがめることなくお与えになる神に願いなさい．そうすればきっと与えられます．(ヤコブ 1⁵)

103 KEKKON 結婚
MARRIAGE

baishakunin 媒しゃく人 go-between

demodori 出もどり divorcee (woman)

ENDAN o matomeru 縁談をまとめる After much discussion, the go-betweens *fixed the engagement* (*made the match*).

engumi 縁組み marriage

    niai no engumi 似合いの縁組み well-matched marriage

emmusubi 縁結び wedding arrangement

naien 内縁 common-law marriage

ryōen o kotowaru 良縁を断わる turn down a good marriage proposal

hanamuko (muko) 花婿(婿) bridegroom (groom)

iinazuke いいなずけ fiancé; betrothed

KEKKON 結婚 marriage

    ~ hirō (en) ~ ひろう(宴) wedding reception

    ~ kinembi ~ 記念日 wedding anniversary

~ no aite ~の相手 fiancé; marriage prospect

~ o mōshikomu ~を申し込む propose; ask for [her] hand in marriage

~ o nobasu ~を延ばす postpone marriage

~ o shōdaku suru ~を承諾する accept a person's hand in marriage

~ o torikesu ~を取り消す annul a marriage

~ o torimotsu ~を取り持つ arrange a marriage

~ sagi ~詐欺 After being *deceived by his marriage promises*, she lost confidence in men.

~ seikatsu ~生活 married life

~ yubiwa ~指輪 wedding ring

kinshin (ketsuzoku) kekkon 近親(血族)結婚 marriage of near relatives

kokusai kekkon 国際結婚 mixed marriage

miai kekkon (miai o suru) 見合い結婚(見合いをする) She was leery about an *arranged marriage*, but after she (*met the marriage prospect*) she found they had much in common.

mibun chigai no kekkon 身分違いの結婚 That mechanic *married out of his class* when he chose the professor's daughter.

nijū kekkon 二重結婚 bigamy

ren'ai kekkon 恋愛結婚 love marriage

bankon (sōkon) 晩婚(早婚) late (early) marriage

chigiri o musubu ちぎりを結ぶ The Lincoln couple *tied the nuptial knot* (*made their marital vows*) at their own home in Springfield.

kekkonshiki (konrei) 結婚式(婚礼) wedding ; marriage ceremony

~ o ageru ~をあげる perform a wedding ceremony

kekkontodoke (sho) 結婚届け(書) marriage certificate

kon'in 婚姻 marriage

konyaku (suru) 婚約(する) engagement (get engaged)

kyukon (suru) 求婚(する) proposal (propose ; ask one's hand in marriage)

musubareru 結ばれる be joined together

rikon (suru) 離婚(する) divorce (get divorced)

saikon (suru) 再婚(する) remarriage (remarry)

metoru めとる take a wife

migomoru 身ごもる be pregnant; be in the family way

moraite ga aru もらい手がある She has had many *offers of marriage* (*suitors*).

nakōdo 仲人 go-between

OTTO (tsuma) 夫(妻) husband (wife)

tsuma ni mukaeru 妻に迎える The young man finally saved enough to *take her as his wife*.

fūfu (fusai) 夫婦(夫妻) man and wife; married couple

fūfu yakusoku 夫婦約束 wedding engagement

ippu ippu 一夫一婦 monogamy

ippu tasai 一夫多妻 polygamy

shojo 処女 virgin

tekireiki 適齢期 marriageable age

tsuresou 連れ添う become wedded

YOME ni iku 嫁に行く [a woman] gets married ; marries into a family

~ ni yaru ~にやる give one's daughter away in marriage

~ no kuchi ga aru ~の口がある have an offer of marriage

~ o morau (ni morau) ~をもらう(にもらう) When I *get married*, I want to (*get married to that*) girl.

hanayome (yome) 花嫁(嫁) bride

~ **sugata de** ~ 姿で in bridal dress

shimpu (shinrō) 新婦(新郎) bride (bridegroom)

yomeiri 嫁入り marriage of a woman

yomeiri jitaku 嫁入りじたく trousseau ⇨ 1

「それゆえ，人はその父と母を離れて，その妻と結ばれ，ふたりの者が 一心同体になるのだ.」と言われたのです. それを，あなたがたは読んだことがないのですか. それで，もはやふたりではなく，ひとりなのです. こういうわけで，人は，神が結び合わせたものを引き離してはなりません. (マタイ 19 ⁵, ⁶)

104 KEN'I 権威
AUTHORITY

ago de [hito o] tsukau あごで[人を]使う The boss *has* that new clerk *at his beck and call.*

ayatsuru あやつる pull strings

hito o ayatsuru 人をあやつる manipulate people; pull strings

haba ga kiku [c] 幅がきく The young executive *is influential* in every department of the firm.

~ **o kikasu** ~をきかす throw one's weight around

hoshii mama ni suru ほしいままにする do as one pleases

[...o] kasa ni kiru [c] [...を]かさにきる *Using the prestige of* the President, the press secretary tried to control the press.

KEN'I 権威 authority

~ **aru** ~ある authoritative [book, theory, etc.]

~ **ni shitagau** ~に従う submit to authority

~ **o ataeru** ~を与える give the right [to]

~ **o nigiru** ~を握る seize power

~ **o motsu** ~を持つ hold authority [to do]

ekken (kōi o suru) 越権(行為をする)

arrogation (overstep one's authority)

gyōseiken 行政権 administrative authority

haken o nigiru 覇権を握る The Soviets *have gained supremacy* (*hold the lead*) in the weightlifting event.

iryoku 威力 might; authority; power

~ **o hakki suru** ~を発揮する display great power

jinken 人権 human rights

~ **o mushi suru** ~を無視する ignore human rights

kairai seiken かいらい政権 puppet government

kengen 権限 authorization; jurisdiction

~ **o kakudai suru** ~を拡大する extend one's power

~ **o seigen suru** ~を制限する limit one's authority; clip one's wings

ken'isuji 権威すじ authorities; authoritative source

kennō 権能 authority; function; power

kenri (kin) 権利(金) rights; claims; franchise (key money)

~ **o kau** ~を買う buy rights; purchase a claim [to]

~ **o mushi suru** ~を無視する ignore rights; disregard authority

~ **o shuchō suru** ~を主張する demand one's rights; assert one's claims

~ **o ushinau** ~を失う lose one's rights

~ **o yōkyū suru** ~を要求する demand one's rights [to]

kenryoku 権力 authority; power

~ **ni kussuru** ~に屈する This is the commander's order, and we must *yield to* his *authority* (*accept* his *authority*).

~ **o ataeru** ~を与える grant authority; invest with authority; empower; make [someone] sovereign over

~ **o furuu** ~を振るう The new government began *wielding authority* (*throwing its weight around*) against civic institutions.

~ o kakuho suru ~ を確保する retain power

seiken 政権 regime

  ~ o tarai mawashi ni suru ~ をたらいまわしにする passing political power around; dispensing political favors [within a party]

shokken o ranyō suru 職権を乱用する Many felt that the president *abused his authority*.

shoyūken 所有権 property rights; ownership

tokken 特権 rights; special privileges

  ~ kaikyu ~ 階級 privileged class

  ~ ni azukaru ~ にあずかる share in the privileges; participate in the rights [of]

zenken o yudaneru 全権をゆだねる give a carte blanche; turn everything over [to]

kuromakuteki sonzai 黒幕的存在 the power behind the throne; the real boss behind the scenes

meirei (suru) 命令(する) order; command (order; command)

osameru 治める rule; reign over

oshi ga tsuyoi [C] 押しが強い He is hard to work for because he's *too pushy* (*a driver*).

seiryoku 勢力 influence; power

  ~ arasoi o suru ~ 争いをする The party *is engaged in a power struggle* between two leading factions.

  ~ han'i ~ 範囲 sphere of influence

  ~ o eru ~ を得る gain influence

  ~ o furuu ~ を振るう exert influence over

seisuru 制する govern; control

shihai (suru) 支配(する) reign; rule (rule over; control)

  saihai o furuu さい配を振るう The Prime

Minister *is waving the baton* (*is calling the shots*) in the election campaign.

tsuru no hitokoe つるの一声 His word is the *voice of authority* in the Liberal-Democratic party.

⇨ **6, 19**

イエスは近づいて来て，彼らにこう言われた。「わたしには天においても，地においても，いっさいの権威が与えられています。（マタイ 28 ¹⁸）

105 KENKŌ 健康 HEALTH

eisei 衛生 sanitation; hygiene

  ~ ni chūi suru ~ に注意する be careful of one's health; be hygienic

ganjō na karada がんじょうなからだ a strong constitution

genki (da) 元気(だ) vigor; vitality; pep (vigorous; peppy)

  ~ ippai ~ いっぱい full of pep; full of energy

  ~ ni naru ~ になる recover; get well

shigokugenki 至極元気 sound as a dollar

guai ga warui ぐあいがわるい be not up to par; don't feel good; be out of shape

jōbu (da) じょうぶ(だ) healthy; strong

kakushaku to shita かくしゃくとした He *is hale and hearty* at the age of eighty-five.

karada ni ii (warui) からだに良い(悪い) It's good (not good) for you.

  ~ ni sawaru ~ にさわる Many scientists have warned us that cigarette smoking *is detrimental to health*.

KENKŌ 健康 health

  ~ hō ~ 法 hygiene

  ~ hoken ~ 保険 health insurance

  ~ ni chūi suru ~ に注意する be careful of one's health

  ~ ni hibiku ~ に響く That strenuous schedule *has affected his health*.

  ~ ni ii (warui) ~ に良い(悪い) be good for one's health; be wholesome; (be

bad for one's health; be unwhole-
some)

~ ni tekishita ~ に適した wholesome;
good for one's health

~ o ataeru ~ を与える Swimming and
tennis *are good for your health.*

~ o gaisuru ~ を害する Studying late
at night and eating irregularly will
eventually *injure one's health.*

~ o kaifuku suru ~ を回復する
recover one's health; be restored
to health

~ shindan ~ 診断 medical examination

subarashii kenkō jōtai (da) すばらし
い健康状態(だ) in tip-top condition;
in excellent health; in the best of
health

kenkōtai 健康体 healthy body; robust
body

kenzai (da) 健在(だ) alive and well

kenzen(da) 健全(だ) soundness (sound;
healthy; wholesome)

mi mo kokoro mo kenzen (da) 身
も心も健全(だ) be of sound body and
mind

sōken (da) 壮健(だ) hale and hearty; in
the pink of health

mubyō sokusai [L] 無病息災 hale and
hearty condition

odaiji ni お大事に Take care of yourself!

sukoyaka (da) すこやか(だ) be healthy; be
sound

tassha (da) 達者(だ) be alive and well; be
in good condition

tokoage suru 床上げする recover from a
long illness

zenkai (suru) 全快(する) full recovery
(fully recover)

⇨ 85

自分を見て賢いと思ってはならない，主を恐れて，悪を
離れよ．そうすれば，あなたの身を健やかにし，あなたの
骨に元気を与える．(箴言 3 ⁷, ⁸)

106 KENSON 謙そん
MODESTY, HUMILITY

enryo (suru) 遠慮(する) reserve; hesitation (hesitate; defer; back out)

~ no nai hito ~ のない人 forthright
person; unrestrained person

enryobukai 遠慮深い reserved person;
modest

enryogachi (da) 遠慮がち(だ) reserva-
tion (diffidence)

futoku no itasu tokoro 不徳のいたすところ
I *am to blame* for everything. *It was my
fault that* the project failed.

hana o motaseru 花を持たせる It was
Lincoln's battle plan, but he *allowed*
McClellan *to get the credit for* the
victory.

herikudaru へりくだる humble oneself;
condescend

hige suru 卑下する humble oneself; disparage oneself

hikaeme (da) 控え目(だ) reserved;
reticent

~ ni suru ~ にする hold back; be
reserved

jimi (da) じみ(だ) modest; conservative

KENSON 謙そん modesty; humility

~ na taido ~ な態度 In his speeches
Lincoln showed a *humble attitude.*

fuson (da) 不そん(だ) arrogant; haughty

kenjō [L] 謙譲 modesty; humility

~ no bitoku [L] ~ の美徳 the virtue
of modesty

kenkyo (da) 謙虚(だ) humble; modest

koshi no hikui hito 腰の低い人 humble
person; self-effacing person

**Minoru hodo atama o sageru inaho
kana** [P] 実るほど頭を下げる稲穂かな The
greater the number of grain to be
harvested the lower the wheat bends
on the stalk. [The mature are humble.]

ohazukashii koto desu ga... お恥ずかしい
ことですが...I am ashamed to say this,
but...

osore irimasu ga... 恐れ入りますが... I am sorry, but...

oyobazunagara 及ばずながら I will *do what little I can* to help. I will try *to the best of my ability.*

shirigomi suru しりごみする shrink back; hold back; hesitate

tsutsumashiyaka (da) つつましやか(だ) modest; reserved

tsutsushimi (mu) 慎しみ(慎む) prudence; care (be careful; be circumspect)

いと高く, いと上なる者, とこしえに住む者, その名を聖ととなえられる者がこう言われる, 「わたしは高く, 聖なるところに住み..., へりくだる者の霊をいかし, 砕けたる者の心をいかす. (イザヤ 51 ¹⁵)

107 KESSHIN 決心
DECISION

erabu 選ぶ choose; select

fungiri ga tsukanai 踏切りがつかない Lincoln was *unable to make up his mind* about relieving McClellan of command.

haisui no jin o shiku 背水の陣を敷く He made a daring decision and *burned his bridges behind him.*

handan (suru) 判断(する) judgment; decision; estimation (judge; decide; estimate)

~ **no kijun** ~ の基準 basis for making a decision; criterion of judgment

~ **o ayamaru** ~ を誤る misjudge; err in judgment

seitō **na handan o kudasu** 正当な判断を下す In such emotional matters it is difficult to *give a right verdict (judge fairly).*

gohandan **ni makasemasu** ご判断に任せます I will *leave it up to your discretion.*

handanryoku o ushinau 判断力を失う lose one's judgment

hantei (suru) 判定(する) verdict;

decision (decide; render a verdict)

shinpan (sha) 審判(者) umpire; referee

hara ga suwatta 腹がすわった He *was resolute* in making that choice.

~ **o kimeru** ~ を決める make up one's mind

ishi ni kajiritsuite mo yaritogeru 石にかじりついてもやり遂げる We tried to discourage him from immigrating to Brazil, but he said he would *stick to his resolve (do it despite all odds).*

kakugo (suru) 覚悟(する) resolve (be resolved; be prepared [for])

~ **no ue** ~ のうえ prepared for the worst; having set one's course

~ **o kimeru** ~ を決める make firm resolve; be fully prepared

KESSHIN (suru) 決心(する) decision (decide; make a decision)

~ **ga guratsuite iru** ~ がぐらついている He had decided to go abroad, but after failing the English proficiency test, he *is wavering* (he *is vacillating*).

~ **ga tsukanai** ~ がつかない We want to go ahead with the plans, but the boss *cannot come to a decision (cannot reach a decision).*

~ **o hirugaesu** ~ をひるがえす reverse one's decision

~ **o katameru** ~ を固める be firmly determined; form a resolution

katai **kesshin de** 固い決心で with grim determination

kekkō (suru) 決行(する) decisive action (carry out; execute)

kessan (suru) 決算(する) financial settlement (settle accounts)

kesshōsen 決勝戦 finals [game, contest, etc.] 「sion

kessuru 決する decide; come to a deci-

koto **wa sude ni kesshita** 事はすでに決した With the attack on Pearl

Harbor the *die was cast*, and the Pacific War began.

ketsudan (suru) 決断(する) resolution; determination (resolve; determine)

ketsudanryoku 決断力 determination

ketsugi (suru) 決議(する) resolution; decision (pass a resolution)

ketsui (suru) 決意(する) resolution (resolve; decide)

~ **o arata ni suru** ~ を新たにする After Kennedy's death, Johnson appealed to the American people to *make a new resolve* (*make a fresh resolve*) to carry out the civil rights' program.

kettei (suru) 決定(する) conclusion; settlement (settle; reach an agreement)

ketteiteki (da) 決定的(だ) decisive

kimeru 決める fix; decide; make up one's mind

hakkiri shita koto wa kimatte inai はっきりした事は決まっていない We would like to take a trip to Hokkaido, but *nothing definite has been decided*.

kangae o kimeru 考えを決める be set on [doing]; make up one's mind

kokoro no mochikata hitotsu de 心の持ち方一つで You will face many difficulties, but success after all *depends upon your frame of mind*.

omoikitte...suru 思い切って...する During the Meiji era certain leaders *resolutely* (*boldly*) instituted a drastic new foreign policy.

sadameru 定める set; appoint; decide

dantei (suru) 断定(する) decision; conclusion (decide; conclude)

suiron (suru) 推論(する) inference (infer; decide; conclude)

tsumori つもり intention

⇨ 73, 121, 178

なぜなら私は、あなたがたの間で、イエス・キリスト、すなわち十字架につけられた方のほかは、何も知らないことに

決心したからです。(コリント I 2²)

108 KIBŌ 希望 HOPE

akogare (ru) あこがれ(あこがれる) yearning; longing (long for)

hossuru 欲する want; wish

KIBŌ (suru) 希望(する) hope (hope [for]; wish)

~ **ga takamaru** ~ が高まる hopes are raised [for]

~ **ni hanshite** ~ に反して against one's wishes

~ **ni mezameru** ~ に目ざめる find hope

~ **ni michita** ~ に満ちた filled with hope; abounding with hope

~ **no nai** ~ のない hopeless

~ **o kujiku** ~ をくじく crush one's hopes; dash one's hopes; disappoint one

~ **o mitasu** ~ を満たす fulfill one's hopes

~ **o noberu** ~ を述べる express hope [that]

~ **o torimodosu** ~ を取りもどす restore hope in; reassure

~ **o tsunagu** ~ をつなぐ hinge one's hopes on; pin one's hope on

kibō dōri ni iku (ikanai) 希望通りにいく(いかない) I received just the pay-raise *I was hoping for*. (The pay-raise *did not come up to my expectations*.)

gambō 願望 aspiration; desire

hommō 本望 long cherished desire

~ **o tassuru** ~ を達する realize a long cherished desire

kibōsha 希望者 aspirant; applicant

machinozomu 待ち望む long for; hope for

netsubō (suru) 熱望(する) fervent hope; earnest desire (earnestly desire)

nozomashii 望ましい desirable

nozomi (mu) 望み (望む) hope (hope for)

　~ ga ari sō mo nai ~がありそうもない [it] doesn't look very hopeful

　~ o idaku ~をいだく We all *cherish a desire* for world peace.

　~ o kakeru ~をかける "We *had been hoping* that he was the man to liberate Israel... ;" (Luke 24 : 21)

　~ o kanaeru ~をかなえる Vote for the party which can best *fulfill the wishes* of the people.

　~ o suteru ~を捨てる abandon all hope

　~ o ushinau ~を失う lose hope; give up hope

　ichiru no nozomi 一るの望み He lost heavily in the business but still feels there is *a ray of hope* left.

nozomiusui 望み薄い little hope [for]

shibō (suru) 志望(する) choice; aspiration (aspire [to])

shukubō 宿望 long cherished desire; deep hope

taimō 大望 aspiration

yabō 野望 ambition

　~ o habamu ~をはばむ frustrate one's hopes

yūbō (da) 有望(だ) promising; hopeful **zento yūbō na** 前途有望な promising

kitai (suru) 期待(する) expectation (expect)

　ōi ni kitai shite 大いに期待して The pitcher *was in great hopes* of winning the opening game of the series.

kōmyō o miidasu 光明を見いだす Things looked pretty dark when he fell ill, but he *found* a *ray of hope* in the new medicine.

mikomi 見込み prospects

　~ ga nai ~がない With his poor English *there's not a ghost of a chance* that he will pass the exams.

myaku ga aru 脈がある I failed the test,

but when the manager told me to come back, I thought *there was still hope*.

nengan (suru) 念願(する) long cherished desire (desire; wish for)

　~ ga kanau ~がかなう His *long cherished desire* to visit Africa *was realized*.

Oboreru mono wa wara o mo tsukamu (P) おぼれる者はわらをもつかむ When the situation seems hopeless, we often *clutch at straws*.

rakkan (suru) 楽観(する) optimism (be optimistic)

shitau 慕う aspire after; follow after

soradanomi そら頼み vain hope

yashin 野心 ambition; desire

どうか，望みの神が，あなたがたを信仰によるすべての喜びと平和をもって満たし，聖霊の力によって望みにあふれさせてくださいますように．(ローマ 15 18)

109　KIKAI 機会
OPPORTUNITY

chansu o toraeru チャンスを捕える seize the chance; use the chance

hazumi はずみ impetus; spur; chance

　nanika no hazumi ni 何かのはずみに by some force of circumstance

kikkake きっかけ chance; occasion

　~ o ataeru ~を与える provide an occasion [for]

KIKAI 機会 opportunity

　~ ari shidai ~あり次第 at the earliest opportunity

　~ aru goto ni ~あるごとに Do a favor for your neighbor *every time you have a chance* (*whenever the opportunity presents itself*).

　~ kintō ~均等 equal opportunities [employment, etc.]

　~ o ataeru ~を与える give opportunity [for]

　~ o eru ~を得る get a chance; find (have) an opportunity [to do]

　~ o minogasu (issuru) ~を見のがす

(逸する) let the opportunity slip through one's fingers

~o mu ni suru ~を無にする waste the opportunity

~o nerau (matsu) ~をねらう(待つ) watch (wait) for an opportunity [to do]

~o toraeru (tsukamu) ~を捕える(つかむ) seize the opportunity; find opportunity

~o ukagau ~をうかがう look for an occasion [to do]; wait for the chance [to do]

mata to nai yoi kikai またとない良い機会 This is *a now-or-never chance* (*a chance of a lifetime*) to travel around the world.

zekkō no kikai o nogasu 絶好の機会をのがす General McClellan *let a golden opportunity slip through his fingers*, and Lee's army escaped.

jiki 時機 chance; occasion

~ga kureba ~がくれば When the right time comes…

~o issuru ~を逸する miss the chance; let the opportunity slip by

ki ni jōjiru 機に乗じる She *took advantage of* (*made the best of the opportunity of*) her husband's trip to New York to buy some new clothes.

~wa jukushite iru ~は熟している Johnson felt that the *time was ripe* for peace negotiations.

kiki 危機 crisis; crucial time

kiun ga takamaru 機運が高まる With the Olympics approaching, *interest is rising in* (*the time is ripe for*) sports programs in the schools.

kōki 好機 favorable chance; good opportunity

machi ni matta kōki 待ちに待った好機 a long awaited opportunity

senzai ichigū no (mare na) kōki 千載一遇の(まれな)好機 a chance in a thousand

koroai ころあい suitable time; opportune moment

ori 折り chance; occasion

setogiwa 瀬戸ぎわ critical moment; threshold [of]

shiodoki 潮時 good chance; favorable opportunity

~o hazusu ~をはずす If you wait too long, you will *miss the opportunity.*

~o matsu ~を待つ wait for a good chance

~o mite…suru ~を見て…する If you *strike while the iron is hot* (*look for an opportune moment*), you might be able to make a fortune.

ですから、私たちは、機会のあるたびに、すべての人に対して、特に信仰の家族の人たちに善を行ないましょう. (ガラテヤ 6 10)

110 KIKEN 危険 DANGER

abunai あぶない risky; dangerous

inochi ga abunai 命があぶない one's life is in peril

abunagaru あぶながる be afraid; be apprehensive of

abunage (da) あぶなげ(だ) perilous; dangerous

inochigake (da) 命がけ(だ) perilous; for dear life

inochi karagara nigeru 命からがら逃げる At the burst of machine-gun fire, the troops *fled for their lives* (*barely escaped alive*).

karōjite ikiru かろうじて生きる The miners trapped in the cave *barely managed to keep alive* on the meager rations.

KIKEN 危険 danger

~ga semaru ~が迫る danger is imminent

~ga tomonau ~が伴う Flying in space ships is *fraught with danger* (*attended by many risks*).

~kiwamari nai ~窮まりない The

lost hikers were in an *extremely dangerous* situation.
~ ni ochiiru ~ に陥る fall into danger
~ ni sarasareru ~にさらされる be exposed to danger; be put in a dangerous position
~ o okashite ~ を冒して at the risk of; run the risk of; take the risk
~ o sakeru ~ を避ける avoid danger
~ shingō ~ 信号 danger signal
ayauku suru 危うくする endanger; jeopardize
   Kunshi ayauki ni chikayorazu[P] 君子危うきに近寄らず The wise man avoids danger.
bōken 冒険 an adventure; a risky attempt
~ ni noridasu ~に乗り出す The young Norwegian men *started out on a great adventure*, attempting to cross the Pacific on a raft.
kigai 危害 injury; harm
~ o kuwaeru ~ を加える injure; harm
kikenbutsu 危険物 dangerous articles
kikensei 危険性 dangers
kiki 危機 crisis
~ ga semaru ~ が迫る As the Cuban *crisis approached*, many people were in fear of war.
~ ippatsu (da) ~ 一髪だ The car swerved away from the truck *just in time.* What a *close shave*!
~ ni chokumen suru ~ に直面する confront danger; face the crisis
~ ni osowareru ~ に襲われる be caught in a crisis
~ ni sonaeru ~ に備える prepare for a crisis; provide against emergencies
~ o dassuru ~ を脱する " Now that America has *passed through the crisis* of losing her President, she must go onward," said President Johnson.

~ o kirinukeru ~ を切り抜ける get past the danger
kinan [L] 危難 peril; hazard
kitoku (da) 危篤(だ) be dangerously ill; be in a critical (serious) condition.
Koketsu ni irazumba koji o ezu [P] 虎穴に入らずんば虎児を得ず Nothing ventured, nothing gained [P].
kyū o tsugeru 急を告げる When the enemy troops came over the border, we were *on the brink of a crisis.*
kyūshi ni isshō o eru 九死に一生を得る He *escaped by the skin of his teeth* (*just got out alive; had a close call*) when the bomb exploded.
Mekura hebi ni ojizu [P] 盲へびにおじず Fools rush in where angels fear to tread [P].
seppa tsumaru せっぱ詰まる be driven into a corner; be in a fix
shisen o koeru 死線を越える He was gravely ill a few months ago but somehow managed to *survive the crisis* (*get through the crisis*).
たといわたしは死の陰の谷を歩むとも，わざわいを恐れません．あなたがわたしと共におられるからです．あなたのむちと，あなたのつえはわたしを慰めます．(詩篇 23 ⁴)

111 KIMOCHI 気持ち
MOOD, FRAME OF MIND

chōshi ni noru 調子に乗る He *got carried away* with his own jokes and kept telling them one after another.
jōcho 情緒 emotion; feeling
kanji 感じ feelings; sense
   yokan ga aru 予感がある Lincoln *felt it in his bones* that he might never return to Illinois.
KANSHAKU かんしゃく temper
   ~ o okosu ~を起こす lose one's temper; get mad [at]
   kanshakumochi かんしゃく持ち person with a short temper; hot-tempered

person; quick-tempered person

KAO o kumoraseru 顔を曇らせる look gloomy; look downcast; frown

kaoiro 顔色 countenance; expression

~ **o ukagau (yomu)** ~ をうかがう(読む) ascertain a person's mood; fathom one's thoughts

KIGEN ga warui きげんが悪い Yesterday the boss seemed to be *out of sorts* (*in ill humor*).

~ **o toru** ~ を取る humor; flatter; try to please

~ **o waruku suru** ~ を悪くする put one in a bad mood; displease

~ **yoku** ~ よく cheerfully; in good humor

ippai kigen de いっぱいきげんで He seemed to *be drunk* (*be high*) at the party.

fukigen (da) ふきげん(だ) displeasure; sullenness; bad humor

~ **ni naru** ~ になる become displeased

gokigen ikaga desu ka ごきげんいかがですか How are you?

~ **naname (da)** ~ 斜め(だ) ill humor; be in bad humor

~ **yō** ~ よう! So long! Take care of yourself!

KIMOCHI 気持ち mood; frame of mind

~ **ga ii** ~ がいい *It feels good* to breathe this fresh mountain air.

~ **ga warui** ~ が悪い It *made me sick* to see all those snakes.

~ **yoku** ~ 良く cheerfully

~ **ii kimochi ni naru** ~ いい気持ちになる Every time I hear that song, I *get in a good mood*.

kurai kimochi ni naru 暗い気持ちになる a gloomy feeling comes over one; get down in the dumps

suru kimochi ga nai する気持ちがない I asked him if he wanted to go hiking, but he said *he didn't feel like doing it* (*he felt disinclined to do it*).

ki 気 spirit; mind; soul; feeling

~ **ga au** ~ が合う I *get along with* him very well. We *hit it off* right from the beginning.

~ **ga kawariyasui** ~ が変わりやすい be fickle; be changeable

~ **ga kusaru** ~ が腐る Seeing that sad play made me *feel blue* (*feel depressed; feel downcast*).

~ **ga mukanai** ~ が向かない I suggested going skiing but he *felt disinclined* (*was not in the mood*) to go.

[...**to iu**] ~ **ga okoru (suru)** [...という] ~ が起こる(する) feel inclined to; feel like doing something

~ **ga omoi** ~ が重い I *am reluctant to go* (*have no peace about going*) with you to that wild party.

~ **ga susumanai** ~ が進まない feel disinclined to; do not feel like [doing]

~ **ga susumu** ~ が進む feel inclined to; feel like [doing]

~ **ni naru (kakaru)** ~ になる(かかる) It *weighed on my mind* (*bothered me*) that you didn't come home on time.

~ **o kaeru** ~ を変える change one's mind

~ **o kujiku** ~ をくじく crush one's feelings; dampen one's spirits; be a wet blanket

~ **o yoku (waruku) suru** ~ を良く(悪く)する (be) pleased; (be) in a good humor (offend one)

ii ki ni naru いい気になる Every time he gets a little money in his pocket, he *gets carried away* (*gets a swelled head*).

suru ki ni naru する気になる At first I was reluctant, but gradually *brought myself around to doing it* (*began to feel like doing it*).

kiai ga komoru 気合いがこもる It was a very *spirited* Rugby match.

kibun 気分 humor; mood

~ **o kowasu** ~をこわす hurt one's feelings

kidate 気だて temper; nature

~ **no yasashii** ~の優しい tender-hearted; kind-hearted

~ **no yoi** ~の良い good natured

kimagure (da) 気まぐれ(だ) caprice

kimazui 気まずい disagreeable

kimijika (da) 気短(だ) short-tempered; touchy; quick-tempered; hot-tempered

kishō ga awanai 気性が合わない I don't think they should get married; their *natures clash.*

kiyasuku 気安く freely; light-heartedly

kokoromochi 心持ち mood; frame of mind

muraki むら気 temperamental; moody

shiki 士気 morale

kokochi ここち feeling; sensation

[...**yō na**] ~ **ga suru** [...ような]~がする When I heard the astronaut's report from the space capsule, I *felt as if I were* right up there with him.

mushi no idokoro ga warui 虫の居所が悪い It seems he *got up on the wrong side of the bed* this morning.

⇨ **89, 121, 218**

あなたの荷を主にゆだねよ. 主はあなたをささえられる. 主は正しい人の動かされるのを決してゆるされない.

（詩篇 55 ²²）

112 KINSEN 金銭 MONEY

akaji ni naru 赤字になる The business *went into the red* and failed.

~ **o umeru** ~を埋める Let us *make up the deficit* by economizing in all departments.

anaume o suru 穴埋めをする Trying to *make up a deficit* will be difficult if we try to expand at the same time.

ashi ga deru 足が出る Be careful this month that you don't *go over the budget.*

Chiri mo tsumoreba yama to naru [P] ちりも積もれば山となる Great oaks from little acorns grow [P].

chōjiri o awaseru 帳じりを合わせる He *balanced the accounts* by dipping into his own pocket.

HARAI (u) 払い(払う) payment (pay; make payment)

genkin de harau 現金で払う pay cash; pay in cash

geppu de harau 月賦で払う pay in monthly installments

bunkatsubarai 分割払い paying by installments

shiharai (u) 支払い(支払う) payment (pay; disburse)

tsukibarai 月払い monthly installments

hesokuri [c] へそ繰り The mother gave up even her *nest egg* (*pin money; secret savings*) to help her son through college.

ichimon nashi de 一文なしで I came home *penniless* (*without a cent to my name*).

ikura desu ka いくらですか How much is [it]? How much does [it] cost?

jibara o kiru 自腹を切る He met the expenses by *dipping into his own pocket.*

KAHEI 貨幣 currency

~ **o chūzō suru** ~を鋳造する mint

~ **seido (tan'i)** ~制度(単位) monetary system (monetary unit)

kōka 硬貨 metallic currency; hard money

shihei 紙幣 paper money

teika 定価 fixed price; marked price; list price

tsūka 通貨 currency

keihi 経費 expenses; cost

hiyō 費用 expenses; cost

KEISAN (suru) 計算(する) computation; calculation (compute; calculate)

~ ni ireru ~に入れる In your estimate *take into consideration* the recent price increase.

yosan 予算 budget; estimate
    ~ o tateru ~を立てる make an estimate; form a budget

KEIZAI 経済 economics
    ~ ni naru ~になる be economical

keizaiteki (da) 経済的(だ) economical

kifu (suru) 寄付(する) donation (donate)

KINSEN 金銭 money
    ~ mondai ~問題 money matter; financial problem

Kinsen wa oyako mo tanin [P] 金銭は親子も他人 In money matters even father and son are strangers.

Akusen mi ni tsukažu [P] 悪銭身につかず Ill gotten, ill spent. Easy come, easy go.

arigane 有り金 cash; all the money you have with you

bokin (suru) 募金(する) fund raising (raise funds)

chochiku (suru) 貯蓄(する) savings (deposit; save)

chokin (suru) 貯金(する) savings; deposit (save money; deposit money)

gankin 元金 principal

genkin 現金 cash

hashitagane はした金 small change; pocket money

kane (okane) 金(お金) money
    ~ areba, baka mo danna [P] ~あればばかもだんな Money makes the man.
    ~ ga dekiru ~ができる money is raised
    ~ ni me ga kuramu ~に目がくらむ be blinded by money; be dazzled by money
    ~ ni me no nai ~に目のない He's a good worker, but he *has a weakness for money.*
    ~ ni mono o iwaseru ~に物をいわせ

る make money talk
    ~ ni suru ~にする liquidate; change into money
    ~ o dasu ~を出す pay; invest money [in]; finance a project; lend money
    ~ o koshiraeru ~をこしらえる raise money; make money
    ~ o toru ~を取る charge for

Kane wa tenka no mawarimono [P] 金は天下のまわりもの You lost money this time, but don't worry —*your time will come.*

komakai kane 細かい金 small change

muda na kane o tsukau むだな金を使う pour money down the drain

nakenashi no kane なけなしの金 The poor widow gave *what little money she had* to aid the victims.

kanekashi 金貸し creditor; loaner

kanemawari ga yoi (warui) 金回りが良い(悪い) Business is good. Business is moving. (Times are tough).

kanezuku de [C] 金ずくで The politician tried to *buy his way* but was unsuccessful.

kenkin (suru) 献金(する) offering (make an offering)

kingaku ga kasamu 金額がかさむ run into a large sum of money

kinko 金庫 safe; vault; cash box

kinyū 金融 monetary; financial

kogane 小金 small sum of money
    ~ o tameru ~をためる save little by little

kozeni 小銭 small change

shakkin (suru) 借金(する) debt; loan (go into debt; borrow money [from])
    ~ o tsukuru ~を作る go into debt

shikin 資金 funds; fund

sokkin 即金 spot cash; ready money

sutegane 捨て金 forfeited funds; wasted money

taikin 大金 large amount of money

zeni 銭 money; dough

Koronde mo tada wa okinai [P] こ
ろんでもただは起きない After the fire, he
put on a fire sale. He *turns everything
into profit* (*turns everything to good
account*).
kozukai こづかい pocket money; spending
money
kuzusu くずす Would you please *change*
this 1,000 yen bill for me?
MŌKERU もうける make money
  kanemōke 金もうけ money making
    ~ shugi 主義 money-first principle
muryō (da) 無料(だ) free of charge
nisoku sammon de uru 二束三文で売る
  I finally had to *sell* the car *for a song*
  (*sell* the car *dirt cheap*).
RIEKI 利益 profit; gain; return
  kōrigashi 高利貸し usurer; loan shark
  rijun 利潤 profit margin
  rishi 利子 interest
saikaku (suru) 才覚(する) fund raising
  (raising money)
SHIHON 資本 capital
  shisan 資産 property
    ~ o nokosu ~ を残す leave an estate
  tōshi (suru) 投資(する) investment
    (invest [in]; put money into)
shotoku 所得 income; earnings
son 損 loss
  ~ o suru ~ をする lose money
takai (yasui) 高い(安い) expensive; high
  (cheap)
te ga dasenai 手が出せない I like it, but I
  can't put out that much for it.
toku 得 profit; gain
tomi 富 wealth; riches
  ~ o nokosu ~ を残す leave an inheri-
    tance; leave a fortune
  ~ o tsukuru ~ を作る make a fortune;
    accumulate wealth
torihiki (suru) 取引(する) trade; transac-
  tion; deal (trade with; transact; deal
  with; do business with)
zaisei (jō) 財政(上) pecuniary; financial

  ~ o azukaru ~ をあずかる be entrusted
    with property
  ~ konnan ~ 困難 financial straits;
    financial difficulties
金銭を愛することが，あらゆる悪の根だからです．ある人
たちは，金を追い求めたために，信仰から迷い出て，非
常な苦痛をもって自分を刺し通しました．
(テモテ I 6 ¹⁰)

113 KIOKU 記憶
MEMORY,
REMEMBRANCE

ANKI (suru) 暗記(する) memorizing
  (memorize)
  anshō (suru) 暗唱(する) memorization
    (learn [it] by heart; recite [it] from
    memory)
  bōanki suru 棒暗記する memorize [it]
    verbatim
atama ni oku 頭に置く keep in mind
  ~ ni fukunde oku ~ に含んで置く I'm
    asking you to *keep in mind* (*keep in
    sight*) our real objectives.
KAIKO suru 回顧する reminisce; look
  back upon; look in retrospect
  kaikoroku 回顧録 memories; reminis-
    cences
  kaisō (suru) 回想(する) reflection
    (recollect; reflect; reminisce)
katami 形見 keepsake
KIOKU 記憶 memory; remembrance
  ~ ga yoi ~ が良い have a good memo-
    ry; have good retentive powers
  ~ ni atarashii ~ に新しい I saw the
    accident just the other day, and
    it *is still fresh in my mind*.
  ~ o tadoru ~ をたどる carry one's
    thoughts back; trace back in one's
    memory
  ~ o yobiokosu ~ を呼び起こす recall;
    summon to mind
  kasuka ni kioku shite iru かすかに記

憶している I *have a vague recollection of* the accident.

namanamashii kioku なまなましい記憶 fresh memory [of]

kinen (suru) 記念する commemoration (commemorate; honor)

  eikyū ni kinen suru 永久に記念する be an everlasting memorial [to]

  naki hito no kinen ni なき人の記念に in memory of

kinenbi 記念日 memorial day

kinenhi 記念碑 monument

kinenhin 記念品 souvenir

kiokuryoku 記憶力 memory; retentive power

  ~ ga gentai suru ~ が減退する become forgetful

kiroku 記録 record

  ~ yaburi (da) ~ 破り(だ) record-breaking

kokoro ni tomeru 心に留める I want you to *be mindful* of what he said.

monogokoro tsuita toki kara 物心ついた時から Ever *since* Abe *could remember*, the Bible had been read in his home.

mukashi o shinobu 昔をしのぶ be nostalgic over the past; reminisce

mune ni kizamu 胸に刻む engrave upon one's heart; indelibly stamp upon one's mind

[...no] nagori o todomeru [...の] 名ごりをとどめる Faint traces of the old Tōkaidō route *are still observable*.

OBOE (ru) 覚え(覚える) recollection; memory (learn; bear in mind)

  ~ ga nai ~ がない *I don't remember* seeing that book before.

monooboe 物覚え memory

  ~ ga ii ~ がいい have a good memory

urooboe うろ覚え vague remembrance

OMOIDE 思い出 remembrance; recollection

  ~ ni fukeru ~ にふける indulge in reminiscing

isshō no omoide 一生の思い出 One of the *outstanding recollections of my life* is the time I met the President in person.

omoidasu 思い出す remember; recall

  [...o] omoidashite [...を] 思い出して *Remembering that* I had an appointment at 3:00 P.M., I quickly left the office.

omoidebanashi o suru 思い出話をする We spent the evening *going over old times (reminiscing)*.

omoiokosu 思い起こす call to mind; put one in mind of

omokage 面影 vestiges; remains; traces

rensō (suru) 連想(する) association of ideas (make an association of ideas)

  tsuisō (suru) 追想(する) recollection; retrospect; reminiscence (recollect)

sō iwareru to そう言われると *Come to think of it* I did promise to help.

UKABU 浮かぶ come to one's mind

  ariari to mune ni ukabu ありありと胸に浮かぶ The incidents surrounding the death of Kennedy *are still vividly impressed on our minds*.

  mabuta ni ukabu まぶたに浮かぶ The pathetic sights I saw in the war *come before my eyes* continually.

  mazamaza to ukande kuru まざまざと浮かんでくる come vividly to mind

  me ni ukabu 目に浮かぶ come before one's eyes

wasureru koto ga dekinai 忘れることができない will always remember; will never forget

⇨ **144**

女がその乳のみ子を忘れて，その腹の子をあわれまないようなことがあろうか。たとい彼らが忘れるようなことがあっても，わたしは，あなたを忘れることはない。
（イザヤ 49 15）

114 KISOKU 規則
REGULATION

chōsei (suru) 調整 (する) regulation; adjustment (adjust)

HŌRITSU 法律 law

~ ni fureru ~ に触れる become a legal matter

~ no tekiyō ~ の適用 application of law

~ no ura o yuku ~ の裏を行く That clever criminal knows how to *outwit the law*.

~ o mamoru ~ を守る abide by the law; keep the law; observe the law

~ o okasu ~ を犯す break the law; flout the law

fubunritsu 不文律 unwritten code

hō ni fukusuru 法に服する Democracy will not work unless each citizen *obeys the law*.

~ ni hansuru ~ に反する be against the law

~ ni kanatta ~ にかなった lawful; legal

hōki 法規 legislation; laws and regulations; code

hōrei 法令 law; statutes

hōritsujō no tetsuzuki 法律上の手続き legal procedures

hōritsuka suru 法律化する pass a law

hōtei de arasou 法廷で争う bring suit against

~ ni tatsu ~ に立つ be called into court; be tried

kempō 憲法 constitution

rippō 律法 law; the Ten Commandments; Biblical law

imashime (ru) 戒め(戒める) commandment; admonition; warning; (admonish; warn)

jōrei 条令 ordinance

kanrei 慣例 code; custom; precedent

kanshū 慣習 convention; usage

KISOKU 規則 regulation

~ de shibarareru ~ で縛られる The trouble with working here is that *you are tied down by* so many *rules*.

~ ihan desu ~ 違反です [It's] against the rules.

~ ni uttaeru ~ に訴える appeal to law

~ ni yotte bassuru ~ によって罰する He was convicted and *punished according to law*.

~ o mamoru ~ を守る observe the regulations; keep the rules

~ o mōkeru ~ を設ける lay down rules

~ tadashii ~ 正しい be regular

~ o yaburu ~ を破る flout the rules

genjū na kisoku 厳重な規則 strict rules

reigai no nai kisoku wa nai 例外のない規則はない Every rule has its exceptions.

gensoku 原則 guiding principle; general rule

~ toshite ~ として as a rule

kikakuhin 規格品 standardized goods

kiritsu 規律 discipline; order; regulations

kisokuteki (da) 規則的(だ) regular; orderly; systematic

kisokuzukume (da) 規則ずくめ(だ) be loaded with rules; be full of regulations

kitei 規定 regulation

[...ni] ~ sarete iru [...に] ~ されている Protection of land tenants *is provided for* in the law.

~ o haishi suru ~ を廃止する abolish the rules

~ o jisshi suru ~ を実施する carry out the regulations

saisoku 細則 bylaws; detailed regulations

seiki (da) 正規(だ) proper; legal; regular

~ no rūto ~ のルート legal channels

tessoku 鉄則 ironclad rule

okite おきて law

sadame (ru) 定め(定める) rule; regulation (fix; decide)

kyōtei (suru) 協定(する) agreement; arrangement (arrange)

seigen (suru) 制限(する) restriction (restrict)

~ o kuwaeru ~ を加える The government has *imposed restrictions* on travel.

seirei 政令 government order

YAKUSOKU (suru) 約束する promise; agreement; compact (promise)

~ o mamoru ~ を守る keep one's promise

~ o yaburu ~ を破る break one's word

jōyaku 条約 treaty

kiyaku 規約 rules; pact

kyōyaku (suru) 協約(する) mutual agreement (make a mutual agreement)

見よ、わたしは、きょう、命とさいわい、および死と災をあなたの前に置いた。すなわちわたしは、きょう、あなたにあなたの神、主を愛し、その道に歩み、その戒めと定めと、おきてとを守ることを命じる。それに従うならば、あなたは生きながらえる。(申命記 30 ¹⁵, ¹⁶)

115 KIYOSA 清さ PURITY

bōtoku suru 冒とくする profane; desecrate; blaspheme

hinkō hōsei na hito 品行方正な人 man of moral purity

issō suru 一掃する purge [evil, etc.]

jōka (suru) 浄化(する) cleansing (cleanse; deterge; purify)

seijō (da) 清浄(だ) purity (pure)

~ muku (no) ~ 無くの pure and undefiled

JUNKETSU (da) 純潔だ purity; chastity; innocence (pure; chaste; innocent)

~ o kegasu ~ を汚す sully the purity of; violate the purity of

~ o mamoru ~ を守る keep one's body pure

KEGARE (ru) 汚れ(汚れる) impurity; defilement; stain; spot (become impure; be defiled; become stained)

~ no nai ~ のない spotless; clean

kegareta kokoro 汚れた心 impure heart

kegasu 汚す defile; desecrate

KIYOSA 清さ purity

araikiyomeru 洗い清める purify by washing

kiyoi 清い clean; pure

~ shōgai ~ 生がい sanctified life

kiyome (ru) 清め(清める) purification (cleanse; purify)

kokoro o kiyomeru 心を清める purify one's heart

mi o kiyomeru 身を清める purify oneself

tsumi o kiyomeru 罪を清める cleanse from sin

kiyoraka (da) 清らか(だ) purity (clean; pure)

seijun (da) 清純(だ) purity (pure)

seiketsu (da) 清潔(だ) cleanliness (clean)

SEIBETSU (suru) 聖別(する) consecration; sanctification (consecrate; set apart; sanctify)

seichi 聖地 sacred ground; holy land

seija (seijin) 聖者(聖人) sage; saint

seijo 聖所 sanctuary

seika (suru) 聖化(する) sanctification (sanctify)

seisho 聖書 the Holy Bible; the Scriptures

seito 聖徒 saint

shinsei (da) 神聖(だ) divinity (divine; holy)

~ o okasu ~ を冒す defile; profane; desecrate [something holy]

心のきよい者は幸いです。その人は神を見るからです。(マタイ 5 ⁸)

116 KOCHŌ 誇張
EXAGGERATION

gyōgyōshiku iu ぎょうぎょうしく言う exaggerate; make too much of

HORA o fuku ほらをふく There he goes *making big claims (tooting his own horn)* again.

fuichō suru 吹聴する He has been *broadcasting around* about his scholarship to college.

hora fuki [c] ほらふき boaster; braggart; liar

KADAI (da) 過大(だ) exaggerated; excessive

iisugi (ru) 言いすぎ(言いすぎる) overstatement (overstate; say too much)

kagon de wa nai 過言ではない What I am saying *is no exaggeration*.

kaikaburu 買いかぶる overestimate

kien o ageru (haku) 気炎をあげる(吐く) Don't believe all you hear; he's *talking big (laying it on thick)*.

kikoe ga ii きこえが良い The salary *sounds good* but when you figure there are no bonuses it is actually low.

KOCHŌ (suru) 誇張(する) exaggeration (exaggerate)

~ **nashi ni iu** ~なしに言う He *told* the story *without any exaggeration (told …without stretching it)*.

kochōteki (da) 誇張的(だ) bombastic; exaggerated

kodai mōsōkyō 誇大もう想狂 big talk about little things; megalomania

kuchi habattai koto o iu 口幅ったいことを言う Don't take him seriously; he's just *talking big*.

mie o kiru 見えをきる Her trouble is that she *acts pretentious (is ostentatious)*.

monomonoshii 物々しい pretentious; ostentatious; imposing

MOTTAI o tsukeru もったいをつける attach undue importance [to]; make much of

~ **rashiku iu** ~らしく言う speak with an air of importance

mottaiburu もったいぶる swagger; put on airs

ŌGESA 大げさ exaggeration; bombast

~ **ni iu** ~に言う make a tall story out of; talk big

~ **ni suru** ~にする make much of; overdo

hanashi ga ōkii 話が大きい His *talk is greatly exaggerated*.

ōburoshiki 大ぶろしき tall story; big talk

~ **o hirogeru** ~を広げる When he told you he climbed Mt. Fuji in one hour he was *talking through his hat (giving you a line)*.

shinshō bōdai (da) 針小棒大(だ) exaggeration (making a mountain out of a molehill)

taigen sōgo suru 大言壮語する brag [about]; boast [of]

shibaike ga aru 芝居気がある Whenever he tells a story, he *is rather dramatic*.

⇨ **42**

あなたがたのことばが、いつも親切で、塩味のきいたものであるようにしなさい。そうすれば、ひとりひとりに対する答え方がわかります。(コロサイ 4⁶)

117 KODOKU 孤独
LONELINESS

HITORIBOTCHI (da) ひとりぼっち(だ) solitary; alone

~ **ni naru** ~になる shut oneself off from people; be all alone

hitonatsukashii ki ga suru 人なつかしい気がする After being alone in Karuizawa for the winter, I began to *have a longing to be around people*.

hitozato hanareta 人里離れた Abe grew up in a little log cabin in the *remote* wilderness of Kentucky.

ikkenya 一軒家 solitary house

intonsha 隠とん者 hermit; recluse

KODOKU 孤独 loneliness
  ~o ajiwau ~を味わう experience loneliness
  ~o kanjiru ~を感じる feel lonely; feel the solitude
  ~o tanoshimu ~を楽しむ I *enjoy* getting away and *being alone.*
  kogun funtō (suru) 孤軍奮闘(する) holding the fort alone; fighting the battle alone
  koji (in) 孤児(院) orphan (orphanage)
  koritsu (suru) ~孤立(する) isolation (be isolated)
  ~shugi ~主義 isolationism
  tandoku (da) 単独(だ) by oneself; alone
koishiku naru 恋しくなる After being in America for six months, Jiro *became homesick* for Japan.
kokorobosoi 心細い lonely; forlorn; hopeless
miyori ga nai 身寄りがない The city had to help the old lady, for she *had no relatives* (*had no one to depend on*).
SABISHII 寂しい lonely
  sabishisa no amari 寂しさのあまり In his *unbearable loneliness* he took to drink.
  ~o koraeru ~をこらえる bear the loneliness
satogokoro ga tsuku 里心がつく After being in Tokyo for awhile, he *got homesick* and went home.
tayorinai たよりない be forlorn; be desolate
tobotobo aruku とぼとぼ歩く trudge along; walk downcast
tsure no nai 連れのない be alone; be unescorted
wabishii わびしい wretched; desolate; forlorn
主は公義を愛し、その聖徒を見捨てられないからである。正しいものはとこしえに助け守られる。しかし、悪しき者の子孫は断ち滅ぼされる。(詩篇 37 ²⁸)

118 KŌFUKU 幸福
HAPPINESS

fugū no mi 不遇の身 That crippled boy has had an *unfortunate life.*
KŌFUKU 幸福 happiness
  ~ni afureru ~にあふれる Life can be *full of happiness* if you will live by its rules.
  ~ni kurasu ~に暮らす live happily; sit pretty
  ~o kizutsukeru ~を傷つける Lincoln's assassination *spoiled the happiness* which came with the ending of the war.
  ~o tsukamu ~をつかむ gain happiness
  ~o ushinau ~を失う lose happiness; forfeit happiness
  tsuka no ma no kōfuku つかの間の幸福 fleeting happiness
  zento no kōfuku 前途の幸福 the happiness ahead; the future happiness [of]
fukō (da) 不幸(だ) unhappiness (unhappy)
  ~na me ni au ~な目に合う meet with adversity; have an unfortunate experience
  ~ni otoshiireru ~に陥れる His drinking habits finally *brought misery* upon his family.
  kō ka fukō ka 幸か不幸か for better or for worse
fukōchū no saiwai 不幸中の幸い *One good thing about* the fire *disaster* is that all of the children were saved.
fukuri 福利 welfare; well-being
fukushi 福祉 well-being; public welfare
  ~o zōshin suru ~を増進する The candidate promised to *promote public welfare* if elected.
kōun 幸運 luck; good fortune

~ **ni megumareru** ～に恵まれる be fortunate; fortune smiles upon one

sachi [L] 幸 happiness; fortune

saiwai (da) 幸い(だ) happiness; blessedness (happy; blessed)

magureatari (da) まぐれ当たり(だ) lucky shot; chance hit

me o fuku 芽をふく He had a hard time at first, but now his *luck is picking up* and the business is booming.

medetai めでたい happy; joyous

medetaku owaru めでたく終わる come to a happy ending; end well

shiawase (da) しあわせ(だ) good fortune; blessing (fortunate; blessed; blest)

~ **ni naru** ～になる become happy

un ga muku 運が向く He *hit a streak of luck* and began winning every game.

unyoku 運よく luckily; happily; fortunately

wazawai o maneku 災いを招く The Shinto priest warned the family that they were *inviting disaster* (*courting disaster*) if they failed to pray for the dead.

~ **o tenjite fuku to nasu** [P] ～を転じて福となす She became ill, but *the misfortune was turned into a blessing;* she married the doctor.

⇨ 198, 210

平和をつくる者は幸いです．その人は神の子どもと呼ばれるからです．
義のために迫害されている者は幸いです．天の御国はその人のものだからです．(マタイ 5 ⁹, ¹⁰)

119 KŌFUN 興奮
EXCITEMENT

agaru あがる When I began making that speech I *got nervous* and forgot part of it.

bimbōyusuri 貧乏ゆすり He has a *nervous mannerism.*

chi ga wakitatsu 血がわき立つ The team rushed to their positions, *tingling with*

excitement.

~ **o wakaseru** ～をわかせる He *gets worked up* whenever he goes to the ball game.

kao ni chi ga noboru 顔に血がのぼる become flustered; get all hot and bothered

dogimagi suru どぎまぎする be disconcerted

GEKISURU 激する get keyed up; be worked up

gekijō 激情 strong emotion; frenzy

gekishiyasui 激しやすい be excitable

gekkō suru 激高する get riled up; raise the roof

shigeki (suru) 刺激(する) incitement; stimulant; incentive (incite; stimulate; excite)

kao ga hoteru 顔がほてる Her *face became flushed* when she met him.

iraira suru いらいらする get irritated; become excited

kenken gōgō けんけんごうごう uproar

kishoku ga warui [L] 気色が悪い feel disgusted at; be repelled by

koe o furuwasete 声をふるわせて in a trembling voice

KŌFUN (suru) 興奮(する) excitement (get excited)

~ **ga sameru** ～がさめる commotion settles down

~ **shite** ～して The TV announcer *got excited* and made all kinds of mistakes.

~ **shiyasui** ～しやすい excitable; be easily excited

funki suru 奮起する be stirred up; get aroused

kōfunzai 興奮剤 stimulant

kokoro o hazumaseru 心をはずませる Hearing the roar of the engines *made him excited.*

~ **o ugokasu** ～を動かす alarms one; shakes one up

muchū ni natte 夢中になって He *got all excited about* (*got engrossed in*) the football game and wouldn't leave the TV set.

MUNE ga dokidoki suru 胸がどきどきする one's heart pounds; one's heart beats hard

  ~ ga odoru ~ がおどる My *heart danced for joy* when I heard the good news.

  ~ o tokimekasete ~ をときめかせて with fluttering heart

nobose (ru) のぼせ(のぼせる) infatuation (be infatuated [with]; be mad about; be crazy about)

  noboseagaru のぼせ上がる When she winked at him, it *went to his head* and he spoke incongruously.

ochitsuki ga nai 落ち着きがない be fidgety; be on edge; be nervous

rōbai suru ろうばいする become disconcerted

SAWAGI (gu) 騒ぎ(騒ぐ) clamor; uproar (raise a clamor; make a fuss about)

  ōsawagi o suru 大騒ぎをする When the faculty expelled the student, his friends *raised the roof.*

  sawagashii 騒がしい noisy; uproarious

  sawagasu 騒がす disturb; upset

sendō (suru) 扇動(する) agitation; incitement (agitate; incite; instigate; stir up)

urusai うるさい irksome; annoying; irritating

ware ni kaeru 我に帰る come to one's senses

  ~ o wasurete ~ を忘れて *Without thinking* the mother jumped in front of the train to save her child.

yakamashii やかましい disturbing; noisy; boisterous

⇨ 88, 124, 187

また、どんなことがあっても、反対者たちに驚かされることはないと。それは、彼らにとっては滅びのしるしであり、あなたがたにとっては救いのしるしです。これは神から出たことです。(ピリピ 1 ²⁸)

---

120 KŌI 行為
ACTION, BEHAVIOR

erai koto o yaru えらいことをやる Now *you've really done it;* you may get fired.

furumai (u) ふるまい(ふるまう) behavior; conduct; deportment (behave; conduct oneself)

honsō suru 奔走する busy oneself; go in all directions at once

KATSUDŌ (suru) 活動(する) activity; action (act)

  dōsa 動作 action; movement

  katsuyaku suru 活躍する be active in

  tahomen ni watatte katsuyaku suru 多方面にわたって活躍する That brilliant engineer *is active in various fields.*

KŌI 行為 action; behavior

  hanzai kōi 犯罪行為 criminal act

  kitoku na kōi 奇特な行為 commendable action

  genkō tomo ni 言行共に in word and deed

  ~ fuitchi (da) ~ 不一致(だ) You can't trust him; he *says one thing and does another.*

  gukō [L] 愚行 foolish action; folly

  gyōjō 行状 behavior; conduct

  misageta gyōjō 見下げた行状 ignoble act

  hikō 非行 delinquency

  hinkō 品行 behavior; conduct; deportment

  jikkō ni utsusu 実行に移す We must *translate* our ideals *into action.*

  kōdō (suru) 行動(する) action; behavior (act; behave)

  ~ ni arawasu ~ に表わす He *demonstrated by his actions* that he was aspiring for a higher position.

  ~ no jiyū o yurusu ~ の自由を許す Under communism the government does not *allow freedom of action.*

~**o okosu** ~を起こす move one to action

[...**to**] ~ **o tomo ni suru** [...と] ~を共にする act together; act jointly

~**o toru** ~をとる Government authorities *took action* against the insurrection.

~**o tsutsushimu** ~を慎しむ The teacher told us to *be careful about our conduct* (*mind our p's and q's*) while on the trip.

okonai (u) 行ない(行なう) deed; action (do; act; carry out)

~**o aratameru** ~を改める You'd better *change your ways* or you'll be fired.

yoi (warui) okonai o suru 良い(悪い)行ないをする do good (bad) deeds; do good (bad)

TE o kudasu 手を下す Though he didn't actually assault the victim, he did *have a hand in* the crime.

[...**ni**] ~ **o tsukeru** [...に] ~をつける begin a task

~**o utsu** ~を打つ It's about time we *took measures* to solve the traffic problem in Tokyo.

waza わざ work; act

shiwaza しわざ act; work; deed

このように, あなたがたの光を人々の前で輝かせ, 人々があなたがたの良い行ないを見て, 天におられるあなたがたの父をあがめるようにしなさい. (マタイ 5 ¹⁶)

121 KOKORO 心
HEART, MIND

hara 腹 heart

junshin (da) 純真(だ) naive; simple-minded

kimo 肝 mind; guts

KOKORO 心 heart; mind; spirit

~ **ga fureau** ~が触れ合う After working in the office together for a few months, they began to *see things the same way.*

~ **ga hikishimaru** ~が引き締まる become tense; become braced for

~ **ga midareru** ~が乱れる become upset

~ **ga kakimidasareru** ~がかき乱される be troubled in heart; be all stirred up

~ **ga kayou** ~が通う *There is mutual understanding* between them.

~ **ga semai** ~がせまい be narrow minded

~ **kara** ~から from the heart; with all one's heart

~ **ni fureru** ~に触れる touch one's heart

~ **ni kakeru** ~にかける have (something) close to one's heart

~ **ni kizamu** ~に刻む Do *lay to heart* the things he said.

~ **ni ukabu** ~に浮かぶ As I was walking through the park, your words *came back to me* (*came across my mind*).

~ **ni yoyū ga aru** ~に余裕がある He *has room in his heart* (*is broadminded enough*) to consider even his enemies.

~ **no kate** ~のかて food for the soul; food for thought

~ **no mazushii hito** ~の貧しい人 Blessed are the *poor in spirit* for theirs is the kingdom of heaven. (Matthew 5 : 3)

~ **no yoridokoro** ~のよりどころ The Bible is the *stay of his heart.*

~ **o aratameru** ~を改める have a change of heart

~ **o atatameru** ~を暖める It *warmed my heart* to see him again.

~ **o awasete** ~を合わせて You'd better *put your minds and hearts together* on this venture or you'll get nowhere.

~o hiku ~をひく The beauty of the Swiss Alps really *appeals to* (*attracts*) me.

~o hiraku ~を開く The villagers *opened their hearts* to the Peace Corpsmen.

~o itameru ~を痛める What she said *hurt* (*grieved*) me.

~o komete (tsukushite) ~を込めて (尽くして) with all one's heart

~o kudaku ~を砕く become broken-hearted; become penitential

~o kumu ~をくむ He was able to *enter into her feelings* (*sympathize with her*).

~o nayamasu ~を悩ます worry about; be anxious about

~o oni ni suru ~を鬼にする The judge wanted to be lenient but *took a stern attitude* toward the youth.

~o shizumeru ~を静める He *composed himself* before the concert by walking alone.

~o sosogu ~を注ぐ He *poured his heart into* the task of helping the crippled children.

~o ubau ~を奪う He *stole her heart* (*captivated her*) by his daring exploits.

~o ugokasu ~を動かす unsettle one; move one; stir one up

~yoku ~よく willingly; gladly

susanda kokoro すさんだ心 Pharaoh had a *hardened heart* and refused to heed Moses' warnings.

futagokoro no aru ふたごころのある A *double-minded* man is unstable in all his ways. (James 1 : 8 AV)

kokorozuyoi 心強い The *stout-hearted* men went forward into the battle.

magokoro o tsukusu 真心を尽くす devote oneself to; do one's utmost [for]

ryōshin 良心 conscience

shinjō 心情 feelings; heart; sentiment

~o sassuru ~を察する enter into the feelings of one; share the same feelings with one

konjō 根性 disposition; nature; spirit

mune 胸 heart; mind

omoi 思い thought; mind; idea

~wa kuchi ni deru [P] ~は口に出る What the heart thinks, the mouth speaks.

seishin 精神 mind; spirit

~o kitaeru ~を鍛える train oneself; discipline oneself.

⇨ **89, 111, 163**

油断することなく, あなたの心を守れ, 命の泉は, これから流れ出るからである. (箴言 4 ²³)

122 KOKUHAKU 告白 CONFESSION

doro o haku [C] どろを吐く After hours of questioning, the suspect *owned up* to everything.

honne o haku 本音を吐く We finally got her to *tell the whole truth*.

KOKUHAKU (suru) 告白(する) confession (confess)

shinkō no kokuhaku 信仰の告白 declaration of faith; statement of faith

hakujō suru 白状する acknowledge; confess

tsutsumazu hakujō suru 包まず白状する frankly confess

jihaku (suru) 自白(する) confession (make a confession; own up to)

~o shiiru ~をしいる wring out a confession [from]; force a confession [out of]

tsumi o jihaku suru 罪を自白する confess one's crime; make a confession of one's sin

jikyō (suru) 自供(する) confession (confess)

jinin (suru) 自認(する) admit; own up to
kuchi o waru [C] 口を割る They finally got him to *talk (confess)*.
minouebanashi o suru 身の上話をする tell one's life story
shōtai o arawasu 正体を現わす He *showed his true colors* when he criticized the very one he tried to curry favor with.
(nani mo kamo) tsutsumazu ni iu (何もかも)包まずに言う candidly tell everything; frankly tell all
UCHIAKERU 打ち明ける open up; make a clean breast of; take one into confidence

  ari no mama o uchiakeru ありのままを打ち明ける frankly tell all
  kokoro kara uchiakeru 心から打ち明ける He had few close friends to whom he could *lay his heart bare*.
  subete o uchiakeru すべてを打ち明ける confess all; come out with the whole story
  sujō o akasu 素性を明かす disclose one's past; reveal one's identity
  uchiakebanashi o suru 打ち明け話をする After dinner I took him aside and *had a heart to heart talk with (spoke frankly to)* him.
  uchitokeru 打ち解ける be candid [with]; open up one's heart [to]
zange suru ざんげする confess one's faults; confess one's sins
⇨ **142, 175**
もし, 私たちが自分の罪を言い表わすなら, 神は真実で正しい方ですから, その罪を赦し, すべての悪から私たちをきよめてくださいます. (ヨハネ I 1⁹)

123 KONNAN 困難
DIFFICULTY, ADVERSITY

anshō ni noriageru 暗礁に乗り上げる He started out well on his career but *ran afoul on the reefs* of life and ended up penniless.

fūha 風波 stormy times; troubles
hidoi me ni au ひどい目に会う go through a bitter experience; have a terrible time
kōgeki no yaomote ni tatsu 攻撃の矢面に立つ The chairman *stood in the breach (faced the fire)* of the opposition's attack upon his party's policy.
KONNAN 困難 difficulty; adversity

  ~ ni au ~に会う run into trouble; encounter difficulty
  ~ ni ochiiru ~に陥る fall into difficulties
  ~ ni taeru ~に堪える endure hardships
  ~ ni uchikatsu ~に打ち勝つ overcome difficulties
  ~ o kirihiraku ~を切り開く make one's way through the difficulties
  ~ o nozoku ~を除く relieve one's difficulties
  ~ o yosō suru ~を予想する anticipate trouble
  tadai no konnan o tomonau 多大の困難を伴う If you undertake that project, *you'll meet with many difficulties (it will be attended with considerable difficulties)*.
kannan かん難 hardships
  ~ nanji o tamanisu [P] ~なんじを玉にす Adversity makes the man wise.
  ~ shinku ~辛苦 trials and difficulties
komaru 困る be in difficulty; be troubled
  ikkō ni komaranai 一向に困らない You *will have no problem at all* going through customs.
konku 困苦 hardships
kunan 苦難 adversity
  ~ ni taeru ~に堪える stand up under trial; endure trials
  ~ o tōru ~をとおる go through trials
nandai 難題 difficult problem
  ~ o hikiokosu ~を引き起こす raise a

difficult problem; cause a serious problem

nangi 難儀 trouble

nangyō kugyō 難行苦行 austerities; penance

nanji 〔L〕 難事 difficult thing

nankyoku 難局 difficult situation

~ **ni ataru** ~ に当たる deal with a difficult situation

nanten 難点 difficult point

KURUSHII 苦しい painful; hard; afflicting

~ **tachiba ni okareru** ~ 立場に置かれる be put in a plight; be put in a hard position

(nan no) ku mo naku (なんの)苦もなく He finished the job *without any difficulty.*

kukyō 苦境 straits; straitened circumstances

~ **ni chokumen suru** ~ に直面する face a difficult situation; meet a difficult challenge

~ **ni ochiiru** ~ に陥る be thrust into dire straits; be driven to the wall

~ **ni tachimukau** ~ に立ち向かう face the difficulties

~ **ni tatsu** ~ に立つ be in difficulty

kushin 苦心 pains; labor

kutō (suru) 苦闘(する) bitter struggle (fight against odds)

akusen kutō suru 悪戦苦闘する Upon becoming president, Lincoln found himself *fighting against odds* (*fighting a losing battle*) to keep the Union intact.

kyūchi ni ochiiru 窮地に陥る get into a fix; be up a tree

Kyūsureba tsūzu 〔P〕 窮すれば通ず Don't worry about it; *there's always a way out.*

te ni amaru hito 手に余る人 He's *a hard person to manage.*

toriatsukainikui hito 取り扱いにくい人 person hard to handle

TSURAI つらい hard; trying; painful

~ **me ni au** ~ 目に会う We *had a hard time of it* because we ran out of water halfway through the desert.

shinku (suru) 〔L〕 辛苦(する) hardships; trials; toil (suffer trials; suffer hardships)

⇨ 185

ですから, 私たちは勇気を失いません. たとい私たちの外なる人は衰えても, 内なる人は日々新たにされています. 今の時の軽い患難は, 私たちのうちに働いて, 測り知れない, 重い永遠の栄光をもたらすからです. (コリント II 4 16, 17)

124 KONRAN 混乱
CONFUSION, CHAOS

abekobe (da) あべこべ(だ) topsy-turvy

awateru あわてる be flustered; be in a hurry

barabara ni naru ばらばらになる The troops *were scattered in all directions* by a hail of bullets.

fukuzatsu (da) 複雑(だ) complicated; involved

gochagocha ni suru ごちゃごちゃにする mix up; ball up

harahara suru はらはらする be on edge; be nervous

hommatsu o tentō suru 本末を転倒する Choosing your dormitory before passing your entrance exams is *putting the cart before the horse.*

kachiau かち合う The date of the opera *conflicts* with the baseball game; we'll have to change it.

keisotsu (da) 軽率(だ) rashness (rash; headlong)

ki ga chiru 気が散る Just as he was about to speak, an airplane zoomed overhead and our *attention was distracted.*

~ **ga tentō suru** ~ が転倒する Getting

all those directions at once *made my head swim.*

kizewashii 気ぜわしい fidgety; restless

KONRAN (suru) 混乱 (する) confusion (be confused)

~ **ni jōjite** ~ に乗じて *In the confusion of* the earthquake, the prisoner fled.

~ **ni konran o kasaneru** ~ に混乱を重ねる throw into utter chaos

~ **ni makikomareru** ~ に巻き込まれる get involved in the confusion

~ **ni ochiiru** ~ に陥る fall into confusion; become turbulent; get out of hand

~ **o hikiokosu** ~ を引き起こす raise a row; make a fuss; throw into confusion

irimidareru 入り乱れる be jumbled together; get all mixed up

kondō 混同 confusion; disorder

konsen 混戦 free-for-all fight

konsen (suru) 混線 (する) We *have a poor connection,* operator, can you give us a better one?

konton toshite 混とんとして After the coup, things were *in a chaotic state.*

konzatsu (suru) 混雑 (する) confusion; disorder; jam (become confused; be jammed [with people, cars, etc.])

mazeru 混ぜる be mixed

midareru 乱れる fall into disorder; be disturbed

chitsujo ga midareru 秩序が乱れる Because the captain neglected his duties, the ship's company *became disorderly.*

midasu 乱す throw into confusion; agitate

chian o midasu 治安を乱す cause a public disturbance; break the public peace

kokoro o midasu 心を乱す rattle one; ruffle one

ranzatsu 乱雑 disorder

sakuran (suru) 錯乱 (する) derangement; distraction (be deranged; be distracted)

torimidasu 取り乱す Hearing the noise, he *became confused (got distracted)* and forgot what he was supposed to say.

koshi ga ochitsukanai 腰が落ち着かない Until that telegram comes, I *cannot sit still (don't know whether I'm coming or going).*

magotsuku まごつく wander around; get confused; be at a loss

mechakucha (da) [C] めちゃくちゃ (だ) incoherent; confusing

menkurau めんくらう be flustered; be confounded; be in a hurry

muchakucha (da) [C] むちゃくちゃ (だ) mess; muddle (mixed up; fouled up)

muchitsujo (da) [C] 無秩序 (だ) chaos

ododo suru おどおどする be in fear and trembling

rōbai (suru) ろうばい (する) consternation (be thrown into consternation)

sakusō (suru) [L] 錯そう (する) complication; tangle (be complicated; be tangled)

SAWAGI (gu) 騒ぎ (騒ぐ) uproar; fuss; hubbub (make a fuss; clamor)

hachi no su o tsutsuita yōna sawagi はちの巣をつついたようなさわぎ They *stirred up a hornets' nest* when they investigated the financial structure of that firm.

ranchiki sawagi らんちきさわぎ The students went on a *spree* that night.

ōsawagi o suru 大騒ぎをする make a scene; raise the roof

ue o shita e no ōsawagi 上を下への大騒ぎ Dallas *was turned upside down* by the Kennedy incident.

sawagashisa 騒がしさ turmoil

kono yo no sawagashisa この世の

騒がしさ turmoil of life; the rat race of life

sawagasu 騒がす disturb; trouble

sōdō 騒動 commotion; uprising; riot

~ **ga okoru** ~ が起こる riot breaks out

sōran 騒乱 disturbance; commotion

sendō (suru) 扇動(する) incitement (incite; stir up)

shidoro modoro ni naru しどろもどろにな る When asked about his past, he *was thrown into confusion (faltered)* and gave a vague answer.

shirimetsuretsu (da) 支離滅裂(だ) incoherent; disarrayed

tentekomai suru [c] てんてこまいする He *is in a whirl of business (is in a rat race)* and takes no time out for his family.

tenya wanya (da) [c] てんやわんや(だ) It was *a madhouse* at the office while we were trying to meet the deadline.

torichigaeru 取り違える confuse; mistake

tōwaku suru 当惑する be perplexed

uōsaō suru 右往左往する When the shot was fired, the men *ran in all directions at once (ran about in confusion)*.

uwatsuku うわつく be restless; be at sea

⇨ 119, 187

偶像を造る者は皆恥を負い、はずかしめを受け、ともに、 あわてふためいて退く。(イザヤ 45 ¹⁶)

125 KORASHIME 懲らしめ PUNISHMENT

aijō no muchi 愛情のむち The boy resented it, but his father's action was *punishment out of love.*

KEIBATSU 刑罰 penalty; punishment

~ **o ukeru** ~ を受ける be punished

[...**ni] sōtō suru keibatsu** [...に]相当 する刑罰 punishment which meets the offense

bachi ga ataru ばちが当たる It *served him right.*

bakkin 罰金 fine

~ **o kasuru** ~ を科する punish by fine; fine one

bassuru 罰する punish

omoku bassuru 重く罰する punish severely

batsu 罰 punishment

genbatsu ni shosuru 厳罰に処する punish severely

kei 刑 penalty; sentence

~ **ga karuku sumu** ~ が軽く済む I thought I would catch it from the judge, but I *got off lightly.*

~ **o nogareru** ~ をのがれる escape punishment; beat the rap

~ **o ukeru** ~ を受ける be punished; suffer punishment

keimusho ni ireru 刑務所に入れる imprison; lock one up; throw one into prison

shikei 死刑 capital punishment; death penalty

~ **ni shosuru** ~ に処する put one to death; execute

~ **o senkoku suru** ~ を宣告する hand down a death sentence; sentence to death

shobatsu (suru) 処罰(する) punishment; penalty (inflict punishment)

taikei 体刑 physical punishment

tenbatsu ga kudaru 天罰が下る He *received just retribution* for his evil deed.

kogoto o kuu 小言をくう He *caught it (was bawled out)* for coming home late.

kōman no hana o oru 高慢の鼻を折る Someone should *take* that braggart *down a peg or two.*

korigori shite iru こりごりしている I've *learned the hard way* about going into debt.

KORASHIME (ru) 懲らしめ(懲らしめる) punishment (punish; discipline)

~ **o ukeru** ~ を受ける be chastened; be punished

chōbatsu 懲罰 discipline
 ~ **shobun ni suru** ~ 処分にする The school authorities *took disciplinary action* against the unruly students.
korasu 懲らす chasten
 aku o korasu 悪を懲らす punish evil
kōchisho ni ireru 拘置所に入れる be thrown into jail
me ni monomiseru 目に物見せる When that boy comes home, I'll *show him a thing or two!*
miseshime 見せしめ warning; example; object lesson
 ~ **ni naru** ~ になる serve as a warning [to]; become an object lesson
omedama o kuu お目玉をくう I *got into hot water (really caught it)* for going without permission.
sekkan (suru) 折かん(する) thrashing; correction (thrash; spank; whip)
shikaru しかる scold; bawl out
tashinameru たしなめる take one to task; reprove one
totchimeru[C] とっちめる The boss *let him have it* for his big bungle at the office.
tsurushiage (ru) つるし上げ(つるし上げる) kangaroo court (victimize)
yaridama ni ageru やり玉にあげる The morning papers *victimized* the police chief for the riots.
⇨ **129, 178**
しかし彼はわれわれのとがのために傷つけられ、われわれの不義のために砕かれたのだ。彼はみずから懲らしめをうけて、われわれに平安を与え、その打たれた傷によって、われわれはいやされたのだ。(イザヤ 53 ⁵)

126 KOTO 事
MATTER, OCCURRENCE

BAAI 場合 case; circumstances; occasion
 ~ **ni yotte wa** ~ によっては depending on the circumstances
 donna baai demo どんな場合でも in any event; rain or shine; no matter what

man'ichi no baai 万一の場合 just in case; if worse comes to worst
sono baai その場合 in that case; in the event that...
bankurawase 番狂わせ The Giants' victory over the Whales was an *upset*.
jitchū hakku 十中八九 The Giants are *eighty to ninety per cent sure (are almost certain)* to win the pennant this year.
KOTO 事 matter
 [...**to iu**] ~ **da** [...という] ~ だ I hear that...
 ~ **koko ni itatte wa** [L] ~ ここに至っては *Now that things have come to this*, there is nothing else to do but go through with it.
 ~ **naku** ~ なく smoothly; without incident
 ~ **no temmatsu** ~ のてんまつ the whole story; details of the incident from beginning to end
 ~ **o okosu** ~ を起こす cause a problem; cause problems
 donna koto ga atte mo どんな事があっても *No matter what happens*, remember that I am ready to help you.
 moshimo no koto ga okottara もしもの事が起こったら *In case anything should happen to me*, please notify my wife.
chinji ちん事 accident; mishap
chinji 珍事 marvel; rare event
daiji o hikiokosu 大事を引き起こす have serious repercussions
 ~ **wa shōji yori okosu** [P] ~ は小事より起こす Great things have small beginnings.
 ichi daiji ga mochiagaru 一大事が持ち上がる a great incident occurs
dekigoto 出来事 happening; incident
 hibi no dekigoto 日々の出来事 daily occurrence
 isshō ni eikyō o ataeru dekigoto

一生に影響を与えるできごと Lincoln's election to the Illinois State Legislature was *an event which affected his whole career.*

isshun no dekigoto 一瞬のできごと sudden happenstance

omo na dekigoto おもなできごと major event

sekai no dekigoto 世界のできごと world event

jihen 事変 incident; disturbance; emergency

~ **ga boppatsu suru** ~ がぼっぱつする The Manchurian *incident suddenly broke out into the open,* causing international tension.

jijō 事情 circumstances

~ **ga yuruseba** ~ が許せば if circumstances permit; circumstances permitting

~ **ni akarui** ~ に明るい He *has a good knowledge of the whole affair.*

~ **ni seitsū suru** ~ に精通する be familiar with the circumstances

~ **ni tsūjiru** ~ に通じる know the situation; be well-versed in the matter

~ **ni yotte** ~ によって We'll decide what to do next *according to circumstances (depending on circumstances).*

~ **no yurusu kagiri** ~ の許すかぎり as far as circumstances permit

yamu o enai jijō no tame やむをえない事情のため owing to unavoidable circumstances; due to circumstances beyond one's control

jiken 事件 event; incident; accident

~ **no gaiyō** ~ の概要 outline of events

~ **no ikisatsu** ~ のいきさつ He *gave us the circumstances leading up to the incident (told us how the incident occurred).*

~ **o akarumi ni dasu** ~ を明るみに出す bring an incident out into the

open

~ **o okosu** ~ を起こす create an incident; start trouble

~ **o uyamuya ni hōmuru** ~ をうやむやに葬る Many people were embarrassed and wanted to *hush up the affair (cover up the affair).*

jiko 事故 accident

furyo no jiko 不慮の事故 unexpected accident

jitai 事態 the situation; state of affairs

~ **wa jūdaika suru** ~ は重大化する The situation has become more serious.

kotogara 事柄 happenings

tadagoto de wa nai ただ事ではない This *is no light matter.*

mi ni furikakaru 身に降りかかる A series of bad accidents *happened to me* when I turned twenty.

NARIYUKI 成りゆき course of events

~ **o miru** ~ を見る await the course of events

~ **shidai** ~ 次第 as the matter develops

okoru 起こる happen; occur

⇨ **41**

神を愛する人々，すなわち，神のご計画に従って召された人々のためには，神がすべてのことを働かせて益としてくださることを，私たちは知っています．(ローマ 8 ²⁸)

127 KOTOBA 言葉 WORD

benzetsu 弁舌 speech; tongue

yūben (da) 雄弁 (だ) eloquence (eloquent)

GO 語 word

dōigo 同意語 synonym

gogen 語源 etymology; derivation

han'igo 反意語 antonym

jukugo 熟語 idiom

kanyōgo 慣用語 colloquial expression

kataru 語る speak; relate

monogatari (ru) 物語 (物語る) story; tale (tell a story; relate)

ruigo 類語 synonym
tango 単語 word; vocabulary
zokugo 俗語 slang; vulgarism
gū no ne mo denai ぐうの音も出ない When they produced the evidence, he *was left without a word to say.*
hagire ga yoi 歯ぎれが良い Billy Graham is understood by everyone because he *enunciates* his words *clearly.*
HANASHI (su) 話(話す) talk; speech (talk; speak)
  [...**to iu**] **~ da** [...という] **~** だ they say that...; it is said that...
  ~ kawatte ~ 変わって *On the other hand,* look at it this way...
  [...**no**] **~ ni fureru** [...の] **~** にふれる He *touched upon the subject of* communism in Japan but didn't go into it deeply.
  ~ o kaeru ~ を変える change the subject
  ~ o kiridasu ~ を切り出す broach the subject
  ~ o mochidasu ~ を持ち出す While we were talking about sports, he *brought up the subject of* the Olympics.
  ~ wa chigaimasu ga ~ は違いますが This is something off the subject but...
  sura sura to hanasu すらすらと話す speak fluently
kaiwa 会話 conversation
wadai 話題 topic; subject
  ~ ni noboru ~ にのぼる The *subject* of atomic warfare *came up.*
  ~ o kaeru ~ をかえる change the subject
hatsuon o ayamaru 発音を誤る mispronounce
hiyu 比ゆ metaphor; simile
hyōgen (suru) 表現(する) expression (express)
  hyōgenryoku 表現力 ability to express

oneself; power of expression
KOTOBA 言葉 word
  ~ ni iiarawasenai ~ に言い表わせない Our feelings over the earthquake disaster *cannot be put into words* (*are beyond words*).
  ~ o kawasu ~ をかわす talk with; have a word with; speak together
  ~ o kakeru ~ をかける address; speak to
  ~ o nigosu ~ をにごす speak ambiguously; use casuistry; equivocate; prevaricate
gengai no imi o toru 言外の意味をとる catch the implied meaning; read between the lines
gengo 言語 language; words
gengogaku 言語学 philology; linguistics
gengoshōgai 言語障害 speech impediment
genron 言論 discussion; views
ichigon 一言 one word
iiarawasu 言いあらわす express; put [it] into words
iidasu 言い出す speak out; blurt out
iifurasu 言いふらす harp on; say the same thing
iikaereba 言いかえれば in other words...
iikaesu 言い返す talk back to; answer back
iikata 言い方 way of speaking; expression
iikiru 言い切る say definitely
iimawashi 言い回し mode of expression; phraseology; figure of speech
iinaosu 言いなおす restate; correct oneself
iinikui 言いにくい be hard to say; be awkward to say; be difficult to express
iinogare (ru) 言いのがれ(言いのがれる) evasion (evade the issue)
iiotosu 言い落とす forget to mention; fail to mention

iishiburu 言いしぶる hesitate to say

iitōsu 言い通す persist in saying; reiterate

iitsuke (ru) 言いつけ(言いつける) order (order to do)

iitsutaeru 言い伝える relate by word of mouth

iiwake 言いわけ apology

iiwatasu 言い渡す speak out; render judgment

iu 言う say

　～ **kachi no nai** ～価値のない be not worth mentioning

　～ **made mo naku** ～までもなく it goes without saying that..., needless to say...

　ii koto o iu いいことを言う speak fitting words; put it well; speak succinctly

　ozanari o iu おざなりを言う say something trite

　share o iu しゃれを言う joke; make [a] pun

　sorerashii koto o iu それらしいことを言う say something as anticipated

　temijika ni ieba 手短に言えば To make a long story short...

iwaba 言わば so to speak; as it were

kotobajiri ことばじり end of a word

kotobazukai ことばづかい choice of words; wording; diction

mugon (da) 無言(だ) wordless; without a word

yogen (suru) 予言(する) prophecy (prophesy)

zengen o torikesu 前言を取り消す I'll have to *eat my words* (*take back what I said*) if I'm unable to keep my promise.

kotozuke (ru) ことづけ(ことづける) message (give a message to)

KUCHI ga omoi 口が重い be slow of speech

　～ **ni dasu** ～に出す mention

　～ **ni shinai** ～にしない not mention

　～ **o kiru** ～を切る speak out

　～ **o tsutsushimu** ～をつつしむ watch your words; weigh your words

　～ **wa wazawai no moto** [P] ～は災いのもと The mouth is the cause of much trouble.

kuchibashi o ireru [C] 口ばしを入れる Right in the middle of our conversation he *chimed in* (*butted in; interrupted us*).

kuchisaki dake (da) 口先だけ(だ) All he says about helping the poor is *talk* (*just a lot of words*).

MONKU 文句 sentence; phrase

bijireiku o naraberu 美辞麗句を並べる The speaker *used flowery language* and failed to get the attention of his audience.

bunshō 文章 composition; writing; sentence

mojidōri (da) 文字通り(だ) literally

ni no ku ga tsugenai 二の句がつげない I *was lost for words* (*was speechless; was dumbfounded*).

mōsu 申す speak [humble]

noberu 述べる say; relate

　chinjutsu (suru) 陳述(する) statement; declaration (state; declare; set forth)

ossharu (ōse ni naru) おっしゃる(仰せになる) say [honorific]

otozure [L] 訪れ news; tidings; message

share しゃれ play on words; pun

shi 詩 poem

sunawachi すなわち that is; in other words

Suntetsu hito o sasu [P] 寸鉄人をさす Brevity is the soul of wit [P].

tatetsuzuke ni shaberu 立てつづけにしゃべる blabber; chatter; prattle

tatoe (ru) たとえ(たとえる) parable; allegory (liken to; compare to)

　tatoeba たとえば for example; for instance

tsutaeru 伝える relate; tell; convey

tsuzuri o ayamaru つづりを誤る misspell [a] word
⇨ 195

わたしはあなたがたに，こう言いましょう．人はその口にするあらゆるむだなことばについて，さばきの日には言い開きをしなければなりません．あなたが正しいとされるのは，あなたのことばによるのであり，罪に定められるのも，あなたのことばによるのです．(マタイ 12 ⁸⁶, ⁸⁷)

128 KUIARATAME 悔い改め
REPENTANCE

ashi o arau 足を洗う She *quit a life of shame* and made a fresh start in life.

ato no matsuri [P] あとの祭り That is a case of *locking the barn door after the horse is stolen* [P].

ayamari (ru) あやまり(あやまる) apology (apologize)

 hira ayamari ni ayamaru 平あやまりにあやまる get down and apologize; eat humble pie

Fukusui bon ni kaerazu [P] 覆水盆に返らず There is no use crying over spilt milk [P].

KOKORO o arata ni suru 心を新たにする undergo a change of heart

 ~ o irekaeru ～を入れ替える After being caught stealing, the youth *had a change of heart (reformed himself; turned over a new leaf)*.

 honshin ni tachikaeru 本心に立ち返る come to one's senses; come to oneself; repent

 ryōshin ni semerareru 良心に責められる be conscience-stricken

KUIARATAME (ru) 悔い改め(悔い改める) repentance (repent; undergo a change of heart)

 aratameru 改める change; alter; correct; revise

 kaikon 悔恨 regret; remorse

 ~ no jō ～の情 feeling of regret

kaishin (suru) 改心 (する) reform (reform; mend one's ways)

kōkai (suru) 後悔(する) regret (regret; be sorry for)

 ~ saki ni tatazu [P] ～先に立たず Regret will not mend matters.

kuiru 悔いる repent; be sorry for

kuyamu 悔やみ rue; be sorry for

kuyashigaru 悔しがる feel chagrined; be vexed

kuyokuyo suru くよくよする fret over; brood over

ma'ningen ni naru 真人間になる After failing in that shady business, he decided to *turn over a new leaf (go straight)*.

tenkō (suru) 転向(する) conversion; about-face (make an about-face)

 hyakuhachijūdo no tenkai o suru 百八十度の転回をする He *made a complete turn-about-face* and became a respectable man in the community.

tsugunai (u) つぐない(つぐなう) compensation; restitution (compensate for; make up for; put matters right)

umarekawari (ru) 生まれ変わり(生れ変わる) new birth; complete reformation (be born again)

 saisei no omoi ga suru 再生の思いがする feel like a new man

wabi (ru) わび(わびる) apology (apologize; make an apology)

zange suru ざんげする confess one's sins; feel penitent

zannen ni omou 残念に思う feel sorry [about]

 zannengaru 残念がる feel bad about; feel sorry for
⇨ 166

神は，そのような無知の時代を見過ごしておられましたが，今は，どこでもすべての人に悔い改めを命じておられます．(使徒行伝 17 ³⁰)

129 KUNREN 訓練 DISCIPLINE, TRAINING

gunki 軍紀(軍規) military discipline

keiko (suru) けいこ(する) practice; training (practice; train)
~ **o tsumu** けいこをつむ He *trained hard* at the gym for months.

KIBISHII きびしい strict; rigid
~ **shugyō o tsumu** ~ 修行を積む As a young monk Luther *went through rigorous austerities* but found no peace of heart.
genkaku na kiritsu 厳格な規律 rigorous discipline
tekibishii 手きびしい He *is very strict with (has a firm grip on)* his children.

kitaeru きたえる train; harden; temper

kokkishin no tsuyoi hito 克己心の強い人 He is a *man of self-control (well-disciplined person)*.

KUNREN (suru) 訓練(する) discipline; training (train)
~ **o kasaneru** ~ を重ねる drill over and over again
~ **o ukeru** ~ を受ける get training; receive training
yukitodoita kunren 行き届いた訓練 thorough training

jukuren (suru) 熟練(する) skill; mastery (become skillful; master)

kaji minarai o suru 家事見習いをする She is staying home *learning housework* before getting married.

kun'iku (suru) 訓育(する) education (educate; train)

kunkai (suru) 訓戒(する) admonition (admonish)

kunrenjō 訓練場 training institute

kyōren 教練 military drill; military training

mōrenshū o suru 猛練習をする The team *trained rigidly* for the big game.

narai (u) 習い(習う) custom; practice; habit (learn; practice; get training [in])

neru 練る polish
kokoro o neru 心を練る discipline one's mind

renshū (suru) 練習(する) practice; exercise (practice; exercise; drill)

shūren 修練 skill; dexterity

tanren (suru) 鍛練(する) tempering; hardening (temper; harden [steel])
shinshin o tanren suru 心身を鍛練する You *must train mind and body* if you want to succeed.

sessei (suru) 節制(する) moderation (use moderation; be temperate)

jisei (suru) 自制(する) self-control (exercise self-control)

shitsuke (ru) しつけ(しつける) training; breeding (train; discipline)
~ **ga yoi (warui)** ~ が良い(悪い) Those children are *well disciplined (well trained)*. Those children are *not disciplined (poorly trained)*.
oya (katei) no shitsuke 親(家庭)のしつけ parental discipline (home training)

mi ni tsukeru 身につける He *learned* the printer's trade while in high school.

muchiutsu むち打つ urge; spur on

SHŪYŌ (suru) 修養(する) training; culture; improvement (train; improve oneself)
~ **o tsumu** ~ を積む do much to improve oneself
jiko shūyō 自己修養 self-discipline

yōiku (suru) 養育(する) training (train; nurture; rear)

yosei kikan 養成期間 training period

ude ga ochiru 腕が落ちる Tanaka *has lost his touch* and will be dropped from the baseball team soon.
~ **o migaku** ~ をみがく You had better *brush up on* your batting *technique* if you want to make the team.

⇨ 125, 133

主はその愛する者を懲らしめ，受け入れるすべての子に，むちを加えられるからである．（ヘブル 12 ⁶）

130 KURŌ 苦労 LABOR, STRUGGLE, HARDSHIP

asedaku ni natte 汗だくになって They *are bending every effort* to get the job done.

donna me ni atte mo どんな目にあっても We'll reach the top of the mountain *no matter what (come what may)*.

  sanzan na me ni au さんざんな目にあう have a rough time of it

HONEORI (ru) 骨折り (骨折る) pains; exertion; effort (go to pains [to]; exert oneself; work hard)

  hone ga oreru 骨が折れる You'll *have a hard time* finding cheap land in Tokyo.

  Honeorizon no kutabire mōke [P] 骨折り損のくたびれもうけ It was like *looking for a needle in a haystack* [P].

  kibone ga oreru 気骨が折れる Working for that ill-tempered boss *is a strain on my mind*.

  mudabone (da) [c] むだ骨 (だ) vain effort; fruitless labor

ibara no michi いばらの道 He will find working amongst those rag pickers *a difficult path*.

KURŌ (suru) 苦労 (する) labor; struggle; hardship (labor; struggle)

  ~ no tane ~ のたね seed of trouble

  naminami naranu kurō o suru 並み並みならぬ苦労をする make an extraordinary effort

  yo no naka no kurō 世の中の苦労 hardships of life

  kigurō ga taenai 気苦労が堪えない The retarded child *was a constant concern* to her mother.

kinrō 勤労 labor

konku 困苦 hardship; distress; affliction

kunō 苦悩 sufferings; hardships

  ~ no iro ~ の色 She wore a *look of distress* when she rushed into the office.

kurōnin 苦労人 man of experience

kurōshō 苦労性 worry wart; constant worrier; person who takes things too seriously

kushin 苦心 pains; exertion; trouble

  ~ o kasaneru ~ を重ねる He *took great pains* in designing the building.

rōdō (suru) 労働 (する) manual labor; labor; physical labor (do manual labor; labor; toil)

rōku 労苦 labor; toil

rōsuru 労する take pains; labor; exert oneself

seikatsuku to tatakau 生活苦とたたかう struggle to make a living

shikuhakku suru 四苦八苦する They *experienced great hardships* during the war.

shinku 辛苦 hardships; troubles

torikoshikurō o suru 取り越し苦労をする Everything was turning out all right, but he *worried about it anyway*.

torō 徒労 fruitless labor; labor lost

  ~ ni owaru ~ に終わる He could find no publisher; his *work was in vain*.

namitaitei no koto de wa nai 並みたいていのことではない It's no easy matter.

omoni 重荷 burden; weight

sesse to hataraku せっせと働く keep plugging along; keep one's nose to the grindstone.

shotaijimita 所帯じみた She was a socialite once but now never takes off her apron and *looks domesticated*.

sui mo amai mo nametsukusu すいも甘いもなめつくす He is a man of varied experience and has *tasted the bitter and the sweet in life*.

tsurai つらい difficult
⇨ 29, 123

ですから，私の愛する兄弟たちよ．堅く立って，動かされることなく，いつも主のわざに励みなさい．あなたがたは自分たちの苦労が，主にあってむだでないことを知っているのですから．(コリント I 15 ⁵⁸)

131 KUTSŪ 苦痛 PAIN

aburaase o nagasu あぶら汗を流す He was *bathed in perspiration* during the painful operation.

aegu あえぐ pant ; gasp

chi no deru yōna omoi 血の出るような思い Being left penniless, I went through some *excruciating experiences* (*trying experiences*) raising my children.

~ **o haku omoi** ~を吐く思い *Our hearts bleed for* the children whose parents were killed in the accident.

danchō no omoi de 断腸の思いで with a heart-rending feeling

GAI o oyobosu 害を及ぼす harm ; injure ; hurt

higai 被害 damage ; injury ; harm

~ **o ataeru** ~を与える damage

~ **o ukeru** ~を受ける suffer loss ; be injured

gōmon (**suru**) 拷問(する) torture (torture)

~ **ni kakeru** ~にかける torture

hanshihanshō no me ni au 半死半生の目にあう The survivors of the mine blast *went through* an *experience that left them more dead than alive.*

kao o shikameru 顔をしかめる He *grimaced* when the doctor injected the needle.

KUTSŪ 苦痛 pain

~ **o kanjiru** ~を感じる feel pain

~ **o torinozoku** ~を取りのぞく relieve pain ; remove pain

chintsūzai 沈痛剤 pain-reliever

fukutsū 腹痛 stomach-ache

gekitsū 激痛 severe pain ; intense pain

hitsū (**da**) 悲痛(だ) intense grief (bitter)

ikigurushii 息苦しい stifling ; suffocating ; asphyxiating

itametsukeru 痛めつける harm ; inflict pain [on]

itami (**mu**) 痛み(痛む) pain (be painful ; hurts)

~ **o karuku suru** ~を軽くする The doctor gave him a shot to *lessen the pain.*

hari de sasareru yōna itami 針でさされるような痛み gnawing pain ; stinging pain

jintsū 陣痛 labor pains

kuhai o nameru 苦杯をなめる He hoped to win in the first round but instead *tasted the bitter cup* of defeat.

kunan 苦難 suffering ; passion

~ **ni taeru** ~に耐える bear up under hardships

kunō 苦悩 distress ; worry

kurushii 苦しい painful ; distressing

~ **hame ni ochiiru** ~はめにおちいる He *got into a painful situation* when he tried to help the criminal.

kurushimagire ni 苦しまぎれに *Driven by pain* (*In desperation*), he tore off the bandages.

kurushimeru 苦しめる torment ; inflict pain [on]

kurushimi (**mu**) 苦しみ(苦しむ) suffering ; pain (suffer ; be in pain)

~ **o ajiwau** ~を味わう experience sufferings ; go through sufferings

[...**no**] ~ **o tomo ni suru** [...の] ~を共にする share the sufferings [of]

umi no kurushimi 生みの苦しみ birth pangs

shinku [L] 辛苦 hardships

shitsū 歯痛 toothache

zutsū 頭痛 headache

kyūkutsu na omoi 窮屈な思い I had a *cramped feeling* (*stifled feeling*) in that little room.

modaeru もだえる be in agony

mune ga harisakeru omoi ga suru 胸がはりさける思いがする Lincoln *felt as if his* *heart would break* when little Willie lay dead in his arms.

nigai にがい bitter

suna o kamu omoi 砂をかむ思い He *had a bitter experience* in the war and will not talk about it.

tsurai つらい hard; difficult

    shinu yori tsurai omoi 死ぬよりつらい思い That *experience was more than flesh and blood can bear.*

ukime o miru うき目を見る go through a bitter experience

umeki (ku) うめき(うめく) groaning; moaning (groan; moan)

⇨ **130**

むしろ, キリストの苦しみにあずかれるのですから, 喜んでいなさい. それは, キリストの栄光が現われるときにも, 喜びおどる者となるためです. (ペテロ I 4 ¹⁸)

132 KYŌFU 恐怖 FEAR

bikubiku びくびく nervously

chi no ke ga nakunaru 血の気がなくなる He *turned pale* when he heard the noise of the crash.

dōjiru 動じる be perturbed; be agitated

gyotto suru 〔C〕ぎょっとする I *gave a start* (*was startled*) when I heard the knock on the door.

hakuhyō o fumu yōna ki ga suru 薄氷を踏むような気がする The boss felt we *were walking on thin ice* in this new venture.

hiyaase o kaku ひや汗をかく I *broke into a cold sweat* when I heard that scream.

hiyari to suru ひやりとする I *shuddered* (*felt a cold chill*) when I heard someone walking in the attic.

ijikeru いじける be cowed [by]

kao no iro o kaeru 顔の色を変える He *was aghast* (*turned pale*) when he learned that the enemy forces had reached the town.

katazu o nonde かたずをのんで We waited *with bated breath* for the enemy sentry

to pass by.

kenen (suru) 懸念 (する) fear; anxiety (fear; be anxious [about])

kimo o hiyasu 肝を冷やす It *made my blood run cold* to see that human arm lying in the road.

koshi o nukasu 腰を抜かす During the raid, some men *became paralyzed with fear* and could not fight.

kowai こわい fearful; frightening

    kowagaru こわがる be afraid [of]

    kowagowa こわごわ gingerly; timidly

KYŌFU 恐怖 fear

    [...no] ~ ni osowarete (kararete) [...の] ~に襲われて (かられて) The people *were terror-stricken* (*were panic-stricken*) by the earthquake.

    ~ no nen o yobiokosu ~の念を呼び起こす excite terror in; put fear into

kyōfukan 恐怖感 sense of fear

kyōkatsu (suru) 恐かつ(する) blackmail; extortion (blackmail; extort)

kyōkō 恐慌 panic; scare [financial]

    sensen kyōkyō toshite (kurasu) 戦々恐々として (暮らす) in fear and trembling (live in constant fear)

osore (ru) 恐れ(恐れる) apprehension; dread; fear (be apprehensive; dread; fear)

    [...no] ~ ga aru [...の] ~がある It is feared that ...; be in danger [of]

    ~ o kanjiru ~を感じる be in awe of; sense a fear that...

osoreru koto wa nai 恐れることはない Yes, they are going on a long hike, but *there is nothing to be afraid of.*

[...o] osorete [...を] 恐れて *For fear* that they would get lost, we sent a guide along.

osoroshii 恐ろしい fearful; terrible; awful; horrible

    miburui suru hodo osoroshii 身震いするほど恐ろしい That spy thriller *was enough to make one shake with* _fear_ (_enough to give one the creeps_).

osoruosoru おそるおそる nervously; cautiously

mi no ke ga yodatsu 身の毛がよだつ My _hair stood on end_ when she screamed.

obieru おびえる become startled; be frightened

obiyakasu 脅かす threaten; intimidate; scare

　kyōhaku (suru) 脅迫(する) threat; menace (threaten; menace)

odosu おどす intimidate; menace

ojike (ru) おじけ(おじける) trepidation; fear (be scared; grow timid)

　~ ga tsuku ~がつく panic; be seized with fear; become afraid

okkanai [C] おっかない I don't like talking to that professor; he's _stern_ (_scary; frightening_).

panikku パニック panic [financial]

samuke o kanjiru 寒気を感じる I _felt a cold chill_ when I went into the room.

senritsu (suru) [L] 戦りつ(する) shudder of fright (shudder; shiver)

sesuji ga samuku naru 背筋が寒くなる _Chills ran up and down my spine_ as he told us the ghost story.

shimpai o fukitobasu 心配を吹き飛ばす The telephone call immediately _dispelled any fear_ that she was in danger.

susamajii すさまじい terrifying; dreadful; horrible

torihada ga tatsu 鳥はだが立つ I _felt goose pimples_ when I heard the weird noise.

yusuri (ru) ゆすり(ゆする) blackmail (blackmail)

zotto suru ぞっとする shudder; get the chills

⇨ **157**

愛には恐れがありません。全き愛は恐れを締め出します。なぜなら恐れには刑罰が伴っているからです。恐れる者の愛は、全きものとなっていないのです。（ヨハネ I 4 ¹⁸）

133　KYŌIKU 教育
EDUCATION

benkyō (suru) 勉強(する) studying (study)

bungei 文芸 literary arts; literature

bunseki (suru) 分析(する) analysis (analyze)

GAKUMON 学問 learning; study

　~ ga dekiru ~ができる be a good student

　~ no aru hito ~のある人 man of learning

　~ no jiyū ~の自由 academic freedom

　~ o hana ni kakeru ~を鼻にかける That young professor uses big words to _show off his learning._

　~ o migaku ~をみがく brush up on one's studies; polish up one's studies

bangaku 晩学 learning late in life

bungaku 文学 literature

chūgakkō 中学校 junior high school

daigaku 大学 university

dokugaku no hito 独学の人 self-taught man

gakkō 学校 school

gakugei 学芸 arts and sciences

gakujutsu 学術 learning; scholarship

gakurei 学齢 school age

gakureki 学歴 academic career; academic record

　~ no nai hito ~のない人 Lincoln _was without formal education_ and studied English grammar after he was twenty-three.

gakuryoku 学力 scholastic ability

gakusei 学生 student; scholar

gakusei 学制 educational system

gakusha 学者 scholar; savant

gakushabutta 学者ぶった pedantic

gakushi 学資 school expenses

gakushiki 学識 scholarly attainments

　~ keikensha ~経験者 man of learning and experience

gakushū (suru) 学習 (する) studying; study

hakugaku 博学 erudition; extensive learning

kagaku 科学 science

kōgakushin ni moeru 向学心にもえる He *is burning with a zeal for study.*

kōtōgakkō 高等学校 high school; senior high school

kugaku suru 苦学する Having no help from his parents, he *studied under difficulties.*

manabi (bu) 学び (学ぶ) study (learn)

nyūgaku (suru) 入学 (する) matriculation; entrance [into a school] (matriculate; enroll in a school)

shōgakkō 小学校 primary school; elementary school

mugaku (da) 無学 (だ) illiteracy (illiterate; uneducated)

gōkaku suru 合格する pass an examination

hakushi (hakase) 博士 (はかせ) doctor of philosophy (Ph.D.)

hitozukuri 人づくり character development

hobo 保母 nursery school teacher

kanka (suru) 感化 (する) influence; inspiration (influence; inspire)

~ **o ukeru** ~ を受ける be influenced [by]

kenkyū (suru) 研究 (する) research (do research)

~ **ni kenkyū o kasaneru** ~ に研究を重ねる do intensive research

kunren (suru) 訓練 (する) training; discipline (train; discipline)

KYŌIKU 教育 education

~ **o fukyū suru** ~ を普及する educate; educate widely

~ **o keishi suru** ~ を軽視する belittle education

[...**no**] ~ **o ukeru** [...の] ~ を受ける I *was educated under* the old system.

bannin kyōiku 万人教育 universal education

gimu kyōiku 義務教育 compulsory education

jinkaku kyōiku 人格教育 character training

jitsugyō kyōiku 実業教育 industrial training

kōtō kyōiku 高等教育 higher education

suparutashiki kyōiku o ukeru スパルタ式教育をうける learn through strict discipline; receive a Spartan-like education

bunkyō 文教 education

kyōju (suru) 教授 (する) professor (lecture; give instruction)

kyōkun 教訓 teaching; lesson; precepts

~ **o ataeru** ~ を与える give a lesson; teach

~ **o ukeru** ~ を受ける receive instruction

kyōshi 教師 instructor; teacher

kyōyō 教養 refinement; culture

~ **aru hito** ~ ある人 person of cultu. refined person

~ **ga nijimideru** ~ がにじみ出る Thomas Jefferson's *refinement is revealed* in the beautiful language found in the Declaration of Independence.

~ **o tsumu** ~ をつむ cultivate oneself

kyōyu 教諭 teacher [kindergarten, primary, junior high, high school]

oshie (ru) 教え(教える) teaching; lesson (teach)

kande fukumeru yōni oshieru かんてふくめるように教える He *teaches* his subject *painstakingly.*

sodachi 育ち upbringing

sodateru 育てる bring up; raise [children]

sodatsu 育つ grow up; be brought up

taiiku (kan) 体育 (館) physical education [gym]

tokuiku 徳育 moral training

michibiki (ku) 導き (導く) guidance (guide)

shidō (suru) 指導 (する) guidance (guide; lead)

mommō (da) 文盲 (だ) illiteracy (illiterate)

Monzen no kozō narawanu kyō o yomu [P] 門前の小僧習わぬ経をよむ If you live with Japanese people, you will *learn* Japanese *by osmosis.*

NARAI (u) 習い (習う) practice (practice; learn; get training in)

Narau yori nareyo [P] ならうよりなれよ Practice makes perfect [P]. Better to practice than to learn.

Rokujū no tenarai [P] 六十の手習い *It is never too late to learn.*

oboeru 覚える learn; memorize

osowaru 教わる be taught

sensei 先生 teacher

seito 生徒 pupil; student; school children

shiken (suru) 試験 (する) exam; test (examine; test)

~ ni ukaru ~に受かる pass an exam

~ o ukeru ~を受ける take a test; be examined

mogishiken 模擬試験 practice test

shūyō (suru) 修養 (する) culture (improve oneself)

tebiki 手引き guide

yōchien 幼稚園 kindergarten

⇨ 129

聖書はすべて，神の霊感によるもので，教えと，戒めと矯正と義の訓練とのために有益です．それは，神の人が，すべての良い働きのためにふさわしい十分に整えられた者となるためです．(テモテ II 3 16, 17)

134 KYŌKI 狂気 MADNESS

ATAMA ga hen ni naru 頭が変になる Since that accident he *has been a little strange* (*doesn't seem to be all there*).

~ ga kurutte iru ~が狂っている He's *out of his mind.* He's *not all there.*

~ ga okashii ~がおかしい He's *not in his right mind.* He's *a little off.*

henshitsukyō 変質狂 partial insanity

henshitsusha 変質者 pervert

ijō (da) 異常 (だ) abnormality (abnormal)

kokoro o torimidasu 心を取り乱す be distracted; lose composure

KYŌKI 狂気 madness

~ o yosoou ~ をよそおう feign madness

hakkyō suru 発狂する go crazy; go mad; crack up

totsuzen no hakkyō de 突然の発狂で The lawyers claimed that Ruby shot Oswald *in a fit of temporary insanity* (*in a fit of sudden derangement*).

kichigai 気違い madness; insanity; madman; lunatic; nut

~ atsukai ni suru ~ 扱いにする treat one like an imbecile

~ ni naru ~ になる go crazy; crack up; go nuts

~ ni suru ~ にする drive one crazy; drive one mad

kichigaijimita 気違いじみた mad; crazy

kichigaizata 気違いざた That was a *crazy thing* he did.

kuruu 狂う lose one's head; go mad

ki ga kuruu 気が狂う be mad; be out of one's mind

kyōbō (da) 狂暴 (だ) rage; frenzy (raging; furious)

kyōjin 狂人 madman; lunatic

kyōran 狂乱 frenzy; wildness

~ jōtai de ~ 状態で in a frenzied condition

nekkyō (suru) 熱狂 (する) mania; craze (be crazy about)

sakkidatsu 殺気立つ become furious at; become mad at

shōki ni kaeru 正気にかえる return to normality; regain one's sanity

shōkizuku 正気づく regain consciousness

noirōze ノイローゼ neurosis

~ **gimi (da)** ~ ぎみ (だ) beginning stages of a nervous breakdown (on the verge of a nervous breakdown)

omedetai hito [C] おめでたい人 He is always doing crazy things like that; he's a *softheaded person* (*nitwit*).

SEISHIN bunretsu 精神分裂 schizophrenia

~ **hakujaku (ji)** ~ 薄弱 (児) feeblemindedness (retarded child)

~ **ijō (da)** ~ 異常 (だ) abnormal; mentally deranged

~ **ijō o kitasu** ~ 異常をきたす go a little bit off; have a mental quirk

~ **sakuran** ~ 錯乱 mental derangement

~ **shōgai** ~ 障害 mental disorder

seishinbyō 精神病 mental illness

shinkei suijaku 神経衰弱 nervous breakdown

⇒ **48**

あなたは全き平安をもって、こころざしの堅固なものを守られる. 彼はあなたに信頼しているからである.
(イザヤ 26 ³)

135 KYŌRYOKU 協力 COOPERATION, HELP

ashinami o soroeru 足並みをそろえる Let us work *with close cooperation* (*with a concerted effort*) to win the election.

dōmei (suru) 同盟 (する) alliance (be allied [with]; combine [with])

hitohada nugu 一はだぬぐ Abe *went out of his way* (*did all he could*) to help his nephew.

isshindōtai ni naru 一心同体になる Unless we *become of one mind* in this task, we will fail.

kata o motsu 肩を持つ He *backed us up* in the new project.

kokoro o awaseru 心を合わせる be of one heart

kumiai 組合 cooperative; co-op

KYŌRYOKU (suru) 協力 (する) cooperation (cooperate [with])

~ **o eru** ~ をえる get one's cooperation

kokusai kyōryoku 国際協力 international cooperation

missetsu ni kyōryoku suru 密接に協力する cooperate closely

chikara o awaseru 力を合わせる If we don't *consolidate our forces* (*work together as a team*), the job will never get done.

~ **o hitotsu ni suru** ~ をひとつにする concentrate efforts; join forces

~ **o kasu** をかす lend a hand; offer help

kyōdō (suru) 協同 (する) cooperation; association (cooperate; work together)

[...**to**] **kyōgi suru** [...と] 協議する be in agreement with

kyōkai 協会 conference; association; cooperative

kyōryokusha 協力者 fellow worker; co-worker

kyōtei (suru) 協定 (する) pact; agreement (make a pact; enter into an agreement)

sanka (suru) 参加 (する) participation (participate in; attend)

shiji (suru) 支持 (する) support (support; back up; get behind; go to bat for)

sōgo 相互 mutual

TASUKE (ru) 助け(助ける) help; assistance (help; assist)

enjo (suru) 援助 (する) assistance; aid (assist; aid; help)

joryoku 助力 assistance; aid

tasukeau 助け合う assist each other; help one another

TE o hiku 手を引く He helped for awhile but finally *quit* (*pulled up stakes*) and left us.

~ **o kasu** ~ をかす lend a hand; pitch in

~ **o kunde** ~ をくんで The two parties

have joined hands in their efforts to revise the constitution.

~ **o toriau** ~ をとり合う go hand in hand together; do [something] together

tetsudai(u) 手つだい(手つだう) assistance; help (assist; help)

tewake suru 手分けする divide up [the] work

teikei suru 提携する work hand in hand; act in unison

TOMO ni 共に together

~ **ni hataraku** に働く work together

tomokasegi suru 共かせぎする The young couple *are working together for a living.*

kyōmei suru 共鳴する agree with; be in sympathy with; get behind

⇨ 22, 74

主が私たちのために死んでくださったのは、私たちが、目ざめていても、眠っていても、主とともに生きるためです。ですから、あなたがたは、今しているとおり、互いに励まし合い、互いに徳を高め合いなさい。(テサロニケ I 5 ¹⁰, ¹¹)

136 KYŌTAN 驚嘆 WONDER

aita kuchi ga fusagaranai [C] あいた口がふさがらない I *gaped in astonishment* as the stunt man stood on the wing of the flying plane.

akireta kao o suru あきれた顔をする Everyone *looked amazed* (*looked dumbfounded*) when they heard that their prize pupil came in last in the English contest.

akirete mono ga ienai あきれて物が言えない It *simply beats me* that he chose communism after preaching about individual rights.

akke ni torarete あっけにとられて in amazement; gaping in wonder

atto iwaseru あっと言わせる The space feat *took our breath away.*

azen to shite あ然として dazed; speechless

bikkuri suru びっくりする be surprised; be startled

fushigi (da) 不思議 (だ) strange

gyōten suru [C] 仰天する We *were spellbound* (*were amazed*) by his feat on the high wire.

kimo o tsubusu 肝をつぶす The explosion of the gas tank *frightened us out of our wits.*

kiseki 奇跡 miracle

kimyō (da) 奇妙 (だ) strange; odd; curious

KYŌTAN 驚嘆 wonder

kantan (suru) 感嘆 (する) wonder; marvel (wonder [at]; marvel [at])

kyōgaku 驚がく amazement; surprise; astonishment (be amazed; be surprised; be astonished)

kyōi 驚異 wonder; amazement

~ **no mato** ~ の的 sensation

~ **no me o miharu** ~ の目を見張る The children *stared in wonder* as twelve elephants paraded by.

kyōiteki (da) [L] 驚異的 (だ) phenomenal

odoroki (ku) 驚き (驚く) astonishment (be astonished; be amazed)

odoroita kao o suru 驚いた顔をする express surprise; show surprise

odoroku ni tarinai 驚くに足りない *There's nothing amazing about* crossing the Atlantic in a few hours.

odorokiakireru 驚きあきれる be appalled [at]

odorokubeki (da) 驚くべき (だ) marvelous; surprising

ME o maruku suru 目を丸くする The country boy's *eyes popped out* as he walked down the Ginza.

~ **o mawasu** ~ を回す *We were bewildered* (Our *eyes were popping out*) at the fantastic display of diamonds.

~ **o miharu** ~ を見張る be struck with wonder; be awestruck

shita o maku 舌を巻く We *were flabbergasted* when the athlete heaved the shotput over sixty feet.

⇨ **38, 67**

わたしは命令を出す. わが国のすべての州の人は, 皆ダニエルの神をおののき恐れなければならない. 彼は生ける神であって, とこしえに変わることなく, その国は滅びず, その主権は終わりまで続く. 彼は救いを施し, 助けをなし, 天においても 地においても, しるしと奇跡とを おこない, ダニエルを救ってししの力をのがれさせたかたである. (ダニエル 6 26, 27)

137 KYŪSOKU 休息 REST

ansei 安静 physical rest
   zettai ansei 絶対安静 absolute rest
   seiyō (suru) 静養 (する) convalescence (convalesce; recuperate)
ikoi (u) いこい (いこう) relaxation; rest (relax; rest)
   ~ no basho ~ の場所 place of rest
kaifuku (suru) 回復 (する) recuperation (recuperate; recover one's strength)
KIBARASHI 気晴らし diversion; recreation
   ~ ni... ~ に... *For diversion* from the cares of the war Lincoln read the satire of David Locke.
   harebare to shita kimochi 晴れ晴れとした気持ち After a good night's rest I *felt like a new man* (*felt like a new person*).
   usabarashi ni うさ晴らしに *For diversion* (*To ease the tension*) we left the office early and played tennis.
kinchō o hogosu (hogusu) 緊張をほごす (ほぐす) That coffee-break *relieved the tension* of the conference.
koshi o kakete 腰をかけて Take the load off your feet!
KYŪSOKU 休息. rest
   ~ iikan ~ 時間 rest period; quiet hours
   ansoku 安息. rest; repose

ansokunichi 安息日 the Sabbath; a sabbath day
hiruyasumi 昼休み noon break
hitoiki ireru 一息入れる Let's *take time out* for a cup of tea!
hitoyasumi suru 一休みする take a short break
iki o tsuku 息をつく take a breathing spell; take a breather
kyūgaku (suru) 休学 (する) He got sick and *dropped out of school* for awhile.
kyūgyō (suru) 休業 (する) business holiday (close for a holiday)
kyūjitsu 休日 holiday
kyūka 休暇 holidays; vacation
kyūkei (suru) 休憩 (する) recess; break (recess [from]; take a break)
kyūshoku (suru) 休職 (する) retirement from work (temporarily retire from work)
kyūyō (suru) 休養 (する) rest; recreation (rest; have some recreation)
nakayasumi 中休み rest; recess; respite
shōkyūshi 小休止 short break
yasumi (mu) 休み (休む) rest; time off (rest; take time off)
   shigoto o yasumu 仕事を休む rest from work; take time off from work
   ki o yasumeru 気を休める relax one's vigilance; rest one's nerves
   kokoro o yasumeru koto ga dekinai 心を休めることができない He *is in constant unrest* over the new business.
   shinkei no yasumaru toki ga nai 神経の休まる時がない have no time to calm one's nerves down
   te o yasumeru 手を休める take a break
NEMURI (ru) 眠り (眠る) sleep (go to sleep)
   gussuri nemuru ぐっすり眠る I *slept like a log.*
   ammin (suru) 安眠 (する) a good

night's rest (have a good night's rest;
sleep well)

fumin fukyū (da) 不眠不休 (だ) They
are working *night and day* to finish
the new highway.

inemuri (suru) 居眠り(する) doze;
catnap (doze; take a catnap)

neru 寝る go to bed

 hirune (suru) 昼寝 (する); nap; siesta
 (take a nap; take a siesta)

 neiru 寝入る fall asleep; drop off

 netsukarenai 寝つかれない be unable to
 sleep; cannot get to sleep

seisei suru せいせいする feel refreshed

 ~ shita kibun ~ した気分 refreshed
 feeling·

yasuraka (da) 安らか (だ)·calm; peaceful;
quiet

yoko ni naru 横になる lie down; recline
⇨ 4, 156

主はわたしの牧者であって，わたしには乏しいことがない．
主はわたしを緑の牧場に伏させ，いこいのみぎわに伴われ
る．主はわたしの魂をいきかえらせ，み名のためにわたしを
正しい道に導かれる．(詩篇 23 ¹, ², ³)

138 MANZOKU 満足
SATISFACTION

akiaki suru [c] 飽き飽きする I *am fed up
with* (*am sick of*) this job.

[...ni] amanjiru [...に] 甘んじる be
contented with; be satisfied with

ariamaru ありあまる be more than enough;
be enough and to spare

hitoriyogari no ひとりよがりの You can't
tell him; he's quite *self-complacent* (*self-
satisfied*)

i-shoku-jū ni komaranai 衣食住に困
らない They *have no worries about the
common necessities of life.*

jūbun (da) 十分 (だ) sufficiency (sufficient; plentiful; enough)

kanbashiku nai かんばしくない The nurse

reported that his condition *was not
satisfactory.*

kayui tokoro ni te ga todoku かゆい所に
手が届く The service at the hotel *left
nothing to be desired.*

ki ni iru 気に入る be pleased with; take a
liking to

maniau 間に合う be enough; be serviceable; meet the need; go around

MANZOKU(suru) 満足(する) satisfaction
(be satisfied)

 ~ o ataeru ~ を与える He thought
 money alone would *give him satisfaction* (*satisfy him*), but he was soon
 disappointed.

 ~ saseru koto wa dekinai ~ させる
 ことはできない *It's impossible to satisfy*
 all the customers who eat at our
 restaurant.

 iikagen de manzoku suru いいかげ
 んで満足する You will never succeed
 if you *are* always *satisfied with
 mediocrity.*

fumanzoku (da) 不満足 (だ) insufficiency; dissatisfaction (dissatisfied;
disgruntled)

jikomanzoku 自己満足 self-satisfaction

mampuku(suru) 満腹(する) satiety (eat
to one's heart's content)

michiafureru 満ちあふれる be full to the
brim; overflow [with]

michitariru 満ち足りる abound; be full
to the brim

 michitarita kimochi 満ち足りた気持
 satisfied feeling

mitasu 満たす fill up; satisfy require-
ments

mōshibun ga nai 申し分がない I *have
nothing to add* to his comments.

omou zonbun ni 思う存分に to one's
heart's content; without reserve

takusan (da) たくさん (だ) sufficient;
enough

mō takusan da [C] もうたくさんだ I've had it!

TARIRU 足りる be adequate; suffice

akitarinai あきたりない unsatisfying; ungratifying

monotarinai tokoro ga aru 物足りないところがある There is still something to be desired in your English thesis.

tarafuku [C] たらふく He told us to eat and drink to our heart's content (all we want).

taru koto o manabu [L] 足ることを学ぶ …for I have learned to find resources in myself, whatever my circumstances. (Philippians 4 : 11)

urusai [C] うるさい The building inspectors here are hard to satisfy (hard to please; sticklers for details).

⇨ **65**

金銭を愛する生活をしてはいけません。いま持っているもので満足しなさい。主ご自身がこう言われるのです。「わたしは決してあなたを離れず、また、あなたを捨てない。」(ヘブル 13 ⁵)

139 MAYOI 迷い ILLUSION, DELUSION, WANDERING

arukimawaru 歩き回る walk about

atedo mo naku aruku あてどもなく歩く Having no place to stay, he walked aimlessly about the city.

bōzen to shite iru ぼう然としている be bewildered; stand aghast

burabura suru [C] ぶらぶらする Let's wander around (stroll along) the Ginza for awhile. He's out of a job and idle.

gensō 幻想 delusion; fantasy

gori muchū 五里夢中 I am in the dark as to what he intends to do.

hinammin 避難民 refugee

hōkō o ayamaru 方向を誤る go astray; wander from the straight and narrow path

hōgaku ga wakaranaku naru 方角が

わからなくなる On the way home from Karuizawa we lost our bearings (lost our way).

HŌRŌ (suru) 放浪(する) wandering (wander)

furōsha 浮浪者 hobo; tramp; vagrant

hōrōheki 放浪癖 wanderlust

hōrōsei o obiru 放浪性を帯びる have a wanderlust; cannot stay in one place

hōrōsha 放浪者 wanderer

rurō 流浪 wandering

ie no nai hito 家のない人 homeless person; refugee

jinsei no kiro ni tatsu 人生の岐路に立つ stand at life's crossroads

MADOI (u) 惑い(惑う) perplexity (be perplexed; entertain doubts)

madowasu 惑わす lead one astray

tomadou とまどう When the lights went out, we fumbled around in the dark looking for the fuse box.

tōwaku (suru) 当惑(する) perplexity (be perplexed; be puzzled)

MAYOI (u) 迷い(迷う) illusion; delusion (get lost; lose one's way; be deluded)

~ **ga deru** が出る Lincoln felt that the South was under a delusion over secession.

~ **ga sameru** ~ がさめる come to one's senses

michi ni mayou 道に迷う get lost; go astray

fumimayou 踏み迷う stray; wander from

meishin 迷信 superstition

samayoi (u) さまよい(さまよう) wandering (wander about; wander)

MICHI ni hazureru 道にはずれる take a false step; do wrong

~ **o fumihazusu** を踏みはずす He turned from the path of duty and disappointed everyone.

michikusa o kuu 道草を食う Johnny

is late from school because he *dilly-dallied* (*fooled around*) on the way home.

muyūbyōsha 夢遊病者 sleep-walker

mōsō もう想 illusion; fantasy

~ **ni fukeru** ~にふける labor under a delusion

sasurau さすらう rove; ramble [around]

tadayou 漂う drift

tesaguri suru 手探りする grope; fumble

tohō ni kureru 途方にくれる When we got the shocking news, we *were at a loss* (*we were bewildered; didn't know which way to turn*).

urouro suru [C] うろうろする Don't spend your time *roaming round* (*milling around*); find something to do. ⇨ **43**

われわれはみな羊のように迷って，おのおの自分の道に向かって行った．主はわれわれすべての者の不義を，彼の上におかれた．(イザヤ 53 ⁶)

140 ME 目 EYE

hitomi ひとみ pupil of the eye

mabayui まばゆい glaring; blinding

mabuta まぶた eye lid

MANAKO まなこ eye

chimanako ni naru 血まなこになる He *became frantic* in his search for the lost boy.

gankō 眼光 glitter in one's eye

gankyū 眼球 eyeball

ganshiki 眼識 insight; discrimination

manazashi まなざし look of the eyes

aijō ni afureru manazashi 愛情にあふれるまなざし Abe looked at the wounded soldiers with *eyes full of affection.*

megane めがね glasses; spectacles

nikugan 肉眼 naked eye; unaided eye

ME 目 eye

~ **ga kiku (takai)** ~がきく (高い) He *has sharp eyes* for finding good items at reasonable prices.

~ **ga koeru** ~が肥える have perceptive eyes; be discerning

~ **ga kuramu** ~がくらむ be dazzled [by]; be blinded [by]

~ **ga mawaru** ~が回る get dizzy

~ **ga mono o iu** ~が物を言う You can tell he is unhappy about it; his *eyes tell the story.*

~ **kara hana e nukeru yōna** ~から鼻へ抜けるような He *doesn't miss a thing,* so be careful how you act.

~ **ni amaru** ~にあまる I *can't stand* the way that rowdy boy acts. That rowdy boy's behavior *is intolerable.*

~ **ni mienai** ~に見えない be invisible

~ **ni miete** ~に見えて conspicuously; markedly

~ **ni tsukiyasui** ~につきやすい easily strikes the eye

~ **no doku** ~の毒 That big offer is *tempting,* but don't let it deter you from the path of duty.

~ **o fuseru** ~を伏せる look down [in shame]

~ **o hiku** ~を引く draw attention to; attract notice

~ **o kakeru** ~をかける take care of; be kind to; look after

~ **o miharu** ~を見張る stare in wonder; look out for

~ **o sara no yōni shite** ~をさらのようにして *Keep* your *eyes peeled* for the missing car.

~ **o tōsu** ~を通す I *glanced over* the newspaper but didn't see his name mentioned.

~ **o utagau** ~を疑う cannot believe one's eyes

~ **wa kuchihodo ni mono o iu** [P] ~は口ほどに物を言う Eyes tell as much as the tongue.

manoatari ni まのあたりに straight in the face; before one's very eyes; face to face

matataki (ku) またたき(またたく) twinkling (blink)

medama 目玉 eyeball

megashira 目がしら the part of the eye near the nose

mesaki 目先 foresight; foreseeing; looking ahead

~ **no koto bakari kangaeru** の事ばかり考える think only of the immediate future

metsuki 目つき expression of the eyes; [a] look [in one's eye]

~ **ga warui** ~ が悪い have an evil eye; have a bad look

urameshī sōna metsuki うらめしそうな目つき resentful look

meutsuri 目移り distraction

mezameru 目ざめる wake up; come to one's senses

mezatoi 目ざとい sharp-eyed; keen; quick-eyed; shrewd

mezawari 目ざわり eyesore; obstruction to the view

MIRU 見る see; look at

chiratto miru ちらっと見る As she walked by, she *cast a glance* in my direction.

jirori to miru じろりと見る throw a searching glance

yokome de miru 横目で見る glance to the side; look to the side

mitsumeru 見つめる stare at; gaze at; set one's eyes on

ana ga aku hodo mitsumeru 穴があくほど見つめる When I walked into the office, the boss *looked a hole through me.*

jitto mitsumeru じっと見つめる stare at; look hard at; watch one's face intently

nagameru ながめる view; gaze at; watch; look at; look around

shiryoku 視力 visual power; eyesight

shisen o sorasu 視線をそらす When I tried to catch her attention, she *glanced in another direction.*

sugame (shashi) すが目(斜視) squint-eyed; crosseyed

yabunirami やぶにらみ squint-eyed; cross-eyed

⇨ **30, 92**

からだのあかりは目です。それで、もしあなたの目が健全なら、あなたの全身が明るいが、もし、目が悪ければ、あなたの全身が暗いでしょう。それなら、もしあなたのうちの光が暗ければ、その暗さはどんなでしょう。(マタイ 6 ²²,²³)

141 MEGUMI 恵み GRACE

HODOKOSHI (su) 施し(施す) favor; charity (grant a favor [to]; bestow [upon])

~ **o kou** ~ を請う When he saw Peter and John on their way into the temple, he *asked for charity.* (Acts 3 : 3)

~ **o suru** ~ をする give alms; give charity

MEGUMI (mu) 恵み(恵む) grace; blessing (grant; bless)

[...**ni**] **megumareru** [...に] 恵まれる be blessed [with]; be favored [by]

Kami no megumi ni yoru 神の恵みによる In our dealings with you, our conduct has been governed *by...the grace of God* and not by worldly wisdom. (II Corinthians 1 : 12)

megumibukai 恵み深い merciful

ON 恩 kindness; favor; obligation

~ **o hodokosu** ~ を施す do a favor [for]; grant a request [to]

~ **o kiru** ~ を着る feel indebted [to]

on'ai 恩愛 loving kindness

onchō 恩ちょう favor; grace

ongi 恩義 obligation; favor

onjō 恩情 compassion

onkei 恩恵 grace; favor

~ **ni yokusuru** ~ に浴する be favored [by]; be in the good graces [of]

~ o hodokosu ~ を施す bestow a favor [upon]

~ o kou ~ を請う ask a favor [of]

shukufuku (suru) 祝福 (する) blessing (bless)

⇨ **9, 97, 216**

律法がはいって来たのは，違反が増し加わるためです．しかし，罪の増し加わるところには，恵みも満ちあふれました．

それは，罪が死によって支配したように，恵みが，私たちの主イエス・キリストにより，義の賜物によって支配し，永遠のいのちを得させるためなのです．（ローマ 5 20, 21）

142 MEIHAKU 明白
CLARITY

abaku あばく expose; divulge; reveal; disclose

   himitsu ga abakareru 秘密があばかれる secret is laid bare; the secret is out

aimai (da) あいまい (だ) vague; ambiguous

   ~ na henji ~ な返事 vague answer; evasive answer

   koto o aimai ni suru 事をあいまいにする be vague and ambiguous

arawareru 表われる (現われる) come to light; come into view

   arawasu 表わす (現わす) reveal; disclose; express; display

ashi ga tsuku 足がつく Through the jacket he left, the crime *was traced* to him.

assari shita あっさりした simple; direct

bakuro suru 暴露する expose; disclose

   akusei o bakuro suru 悪性を暴露する show one's true colors

chokugen (suru) 直言(する) plain speaking (state plainly)

hakkiri to はっきりと distinctly; plainly; clearly

   ~ yomitoru ~ 読み取る grasp with clarity; read clearly

hanzen to [L] 判然と distinctly

   kōzen to 公然と openly; publicly

hikari ni sarasareru 光にさらされる be exposed to the light

himitsu ga moreru 秘密が漏れる secret leaks out

itten no utagai mo nai 一点の疑いもない There *is not a shadow of doubt* that he is innocent.

miesuita koto 見えすいた事 *It is perfectly obvious* that he intended to break the agreement before he even made it.

misebirakasu 見せびらかす air; expose; show off; display

   te o miseru 手を見せる He finally *laid his cards on the table*, telling us the whole plan.

MEIHAKU (da) 明白 (だ) clarity (clear; lucid)

   ~ na setsumei ~ な説明 lucid explanation

   ~ na shōko ~ な証拠 patent proof; clear evidence

   ~ ni naru ~ になる become clear

akarasama (da) あからさま (だ) plain; clear

akarui 明るい bright; light

akarumi 明るみ light

   ~ ni dasu ~ に出す " Bad men all hate the light and avoid it, for fear their practices should *be shown up*." (John 3 : 20)

   ~ ni deru ~ に出る The whole affair *came to light*, and the official resigned.

akasu 明かす divulge; reveal

akiraka (da) 明らか (だ) clear; lucid; obvious

   ~ ni naru ~ になる become evident; become clear

   ~ ni suru にする Lincoln *made it clear* to everyone that the government would not attack the South.

   hi o miru yori akiraka 火を見るより明らか as clear as day; perfectly clear

hakuchū kōzen to okonau 白昼公然と行なう He *did* the foul deed *right out in broad daylight*.

jimei no ri 自明の理 self-evident truth
kaimei suru 解明する make clear
meiryō (da) 明りょう (だ) distinct; clear
  kantan meiryō ni 簡単明りょうに simply and clearly
tōmei (da) 透明 (だ) clear; transparent
tokiakasu 解き明かす elucidate
meiron takusetsu 名論卓説 sound argument
ōppira (da) おおっぴら (だ) open; public
shimesu 示す reveal; disclose; display
sukitōtta 透き通った clear
sumikitta 澄みきった clear; transparent; serene
suppanuku すっぱ抜く bring out in the open; uncover
te ni toru yōni kikoeru 手に取るように聞こえる hear clear as a bell
tsukitomeru 突きとめる ascertain; make sure of
tsutsunuke ni kikoeru つつぬけに聞こえる Even the king's private conversations *found their way right into the ears of* Elisha the prophet.
wakarikitta jijitsu わかりきった事実 recognized fact; clear fact
yō o eta 要を得た He spoke right *to the point*.
  yōryō o enai 要領を得ない vague; inconclusive; incoherent
⇨ 96, 122, 161
ですから、あなたがたは、主が来られるまでは、何についても、先走ったさばきをしてはいけません。主は、やみの中に隠れた事も明るみに出し、心の中のはかりごとも明らかにされます。そのとき、神から各人に対する称賛が届くのです。(コリント I 4⁵)

143 MEIYO 名誉 FAME

EIKŌ 栄光 glory
  ~ o arawasu ~を表わす reveal the glory [of]; glorify
eiga 〔L〕 栄華 splendor; pomp
eikan 栄冠 crown; garland

eiyo 栄誉 glory; honor
kōei 光栄 privilege; honor
kōki aru 光輝ある glorious; splendid
sakae (ru) 栄え (栄える) prosperity (prosper; thrive)
en no shita no chikaramochi 縁の下の力持ち He is the *unsung hero* of the whole project.
eragari 偉がり self-importance
hana o motaseru 花を持たせる Glenn tried to *give* his working staff at Cape Kennedy *the glory* for his space feat.
hipparidako ni naru 引っぱりだこになる After Horie crossed the Pacific alone, he *became eagerly sought after (became in great demand)* all over Japan.
HYŌBAN 評判 reputation
  ~ ga ochiru ~が落ちる Grant's *reputation dropped* at Vicksburg when they discovered he had been drinking.
  ~ o takameru ~を高める gain fame
kōhyō o hakusuru 好評を博する receive favorable criticism
KAO 顔 face; reputation
  ~ ni kakawaru ~にかかわる His bad conduct *affected the honor* of his family.
  ~ o tateru ~を立てる Lincoln removed Secretary Cameron, but *to help him save face*, he assigned him as minister to Russia.
kassai o hakusuru かっさいを博する receive a big ovation
  manjō no kassai o abiru 満場のかっさいをあびる win the applause of the whole audience
koken ni kakawaru こけんにかかわる It *was beneath his dignity* to accept that position.
kokyō ni nishiki o kazaru 故郷ににしきを飾る Hillary *returned home* from his Everest feat *loaded with honors*.
kō o isogu 功を急ぐ be too eager for success

kōseki o nokosu 功績を残す By translating the Bible into Japanese, Dr. Hepburn *left a splendid work behind.*

kuchiguchi ni hometataeru 口々にほめたたえる *Praises* of the spacemen *were on everyone's lips.*

kyakkō o abiru 脚光を浴びる That actor *has been in the limelight (has been stealing the show)* since the first performance.

MEMBOKU 面目 face; honor
- **~ marutsubure ni naru** 丸つぶれになる When they discovered he cheated on the exam, he *lost face completely (was completely discredited).*
- **~ o hodokosu** ~ を施す Kashiwado finally *redeemed himself* by beating Taiho in the last match.

mentsu o tateru めんつを立てる save one's face

taimen 体面 honor
- **~ o tamotsu** ~ を保つ uphold one's honor

MEIYO 名誉 fame
- **~ o bankai suru** ~ をばんかいする vindicate oneself; make a comeback

chomei (da) 著名 (だ) prominent; of repute; distinguished

fukyū no meisaku 不朽の名作 an immortal literary masterpiece

fumeiyo (da) 不名誉 (だ) dishonorable; disgraceful

homare 誉れ praise

isshō no naore 一生の名折れ life long disgrace

kōmyō 功名 great feat; distinction
- **~ o arasou** ~ を争う vie for fame

meimon 名門 blue blood; aristocracy

meisei 名声 celebrity; fame
- **~ ni madowasareru** ~ にまどわされる I was *fooled by the* celebrity's *name,* hoping he would give to our charity drive, but he was penniless.
- **~ no takai** ~ の高い illustrious

sekaiteki meisei o hakusuru 世界的名声を博する achieve world-wide fame

mumei (da) 無名 (だ) unknown; obscure

na 名 name
- **~ ni fusawashii** ~ にふさわしい be worthy of the name
- **~ o ageru** ~ を上げる He left for Tokyo to *make a name for himself.*
- **~ o kōsei ni nokosu** を後世に残す leave an immortal name behind
- **~ o nasu** ~ をなす attain fame

nadakai 名高い well-known; celebrated

yūmei (da) 有名 (だ) famous; famed

miageta okonai 見上げた行ない splendid deed; admirable act

mibun no hikui 身分の低い of humble origins; of poor circumstances
- **~ no takai** ~ の高い noble; illustrious

NINKI 人気 popularity
- **~ ga ochiru** ~ が落ちる one's popularity declines

butai ninki 舞台人気 theatrical fame

ōatari (da) 〔c〕 大当たり (だ) His book was a *big hit.*

sakan (da) 盛ん (だ) rage (thriving; popular; fashionable)

sekaijū ni shirewataru 世界じゅうに知れ渡る have worldwide fame; be world famous

SHIMBŌ 信望 popularity
- **~ no atsui** ~ の厚い highly regarded
- **~ o eru** ~ を得る gain popularity; receive commendation

SHŌSAN (suru) 賞賛 (する) admiration (admire; look up to)
- **~ ni atai suru** ~ に値する be worthy of praise
- **~ no kotoba** ~ の言葉 words of praise
- **~ no mato ni naru** の的になる become the object of praise; become the talk of the town
- **~ o hakusuru** ~ を博する receive high praises

~ o ukeru ~ を受ける be commended;
receive praise
raisansha 礼賛者 admirer
⇨ **136**

互いの栄誉は受けても, 唯一の神からの栄誉を求めない
あなたがたは, どうして信じることができますか.
(ヨハネ 5 ⁴⁴)

144 MOKUSŌ 黙想
MEDITATION

furikaeru ふり返る look back; reflect on;
consider the past
**jibun no tōtte kita michi o furika-
ette miru** 自分の通って来た道をふり返
って見る *When I look back over my
past*, I see I've made many mistakes.
hairyo (suru) 配慮 (する) consideration
(consider)
hansei (suru) 反省する reflection; introspection (examine oneself)
naisei (suru) 内省 (する) reflection
(reflect upon)
jukkō(suru)熟考(する)deliberation(think
over)
jukushi (suru) 熟思 (する) pondering
(turn over in one's mind)
KAIKO (suru) 回顧 (する) recollection
(recollect; look back over; review)
kaikoroku 回顧録 memoirs
kaisō (suru) 回想 (する) reminiscence
(reminisce; reflect upon; recall)
KANGAE ni shizumu 考えに沈む He just
sat at his desk, *lost in thought.*
asahaka na kangae 浅はかな考え
Quitting school to get a job is
shallow thinking on your part.
kangaekomu 考え込む brood over; be
lost in thought
kangaete miru 考えて見る I'll *think
over* what you said.
keisan ni ireru 計算に入れる When you
buy a cheap house, you must *take into
account* that it will depreciate quickly.

MOKUSŌ 黙想 meditation
chinshi mokkō (suru) 沈思黙考 (する)
silent meditation (silently meditate;
contemplate)
kūsō (suru) 空想 (する) idle fancy (daydream)
~ **ni fukeru** ~ にふける daydream;
spend one's time in reverie
meisō (suru) めい想 (する) contemplation; meditation (contemplate; meditate)
~ **ni fukeru** にふける be lost in reverie
mōsō 妄想 fantasy; pipe dream
sōzō o megurasu 想像をめぐらす
contemplate; imagine
OMOI ni karareru 思いにかられる He *was
carried away with the idea* (*urged on by
the idea*) of getting rich quick.
omoimegurasu 思いめぐらす ponder
over; reflect upon; turn [a matter]
over in one's mind
shisaku (suru) 思索 (する) contemplation (contemplate; meditate)
~ **ni fukeru** ~ にふける be lost in
meditation
⇨ **174, 181, 193**

わが岩, わがあがないぬしなる主よ, どうかわたしの口の言
葉と, 心の思いがあなたの前に喜ばれますように.
(詩篇 19 ¹⁴)

145 MOKUTEKI 目的
PURPOSE, GOAL

dōki 動機 motive; inducement
hakaru 図る plan; devise
hara ga wakaranai 腹がわからない He is
so evasive I *can't figure him out* (*can't
understand his intentions*).
HŌSHIN 方針 course; policy; line
~ **ni shitagau** ~ に従う pursue a
course; follow a policy
~ **o tateru** ~ を立てる map out a
course; fix a plan
hōkō 方向 course; aim; direction

~ o kaeru ~を変える change one's course; switch directions

shishin 指針 compass needle; pointer; guide

ITO 意図 intention

  ~ ga wakaru ~がわかる Don't worry about him; *I've got him figured out* (*I've got his number*).

  ikō o saguru 意向を探る Foreign dignitaries came to *sound out* Johnson's *views* on disarmament.

  shin'i o kaisuru 真意を解する I think I *know his true intentions* (*know what he has in mind*).

  sokoi 底意 deeper motive; real intention

KEIKAKU (suru) 計画(する) plan; project (plan; formulate a plan)

  ~ ga kuichigau ~が食い違う In the end, the *plan miscarried.*

  ~ ni shitagatte ~にしたがって according to purpose

  ~ o jikkō suru ~を実行する carry out a plan

  ~ o susumeru ~を進める put a plan into practice

  ~ o tateru を立てる form a plan

keikakuteki (da) 計画的(だ) purposely; on purpose; intentional

kokorogakeru 心がける endeavor; intend [to]

shitagokoro 下心 ulterior motive

kokorozashi 志 intention; purpose; will

kontan 魂胆 plot; secret plan; scheme

  ~ ga aru ~がある The many callers at the White House came *with an eye to some position* (*with an axe to grind*).

kuwadateru 企てる scheme; plot; plan

  kikaku (suru) 企画(する) plan; project (attempt)

mokuromi (mu) [L] もくろみ(もくろむ) plot; intention (plot; plan; scheme)

MOKUTEKI 目的 purpose

  [...no] ~ de [...の] ~で with this in mind

~ ni kanau ~にかなう meet the purpose of; go along with the objective [of]

~ ni yakudatsu ~に役立つ serve the purpose [of]

~ o hatasu (jitsugen suru) ~を果たす(実現する) carry out one's purpose; achieve one's goal

~ o tassuru ~を達する accomplish one's purpose; reach an objective

kompon no mokuteki 根本の目的 primary purpose

mato 的 target; object; aim

  ~ ga hazureru ~がはずれる miss the point; strike wide of the goal

meate 目当て guidepost; aim; goal

mejirushi 目印 landmark; sign; guidepost

meyasu o tateru 目安を立てる *Fix your aim* (*Set your sights*) on the best college and work toward getting admitted.

mezasu 目ざす aim at; direct one's attention to

mokuhyō 目標 goal; objective

  ~ ni tassuru ~に達する reach one's goal

  ~ o mezasu ~を目ざす aim at a goal; set a goal

  ~ o tateru ~を立てる establish a purpose

mokutekichi 目的地 destination

nerai (u) ねらい(ねらう) aim (aim at; take aim)

  neraidokoro ねらい所 His *aim* (*goal*) is getting into foreign service.

omou tsubo ni hamaru 思うつぼにはまる I expected him to accept the proposal, and he *fell right into my clutches.*

shippo o tsukamu しっぽをつかむ He wouldn't tell anything about his plans, but I *found* him *out* by something he said.

shoshin o kantetsu suru [L] 初心を貫徹

する carry out the original plan; follow through with the original plan

shugan to suru 主眼とする paramount object; chief objective

shushi 趣旨 intention; purport

honshi 本旨 chief objective; main purpose

yōshi 要旨 purport

takurami (mu) たくらみ (たくらむ) plot; trick; scheme (contrive; plot; scheme) ⇨ 174

わたしはあなたを教え，あなたの行くべき道を示し，わたしの目をあなたにとめて，さとすであろう． (詩篇 32 ⁸)

146 MUDA むだ WASTE, USELESSNESS

Abu hachi torazu [P] あぶはち取らず If you try two things at once, you will *succeed in getting nowhere.*

fumō no chi 不毛の地 wasteland; barren soil

fuyō (da) 不用 (だ) uselessness (useless; unnecessary)

haibutsu 廃物 waste; refuse

~ **ni naru** ~になる become useless; become scrap

~ **riyō** ~利用 utilization of waste materials

honeori zon (o suru) 骨折り損 (をする) wasted effort (make a wasted effort; beat the air)

~ **no kutabire mōke** [P] ~のくたびれもうけ You can do it if you want, but you will be *making a vain effort* (*doing it uselessly*).

Hotoke tsukutte tamashii irezu [P] 仏作って魂入れず He went to all that trouble and then *left out the most vital part* (*forgot the one vital thing*).

itazura (da) いたずら (だ) purposelessness (in vain; to no purpose)

KŪHI (suru) 空費 (する) waste (throw away)

jikan no kūhi 時間の空費 waste of time

kūkyo (da) 空虚 (だ) emptiness (empty; hollow)

rampi (suru) 乱費(する) waste (waste; squander)

rōhi (suru) 浪費 (する) squandering (squander; fritter away)

tsuiyasu 費やす spend; waste [money, time, etc.]

kuitsubusu 食いつぶす squander

zaisan o kuitsubusu 財産を食いつぶす squander a fortune

goku tsubushi [C] ごくつぶし He is a *good-for-nothing fellow.*

kuzu くず waste; garbage; refuse

mizu no awa to naru [L] 水のあわとなる After all our preparations the project was rejected and *came to naught* (*became a fiasco*).

MUDA ni naru むだになる prove to be labor lost; become a wasted effort

~ **o habuku** を省く eliminate waste

dainashi ni suru だいなしにする I spilled ink on my new suit and *completely ruined* it.

mu [L] 無 nothing

~ **ni suru** ~にする nullify

mudaashi o hakobu むだ足を運ぶ He *went on a wild goose chase* looking for motor parts on the Ginza.

mudabanashi (mudaguchi) むだ話 (むだ口) idle talk

mudabone o oru むだ骨を折る work in vain; prove to be labor lost

mudazukai (suru) むだ使い (する) waste (waste; fritter away)

mueki (da) 無益 (だ) useless; futile; vain

muimi (da) 無意味 (だ) meaninglessness (meaningless; without significance)

mukō (da) 無効 (だ) invalidity (invalid)

muyō (da) 無用 (だ) uselessness (useless; unserviceable)

munashii 空しい empty; vain

nan no tashi ni mo naranai 何の足しにもならない Practicing late at night *will get you nowhere* (*will amount to nothing*) if you ruin your health in the process.

Nito o ou mono wa itto o mo ezu [P] 二兎を追う者は一兎をも得ず You can't do two things at once.

Noren ni ude oshi [P] のれんに腕押し You are just *beating the air* (*wasting your efforts*) trying to effect a change around here.

Nuka ni kugi [P] ぬかにくぎ Trying to help that drunk was *wasted effort*.

Odawara hyōjō [P] 小田原評定 They're discussing politics again; it's just a *fruitless discussion*.

shikata ga nai しかたがない it can't be helped; there's no way out

shiyō ga nai しようがない nothing can be done about it; there is nothing one can do about it

Takara no mochigusare [P] 宝の持ち腐れ I don't know what I can do with that large vase he gave me; it's a *white elephant*.

tsukaimichi ga nai 使いみちがない If you divide up the property that way, *there'll be no way to use* the triangular part.

Tsukiyo ni chōchin [P] 月夜にちょうちん Taking rice with you to the hotel is like *carrying coals to Newcastle* [P].

Yakeishi ni mizu [P] 焼け石に水 The project is too far along; I'm afraid your suggestions *will be wasted effort* (*will be of no avail*).

Yasumonokai no zeni ushinai [P] 安物買いのぜにに失い Penny wise and pound foolish [P].

そして，もしキリストがよみがえらなかったのなら，あなたがたの信仰はむなしく，あなたがたは今もなお，自分の罪の中にいるのです．（コリントⅠ15 ¹⁷）

147 MUTONJAKU むとんじゃく INDIFFERENCE, UNCONCERN

aite ni shinai 相手にしない *Have nothing to do with* him; he's unreliable.

atama kara mondai ni shinai 頭から問題にしない We made a proposal, but the boss *flatly refused to give it any consideration*.

Ato wa no to nare yama to nare [P] あとは野となれ山となれ I couldn't care less; let the chips fall where they may.

dogaishi suru 度外視する leave [it] out of consideration; take no account [of]

dotchi tsukazu no taido どっちつかずの態度 a non-committal attitude

ganchū ni okanai 眼中におかない The ambassador *made light of* (*wouldn't even consider*) their request for aid.

heiki (da) 平気（だ） unconcernedness (unconcerned; do not care)

i ni kaisanai 意に介さない He is successful because he *is not bothered by* criticism (*doesn't take* criticism *seriously*).

ikkō ni kanshin ga nai いっこうに関心がない I tried to talk to him about hiking, but he *has no interest* in it *whatsoever*.

mukanshin (da) 無関心（だ） indifference (indifferent)

isshō ni fusuru 一笑に付する laugh it off; laughingly disregard it

kamawazu ni oku かまわずにおく I know you were insulted, but it would be best just to *leave things as they are* (*pass it off*).

narifuri kamawazu なりふりかまわず He walks into offices *not caring how he looks*.

kao o somukeru 顔をそむける spurn; turn one's face away

ki ni tomenai 気に留めない take no notice [of]; ignore

kikinagasu 聞き流す pay no attention [to]; pass over

kokoro ni kakenai 心にかけない take no interest in

mimi ni hairanai 耳にはいらない not hear; miss; will not listen

~ **o kasanai** ~を貸さない I think you should *turn a deaf ear to* any smutty talk you hear.

MIMUKI mo shinai 見向きもしない I called after her, but she went on *without so much as glancing back.*

minai furi o suru 見ないふりをする pretend not to see

minogasu 見のがす overlook; pass over

mushi suru 無視する ignore; disregard

[...**o**] **naigashiro ni suru** [...を] ないがしろにする make light of; make little of

nan tomo omowanai なんとも思わない Even though he had broken the valuable watch, he seemed to *think nothing of it.*

nentō ni okanai 念頭におかない disregard; not keep in mind

reitan (da) 冷淡 (だ) coolness (cool; indifferent)

~ **ni naru** ~になる become indifferent [to]; become cool [toward]

kokoro no tsumetai (hito) 心の冷たい (人) heartless person; cold person

[...**ni**] **se o mukeru** [...に] 背を向ける He tried to get back into the organization, but because of his actions they *turned their backs on* (*shunned; ostracized; disowned*) him.

SHIRANAI furi o suru 知らないふりをする pretend not to know

shiran kao o suru 知らん顔をする feign ignorance

Shiranu ga hotoke [P] 知らぬが仏 Ignorance is bliss [P].

soburi o misenai そぶりを見せない He is quite a distinguished person, but *he never lets on about it* (*you would never know it*).

soppo o muku そっぽを向く He tried to be kind to her, but she *turned her back on him* (*brushed him off; snubbed him*).

sora to bokete iru そらとぼけている She was an old friend, but at the party she *pretended not to know* me.

tana ni ageru たなに上げる He's always criticizing others and *ignoring his own faults.*

toriawanai 取り合わない They *didn't take* him *seriously*, because he exaggerated so.

Uma no mimi ni nembutsu [P] 馬の耳に念仏 Your advice to the old fellow will be like *water off a duck's back* [P].

uwa no sora de うわの空で The children listened *vacant-eyed* to the boring lecture.

⇨ 28

わたしは右の方に目を注いで見回したが, わたしに心をとめる者はひとりもありません. わたしには避け所がなく, わたしをかえりみる人はありません. 主よ, わたしはあなたに呼ばわります. わたしは言います. 「あなたはわが避け所, 生ける者の地で, わたしの受くべき分です.

(詩篇 142 [4], [5])

148 NAGEKI 嘆き GRIEF

hihō 悲報 sad news

itamu いたむ lament; mourn; grieve

koe o tsumaraseru 声をつまらせる sob

umekigoe o tateru うめき声を立てる groan in anguish

mune ga harisakeru yōna 胸が張り裂けるような I read the story of the Jews in Germany with a *heart-rending feeling.*

NAGEKI (ku) 嘆き(嘆く) grief (be grieved over; sigh; lament)

~ **no amari** ~のあまり overwhelmed with grief; grief-stricken

shi o nageku 死を嘆く She is *mourning the passing* of her father.

gaitan suru 慨嘆する deplore; lament

hitan 悲嘆 grief; sorrow

nagekawashii 嘆かわしい sad; wretched; deplorable; lamentable

NAKU 泣く cry; weep

oioi naku [c] おいおい泣く When her mother died, she *wept bitterly* (*cried her heart out*).

samezame to naku さめざめと泣く cry one's heart out

nakidasu 泣き出す burst out crying; cry out

nakifusu 泣き伏す break down

nakigoe 泣き声 crying voice

nakikanashimu 泣き悲しむ weep over; mourn

nakikuzureru 泣きくずれる break down in tears

nakimane 泣きまね crocodile tears; fake tears

nakimushi 泣き虫 cry-baby

nakineiri suru [c] 泣き寝入りする John went to bed disappointed and *cried himself to sleep*. The decision was against us, but we just have to *put up with it* (*resign ourselves to it*).

nakiotosu 泣き落とす cry for something; persuade by tears

nakisakebu 泣き叫ぶ cry out; scream

shinobinaku しのび泣く weep silently

soranaki そら泣き crocodile tears

susurinaku すすり泣く sob; weep

NAMIDA 涙 tear

~ **ga komiagete kuru** ~ がこみ上げてくる tears well up; be reduced to tears

~ **ga tomedomonaku nagareru** ~ がとめどもなく流れる cannot stop the tears from flowing

~ **ga waku** ~ がわく tears come welling up

~ **moroi** ~ もろい easily reduced to tears; cries easily

~ **ni kureru** ~ にくれる be reduced to tears

~ **ni musebu** ~ にむせぶ be choked with tears

~ **o dasu** ~ を出す shed tears

~ **o nagasu** ~ を流す cry; shed tears

~ **o sasou** ~ を誘う Seeing that pitiful blind girl *moved* us *to tears.*

~ **o ukaberu** ~ を浄かべる tears well up in one's eyes

namidagumashii 涙ぐましい pathetic; tearful

namidagumu 涙ぐむ be moved to tears

oshimu 惜しむ regret

sakebu 叫ぶ cry out

sakebigoe 叫び声 cry; crying out

tansei 嘆声 sigh

tansoku (suru) 嘆息 (する) sigh (heave a sigh; gulp)

⇨ **87**

そのとき私は，御座から出る大きな声がこう言うのを聞いた。「見よ。神の幕屋が人とともにある。神は彼らとともに住み，彼らはその民となる。また，神ご自身が彼らとともにおられて，

彼らの目の涙をすっかりぬぐい取ってくださる。もはや死もなく，悲しみ，叫び，苦しみもない。なぜなら，以前のものが，もはや過ぎ去ったからである。」（黙示録 21 [8, 4]）

149 NAGUSAME 慰め
COMFORT, CONSOLATION

aitō no i o hyōsuru 哀悼の意を表する He *expressed* his *condolences* to the family.

genkizukeru 元気づける strengthen; enliven; put heart into; bolster

kiyasume o iu 気休めを言う He *used reassuring words* (*spoke soothing words*) to us, but we were not convinced.

HAGEMASHI (su) 励まし(励ます) encouragement (encourage; stimulate; cheer up)

~ **o ukeru** ~ を受ける receive encouragement

gekirei no kotoba 激励の言葉 word of encouragement

hagemi (mu) 励み(励む) encouragement; stimulation (be encouraged in)

itawari (ru) いたわり(いたわる) sympathy;

pity (sympathize with; show pity [toward])

kokoro o uruosu 心をうるおす It *did my heart good* to see him again.

~ o yasumeru ~を休める The news of her boy's safety *put* her *at ease.*

mimai (u) 見舞い (見舞う) sympathy call; sick call (make a sick call)

mimaijō 見舞い状 condolence letter

nadameru なだめる soothe; calm one down; placate

nadamesukasu なだめすかす humor; soothe

NAGUSAME (ru) 慰め (慰める) comfort; consolation (cheer up; comfort)

~ no kotoba o kakeru ~の言葉をかける The pastor stopped in to *speak a word of comfort* to her.

semete mo no nagusame ni せめてもの慰めに The *least comfort that can be given* at a time like this is sending him a letter.

ian 慰安 consolation; solace

~ o ataeru ~を与える give comfort

~ o motomeru ~を求める seek solace [in]

imon (jō) 慰問 (状) visit to the sick (get-well card)

isha 慰謝 comfort; consolation

isharyō 慰謝料 consolation money; compensation; alimony

~ o harau ~を払う pay alimony; pay for damages

nagusami 慰み amusement; pleasure

negirau ねぎらう provide comfort for; give comfort to

[...no] rō o negirau [...の] 労をねぎらう *In appreciation for the service* he rendered to the firm, the boss bought him a chair.

okuyami お悔やみ solace; consolation

~ o iu ~を言う I went over and *expressed my sympathy* (*expressed my condolences*) to the family.

⇨ 9
神は、どのような苦しみのときにも、私たちを慰めてくださいます。こうして、私たちも、自分自身が神から受ける慰めによって、どのような苦しみの中にいる人をも慰めることができるのです。(コリント II 1 ⁴)

150 NAYAMI 悩み
ANGUISH, WORRY

hammon (suru) 煩もん (する) agony; anguish (agonize [over]; be in anguish [about]; have an inner conflict)

ite mo tatte mo irarenai 居ても立ってもいられない Lincoln *was beside himself* (*couldn't stay still*) waiting for news from Sherman's lost army.

jitto shite irarenai じっとしていられない Waiting for the report, I *couldn't stay still* (*had to do something*).

kami o kakimushiru 髪をかきむしる I *tore my hair* waiting for word about the lost children.

KI ga ki de nai 気が気でない Because you didn't come I *felt very anxious* (*was unable to relax; was not myself*).

~ o momu ~をもむ She is getting past the marriageable age and *is worried about* it.

kigurō (suru) 気苦労 (する) worry; care (worry about; be concerned about)

kokoro ni kakeru 心にかける That she hasn't come home yet *weighs on his mind.*

kokoronokori 心残り The boy left home, but he has been a *constant worry* (*cause of concern*) to his father.

KUNŌ 苦悩 agony

kokoro o kurushimeru 心を苦しめる He is *torturing himself* with the idea that he caused the accident.

ku ni suru 苦にする take something to heart

kurō o kakeru 苦労をかける By your

negligence you have *caused him trouble.*

modaekurushimu もだえ苦しむ writhe in agony

kuttaku no nai くったくのない In spite of all the problems, he seems to be *free from worry (unconcerned).*

kuyashigaru くやしがる be vexed [about]; regret

kuyokuyo shinai [C] くよくよしない He is not one to *be upset by trifles (fret over trivialities).*

MUNE ga mushakusha suru 胸がむしゃくしゃする be upset; be rankled [by]; be out of sorts

~ **no harisakeru omoi** ~ の張り裂ける思い heart-rending experience

~ **o itameru** ~ を痛める Lincoln *was vexed (was heartsick)* over the Fredericksburg defeat.

munasawagi ga suru 胸騒ぎがする feel uneasy about; be at unrest over; be apprehensive

NAYAMI(mu) 悩み(悩む) anguish; worry (be in anguish; be worried [about])

kokoro no nayami 心の悩み deep anxiety

nayamashii 悩ましい distressing; painful

nayamasu 悩ます torment; harass; worry

atama o nayamasu 頭を悩ます be in mental anguish

kokoro o nayamasu 心を悩ます Set your *troubled hearts* at rest. (John 14: 1)

nayamikurushimu 悩み苦しむ be painfully troubled

SHIMPAI (suru) 心配 (する) worry; concern; misgivings (worry; be concerned [about]; have misgivings [about]; be troubled about)

~ **ga nai** ~ がない *There is nothing to worry about.*

~ **o kakeru** ~ をかける cause anxiety; cause concern

UREI (u) 憂い (憂う) grief; distress (be anxious about)

kōko no urei ga nai 後顧の憂いがない He is gravely sick but *has no anxiety over the future* of his family, since he has made good provision for them.

kokoro no urei 心の憂い great distress; deep distress

WAZURAI (u) わずらい(わずらう) worry (be afflicted with)

kokoro o wazurawasu 心をわずらわす cause worry: be concerned about

omoiwazurau 思いわずらう worry about; be anxious about

wazurawashii わずらわしい troublesome; bothersome

ya mo tate mo tamaranai [L] 矢も盾もたまらない Mary was so anxious to see her boyfriend that she *couldn't contain herself (couldn't sit still).*

yarusenai やるせない After being deserted by his sweetheart, he *was inconsolable.* ⇨ **130**

あなたがたは、世にあっては患難があります。しかし、勇敢でありなさい。わたしはすでに世に勝ったのです。
（ヨハネ 16 ³³）

151 NESSHIN 熱心 ZEAL, ENTHUSIASM

atsuku 熱く fervently; warmly

chi o wakasu 血をわかす The Waseda students *boiled over with enthusiasm* as the rugby team scored.

isshin ni 一心に wholeheartedly

~ **furan ni** ~ 不乱に He *is cramming* for the final exams. He is *going all out* to get the job done.

isshōkemmei (da) 一生懸命(だ) wholeheartedness (wholehearted; with all one's might)

maishin suru まい進する strive for; push on

moeru 燃える be burning; be on fire; be fervent

muchū ni naru 夢中になる He has *become crazy about* (*become absorbed in*) baseball.

NESSHIN (da) 熱心(だ) zeal; enthusiasm (zealous; enthusiastic)

 jōnetsu 情熱 passion; fervor; zeal

  ~ ni moeru ~に燃える burn with passion [for]

  ~ o aoru ~をあおる His description of life in the Peace Corps *inspired* us (*kindled* our *zeal*) to follow his example.

  ~ o kakete ~をかけて putting one's heart into; with fervor

  ~ o kaku ~を欠く lack enthusiasm

  ~ o komete ~をこめて putting all one's enthusiasm into

 nekketsu 熱血 hot blood; fiery spirit

 nessei 熱誠 fervency; devotion

 nessuru 熱する get hot [about]; become excited [about]

 netchū (suru) 熱中 (する) enthusiasm; zeal; mania; fervor (be engrossed in)

 netsu ni ukasareru 熱に浮かされる The baseball fans, *carried away by enthusiasm* for their team, rushed out and put them on their shoulders.

  ~ o ageru ~をあげる become enthusiastic

 netsuai (suru) 熱愛 (する) fervent love (love fervently)

 netsui o motte ataru 熱意をもって当たる I hope you will *do* your duty *with* zeal.

 netsujō 熱情 zest; ardor; zeal; passion

  ~ no aru ~のある fervent

 netsuretsu (da) 熱烈 (だ) vehemency; passion (vehement; passionate; ardent)

yamitsuki ni naru [C] 病みつきになる He's

developed a craze for tennis and plays every day.

⇨ **85, 95, 176**

キリストが私たちのためにご自身をささげられたのは，私たちをすべての不法から贖い出し，良いわざに熱心なご自分の民を，ご自分のために聖別するためでした．
(テトス 2 ¹⁴)

152 NETAMI ねたみ
JEALOUSY, ENVY

NETAMI (mu) ねたみ (ねたむ) jealousy; envy (envy; be jealous of)

 ~ o okosu ~を起こす stir up envy

 netamashii ねたましい enviable

 netamashiku omou ねたましく思う She *felt jealous of* (*was filled with resentment toward*) Jane for getting all those dates.

senbō no mato せん望の的 After his heroic crossing of the Pacific, Horie became the *envy* of Japanese youth.

SHITTO (suru) しっと (する) jealousy; envy (be jealous [of]; be envious [of])

 ~ ni me ga kuramu ~に目がくらむ *Blinded by jealousy*, he did some very irrational things.

 ~ no amari ~のあまり from jealousy; out of envy

 ~ o okosu ~を起こす become envious [of]; stir up jealousy

 ~ shite ~して *Moved by jealousy*, he tried to hinder his opponent.

 shittoshin kara しっと心から out of jealousy

sonemi (mu) そねみ(そねむ) jealousy; envy (be jealous [of]; be envious [of])

tsuno o dasu [C] つのを出す If he even speaks to other women, his wife *gets jealous*.

urayami (mu) うらやみ (うらやむ) envy; covetousness (envy; covet)

 urayamashii うらやましい enviable; envious

yakimochi 焼きもち jealousy
  ~ o yaku ~ を焼く He can't even talk to another woman without his wife's *feeling jealous.*

愛は死のように強く、ねたみは墓のように残酷だからです。そのきらめきは火のきらめき最もはげしい炎です。
(雅歌 8 ⁶)

153   NIKUSHIMI 憎しみ
HATRED

AKUI 悪意 ill will; malice; evil intention
  ~ ni toru ~ に取る The South *took* many of Lincoln's remarks *wrongly.*
  ~ o idaku ~ をいだく mean ill towards; harbor malice
  akukanjō o idaku 悪感情をいだく *There is bad blood between* those two.

hana ni tsuku 鼻につく I used to like him, but his boastfulness *has become disgusting.*
  hanamochi naranai 鼻持ちならない I *can't stomach* the way those men cheat. The way those men cheat *is disgusting.*

ikon 遺恨 hatred

itou いとう hate; dislike

IYA ni naru いやになる become disgusted [with]
  iyagaru いやがる He *seems to dislike* (*seems to loathe*) playing tennis on Sundays.
  [...ni] iyaki ga sasu [...に] いや気がさす I *am sick of* (*feel repugnant to; feel an aversion towards*) the way he does business.
  iyami no aru いやみのある irksome; peeving

ki ni kuwanai 気にくわない The way he ridicules others *is distasteful to me* (*gets under my skin*).

KIRAI (u) きらい(きらう) dislike (have a distaste for)

atama kara kirau 頭からきらう thoroughly dislike

daikirai (da) 大きらい (だ) hatred; abhorrence (detest; abhor)

imikirau 忌みきらう detest; abhor

kegirai suru けぎらいする have antipathy for; be prejudiced against

kuwazugirai (da) 食わずぎらい(だ) *He's a prejudiced person. He dislikes a thing without even trying it.*

ken'o (suru) けん悪 (する) hatred (hate; have a deep dislike for)

mayu o hisomeru まゆをひそめる She *raised her eyebrows* in disgust at his crude remark.

me no kataki ni suru 目のかたきにする He *is out to get* that fellow every time he has a chance.

munakuso ga warui [C] 胸くそが悪い I *cannot stomach* (*get sick of*) the way he brags.

mushi no sukanai 虫の好かない I don't know why, but that new clerk *rubs me the wrong way.*
  mushizu ga hashiru 虫ずが走る It *makes me sick* (*It is revolting*) to see all those drunks staggering around the station.

NIKUSHIMI 憎しみ hatred
  nikui 憎い hateful
  nikumaremono 憎まれ者 object of hatred
  nikumu 憎む hate; abhor
    nikunde mo tarinai 憎んでも足りない abominate; really detest
  nikunikushige ni 憎々しげに hatefully
  nikunikushii にくにくしい loathsome; detestable
  nikurashii 憎らしい hateful; odious; provoking
  Kawaisa amatte nikusa hyakubai [P] かわいさあまって憎さが百倍 A person who is especially loved is hated all the more when he spurns that love.

zōo 憎悪 hatred; abhorrence

nirami(mu) にらみ(にらむ) scowl (glare at)

tekii 敵意 enmity; hostile feeling; animosity

　tekitai (suru) 敵対 (する) antagonism (be antagonistic [to])

⇒ 99, 205

神を愛すると言いながら, 兄弟を憎んでいるなら, その人は偽り者です. 目に見える兄弟を愛していない者に, 目に見えない神を愛することはできません. (ヨハネ I 4 ²⁰)

154 NINTAI 忍耐 PATIENCE, PERSEVERANCE

Bushi wa kuwanedo, takayōji [P] 武士は食わねど高ようじ The samurai glories in honorable poverty.

futō-fukutsu no seishin 不とう不屈の精神 unyielding spirit

GAMAN (suru) がまん (する) endurance (endure; bear; stand)

　~ dekinai ~ できない Stop your criticism; I *can't stand it* (*can't stomach it*) any longer.

　~ naranai ~ ならない She *is out of patience with* her wilful daughter.

　ha o kuishibatte gaman suru 歯を食いしばってがまんする He didn't want to have the operation, but I told him to *grit his teeth and go through with it.*

　yasegaman (suru) やせがまん (する) He was turned down again, but he'll *keep trying because his pride's at stake* (*grin and bear it*).

ganbaru がんばる persevere; keep at it; stick to it

ishi ni kajiritsuite mo 石にかじりついても I'm going to try to get that degree *at any cost* (*no matter what*).

Ishi no ue ni mo sannen 石の上にも三年 [P] Perseverance will even wear out a stone.

itatamarenai いたたまれない unbearable

Itchō isseki ni wa dekinai [P] 一朝一夕にはできない Rome wasn't built in a day [P].

KANNIN bukuro no o ga kireru 堪忍袋の緒が切れる I tried to overlook his rude remarks, but finally *I couldn't take it any longer* (*my patience ran out*), and I told him off.

　Naranu kannin suru ga kannin [P] ならぬ堪忍するが堪忍 Enduring the unendurable is true endurance.

mō kanben dekinai もうかんべんできない My patience has run out!

kinaga ni 気長に patiently

KONKI 根気 grit; perseverance

　~ yoku yaru ~ よくやる keep at it; do [something] patiently

　konkurabe 根くらべ feat of endurance

　konmake suru 根負けする I finally *gave in* to his persistent sales talk.

koraeru こらえる bear; endure; stand [it]; stick it out

kotsu kotsu yaru yori hoka wa nai こつこつやるよりほかはない There's no alternative but to keep plugging away.

kubi o nagaku shite 首を長くして The anxious father *waited impatiently* for his son to return from the war.

kyōkō suru 強行する Everyone was against it, but he *pushed it through* (*went through with it*) anyway.

nakineiri suru 泣き寝入りする Even though we were right, we were overruled and *forced to put up with* the situation.

nebarizuyoi 粘り強い tenacious; tough

NINTAI (suru) 忍耐 (する) patience; perseverance (be patient; persevere)

　nintairyoku 忍耐力 perseverance; pertinacity

　~ o yashinau ~ を養う cultivate patience

　nintaizuyoi 忍耐強い persevering

　　nintaizuyoku matsu 忍耐強く待つ wait patiently

shinobu 忍ぶ withstand; bear; put up with
  fuben o shinobu 不便を忍ぶ Please *put up with the inconvenience of* having to use the other door.
  kutsū o shinobu 苦痛を忍ぶ endure pain
taeru 耐える tolerate; bear; endure
  kurushimi ni taeru 苦しみに耐える bear up under suffering
  taeshinobu 耐え忍ぶ bear up [under]; bear [something] patiently
shibire o kirasu しびれをきらす I *got tired of waiting* for him and came home.
shinbō (suru) しんぼう (する) perseverance; stick-to-itiveness; patience (persevere; exercise patience)
  shinbōzuyoi しんぼう強い persevering; of infinite patience
shitsukoi しつこい tenacious; won't take no for an answer
また, 神の栄光ある権能に従い, あらゆる力をもって強くされて, 忍耐と寛容を尽し, また, その中にある。 聖徒の相続分にあずかる資格を私たちに与えてくださった父なる神に, 喜びをもって感謝をささげることができますように。 (コロサイ 1 ¹¹, ¹²)

155 NŌRYOKU 能力
ABILITY, CAPACITY

dekiru できる can do
enjuku shita 円熟した fully developed; mature; ripe
gei ga nai [C] 芸がない He is a good worker but in negotiations *is not versatile (lacks finesse)*.
  ~ o suru ~をする do a stunt
giryō 技量 [technical] skill; ability
  ~ o shimesu ~を示す He *showed a talent for (displayed his ability in)* that type of work.
hakuryoku ga nai 迫力がない Chuo is losing badly; they *don't have any drive* today.

Heta no yokozuki [P] へたの横好き You go bowling a lot, but you *never seem to improve*.
isai o hanatsu 異彩を放つ In the swimming meet he *stood out from the others (was outstanding)*.
ita ni tsuku 板につく His lectures were stilted at first, but now he *is at home in them (has become used to them; acts like a pro)*.
jōzu (da) じょうず (だ) skill (skillful)
  Suki koso mono no jōzu nare [P] 好きこそ物のじょうずなれ Of course you have to like something to become good at it.
kaishō ga nai [C] かいしょうがない He's a nice fellow but *hasn't got what it takes (lacks the drive)* to be a successful salesman.
mi no hodo o shiranai 身のほどを知らない He's trying to get into Tokyo University, but I'm afraid he *doesn't know his own limitations*.
NŌRYOKU 能力 ability; capacity
  ~ ijō ni shiyō to suru ~ 以上にしようとする He's *biting off more than he can chew*.
  ~ o hakki suru ~を発揮する fully display one's ability
  ~ o ikasu ~を生かす utilize one's ability; make use of one's gift
  ~ o nobasu ~を伸ばす develop one's capacity
  ~ o utagau ~を疑う question one's ability
  [...o] suru nōryoku ga nai [...を] する能力がない have no capacity to do
chikara 力 power; ability
munō (da) 無能 (だ) incompetency (incompetent; incapable)
nō ga nai 能がない He will be a good clerk but *will not be up to (will be a poor hand at; will be inadequate for)* being an executive.

nō aru taka wa tsume o kakusu
[P] 能あるたかはつめを隠す A talented
person knows how to be modest.

nōritsu 能率 efficiency

nōritsuteki (da) 能率的 (だ) efficient

rikiryō 力量 capacity; ability; talent
　~ o tamesu ~ をためす test one's ability

yūnō (da) 有能 (だ)　competency
(competent)
　~ no shi ~ の士 competent man; man
of ability

SAI 才 ability; talent
　gogaku no sai 語学の才 language
ability; linguistic ability
　keiei no sai 経営の才 administrative
ability; managerial ability
　bunsai no aru hito 文才のある人 He is
a man of remarkable literary talents.
　saien 才えん clever girl; talented woman
　saijin (saishi) 才人 (才子) talented
person (clever man)
　sainō 才能 talent; gift
　~ no aru ~ のある gifted; talented
　~ o migaku ~ をみがく cultivate one's
gifts; develop one's talent
　~ o riyō suru ~ を利用する utilize
one's talents
　nami ika no sainō 並み以下の才能
below-average ability
　tenpu no sainō [L] 天賦の才能 natural
talents

taiki bansei [L] 大器晩成 Great talents
develop late.

takumi (da) 巧み (だ) cleverness (cleverly;
cunningly)

TENBUN 天分 natural ability; natural
endowment
　~ o ikasu ~ を生かす You should *make
the most of your natural talent* and
practice singing.
　yutaka na tenbun ga aru 豊かな天分が
ある be richly endowed [with] natural
ability

tokui (da) 得意 (だ) skill (skilled; one's
pride)

UDE ga aru 腕がある He *has ability* but is
not putting it to good use.
　~ ni oboe ga aru ~ に覚えがある He
is over sixty but *prides himself in*
his golf *ability.*

udekiki 腕きき man of ability; able
person

udemae 腕前 capacity; ability
　hibon no udemae 非凡の腕前
extraordinary ability

umaku yatta うまくやった He *did* the job
well (did...skillfully).

⇨ **19**

それぞれが賜物を受けているのですから，神のさまざまな
恵みの良い管理者として，その賜物を用いて，互いに仕
え合いなさい．（ペテロ I 4 ¹⁰）

156　OCHITSUKI 落ち着き
COMPOSURE

chakujitsu (da) 着実 (だ)　steadiness;
stability (steady going; stable)
　chinchaku (da) 沈着 (だ) composure
(composed; poised; cool; collected)

dokyō o sueru [C] 度胸をすえる Before
the doctor came in with the report, I
*mustered up courage (got prepared for
the worst).*

HEION (da) 平穏 (だ) composure (composed)
　heiki na kao de 平気な顔で with an
indifferent look
　heizen toshite iru 平然としている remain calm
　kokoro no heisei o tamotsu (ushinau)
心の平静を保つ (失う) keep one's peace
of mind (lose one's mental composure)

hyōjō hitotsu kaenai 表情一つ変えない
When told he had lost his fortune, he
*didn't bat an eye (showed no change of
expression whatever).*

jibun o torimodosu 自分を取りもどす come
to oneself; find oneself

kanjō ni hashiranai 感情に走らない You

can count on him; he *doesn't go on his emotions.*

kiso ga katamaru 基礎が固まる become established

koto mo nage ni 事もなげに nonchalantly

koshi o sueru 腰をすえる He finally *settled down (knuckled down)* to the job.

mijirogi mo shinai 身じろぎもしない In face of the danger he *didn't stir an inch.*

miugoki mo shinai 身動きもしない He *sat still* and listened intently. He listened *without a quiver.*

monogoto o ku ni shinai hito 物事を苦にしない人 easygoing person

nonki (da) のんき (だ) carefreeness (carefree)

OCHITSUKI (ku) 落ち着き(落ち着く) composure (calm down; settle down)

  ~ harau ~ はらう be perfectly composed

    ~ o torimodosu ~ を取りもどす After *settling down (regaining his composure),* he began to talk more slowly.

    ~ o ushinau ~ を失う lose one's composure; become ruffled; become upset

  ochitsukeru 落ち着ける calm oneself

    kimochi o ochitsukeru 気持ちを落ち着ける Wait until I *settle down and collect my thoughts.*

    koshi o ochitsukeru 腰を落ち着ける He has wandered around from job to job. It's time he *settled down.*

odayaka (da) 穏やか(だ) tranquillity; mildness (tranquil; placid; mild)

reisei (da) 冷静(だ) calmness (calm; cool-headed)

  ~ ni furumau ~ にふるまう keep cool; act calmly

sukoshi mo awatenai 少しもあわてない In the midst of that confusion he *was not flustered at all (kept his head).*

sukoshi mo dōjinai 少しも動じない In the

face of their threats he *was unmoved (acted with perfect composure).*

taizen jijaku [L] 泰然自若 presence of mind; imperturbability; self-possession

  ~ toshite ~ として nonchalantly

yoyū shaku shaku to shite 余裕しゃくしゃくとして Even though he had gone through that experience, he was *calm and collected.*

yuttari toshite ゆったりとして at ease; calmly

yūyū to shita ゆうゆうとした calmly; composedly; serenely

yūzen to shite ゆう然として with an air of composure

⇨ **4**

静まってわたしこそ神であることを知れ，わたしは，もろもろの国民のうちにあがめられ，全地にあがめられる．(詩篇 46 ¹⁰)

157 OKUBYŌ 憶病
COWARDICE

damashi uchi (da) だまし討ち (だ) He has a habit of *stabbing* his friends *in the back* when it suits his purpose.

hikkomijian (da) 引っ込み思案 (だ) reticence (retiring; unenterprising)

hikyō (da) 卑きょう (だ) cowardice (cowardly; sneaky)

  ~ na koto o suru ~ なことをする act cowardly; do something sneaky

hito o habakaru 人をはばかる He *is* so *careful about what others might think* that he won't walk alone with her.

hitome o sakeru 人目を避ける Ever since he had that trouble, he *has been avoiding people (has been avoiding people's eyes).*

ikuji ga nai 意くじがない be spiritless; be timid

KI ga chiisai 気が小さい You had better not take him into that room full of people; he's *timid.*

~ ga hikeru ~がひける I'm doing poorly in the course so *hang back* (*feel shy*) when I have to face the teacher.

~ ga yowai ~弱い faint-hearted; chicken-hearted

kiokure (suru) 気おくれ (する) timidity; fear (lose heart; feel nervous)

koshi ga yowai 腰が弱い He *is morally weak* and will not stand up for what is right.

koshinuke 腰抜け coward; chicken-hearted person

ni no ashi o fumu 二の足を踏む I thought he would go right in, but he stood at the door, *marking time (hesitating)*.

obieru おびえる shrink from; cower before

odo odo suru おどおどする be nervous; be timid

okusuru おくする be shy; flinch

otoko rashikunai 男らしくない That was *unmanly* of him to seize the only life-preserver.

rettōkan o idaku 劣等感をいだく have an inferiority complex

shirigomi suru しり込みする hang back; hesitate; flinch

shōtan 小胆 timidity; cowardice

shōshin 小心 timidity; faint-heartedness

~ yokuyoku toshite ~翼々として He *cautiously* (*fearfully*) advanced toward the dark house.

sukumu すくむ cower; crouch

ashi ga sukumu 足がすくむ shrink before; be cowed by

tamerau ためらう hesitate; waver

Tora no i o karu kitsune [P] とらの威を借るきつね He talks strongly but actually he's *a sheep in wolf's clothing (he's a big bluffer)*.

ukiashi tatsu 浮き足立つ During the rugby match, Keio was doing fine until she *began to waver*; then all was lost.

ushiro o miseru うしろを見せる run away

from; take to one's heels; turn one's back on

yowamushi 弱虫 weakling; coward ⇨ **83, 132**

神が私たちに与えてくださったものは、おくびょうの霊ではなく、力と愛と慎みとの霊です。(テモテ II 1 ⁷)

158 OTO 音 SOUND

CHŌSHI 調子 tone; note; pitch

~ ga au ~が合う The choir *is in tune* this morning.

~ ga takai ~が高い high-pitched

~ hazure (da) ~はずれ(だ) discordance; disharmony; dissonance (discordant; unharmonious; dissonant)

~ o ageru ~を上げる raise the pitch

~ o awaseru ~を合わせる The conductor tried to *get* the violinists *in tune* with the cellists.

~ o toru ~を取る keep time

~ o tsukete yomu ~をつけて読む read with intonation

chōwa ga toreta 調和がとれた harmonious

gochō 語調 intonation

fushi 節 tune; air; melody

~ o tsukeru ~をつける On Christmas Eve, 1818, Mohr asked Franz Gruber to *set* " Silent Night " *to music*.

hibiki (ku) 響き(響く) echo; sound (make an echoing sound; reverberate)

hankyō (suru) 反響 (する) reverberation (reverberate)

himei o ageru 悲鳴をあげる give a shriek

kikoeru 聞こえる be heard

hen ni kikoeru へんに聞こえる sounds queer; sounds funny

KOE 声 voice

~ o hariagete ~を張り上げて raise one's voice

~ o kagiri ni ~を限りに at the top of one's voice

~ **o kakeru** ~ をかける As I was leaving, he *called out* to me to stop.

~ **o karashite** ~ をからして talking oneself hoarse

~ **o tateru** ~ を立てる cry out; raise one's voice

yoku tōru koe よく通る声 penetrating voice

kanakirigoe 金切り声 shrill voice

kodama こだま echo

kuchibue o fuku 口笛を吹く whistle

merodii メロディー melody

mimi ni tsuku 耳につく strike the ear; stick in one's mind

OTO 音 sound

~ **ga suru** ~ がする Listen again. I *hear something* over there.

~ **no kikoeru tokoro de** ~ の聞こえるところで At one time, Washington, D. C. *was within the sound of* cannon shot from the Confederates.

~ **o tateru** ~ を立てる make a noise

boin 母音 vowel

hatsuon (suru) 発音 (する) pronunciation (pronounce)

~ **kigo** ~ 記号 phonetic sign; phonetic symbols

monooto ga suru 物音がする I think I hear a *noise being made* up in the attic.

neiro 音色 tone; tone quality

onchi (da) 音痴 (だ) off pitch; tone deafness (be off pitch)

onchō 音調 sound; rhythm

ongaku 音楽 music

onkyō 音響 sound; noise; echo

onryō 音量 volume of the voice

onseigaku 音声学 phonetics

onsetsu 音節 syllable

shiin 子音 consonant

senritsu 旋律 rhythm

shindō 振動 oscillation; vibration

yakamashii やかましい noisy

yoin 余韻 reverberation; swell

yokuyō 抑揚 intonation

. . .信仰は聞くことから始まり，聞くことは，キリストについてのみことばによるのです。（ローマ 10 ¹⁷）

159　OWARI　終わり　END

akumade あくまで to the last; to the very end

banji kyūsu 万事休す When they presented him with the evidence, he knew *it was all over* (*the game was up*).

bansaku tsukiru 万策尽きる be at one's wits' end

donzumari (da) 〔c〕どん詰まり (だ) the very last; the bitter end; the upshot

gohasan ni suru ご破算にする cancel

hashi 端 end; tip; edge; brink

~ **kara hashi made** ~ から端まで from one end to the other

HATE 果て end; extremity

ageku no hate (ni) あげくの果て (に) in the end; in the long run; on top of

hateshi nai 果てしない inconclusive; perennial; never-ending; interminable

heikai (suru) 閉会 (する) adjournment (close a meeting; adjourn)

ichidanraku o tsukeru 一段落をつける By at least freeing the slaves in the rebel states, Lincoln *settled the matter for the time being*.

ii **tokoro de yameru** いいところでやめる Please *stop where you can* and come over and help us.

ketchaku o tsukeru 決着をつける settle; bring the matter to a conclusion

KETSUMATSU 結末 conclusion; termination

~ **ga tsuku** ~ がつく come to an end

~ **o tsukeru** ~ をつける bring to an end

kanketsu (suru) 完結 (する) end; completion; termination (be brought to a conclusion)

musubi 結び end; close

KIRI きり end; bounds; limits; periphery
  ~ no nai ~ のない boundless; endless; interminable
  ~ o tsukeru ~ をつける reach an agreement; bring to an end
  kiriageru 切り上げる wind up [work, affairs, etc.]
  makugire 幕切れ end of an act
kiwami 窮み limit; extremity
kono gurai ni shite okimashō このぐらいにしておきましょう Let's call it quits here. Let's wind it up here. Let's call it a day.
kyokugen 極限 limitation
  kyūkyoku (da) 究極 (だ) extremity; ultimate; finality (extreme; ultimate; final)
nengu no osamedoki 年ぐの納め時 He is getting away with it now, but there will come a *time of reckoning.*
OWARI (ru) 終わり (終わる) end (end; complete; finish)
  ~ ni chikazuku ~ に近づく approach the end
  ~ o mattō suru ~ を全うする bring to a good end
  ~ o tsugeru ~ を告げる come to an end
  akkenaku owaru あっけなく終わる end suddenly
  hajime kara owari made 初めから終わりまで *From beginning to end* the story was thrilling.
  Hajime yokereba owari yoshi [P] 初めよければ終わりよし Well begun, well done. A good beginning makes a good ending.
  yo no owari 世の終わり end of the age
oeru 終える end [it]; complete [something]
  shigoto o oeru 仕事を終える finish work
saishū 最終 the last
shūbi [L] 終尾 end
shūketsu (suru) 終結 (する) conclusion; settlement (terminate; close)

shūkyoku 終局 conclusion; termination
  ~ ni chikazuku ~ に近づく approach the end
shūmatsu 終末 end; finish; termination
shūryō (suru) 終了 (する) finish (be ended; close)
shūshifu 終止符 period; full stop
shūten 終点 terminal; last station; end of the line
saigo 最後 last; end
  ~ o mitodokeru ~ を見とどける When Paul was finally imprisoned in Rome, only a few *stayed with him to the end* (*were with him to the end*).
shimai (u) しまい (しまう) end (end up)
  oshimai da! おしまいだ That's all!
shimekiri (ru) 締め切り(締め切る) deadline (close)
  shimekukuri 締めくくり completion; conclusion
    ~ o tsukeru ~ をつける tie the loose ends together; finish up
SUE 末 the end; the finale; the last
  mattan 末端 the very end
  nenmatsu (saimatsu) 年末 (歳末) end of the year
  shūmatsu 週末 weekend
todo no tsumari とどのつまり finally in the end; after all; in the final analysis
todome o sasu とどめを刺す He pressed his opponent into a corner and then *dealt him a devastating blow* by producing the evidence.
tokoton made [C] とことんまで She explained *every little detail.*
tsui ni ついに after all; finally
yatto やっと finally; at last; at length
yukizumari (ru) 行き詰まり(行き詰る) impasse; end of the road; deadlock (reach an impasse; come to a deadlock)
⇨ **84, 93**

また、わたしがあなたがたに命じておいたすべてのことを守るように、彼らを教えなさい。見よ。わたしは、世の終わりまで、いつも、あなたがたとともにいます。（マタイ 28 [20])

160 REIGI 礼儀
MANNERS, DECORUM

atsukamashii あつかましい bold; rude

aisatsu (suru) あいさつ（する）greeting (greet)

bukkirabō na taido [c] ぶっきらぼうな態度 He has a *completely unpretentious manner* which I like. He offends people with his *abruptness* (*curt way*).

Dōmo arigatō gozaimasu! どうもありがとうございます Thank you very much!

ENRYO (suru) 遠慮（する）reticence; hesitation (refrain from; not do; show respect for another's feelings)

　buenryo (da) 無遠慮（だ）impoliteness (impolite; rude)

　enryobukai 遠慮深い reserved; very reticent; modest

eri o tadasu えりをただす Before the principal came into the room, all the students *became alert* (*stiffened up*).

Gochisō sama deshita ごちそうさまでした Thanks for the delicious meal!

ingin (da) いんぎん（だ）politeness (polite; civil)

　~ ni aisatsu suru ~にあいさつする greet courteously

Itadakimasu! いただきます [said before eating; no English equivalent]

Itterasshai! いってらっしゃい Hurry back!

　Ittemairimasu! いってまいります I'll see you later!

kangei (suru) 歓迎（する）welcome (welcome)

kinshin (suru) 謹慎（する）good behavior (be on one's good behavior; mind one's P's and Q's.)

midashinami no yoi hito 身だしなみのよい人 well-groomed person

monzenbarai o kuwaseru 門前払いを食わせる Before he could show me his products, I *gave* that salesman *the gate*.

Nan no okamai mo dekimasen deshi-

ta! なんのおかまいもできませんでした It wasn't much, but I hope you enjoyed yourself.

okamai naku! おかまいなく Please don't bother!

okogamashii おこがましい presumptuous

orime tadashii 折り目正しい He gets along in any social circle because he is so *proper* (*meticulous; correct in his manner*).

Osore irimasu ga... 恐れ入りますが... Excuse me [please], but...

REIGI 礼儀 manners; decorum

　~ ni kanawanai ~にかなわない be not the thing to do; be out of place; lack good taste

　~ ni motoru ~にもとる His way of doing it *went against convention*.

　~ o mamoru ~を守る observe decorum; have good manners

　~ o shiranai (wakimaenai) hito ~ を知らない（わきまえない）人 bad-mannered person; uncouth person; boor

　~ o tsukushite ~を尽くして with good grace; very courteously

　~ tadashii ~正しい courteous

burei (da) 無礼（だ）rudeness; insult (rude; insulting)

　~ na koto o suru ~なことをする act impolitely [toward]; be rude [to]

　~ ni mo...suru ~にも...する After waiting until the last minute, he was *rude enough to* ask me for a date.

gyōgi 行儀 manners; decorum

　~ no warui ~の悪い Don't talk with your mouth full! *Where are your manners?* (*You have bad manners*).

　~ o shiranai ~を知らない doesn't know decorum; be uncouth

　~ tadashii ~正しい properly behaved; well-mannered

jingi ni hazureru 仁義にはずれる be against common decency

[...no] orei toshite [...の] お礼として *In appreciation for* your help, please take this little gift.

rei ni kakeru 礼に欠ける lack manners; [it] is not the proper thing; be out of place

  ~ o atsuku suru ~を厚くする be civil; be courteous

  ~ o shissuru ~を失する It *is rude* to be late for appointments.

reigijō 礼儀上 out of courtesy

reijō 礼状 courtesy letter; letter of thanks

reisetsu 礼節 good etiquette; propriety; courtesy

  Ishoku tarite reisetsu o shiru [P] 衣食足りて礼節を知る Well fed, well bred [P].

reishiki 礼式 formal manner

shitsurei (suru) 失礼 (する) breach of etiquette; bad form (act rudely)

  ~ na koto o iu ~なことを言う ·say something rude

  Shitsurei! 失礼 Pardon me! Oops!

sahō 作法 manners; decorum

  busahō (da) 無作法 (だ) bad manners (discourteous)

    ~ na koto o suru ~なことをする act rudely

Sumimasen ga... すみませんが... Sorry to trouble you, but...

Tadaima! ただいま! I'm back!

teichō (da) 丁重 (だ) civility (civil)

teinei (da) ていねい (だ) politeness; thoroughness (polite; thorough)

zonzai (da) ぞんざい (だ) roughness; coarseness (roughly; carelessly)

⇨ **101**

愛は寛容であり, 愛は親切です. また人をねたみません.
愛は自慢せず. 高慢になりません.
礼儀に反することをせず, 自分の利益を求めず, 怒らず, 人のした悪を思わず. (コリント I 13 ⁴, ⁵)

161 RIKAI 理解
UNDERSTANDING

chinpun kanpun (da) [C] ちんぷんかんぷん (だ) Nuclear physics is *all Greek to* me!

doryō ga semai 度量が狭い be narrow-minded; be prejudiced

ETOKU (suru) 会得 (する) perception; understanding (perceive; understand; grasp)

  nattoku ga iku 納得がいく He said that he didn't hear the order, and I *am satisfied with his explanation.*

  yōyaku nattoku shita ようやく納得した He *finally got it through his head* that we are not interested in the project.

  settoku (suru) 説得 (する) persuasion (persuade; prevail upon; get across to)

  tokushin (suru) 得心 (する) consent (be convinced [of])

    tokushin no iku 得心のいく What he says *stands to reason (makes sense).*

GATEN (suru) がてん (する) comprehension; understanding (comprehend; understand)

  ~ ga iku ~がいく make sense; be understandable

  ~ no ikanai ~のいかない All his talk about progress under communism when they still do not have freedom of elections *is incomprehensible (is puzzling)* to me.

  hayagatten suru 早がてんする jump to a conclusion

  hitorigaten (suru) ひとりがてん (する) dogmatism; subjective interpretation (take it for granted)

  mōshiawase (ru) 申し合わせ(申し合わせる) understanding (have an understanding [with]; make an arrangement [with])

hirataku iu 平ったく言う speak plainly

IMI (suru) 意味 (する) meaning; signifi-

cance [it] means [that]; it signifies
~ **ga tsūjinai** ~が通じない Your
explanation *has failed to convey the
meaning*.
~ **o torichigaeru** ~を取り違える
mistake the meaning; get it wrong;
get the wrong end of the stick
~ **o tsukamu** ~をつかむ grasp the
meaning; make [it] out
igi 意義 significance; meaning
~ **ga fukai** ~が深い This term *has
deep significance* for the student of
history.
ishi no sotsū 意思の疎通 mutual understanding
jōshiki 常識 common knowledge; common sense
kumitoru くみ取る You have to read his
letters carefully to *catch the implied
meaning*.
me ga hirakareru 目が開かれる Finally his
eyes were opened to the possibilities of
space research.
~ **o hiraku** ~を開く Those bitter
experiences *have opened his eyes* to
the true meaning of life.
MUJUN (suru) 矛盾（する）inconsistency
(be inconsistent)
~ **darake (da)** ~だらけ（だ）be full of
inconsistency; be wholly illogical
~ **o kanjiru** ~を感じる I *feel* that *there
is an inconsistency* in what he says.
~ **shita koto o iu** ~した事を言う make a
contradictory remark
nomikomu のみこむ I can't *grasp (digest;
absorb*) the meaning of all those Chinese
characters so quickly.
pinto hazure da [c] ピントはずれだ He
came close but still *missed the point*.
pinto kuru [c] ぴんと来る After his
explanation, finally *I caught on (I got
the point; it made sense*).
RIKAI (suru) 理解（する）understanding
(understand)

~ **dekiru** ~できる it is understandable
~ **ga tarinai** ~が足りない do not fully
understand; lack full appreciation [of]
~ **no aru** ~のある sympathetic
dōri ni awanai 道理に合わない be
unreasonable
gokai (suru) 誤解（する）misunderstand-
ing (misunderstand; get [it; one]
wrong
~ **o maneku** ~を招く invite misunderstanding; leave room for misunderstanding
~ **sareyasui** ~されやすい misleading;
easily misunderstood
herikutsu o iu へりくつを言う use specious arguments; argue for argument's
sake
hito ni wakaraseru 人にわからせる
Lincoln chose simple words and
illustrations in order to *make himself
understood*.
jimei no (ri) 自明の（理）self-evident
(reason)
kaisetsu (suru) 解説（する）commentary
(comment)
kaishaku (suru) 解釈（する）interpreta-
tion (interpret)
kaisuru [L] 解する understand; comprehend
monowakari no yoi hito 物わかりの良
い人 perceptive person; person who
understands well; discerning person
rikairyoku 理解力 power of understanding
rikutsu 理屈 theory; reason; argument;
pretext
~ **de warikirenai** ~で割り切れない
not fully comprehended by reason
alone
~ **ga tatanai** ~が立たない doesn't stand
to reason
~ **ni au** ~に合う be reasonable; stands
to reason
~ **o tsukeru** ~をつける give a plausible
reason

rikutsuppoi 理屈っぽい argumentative
riro seizen to shita 理路整然とした
His report *is lucid and orderly* (*has systematic consistency*).
risei 理性 reasoning power
risō (**teki**) (**da**) 理想(的) (だ) ideal (ideal)
rizume 理詰め reasoning; persuasion
~ **de toku** ~で説く talk one into; persuade one with cool logic
ryōkai (**suru**) 了解 (する) understanding; comprehension (understand; comprehend)
~ **o eru** ~を得る *With their understanding* we went ahead and put up the fence.
~ **shiau** ~し合う understand each other
toku 解く solve; unravel; explain
sassuru 察する guess; surmise; understand
setsumei (**suru**) 説明 (する) explanation (explain; illustrate)
shinzui ni fureru 真髄に触れる When he said that, he *was touching upon the true meaning* of democracy.
SHIRU 知る know; understand
shōchi suru 承知する agree; consent; understand
goshōchi no tōri ご承知のとおり As you well know....
torikime (**ru**) 取り決め(取り決める) arrangement; understanding (arrange; settle)
toritome no nai koto o iu 取り留めのない事を言う He tends to *ramble in* his *talk* (*say irrelevant things*).
TSŪJIRU 通じる be understood; be well-versed in; be articulate [in]
kotoba ga tsūjiru 言葉が通じる Your *words make sense* (*words are intelligible*) to me.
suji ga tōranai 筋が通らない be illogical; be unreasonable
tsujitsuma ga awanai [C] つじつまが合わない His report *is all confused* (*is inconsistent*).

WAKARU わかる understand; get on to
hanashi ga wakaru 話がわかる *What you say makes sense*, but I still do not agree with you.
sappari wakaranai さっぱりわからない It is quite beyond me. I can't make heads nor tails of it.
wake ga wakaranai 訳がわからない I *can't figure out* (*can't make out*) what he's getting at.
yō o eta 要を得た His speech *was right to the point*.
yōryō o enai 要領を得ない be vague; be inconclusive; be incoherent
⇨ **18, 21, 142**

それは, この人たちが心に励ましを受け, 愛によって結び合わされ, 理解をもって豊かな全き確信に達し, 神の奥義であるキリストを真に知るようになるためです。
(コロサイ 2 ²)

162 RUIJI 類似
SIMILARITY, ANALOGY

aitsūjiru mono ga aru 相通じるものがある *There are some common points between* Marxism and Buddhism.
arayuru あらゆる all sorts of; each and every
hadaai ga chigau はだ合いが違う Don't compare the two; he *is of a different color* (*is of a different stamp*).
doko to naku mioboe ga aru どことなく見覚えがある I *have a faint recollection of* having seen him *before*.
Donguri no seikurabe [P] どんぐりの背比べ There is little to choose between them. It's six of one and a half-dozen of the other. It's a pointless comparison.
hakuchū (**suru**) 伯仲 (する) Those two teams *are equally matched*.
[...**o**] **hinagata ni suru** [...を] ひな型にする They *modeled* that toy plane after a real jet.
hitoshii 等しい be similar; be equal to

ikiutsushi 生き写し exact replica; living resemblance

iroiro (da) いろいろ (だ) various; all sorts of; all manner of

katadoru かたどる pattern after; model after

keiro no kawatta 毛色の変わった strange; curious; eccentric; exotic

kurikaesu くり返す repeat; do over again

　kurikaeshi-kurikaeshi...suru くり返しくり返し...する do over and over again

　Rekishi wa kurikaesu [P] 歴史はくり返す History repeats itself [P].

kyōtsū (da) 共通 (だ) commonness (in common; common)

　kyōtsūten 共通点 common points

MANE (ru) まね(まねる) copy; imitation (copy; imitate; follow an example)

　kuchimane (suru) 口まね (する) mimic; pantomime; parrot (mimic; parrot; do [something] in parrot fashion)

　miyō mimane (de) 見様見まね (で) That boy has learned to play golf *by copying* his Dad.

　saru mane さるまね Monkey see, monkey do; copycat

mohō (suru) 模倣 (する) imitation (model after)

　mokei 模型 pattern; model [airplane, etc.]

ONAJI (da) 同じ (だ) identity; sameness (identical; same; equal)

　~ katachi ni kaeru ~形に変える change into the same shape

　mattaku onaji da 全く同じだ exactly the same; as two peas in a pod

　dō demo yoi どうでもよい Coca-Cola or Pepsi Cola—*they're the same to me* (*either's okay*).

　dōkei (da) 同形 (だ) same type; similar pattern (patterned the same)

　dōitsu (da) 同一 (だ) the very same (identical)

　dōtō (da) 同等 (だ) equally; similarly; on the same footing

　dōyō (da) 同様 (だ) in the same way; likewise

renzoku (suru) 連続 (する) continuation (run continuously)

RUIJI 類似 similarity; analogy

　kokuji 酷似 striking resemblance

　[...ni] niau [...に] 似合う That tie *goes well with* that suit.

　nikayou 似通う be similar to; resemble

　niru 似る resemble; be like

　　nite mo nitsukanai 似ても似つかない be completely dissimilar; does not resemble in the least

　　yoku nite iru よく似ている closely resemble

　niseru 似せる make [it] like; shape [it] like

　rui no nai sonzai 類のない存在 [there is] nothing quite like [it]; be absolutely unique; be incomparable

　　~ wa tomo o yobu [P] ~は友を呼ぶ Birds of a feather flock together [P]. Likes attract.

　ruijiten 類似点 points of similarity

　ruirei o minai 類例を見ない That is a beautiful museum; *it is unparalleled* (*you'll not find another like it*).

sokkuri (da) そっくり (だ) close resemblance

　oya ni sokkuri 親にそっくり That boy is a *chip off the old block* (*the spitting image of* his dad).

Tsuki to suppon [P] 月とすっぽん They are *as different as night and day*.

uri futatsu (da) うり二つ (だ) exactly alike; like two peas in a pod

神はまた言われた、われわれのかたちに、われわれにかたどって人を造り、これに海の魚と、空の鳥と家畜と、地のすべての獣と、地のすべてのはうものとを治めさせよう。
(創世記 1 ²⁶)

163 RYŌSHIN 良心 CONSCIENCE

JIKAKU (suru) 自覚 (する) realization; awareness (realize; sense)

~ **o unagasu** ~ を促す The pastor tried to *get* him *to realize* (*arouse in* him *an awareness of*) the seriousness of his fault.

tsumi o jikaku suru 罪を自覚する be conscious of one's sin

ki ga togameru 気がとがめる He *is bothered about* the way he cheated in his exams.

ushiro gurai kimochi ga suru うしろ暗い気持ちがする I *feel there is something shady about* the way he is conducting his business.

me ga sameru 目が覚める He finally *opened his eyes to* (*came to realize*) his true situation.

mimi ga itai 耳が痛い Don't talk about my poor English; it *hurts to hear* about it.

nezame ga warui 寝ざめが悪い He *has a guilty conscience* about the way the company is doing business.

RYŌSHIN 良心 conscience

~ **ga mahi suru** ~ がまひする one's conscience is dulled

~ **ga togameru** ~ がとがめる He *had qualms of conscience about* taking the money, so he returned it.

~ **ni hajinai** ~ に恥じない have a clear conscience

~ **ni hajiru** ~ に恥じる feel pangs of conscience

~ **ni somuku** ~ にそむく violate one's conscience

~ **ni tou** ~ に問う heed conscience; listen to one's conscience

~ **no kashaku ni kurushimu** ~ の呵責に苦しむ His conduct last night *weighed heavily upon* him, so he sent his apologies.

~ **no kashaku o ukeru** ~ の呵責を受ける feel qualms of conscience; be conscience stricken

~ **o kizutsukeru** ~ を傷つける wound one's conscience

tadashii ryōshin 正しい良心 good conscience

dōgishin 道義心 moral sense

honshin ni tachikaeru 本心に立ち返る come to one's senses; come to oneself

kokoro o itameru 心を痛める He *is deeply troubled* over the rude way in which he treated his mother.

~ **ni yamashii tokoro ga nai** ~ にやましいところがない have a good conscience about; have no qualms about; have no regrets [over]

kokorogurushiku omou 心苦しく思う I *didn't feel right about* (*felt cheap*) taking all that money for the little help I gave.

yamashii to omowanai やましいと思わない Happy is the man who can make his decision *with a clear conscience*. (Romans 14 : 22)

zenaku no betsu o shiru 善悪の別を知る know right from wrong

~ **no kannen** ~ の観念 conception of right and wrong

⇨ **121**

彼らはこのようにして，律法の命じる行ないが彼らの心に書かれていることを示しています．彼らの良心もいっしょになってあかしし，また，彼らの思いは互いに責め合ったり，また，弁明し合ったりしています．(ローマ 2 ¹⁵)

164 SABETSU 差別 DIFFERENCE, DISCRIMINATION

CHIGAI (u) 違い(違う) difference (be different [from])

sōi 相違 difference

sōiten 相違点 point of difference; disparity

erabu 選ぶ select; choose
 sentaku (suru) 選択 (する) choice; elective (choose; elect)
furui ni kakeru ふるいにかける weed out;
 screen; sift
Gojippo hyappo [P] 五十歩百歩 *There
 is not much difference* between those two
 parties in the way they run the government.
hakaru はかる measure; compare
 jibun o kijun ni shite, hito o hakaru
 自分を基準にして人をはかる What fools
 they are to...*find in themselves their
 own standard of comparison.* (II
 Corinthians 10 : 12)
handan no kijun 判断の基準 standard of
 comparison; criterion of judgment
HENKEN 偏見 prejudice; bias
 ~ o motsu ~ を持つ harbor a prejudice
 ~ o suteru ~ を捨てる forget one's
 prejudices; discard one's bias
hike o toranai 引けを取らない Tanaka
 boasted that he *would be second to none*
 in the coming English contest.
hiraki ga aru 開きがある *There is a
 discrepancy in* their stories.
Hitotsu ana no mujina[P] 一つ穴のむじな
 Those punks hanging around the station
 are all *painted with the same brush (of
 the same bad crowd).*
hitteki suru 匹敵する be a match for
irowake (suru) 色わけ (する) sorting (sort
 out; single out; draw a line between)
 Jūnin toiro [P] 十人十色 So many men,
 so many minds. Everyone to his own
 taste. To each his own.
kegirai (suru) 毛ぎらい (する) prejudice;
 dislike (have a disliking for)
KEJIME けじめ difference
 ~ ga tsukanai ~ がつかない can make no
 distinction between; split hairs
 ~ o tsukeru ~ をつける discriminate
keta ga chigau けたが違う differ widely
 from; be a horse of a different color

ketahazure (da) けたはずれ (だ) great
 difference (be widely different)
kokubyaku o akiraka ni suru 黒白を
 ら明かにする By so doing he will *make a
 clear distinction (decide which is right).*
kō otsu o tsukeru 甲乙をつける It is hard
 for me to *tell which* candidate *is better*
 in this campaign; they both say the same
 thing.
kotonaru 異なる dissimilar; different
KURABERU 比べる compare
 hikaku (suru) 比較 (する) comparison
 (compare)
 kurabemono ni naranai 比べものになら
 ない When it comes to rugby, Todai
 *can't hold a candle to (is incomparable
 to)* Waseda.
MIKIWAMERU 見窮める discern
 katayotte miru かたよってみる ...I now
 see how true it is that God *has no
 favorites*...(Acts 10 : 34)
 yokume de miru 欲目で見る She's
 blind to his faults. She *always sees
 him in a good light.*
 mikuraberu 見比べる judge [it; one]
 by comparison
 miotori ga suru 見劣りがする be inferior
 [to]; fall below the mark
 miwakeru 見分ける discriminate;
 distinguish
SABETSU 差別 difference; discrimination
 ~ o tsukeru ~ をつける discriminate
 ~ taigū ~ 待遇 Don't patronize that
 company; they give *preferential treatment* to people with money.
 jinshu sabetsu 人種差別 racial
 discrimination
 kaikyūteki sabetsu 階級的差別 class
 distinction
 betsu (da) 別 (だ) difference; distinction;
 another (different; distinct; another)
 betsu betsu ni suru 別々にする Please
 wrap the gifts *separately.*
 danjo no betsu naku 男女の別なく
 boys and girls alike

hanbetsu (suru) 判別 (する) discrimination (notice the difference)

kubetsu (suru) 区別 (する) difference (discriminate between)

~ **ga nai** ~ がない there is no difference

sa 差 difference; variance

~ **ga aru** ~ がある there is a difference

kamihitoe no sa 紙一重の差 hardly any difference; fine line of difference; no appreciable difference

undei no sa 雲泥の差 vast difference; all the difference in the world

sai 差異 difference; disparity

sensa banbetsu (da) 千差万別 (だ) infinite variety (multifarious)

shikibetsu (suru) 識別 (する) discernment; discrimination (discriminate)

shubetsu (suru) 種別 (する) classification; assortment (classify)

shuruibetsu ni suru 種類別にする divide into types; sort into; classify

taisa ga nai 大差がない there is no great difference [between]

shusha suru 取捨する choose; select; adopt and reject

taishō (suru) 対照 (する) contrast; comparison (contrast [with]; compare [with])

TOKUSHOKU 特色 characteristic

tokushokuzukeru 特色づける characterize

tokushusei 特殊性 distinctiveness; distinctive characteristic

tokuyū (da) 特有 (だ) characteristic (indigenous; special)

Tsuki to suppon [P] 月とすっぽん They are *as different as night and day.*

WAKERU 分ける divide; separate

wakehedate (suru) 分け隔てする be partial; play favorites; make personal distinctions

wakimaeru わきまえる discern; discriminate; be prudent

wariai ni 割合に comparatively; relatively

あなたがたが，真にすぐれたものを見分けることができるようになりますように．またあなたがたが，キリストの日には純真で非難されるところがなく... (ピリピ 1 ¹⁰)

165 SANSEI 賛成 APPROVAL

aizuchi o utsu 相づちを打つ chime in; follow suit; give one the green light

batsu o awaseru [C] ばつを合わせる I didn't like his ideas but *went along with them* anyway.

DŌI 同意 consent; approval (agree with; side with)

ichi mo ni mo naku dōi suru 一も二もなく同意する They all *fully agreed* (*unanimously agreed*) to the proposal.

dōkan 同感 same sentiment

mattaku dōkan (da) 全く同感 (だ) You and I *have precisely the same sentiments* (*see eye-to-eye*) on the subject.

gakumen dōri ni ukeru 額面通りに受るけ You had better not *take* that statement *at face value.*

izon naku 異存なく without objection

ikudōon ni 異口同音に with one voice; unanimously

jōyaku o hijun suru 条約を批准する ratify a treaty

kekkō (da) 結構 (だ) All right!

kubi o tate ni furu 首を縦に振る Everyone *nodded his assent* (*consented*) to the idea.

kyoka (suru) 許可 (する) permission; approbation; okay (permit; approve; give the okay)

~ **o eru** ~ を得る receive permission; get approval

kyōmei (suru) 共鳴 (する) accord (be in sympathy with)

manjōitchi (da) 満場一致 (だ) unanimity (unanimous)

MITOMERU 認める recognize; approve

kōnin (suru) 公認 (する) public recognition (recognize publicly; sanction)

mokunin (suru) 黙認 (する) silent approval (wink at; tolerate)

ninka (suru) 認可 (する) official approval (authorize; legalize)

　seishiki ni ninka suru 正式に認可する give official approval

zenin (suru) 是認 (する) consent; approval (consent [to]; approve)

SANSEI (suru) 賛成 (する) approval (approve)

　~ o eru ~を得る gain approval; get the okay

　~ o motomeru ~を求める seek one's approval

sandō (suru) 賛同 (する) endorsement; backing (endorse; back)

　kokumin no sandō o eru 国民の賛同を得る gain public approval

　san'i o hyōsuru 賛意を表する express approval

sanjo (suru) 賛助 (する) backing; support (back; support)

sanpi ryōron ni wakareru 賛否両論に分かれる have pros and cons; have divided opinions [about]

sanseisha 賛成者 supporter; advocate

shiji (suru) 支持 (する) support; backing (support; back up; stand by)

SHŌCHI (suru) 承知 (する) consent; acknowledgment (consent [to]; agree [to])

shōdaku (suru) 承諾 (する) consent (consent [to]; accept a proposal)

　~ o eru ~を得る gain approval

　~ o motomeru ~を求める seek consent; seek approval; want approval

shōfuku (suru) 承服 (する) approval (submit to; give in to)

shōnin (suru) 承認 (する) approval (certify)

unazuku うなずく nod; nod approval

yoroshii! よろしい okay; it's all right; it will do

⇨ **74**

神の約束はことごとく，この方において「しかり.」となりました. それで私たちは, この方によって「アーメン.」と言い, 神に栄光を帰するのです. (コリント II 1 [20])

166 SEIGI 正義 JUSTICE, INTEGRITY

hyōri no nai 表裏のない Lincoln won the confidence of people because he *was open and above board* (there was no duplicity about him; he *was out in the open*).

jitchoku (da) 実直 (だ) uprightness (upright; steadfast)

KŌHEI (da) 公平 (だ) fairness; impartiality (fair; impartial; just)

　~ mushi (da) 無私(だ) A judge must be *impartial and disinterested*.

　~ ni toriatsukau ~に取り扱う treat one fairly

kōmei seidai (da) 公明正大(だ) fairness (fair)

kōsei 公正 equity; justice; fairness

magokoro 真心 sincerity

　massugu (da) まっすぐ(だ) honesty (honest; straight)

SEIGI 正義 justice; integrity

　~ no nen ~の念 idea of justice; sense of justice

　gi 義 righteousness; justice; duty

　　~ to sareru ~とされる be justified; be declared righteous

　gijin 義人 righteous person

　hōsei [L] 方正 integrity

　seigikan ga tsuyoi 正義感が強い He *has a strong sense of justice.*

seisei dōdō to shita 正々堂々とした open and above board; fair and square

seitō (da) 正当 (だ) fairness; legitimacy (fair; legitimate; due; proper)

seitōka suru 正当化する warrant; justify; legitimatize

shōjiki (da) 正直 (だ) honesty (honest; true; fair and square)

~ wa saizen no saku [P] ~ は最善の策 Honesty is the best policy [P].

Shōjikimono ga baka o miru (son o suru) [P] 正直者がばかを見る (損をする) An honest person will be taken in.

tadashii 正しい right; rightful; correct

~ koto o suru ~ 事をする do the right thing

tansei (da) [L] 端正 (だ) correctness; propriety (correct; proper; right; decent)

SEIJITSU (da) 誠実 (だ) integrity; honesty (honest; faithful; upright)

~ o kaku ~ を欠く lack sincerity; be insincere

shisei [L] 至誠 sincerity; highest integrity

seiren keppaku (da) 清廉潔白 (だ) uprightness (upright)

shishin ga nai 私心がない I'm sure he *has no personal interest* in this proposal but is offering it only for the good of the school.

take o watta yōna kishō 竹を割ったような気性 I like him because he is *straightforward (open and above board)*.

tashika (da) 確か (だ) certainty (certain; positive; definite)

⇨ 175

ただ, 神の恵みにより, キリスト・イエスによる贖いのゆえに, 価なしに義と認められるのです. (ローマ 3 ²⁴)

167 SEIJAKU 静寂
STILLNESS, QUIETNESS

hissori to shite iru ひっそりとしている The whole room *was very quiet.*

hitoashi ga todaeru 人足がとだえる After ten at night the *streets are deserted (it gets quiet)* in this town.

odayaka (da) 穏やか (だ) calmness (calm; serene)

oto ga shinai 音がしない Since he fixed it,

the motor *is noiseless (doesn't make any noise).*

SEIJAKU (da) 静寂 (だ) stillness; quietness (still; quiet)

kansei (da) 閑静 (だ) quietness (quiet; still)

seion 静穏 quietness

seishuku ni 静粛に silently; quietly

seiteki (da) 静的 (だ) quiet [person]

shizuka (da) 静か (だ) tranquillity; stillness (tranquil; still; quiet)

shizukesa 静けさ solitude; hush; calm

~ o yaburu ~ を破る The roaring planes *broke the silence* over the sleeping town.

arashi no mae no shizukesa あらしの前の静けさ This is only the *calm before the storm.*

kiwadatta shizukesa きわだった静けさ weird silence; deep silence

mizu o utta yōna shizukesa 水を打ったような静けさ When I walked to the lake this morning, there was *a serene silence* everywhere.

shi no shizukesa 死の静けさ When he announced his resignation, there was a *death-like silence* in the room.

shizumaru 静まる become quiet; calm down

shin to shizumarikaeru しんと静まり返る become absolutely quiet; become deathly silent

shin to shita しんとした still; silent

⇨ 20

しかし, 主はその聖なる宮にいます. 全地はそのみ前に沈黙せよ. (ハバクク 2 ²⁰)

168 SEIKATSU 生活
LIVELIHOOD, LIVING

chūryū katei 中流家庭 middle-class family

jōryū shakai 上流社会 high society

ikka o sasaeru 一家を支える You had

better not consider marriage until you can *support a family*.

hi o okuru 日を送る He is *passing* his *days* out on the farm.

kasō shakai 下層社会 low society

kikyo 起居 one's daily life

KURASHI (su) 暮らし (暮らす) living; livelihood (live)

   ~ ni komaru ~に困る I *can't make ends meet* on that income.

   ~ o tateru ~をたてる He is *earning his living* by selling insurance.

   anraku ni kurasu 安楽に暮らす live in comfort

   kōfuku ni kurasu 幸福に暮らす live happily

   yatto kurasu やっと暮らす eke out a living; just able to live

   zeitaku ni kurasu ぜいたくに暮らす live in luxury; live in clover; live it up; live high off the hog

   kurashimuki ga yoi (warui) 暮らし向きがよい (悪い) With that good (poor) job, their *situation is looking up (situation is bad)*.

   sono higurashi その日暮らし living from hand to mouth; just keeping one's head above water; just keeping the wolf away from the door

oya no sune o kajiru 親のすねをかじる Too many students are becoming lazy, *living off their parents (depending on their parents)*.

SEIKATSU (suru) 生活(する) livelihood; living (live)

   ~ ni hariai ga aru ~に張り合いがある Now that he has a grandchild, he *has a zest for living* (he's *getting a kick out of life*).

   ~ ni komaru ~に困る be bad off; be having a tough time of it

   ~ no antei ~の安定 stable subsistence; stable economy

   ~ no hitsujuhin ~の必需品 necessities of life

   ~ o yutaka ni suru ~を豊かにする enrich one's life

   heibon na seikatsu 平凡な生活 simple life

   kegare no nai seikatsu o okuru 汚れのない生活を送る lead a pure life

   michitarita seikatsu 満ち足りた生活 abundant life; full life

   nichijō seikatsu 日常生活 daily life; everyday life

   tanchō na seikatsu 単調な生活 monotonous life

   tanoshii seikatsu 楽しい生活 pleasant life; happy life

ikiru 生きる live

seikatsuhi 生活費 living expenses; cost of living

seikatsukankyō 生活環境 living environment

seikatsunan to tatakau 生活難と戦う struggle to make ends meet; fight to make a living

seikatsuryoku 生活力 means of livelihood

seikatsusuijun 生活水準 standard of living

seikatsuteido 生活程度 level of living

seikatsuyōshiki 生活様式 way of life

seikei 生計 living; livelihood

   [...de] ~ o tateru [...で] ~を立てる He felt he could *make a living by (support himself by)* tutoring students.

seizon (suru) 生存 (する) being; existence (exist)

sonzai (suru) 存在 (する) existence (exist; be extant)

shotai o motsu 所帯をもつ Now that she *has a household* of her own, she is finding out the value of money.

sugosu 過ごす pass one's time; live

   heiwa ni sugosu 平和に過ごす If possible, so far as it lies within you, *live at peace* with all men. (Romans 12:18)

sumu 住む dwell; live
yarikuri (suru) [C] やりくり (する) I'm having a difficult time *making ends meet.*
⇨ **78, 170**
だから，神の国とその義とをまず第一に求めなさい．そうすれば，それに加えて，これらのものはすべて与えられます．(マタイ 6 ³³)

169 SEIKŌ 成功 SUCCESS

fukaku o toru 不覚を取る make a grave mistake; make a regrettable blunder
guai yoku iku ぐあいよくいく Recently things *have been going well (have been going smoothly)* at the office.
gyōseki o ageru 業績をあげる Their business went slowly at first, but now they are *making a good showing (making a go of it).*
han'ei (suru) 繁栄 (する) prosperity (prosper; flourish)
　hanjō (suru) 繁盛 (する) flourishing (flourish; thrive [business, etc.])
hito hata ageru 一旗あげる He went overseas and *became a success (made a name for himself).*
ichika bachi ka yatte miru [C] 一か八かやってみる I know it is risky, but I'*m going for broke (going to give it a try; going to sink or swim).*
ichininmae no ningen ni naru 一人前の人間になる If you continue working like that, I'm sure you'll *make the grade (win your spurs).*
isshōkenmei yatta kai ga atta 一生懸命やったかいがあった It was worth the effort. There is something to show for [one's] all-out effort.
mi o tateru 身を立てる He went into law and *made good (established himself).*
minoru 実る bear fruit; achieve results
　doryoku ga minoru 努力が実る efforts yield results
mono ni naru ものになる His English was

poor, but after years of study, *it developed into something (something came of it).*
nurete de awa ぬれ手であわ He *made a killing* in land speculation.
risshin suru 立身する make good; be going places [in life]
　risshidenchū no hito 立志伝中の人 He's a *man that's going to do something in life.*
shusse suru 出世する make the grade in life; give a good account of oneself
　risshin shusse o suru 立身出世をする I'm sure he'll *make good in life (be a success in life).*
SEIKŌ (suru) 成功 (する) success (succeed)
　~ ni owaru ~ に終わる end in success; succeed; bring home the bacon
　~ no hiketsu ~ のひけつ secret of success
　~ no mikomi ~ の見込み prospects of success; chances of succeeding
　~ o aseru ~ をあせる be too eager for success
　~ o ayauku suru ~ を危うくする jeopardize one's success
　migoto ni seikō suru 見事に成功する make a fine success of; go over in a big way
　Shippai wa seikō no moto [P] 失敗は成功のもと We learn by trial and error.
daiseikō 大成功 huge success; whopping success
fuseikō ni owaru 不成功に終わる end in failure; be a flop
jōju (suru) 成就 (する) fulfillment (be accomplished; be fulfilled)
kō o isogu 功を急ぐ be over-eager for quick success
　~ o sōsuru ~ を奏する be successful; give a good account of oneself
nariagaru 成り上がる A few years ago he was a mechanic, but now he has *become wealthy overnight.*

nashitogeru 成し遂げる accomplish; bring about; complete

rakusei (suru) 落成 (する) completion; finishing (complete; finish [a building, etc.])

Rōma wa ichinichi ni shite narazu [P] ローマは一日にして成らず Rome wasn't built in a day [P].

seika o ageru 成果をあげる achieve good results; get good results

seisan [L] 成算 prospects of success

seiseki ga yoi 成績がよい good results; make a good showing; good grades [in school]

Seishin ittō nanigoto ka narazaran [P] 精神一到何事か成らざらん Where there's a will, there's a way [P].

taiki bansei 大器晩成 Success does not come early. Great talents mature late.

tassei (suru) 達成 (する) achievement; attainment (arrive at; attain)

shubi yoku 首尾よく successfully; thoroughly

umaku iku うまくいく get along well; goes fine

yaritogeru やり遂げる complete; carry out; accomplish

　hommō o togeru [L] 本望を遂げる Lincoln *succeeded at long last in* (*achieved his long-cherished desire of*) bringing the states together.

⇨ 93

イエスは彼らに言われた.「わたしを遣わした方のみこころを行ない, そのみわざを成し遂げることが, わたしの食物です. (ヨハネ 4 ³⁴)

170 SEIMEI 生命 LIFE

hito o sukuu 人を救う Your task is to *save life*, not jeopardize it.

SEIMEI 生命 life
　~ no kigen ~ の起源 origin of life
　~ no kiken o okasu ~ の危険を冒す A

test pilot must often *put his life in jeopardy*.

~ o ataeru ~ を与える bestow life

~ o hogo suru ~ を保護する protect life

~ o yomigaeraseru ~ をよみがえらせる bring back to life

ikimono 生き物 living thing; sentient being

ikiru 生きる live; exist

　chikarazuyoku ikiru 力強く生きる He *lived energetically* right up to the end of his career.

inochi 命 life

~ karagara ~ からがら The soldiers were ambushed and *barely escaped with their lives.*

~ no aru kagiri wa ~ のある限りは *As long as I live* (*While there is breath in me*) I will try to help you.

~ o chijimeru ~ を縮める The chemist Linus Pauling proved that smoking twenty cigarettes a day can *shorten* a man's *life* by eight years.

~ o eru ~ を得る I have come that men may *have life*, and may have it in all its fullness. (John 10: 10)

~ o nerau ~ をねらう seek after one's life; have a design on one's life

~ o suteru (nageutsu) ~ を捨てる (なげうつ) lay down one's life

~ o toru ~ を取る take one's life; kill

~ o tsunagu ~ をつなぐ We *just managed to keep going* on those meagre provisions.

~ o uchikomu ~ を打ち込む He *put his heart and soul into* that relief work.

~ o ushinau ~ を失う He lost his life during the rescue operations.

~ shirazu (da) ~ 知らず (だ) He is a *daredevil* (*reckless person*).

inochibiroi (suru) 命拾い (する) narrow escape (make a narrow escape)

inochigake (da) 命がけ(だ) The fireman entered the burning building *at the risk of his life.*

inochitori (da) 命取り(だ) fatal

chōmei 長命 long life; longevity

jinmei 人命 life of man

  ~o sonchō suru ~を尊重する We must *have respect for human life.*

jumyō 寿命 life-span; life expectancy

nagaiki (suru) 長生き(する) longevity (live long)

sei o ukeru〔L〕生を受ける be born; live

seibutsu 生物 living thing

seizon (suru) 生存(する) existence; exist

shinsei 新生 new life

tanmei 短命 short life

yosei 余生 remainder of one's life; rest of one's life

zonmeichū 存命中 during life; while alive

sonzai (suru) 存在(する) existence (exist)

  doko made mo sonzoku suru どこまでも存続する Democracy has come to Japan, but some feudalistic customs *are still firmly in existence.*

⇨ **78, 168**

だから，わたしはあなたがたに言います．自分のいのちのことで，何を食べようか，何を飲もうかと心配したり，またからだのことで，何を着ようかと心配したりしてはいけません．いのちは食べ物よりたいせつなもの，からだは着物よりたいせつなものではありませんか．(マタイ 6 ²⁵)

171   SEKININ 責任   RESPONSIBILITY

Ato wa no to nare, yama to nare〔P〕あとは野となれ山となれ I'm going to do what I should and *let the chips fall where they may* (*I couldn't care less what happens*).

FUTAN (suru) 負担(する) responsibility; charge; expense (bear the expense; assume financial responsibility)

  ~o kakeru ~をかける I am not going to *sponge on* you.

  ~tantō (suru) ~担当(する) charge; control (be in charge [of]; take charge [of])

GIMU 義務 obligation; duty

  ~o ou ~を負う fulfill one's duty; [it] devolves upon one; assume an obligation

giri o kaku 義理を欠く fail in one's duty [to]

  ~o tateru ~立てる Don't worry, he'll *do his duty by you* (*do right by you*).

girigatai 義理堅い be conscientious

hatasu 果たす fulfill; carry out; make good

hitomakase ni suru 人任せにする He often starts something then *leaves it to someone else* to finish.

kanbu 幹部 management; governing body

kanri (suru) 管理(する) administration (administer)

kantoku (suru) 監督(する) supervision; control (supervise; control)

honbun o tsukusu 本分を尽くす do one's bit; keep one's end up; do one's part of the bargain; fulfill one's appointed task

keiei (suru) 経営(する) management (manage; operate; run)

  un'ei (suru) 運営(する) operation (operate; conduct)

kōyō o tsukusu 孝養を尽くす discharge one's filial duty

NI 荷 burden; load; responsibility

  ~ga omosugiru ~が重すぎる The *burden* of the Civil War *was too heavy* for one man, and Lincoln confessed, " I shan't last long after it's over."

  omoni 重荷 heavy burden; responsibility

  ~ga oriru ~が降りる be relieved of one's burden

  ~o orosu ~をおろす Knowing he passed the exam *takes a load off my mind.*

~ o ou ~ を負う …everyone *has* his own proper *burden to bear*. (Galatians 6 : 5)

ninau になう bear a burden; take upon oneself [to]

SEKININ 責任 responsibility

~ **aru** ~ ある responsible

~ **ga nai** ~ がない I'm sorry the books were not there on time, but *I'm not responsible* for their delivery.

~ **no shozai o akiraka ni suru** ~ の 所在を明らかにする make clear who is responsible; fix the responsibility

~ **o hatasu** ~ を果たす fulfill one's duty; carry out one's responsibility

~ **o kaihi suru** ~ を回避する shirk the responsibility [of]

~ **o kanjiru** ~ を感じる feel responsible [for]; sense the responsibility

~ **o oshitsukeru** ~ を押し付ける shift responsibility; pass the buck

~ **o ou** ~ を負う bear the responsibility; be responsible [to]

~ **o owaseru** ~ を負わせる place the responsibility [on]

~ **o tenka suru** ~ を転嫁する Government officials are always *passing the buck*.

~ **o tokareru** ~ 解かれるを I was glad when I *was relieved of the responsibility of* watching the children.

~ **o toru** ~ を取る Lincoln *took the responsibility* for the wrong done by his Secretary.

~ **o tou** ~ を問う call one to account; make one answerable to; call one to task [for]

~ **o wakeau** ~ を分け合う share the responsibility

fuyō no sekinin 扶養の責任 family responsibilities

musekinin (da) 無責任(だ) irresponsibility (irresponsible)

ninmu 任務 duty; burden; task

~ **o hatasu** ~ を果たす God knows I have at least tried very hard to *do my duty*. (Lincoln)

rentaisekinin 連帯責任 joint responsibility [of a committee, etc.]

sekimu 責務 duty; obligation

sekininsha 責任者 the person responsible; person in charge

sekininkan 責任感 sense of responsibility

~ **ga nai** ~ がない lack all sense of responsibility

~ **ga tsuyoi** ~ が強い have a strong sense of responsibility

seme (ru) 責め(責める) blame; responsibility (blame; make responsible [for])

shigoto o itaku sareru 仕事を委託される be put in charge of [work, etc.]; be given [some] work to do

shimei 使命 mission; appointed task

~ **o kanjiru** ~ を感じる feel a calling for; sense a mission [to]

[…**no**] **sōken ni kakaru** […の] 双肩にかか る The future of America *rested upon* Lincoln's *shoulders* (*fell upon* Lincoln's *shoulders*).

shusai (suru) 主催(する) sponsorship (sponsor; organize)

Tobu tori ato o nigosazu [P] 飛ぶ鳥あと をにごさず Don't forget to *leave a clean slate* (*take care of your responsibilities*) before you leave that job.

tsutome (ru) 務め(務める) duty (make it one's business to)

~ **o hatasu** ~ を果たす complete one's task; fulfill one's mission

yakume 役目 function; duty; role

[…**no**] ~ **o hatasu** […の] ~ を果たす carry out one's duty; complete one's task

yakuwari 役割 role; assignment

yaomote ni tatsu [L] 矢面に立つ When the boss criticized the whole office for the blunder, she *bore the brunt of* his criticisms (*stood in the breach*) and took the blame.

けれども，私が自分の走るべき行程を走り尽くし，主イエスから受けた，神の恵みの福音をあかしする任務を果たし終えることができるなら，私のいのちは 少しも惜しいとは思いません．(使徒行伝 20 ²⁴)

172 SENSŌ 戦争
WAR, BATTLE

BUSŌ 武装 arms (take up arms; become a soldier)

buryoku ni uttaeru 武力に訴える go to war; resort to force

kakubusō suru 核武装する arm with nuclear weapons

CHŪRITSU 中立 neutrality

~ **no tachiba o toru** ~の立場を取る be neutral; take a neutral position

~ **o mamoru** ~を守る observe neutrality

~ **o okasu** ~を侵す violate the neutrality [of]

~ **o sengen suru** ~を宣言する declare neutrality

busō chūritsu 武装中立 armed neutrality

chūritsushugi 中立主義 neutrality

genbaku 原爆 atomic bomb

gunshuku 軍縮 disarmament

~ **kaigi** ~会議 disarmament conference

guntai 軍隊 army

rikugun 陸軍 army; land forces

hei (heitai) 兵(兵隊) rank and file soldier (soldier)

heishi 兵士 soldier

heitai ni torareru 兵隊に取られる be drafted; be inducted into military service

nyūtai suru 入隊する join the colors; join up

hibuta o kiru 火ぶたをきる open fire; commence hostilities

kakuheiki 核兵器 nuclear weapons

kakujikken kinshi 核実験禁止 ban on nuclear testing

koroshiau 殺し合う kill one another [in battle]

senryō (suru) 占領(する) possession; capture; occupation (take possession; capture; occupy)

SENSŌ (suru) 戦争(する) war (wage war; fight; go to war)

~ **ga okoru** ~が起こる war breaks out; hostilities begin

~ **jōtai ni hairu** ~状態にはいる enter into a state of war

~ **kōi ni deru** ~行為に出る commit an act of war

~ **ni deru** ~に出る go to war

~ **ni katsu** ~に勝つ win a war

~ **ni makikomareru** ~に巻き込まれる become involved in war; get embroiled in the conflict

~ **ni sanka suru** ~に参加する participate in a war

~ **ni sonaeru** ~に備える prepare for war

tsumetai sensō (reisen) 冷たい戦争 (冷戦) cold war

akusen kutō (suru) 悪戦苦闘(する) losing battle (fight with one's back to the wall)

funsen (suru) 奮戦(する) fight; struggle (fight desperately; fight tooth and nail)

ikusa [L] いくさ war; battle

make ikusa 負けいくさ a losing battle

jissen 実戦 hot war

kaisen (suru) 開戦(する) opening of hostilities (open hostilities)

kessen 決戦 decisive battle; deciding match [baseball, tennis, etc.]

kōsenchū 交戦中 be at war

sakusen 作戦 warfare; maneuvers; tactics

senchi 戦地 battlefront

sengo (senzen) 戦後(戦前) after the war (before the war)

senjō 戦場 battlefield

senjutsu 戦術 tactics; strategy

senka 戦禍 ravages of war

senryakuteki 戦略的 strategic

sensenfukoku (suru) 宣戦布告(する) declaration of war (declare war)

senshi (suru) 戦死(する) war death (die in battle)

senshisha (senbotsusha) 戦死者(戦没者) war dead (number of war dead)

sentō (suru) 戦闘(する) battle (fight)

shinkei senjutsu (shinri sakusen) 神経戦術(心理作戦) psychological warfare

shisōsen 思想戦 ideological warfare

taisen 大戦 great war; pitched battle

tatakai (u) 戦い(戦う) fight; battle (fight; battle)

> **~ ni sonaeru** ~に備える prepare for battle

> **~ o idomu** ~をいどむ challenge to fight; fight against

> **noruka soruka no tatakai** のるかそるかの戦い The two platoons of soldiers were engaged in a *life and death struggle.*

> **seishi o kaketa tatakai** 生死をかけた戦い a fight to the bitter end; life and death struggle

> **sokoku no tame ni tatakau** 祖国のために戦う fight for the fatherland

tatakainuku 戦い抜く fight to the finish

shinryaku (suru) 侵略(する) aggression (invade)

tama no shita o kuguru たまの下をくぐる The troops *moved* ahead, fighting *under a hail of bullets.*

teki mikata 敵味方 friend and foe

⇨ 7, 15

何が原因で, あなたがたの間に戦いや争いがあるのでしょう. あなたがたのからだの中で戦う欲望が原因ではありま

せんか. あなたがたは, ほしがっても自分のものにならないと人殺しをするのです. うらやんでも手に入れることができないと, 争ったり, 戦ったりするのです. あなたがたのものにならないのは, あなたがたが願わないからです. (ヤコブ 4 ¹, ²)

173 SHI 死 DEATH

horobi (bu) 滅び(滅ぶ) death; destruction (die; be destroyed)

iki ga taeru 息が絶える breathe one's last; expire

> **~ o hikitoru** ~をひきとる expire; die

ikka shinjū 一家心中 family suicide

INOCHI o chijimeru 命を縮める Unless you get enough sleep and rest, you will *shorten your life.*

> **~ o suteru** ~を捨てる lay down one's life; throw away one's life

> **~ o ushinau** ~を失う lose one's life; meet one's end

jisatsu (suru) 自殺(する) suicide (commit suicide)

junkyō (suru) 殉教(する) martyrdom (become martyred)

> **junkyōsha** 殉教者 martyr

korosu 殺す kill; slay; put to death

mesareru 召される The pastor told the congregation that the church elder *had been called home* last Thursday.

nakunaru なくなる perish; pass away; expire

> **nakigara** なきがら remains; corpse; cadaver

nemuru 眠る fall asleep; die

> **eimin (suru)** 永眠(する) eternal sleep (sleep eternally; pass away)

rinjū (da) 臨終(だ) He's *at death's door (in his last hour).*

> **~ no kotoba** ~の言葉 last words

saigo 最期 death; end

> **higō no saigo o togeru** 非業の最期を遂げる The world grieved Kennedy's *ill-fated death.*

seikyo suru 逝去する die
  yo o saru [L] 世を去る depart from this world
SHI 死 death; decease
  ~ni chokumen suru ~に直面する face death
  ~ni nozonde ~に臨んで When *one is dying* (*is facing death*), he thinks about the true meaning of life.
  ~o hayameru ~を早める hasten death
  ~o itamu ~をいたむ Lincoln *mourned the death* of so many soldiers at Fredericksburg.
  ~o kakugo suru ~を覚悟する Paul Miki and the other seventeen Japanese *resolved to die* for their faith in the martyrdom of 1597.
  ~o maneku ~を招く invite death; court death
  ~o manukareru ~を免れる escape death
  furyo no shi o togeru 不慮の死を遂げる Many passengers *met sudden death* in the train disaster.
inuji ni suru 犬死にする The brilliant pilot *died a tragic death* in the auto mishap.
jōshi (suru) 情死(する) lover's suicide (die together)
kakushi suru 客死する die abroad
kokubetsushiki 告別式 funeral service; saying farewell to the deceased
kyūshi (suru) 急死(する) sudden death (meet sudden death)
notareji ni suru 野たれ死にする die a vagabond's death; die in a ditch somewhere
senshi suru 戦死する die in battle; die in [the] war
shibetsu (suru) 死別(する) bereavement (bereave)
shibō (suru) 死亡(する) death; decease (die)

shibōtodoke 死亡届け report of death
shigo 死後 after death
shikei (ni suru) 死刑に(する) capital punishment (execute)
shikyo 死去 death
shinikakaru 死にかかる be in the throes of death; be dying
shinikata 死に方 way of dying
shinime 死に目 moment of death; closing of one's eyes
shinin 死人 dead person
shinitaeru 死に絶える die out; become extinct
shiniwakareru 死に別れる be separated by death
shinu 死ぬ die; pass away
shisha 死者 death casualty
  ~o dasu ~を出す Many lives were *lost* in the plane accident.
shishōsha 死傷者 dead and wounded; casualties
shitai 死体 corpse; remains
  ~kaibō ~解剖 autopsy
gashi suru 餓死する starve to death
sōshiki 葬式 funeral service
tenju o mattō suru 天寿を全うする live out a natural life
yuigon (suru) 遺言(する) will; last dying wish (give one's last will and testament) ⇨ 52

しかし、朽ちるものが朽ちないものを着、死ぬものが不死を着るとき、「死は勝利にのまれた。」としるされているみことばが実現します。(コリント I 15 ⁵⁴)

174 SHIKŌ 思考
PLAN, THOUGHT

AN 案 plan
  ~o dasu ~を出す He *proposed* that we raise the funds by floating a bond.
  ~o neru ~を練る think out a way
Anzuru yori umu ga yasui [P] 案ずる

より産むがやすい It is easier to do a thing than to think about it.

fukuan ga aru 腹案がある He is not saying much, but I think he *has some scheme up his sleeve* (*has a plan in the back of his mind*).

meian 名案 good idea; good proposal

myōan 妙案 ingenious plan; a brainstorm

teian (suru) 提案(する) proposal; suggestion (propose; suggest)

anchū mosaku [L] 暗中模索 probing in the dark

chakusō 着想 idea; concept

kōsō o neru 構想を練る map out a plan

chie o shiboru 知恵をしぼる I *racked my brains* to figure that out.

gikō o korashite 技巧をこらして I can tell that he *took many pains* with this drawing.

hatsumei (suru) 発明(する) invention (invent; devise)

KEIKAKU (suru) 計画(する) plan; project (plan; form a plan)

keikakudōri (da) 計画通り(だ) as scheduled; as planned

keisan ni ireru 計算に入れる We must *make allowances for* (*reckon with; take into account*) rising labor costs when we estimate the building.

sekkei (suru) 設計(する) plan; design (plan; design)

kokoro ni tomeru 心に留める keep [something] in mind

kubi o hineru 首をひねる I think they *are pondering over* (*are thinking over*) that idea you gave them.

KUFŪ (suru) 工夫(する) device; scheme; invention (devise; invent)

~ o korasu ~ をこらす tax one's ingenuity; figure out a plan

sōi kufū o korasu 創意工夫をこらす figure out a way

kushin santan suru 苦心さんたんする rack

one's brains [over]; sweat [out]

kuwadate (ru) 企て(企てる) plan (plot; scheme)

mondai o tsukitsumeru 問題を突きつめる pursue the problem

ryōken 了見 notion; ideas; design

sakuryaku 策略 strategem; wiles

sengi suru 詮議する investigate; consider

sennyūkan 先入感 preconception; prejudice

shinshaku (suru) 斟酌(する) allowance (take into account)

SHIKŌ 思考 plan; thought

kangae (ru) 考え(考える) idea (think; plan; consider)

jikkuri kangaeru じっくり考える weigh a matter carefully; ponder over; think twice about

mune ni te o atete kangaeru 胸に手を当てて考える You did wrong, and I want you to *mull it over for a while* (*think it over seriously*).

kangaenaosu 考え直す think better of; change one's mind

kangaenuku 考え抜く think out

kōan (suru) 考案(する) plan; design; conception (plan; design; conceive)

kōryo suru 考慮する take into consideration; deliberate

banji kōryo shite 万事考慮して *All things considered*, I think we had better not buy it.

omoi (u) 思い(思う) thought (think; believe)

omoitatsu 思い立つ plan; think of doing

omoitsuki(ku) 思いつき(思いつく) notion; sudden thought; brain storm (have a brain storm; hit upon an idea)

omoitsumeru 思い詰める ponder over carefully; think over; think twice about

(hito no) omowaku (人の)思わく Don't worry about *what people think*.

shian (suru) 思案(する) consideration
(consider; reflect over)

~ ni amaru ～にあまる be beyond
one's resources of thought; be at
one's wits' end

~ ni fukeru ～にふける be buried in
thought; be absorbed in thought

~ o kasaneru ～を重ねる go over
different ideas

~ o megurasu ～をめぐらす rack one's
brains for an idea

shikōryoku 思考力 power of thought
shiryo 思慮 discretion

yotei (suru) 予定(する) plan; program;
schedule; prearrangement (plan ahead;
program; schedule; prearrange)
⇨ 145, 181, 193

人は心に自分の道を考え計る。しかしその歩みを導く
者は主である。(箴言 16 ⁹)

175　SHINJITSU 真実
TRUTH

ari no mama ni iu ありのままに言う When
Sarah got bruised, little Abe told her to
tell their mother *the plain truth* (*tell the
whole story*).

HONTŌ (da) ほんとう(だ) truth; fact (true;
actual; in point of fact)

~ ni suru ～にする She *accepted* his
wild story *as fact.*

~ no koto o uchiakeru ～の事を打ち
明ける be honest with; give it to
one straight; open up and speak the
truth

honki ni suru 本気にする You get
offended because you *take* my joking
seriously.

honrai no sugata 本来の姿 true nature
[of]

honshin 本心 one's true self

kakushin ni fureru 核心に触れる Abe's
words, "All men are created equal"

touched the heart of the slavery issue.

kotoba o shinjiru 言葉を信じる We'll *take
his word for it* that the money was paid.

makoto (da) 誠(だ) really; truly; indeed

~ shiyaka ni iu ～しやかに言う speak
plausibly; talk as if it were true

mattaku 全く completely; utterly; truly;
indeed

shōgō (suru) 照合(する) verification
(verify)

SHŌKO 証拠 proof

Ron yori shōko [P] 論より証拠 The
proof of the pudding is in the
eating [P].

sore ga shōko ni wa それが証拠には
The proof of this is that his finger-
prints were on the gun.

risshō (suru) 立証(する) verification
(verify)

shōmei (suru) 証明(する) proof (prove)

SHINJITSU 真実 truth

~ o mageru ～を曲げる pervert the
truth; embellish the truth

~ o tashikameru ～を確かめる ascertain the truth

jijitsu 事実 fact; actuality; reality

~ ni terashite ～に照らして The story
changes *in the light of reality.*

~ o mushi suru ～を無視する ignore
the facts

~ o shōmei suru ～を証明する make
the facts known

kisei no jijitsu 既成の事実 evident
fact; unequivocal fact

jissai (wa) 実際(は) truth; fact (as a
matter of fact)

jisseki 実績 actual results

jisshō 実証 actual proof

jitsujō 実情 actual state of affairs

jitsuzai 実在 real existence; reality

jittai 実体 actual condition

magokoro 真心 sincerity; devotion

shinri 真理 truth

~ kar　hazureru ～からはずれる

they *have shot wide of the truth* in saying that our resurrection has already taken place. (II Timothy 2: 28)

~ ni hansuru ~に反する defy the truth; go against the truth; flout the truth

~ ni shitagau ~に従う obey the truth; follow the truth

~ o akiraka ni suru ~を明らかにする ...only by *declaring the truth openly* do we recommend ourselves...(II Corinthians 4: 2)

shinsei (da) 真性(だ) genuineness (genuine)

shinsō 真相 the facts; things as they are

~ o tsukamu ~をつかむ grasp the true picture

shōtai o tsukitomeru 正体を突き止める find out the facts; get the facts

masa ni まさに exactly; certainly; truly

tōzen (da) 当然(だ) proper; just ⇨ **41, 166**

私たちは，真理に逆らっては何をすることもできず，真理のためなら何でもできるのです．（コリント II 13 ⁸）

176 SHINKEN 真剣
SERIOUSNESS

chimanako ni naru 血眼になる He *became frantic* looking for the lost papers.

chūjitsu (da) 忠実(だ) faithfulness (faithful; loyal)

hisshi (da) 必死(だ) desperation (desperate; frantic)

hitasura (da) ひたすら(だ) desperately; wholeheartedly

hone o umeru kakugo o suru 骨を埋める覚悟をする When Livingston went to Africa, he *gave up every hope of returning* to his native land.

HONKI (da) 本気(だ) earnestness (in earnest)

~ de iu ~で言う say in earnest; talk turkey

~ ni naru ~になる He *became dead earnest* about learning English.

hongoshi ni naru 本腰になる get down to business

ippongi na hito 一本気な人 one-track minded person

ki o haru 気を張る Before the game his *nerves are* always *on edge*.

~ o haritsumeru ~を張りつめる get tense; become keyed up

ichizu ni...suru 一途に...する You will succeed if you *do it wholeheartedly* (*do it with singleness of purpose*).

isshin ni 一心に with a single heart; singleheartedly

isshōkenmei (da) 一生懸命(だ) earnestness (as hard as one can; with all one's might)

jitchoku (da) 実直(だ) seriousness (serious; faithful)

jōdan de wa sumasarenai 冗談では済まされない Being in debt like that *is no laughing matter*.

kage hinata naku hataraku 陰ひなたなく働く You can count on him because he *works conscientiously*.

kichōmen (da) きちょうめん(だ) scrupulosity (scrupulous; methodical; punctual)

kinben (da) 勤勉(だ) industry; diligence (industrious; diligent; hard-working)

kinchō (suru) 緊張(する) tenseness (get tense; become keyed-up)

mi ga hairanai 身がはいらない Without higher goals, men *do not do their best* (*do not put themselves into* their work).

~ o irete ~を入れて with vigor; putting oneself into [the work]

~ o ko ni shite hataraku ~を粉にして働く work very hard; work oneself to the bone

nen ga itta 念が入った They *painstakingly* made all the preparations.

omoshirohanbun ni suru おもしろ半分にする do [something] just for fun

seishin o tōitsu suru 精神を統一する devote one's attention to; concentrate one's mind on

shigoto ga daiichi 仕事が第一 Business before pleasure.

SHINKEN (da) 真剣(だ) seriousness; earnestness (serious; earnest)

~ **ni naru** ~になる become serious about

~ **shōbu** ~勝負 life and death struggle; a real battle

ma ni ukeru 真に受ける He *took me seriously* and was offended.

magokoro 真心 sincerity; one's true heart

majime (da) まじめ(だ) earnestness (earnest; serious)

~ **kusatta hito** [c] ~くさった人 He doesn't fit in well at the office because he is *an overly serious person* (*a solemn person*).

shinkenmi 真剣味 seriousness; earnestness

shinketsu o sosogu 心血を注ぐ He *poured his heart and soul* into preparing for the occasion.

[...ni] tamashii o uchikomu [...に]魂を打ち込む He *put his heart into* teaching, and his students knew it.

tansei o komete 丹精を込めて with true devotion

uita kangae 浮いた考え flippant thought; frivolous thought

wakime mo furazu ni わき目も振らずに Abe would study for hours *without even glancing around* when people came in.

yakki to naru やっきとなる He *got heated up* about the problem and talked for two hours.

zenryoku o ageru (sosogu) 全力をあげる

(注ぐ) He worked in the civil rights movement *with all his might.*

⇨ **23, 29, 188**

また, 私が命じたように, 落ち着いた生活をすることを志し, 自分の仕事に身を入れ, 自分の手で働きなさい. 外の人々に対してもりっぱにふるまうことができ, また乏しいことがないようにするためです.

(テサロニケ I 4 ¹¹, ¹²)

177 SHINKŌ 信仰
FAITH, TRUST

agameru あがめる revere; worship

chūjitsu (da) 忠実(だ) faithfulness (faithful)

haisuru 拝する worship

reihai (suru) 礼拝(する) worship (worship)

reihaishiki 礼拝式 worship service

heifuku suru 平伏する prostrate before

heishin teitō suru 平身低頭する get down and bow low

hirefusu ひれ伏す prostrate oneself

hizamazuku ひざまずく bow down before; bend the knee

Hyakubun wa ikken ni shikazu [P] 百聞は一見にしかず Seeing is believing [P].

KEII 敬意 homage; respect

keifuku suru 敬服する admire; respect

keiken (da) 敬けん(だ) piety; reverence (pious; reverent)

keishin 敬神 reverence; piety

Kirisutokyō キリスト教 Christianity

mi o kagameru 身をかがめる prostrate oneself; bow down before

miageru 見上げる look up to; respect; set one's eyes above

osoreononoku 恐れおののく fear and tremble

SHINKŌ (suru) 信仰(する) faith; trust (have faith [in]; trust [in])

~ **ni ikiru** ~に生きる ...my present bodily life *is lived by faith in* the

Son of God, who loved me and gave himself for me. (Galatians 2: 20)

~ no atsui ~ の厚い devout; of fervent faith

~ no jiyū ~ の自由 freedom of faith; religious liberty

~ no michi o hanareru ~ の道を離れる depart from the faith; desert the faith; apostatize

~ no nai ~ のない unbelieving; faithless

~ o motsu ~ を持つ have faith

~ o suteru ~ を捨てる give up one's faith

~ seikatsu ~ 生活 religious life

ayafuya na shinkō あやふやな信仰 uncertain faith

nezuyoi shinkō 根強い信仰 deeprooted faith

yurugi no nai shinkō ゆるぎのない信仰 unwavering faith

aogu 仰ぐ look up to; revere

fushin (da) 不信(だ) bad faith; unreliability (unreliable)

fushinjin 不信心 impiety; unbelief

fushinkō 不信仰 unbelief

haishin 背信 breach of faith

~ kōi ~ 行為 breach of faith

mishinja 未信者 unbeliever

mōshin (suru) 盲信 (する) blind faith (blindly believe)

shinja 信者 believer

shinjigatai 信じ難い hard to believe; dubious; doubtful

shinjin (suru) 信心(する) faith; belief; reverence (believe in; revere)

shinjinbukai 信心深い Abe's father was a *devout* (*pious*) man.

shinjiru 信じる believe in; have faith in; trust

~ ni atai shinai (tarinai) ~ に価しない(足りない) not worth believing; incredulous

~ ni shinjikirenai ~ に信じ切れない *It staggers belief* (*I can hardly believe*) that the cosmonaut actually walked in space.

Kami o shinjiru 神を信じる trust in God; believe God

sukoshi no utagai mo naku shinjiru 少しの疑いもなく信じる She *believes beyond a shadow of a doubt* that she will see him again.

shinjitsu 信実 faithfulness; fidelity; honesty

shinjō 信条 creed; article of faith; principle

shinkōbukai 信仰深い pious; reverent

shinkyō 信教 religious belief; faith

shinnen 信念 belief; conviction; faith

~ ga katai (tsuyoi) ~ が堅い(強い) He *has strong convictions.*

~ o magenai ~ を曲げない be unbending in one's convictions

Ichinen iwa o mo tōsu [P] 一念岩をも通す An arrow of conviction will even go through a rock.

shinpuku suru 信服する be convinced; be devoted to

shinrai (suru) 信頼(する) trust; confidence (trust; have confidence in; depend upon; rely on)

~ ni kotaeru ~ にこたえる prove trustworthy; live up to expectations

~ no nen ga atsui ~ の念が厚い have deep trust [in]; be trusting

~ o eru ~ を得る win the confidence of; obtain the trust of

~ o oku ~ をおく put confidence in

~ o uragiru ~ を裏切る betray the confidence of

~ suru ni taru ~ するに足る be worthy of [one's] trust; be trustworthy

shinyō (suru) 信用(する) trust; confidence; faith (trust; have confidence in)

~ no dekiru ~ のできる He is a *reliable* (*trustworthy*) person.

~ no shittsui ~の失墜 Because of those bad checks, he suffered a *loss of credit* at the bank.

~ o uragiru ~を裏切る betray one's trust

sugaritsuku すがりつく cling to; hold on to

tanomu 頼む rely on; lean upon; trust; count on

tatematsuru 奉る revere

tattobu (tōtobu) 尊ぶ(とうとぶ) esteem; honor

yoridokoro よりどころ foundation; ground [of trust, etc.]

⇨ 191

信仰がなくては，神に喜ばれることはできません．神に近づく者は，神がおられることと，神を求める者には報いてくださる方であることとを，信じなければならないのです．(ヘブル 11 ⁶)

178 SHINPAN 審判
JUDGMENT

benkai (suru) 弁解(する) defense (make a defense; defend oneself)

bengoshi 弁護士 lawyer

HŌTEI 法廷 court

  ~ de arasou ~で争う bring suit against; go to court

  ~ ni tatsu ~に立つ be called into court; be tried

  hōteigai (da) 法廷外(だ) They settled the case *out of court.*

  kaitei (suru) 開廷(する) hearing (hold court)

kenji 検事 district attorney; prosecuting attorney

ketchaku o tsukeru 決着をつける The judge *settled the matter* by fining them both.

kōhei ni miru 公平に見る look at [a matter] fairly

kuroshiro o tsukeru 黒白をつける Unless you have an absolute standard, it is hard to *distinguish right and wrong.*

kyōtei ga seiritsu suru 協定が成立する come to an agreement

sashiosae 差し押え seizure [of property by legal authority]

  karisashiosae o suru 仮差し押えをする sequester provisionally; temporarily seize

seibai suru [L] 成敗する deal with; mete out punishment

senkoku (suru) 宣告(する) sentence; verdict (give sentence; render a verdict)

SHIKEI ni shosuru 死刑に処する condemn to death; hand down the death penalty

  ~ ni suru ~にする execute; administer capital punishment

  ~ o senkoku suru ~を宣告する sentence to death

SHINPAN (suru) 審判(する) judgment (judge; referee)

  kibishii shinpan きびしい審判 harsh judgment

  saigo no shinpan 最後の審判 the Last Judgment

handan (suru) 判断(する) judgment; estimation; evaluation (judge; estimate; evaluate)

handanryoku 判断力 ability to judge

hanketsu (suru) 判決(する) judgment; verdict (decide a case; render a verdict)

  ~ ni fukusuru ~に服する accept the decision [of]

  ~ o matsu ~を待つ await a decision

  ~ o kudasu ~を下す hand down a verdict

hantei (suru) 判定(する) decision; finding; verdict (pass judgment [on])

kōhan 公判 trial

saiban (suru) 裁判(する) hearing; judgment (have a hearing; hold court)

  ~ ni kakeru ~にかける have a litigation against; go to court [over]

  ~ ni naru ~になる come to court; be tried

~ o hiraku (okonau) ~ を開く(行なう) hold court

~ o ukeru ~ を受ける be tried

futō na saiban 不当な裁判 miscarriage of justice

saibanchū 裁判中 We don't know the verdict yet; the case *is still being tried*.

saibankan 裁判官 judge

saibansho 裁判所 court

saibanzata 裁判ざた lawsuit; litigation

sabaki (ku) 裁き(裁く) judgment (judge)

saiketsu (suru) 裁決(する) verdict (hand down a verdict; render a decision)

shingi (suru) 審議(する) review (review a case; deliberate; look into a matter)

shinpansha 審判者 judge; umpire; referee

SHOGEN (suru) 証言(する) testimonial; testimony (testify)

furi na shōgen o suru 不利な証言をする testify against; give damaging evidence

shōko 証拠 proof; evidence

SOSHŌ (suru) 訴訟(する) law suit (have a law suit [against])

kokuso (suru) 告訴(する) accusation; complaint (accuse; make a complaint [against])

uttae (ru) 訴え(訴える) law suit; litigation (make a charge against)

~ o toriageru ~ をとりあげる The judge *took up the accusation* against the accused.

torishirabe (ru) 取り調べ(取り調べる) investigation (investigate; deal with)

wakai (suru) 和解(する) reconciliation (be reconciled)

yūzai to suru 有罪とする find guilty

muzai no senkoku o suru 無罪の宣告をする The judge *handed down a verdict of not guilty*.

⇨ 30, 92, 107, 114

そして，人間には，一度死ぬことと 死後にさばきを受けることが定まっているように. ... (ヘブル 9 ²⁷)

179 SHINPO 進歩
PROGRESS

chakuchaku to 着々と steadily

HAKA ga iku はかがいく Road construction *is making good progress* in some parts of Tokyo.

hakabakashii はかばかしい [is] making great strides

ikkō ni hakabakashiku nai いっこうにはかばかしくない making no advance whatsoever; not getting anywhere

hakadoru はかどる make good progress

hakadoranai はかどらない make little headway; make no progress

HATTEN (suru) 発展(する) growth; progress; expansion; development (grow; progress; develop)

~ o hakaru ~ をはかる plan for growth

~ o jochō suru ~ を助長する foster the development of

hiyakuteki hatten 飛躍的発展 rapid development; speedy growth

hattensei ga aru 発展性がある *There are signs of future development* in that area.

hirakeru 開ける open up; become developed

JIDAI ni okureru 時代に遅れる lag behind the times

gendai 現代 modern; present age; contemporary times

jidaiokure (da) 時代遅れ(だ) old fashioned; out-of-date

kindai 近代 modern age (modern; recent)

shinjidai no nami 新時代の波 wave of the future

KAITAKU (suru) 開拓(する) pioneering; developing (pioneer; develop; open up)

kaihatsu (suru) 開発(する) development [of backward areas] (develop)

kaitakusha 開拓者 pioneer

kakudai (suru) 拡大(する) spread; enlargement (spread; enlarge; expand)

keika 経過 progress; process

kidō ni noru 軌道に乗る be on the right track; get into orbit

KŌJŌ (suru) 向上(する) progress; improvement (progress; improve)

  kōjōshin ni moeru 向上心に燃える That young manager *is burning to get ahead* in the world.

  ~ o ushinau ~を失う lose the desire to get ahead

masshigura ni iku まっしぐらに行く rush pell-mell ahead; dash against; run full tilt [toward]

muri ni te o nobasu 無理に手を伸ばす overstretch oneself

noronoro to iku のろのろと行く move at a snail's pace; inch along

rachi ga akanai らちがあかない In the discussions today we *made no progress (got nowhere)*.

seichō (suru) 成長(する) growth (grow up)

  ~ o togeru ~を遂げる make progress; see growth

[...no] sentan o iku [...の]先端を行く The cosmonaut's first explorations in space *were paving the way for the future.*

SHINPO (suru) 進歩(する) progress (make progress)

  ~ o okuraseru ~を遅らせる delay progress

  chōsoku no shinpo o togeru 長足 の進歩を遂げる Since the war Japan *has been making rapid strides of progress.*

  ichijirushii shinpo 著しい進歩 marked progress; remarkable advance

  jinrui no shinpo 人類の進歩 human progress

  isshin ittai 一進一退 We can't reach an agreement on procedure so we *are at a standstill (are getting nowhere).*

  shinka (suru) 進化(する) evolution;

development (evolve; develop)

shinkaron 進化論 evolutionary hypothesis

shinkō (suru) 進行(する) progress; advancement (advance; go ahead)

shinkōchū (da) 進行中(だ) in progress

shinpoteki (da) 進歩的(だ) advanced; progressive; radical

shinten (suru) 進展(する) progress; development (progress; develop)

sokushin suru 促進する speed up progress

susumeru 進める promote; step up; speed up

susumu 進む advance; make progress; march

zenshin (suru) 前進(する) advance; progress (advance; make progress; go forward)

⇨ **16, 85**

さて，兄弟たち．私の身に起こったことが，かえって福音を前進させることになったのを 知ってもらいたいと思います．(ピリピ 1 ¹²)

180 SHINSETSU 親切
KINDNESS

aiso ga yoi あいそが良い sociable; amiable

attakai kotoba o kakeru 暖かい言葉をかけ る He walked through the orphanage, *speaking kindly* to each child.

kawaige ga nai かわいげがない That spoiled girl *is not very lovable.*

KŌI 厚意 kind intentions

  ~ o motsu ~を持つ Let's ask him; he's *favorably disposed* toward us.

  ~ o mu ni suru ~を無にする He changed the date so you could come, but you *disregarded his kindness (were inconsiderate of his kindness)* and didn't show up.

kōi 好意 kindness; good will

  ~ aru ~ある kind; well-meaning

[...**no**] **~ de** [...の] ~ で *Through the kindness of* Mr. Jones, I was introduced to you.

KOKORO kara kangei suru 心から歓迎する welcome with open arms; roll out the red carpet

> **atatakai kokoro o motsu** 暖かい心を持つ be warm-hearted

> **kokorozukushi** 心づくし warm-hearted kindness

> **yasashii kokorozukai** 優しい心づかい kind consideration

komakai tokoro ni te ga todoku 細かい所に手が届く The hotel *was careful to the smallest detail*; all the guests were well taken care of.

me o kakeru 目をかける The boss *does well by* (*looks out for*) his employees, even finding housing for them.

MOTENASHI (su) もてなし(もてなす) hospitality (be hospitable; entertain)

> **hito o motenasu** 人をもてなす be hospitable to people; entertain

> **teatsui motenashi o suru** 手厚いもてなしをする She certainly *made us feel at home* (*showed us warm hospitality*).

nengoro (da) [L] ねんごろ(だ) cordial; with kind care; hospitable

okage de おかげで *Through your kindness* I was able to pass the English exam.

omoiyari (ru) 思いやり(思いやる) kindness; sympathy (be kind to; sympathize with; feel for)

onjō 恩情 thoughtfulness; kind-heartedness

> **ongaeshi o suru** 恩返しをする pay back a kindness

SEWA o suru 世話をする take care of; look after

> **osewa ni naru** お世話になる I would like to *be under your care.*

> **sewazuki na seishitsu** 世話好きな性質 She *has an obliging disposition* (*is naturally hospitable*).

SHINSETSU (da) 親切(だ) kindness (kind)

> **~ na kimochi kara** ~ な気持ちから I know he did this *out of kindness.*

> **~ ni amaeru (tsukekomu)** ~ に甘える(つけ込む) Be careful that you don't *take advantage of his kindness* and wear out your welcome.

> **~ ni mo** ~ にも He *was kind enough* to let us have the best room.

> [...**o**] **~ ni suru** [...を] ~ にする treat one with kindness; handle one with kid gloves

> **~ o muda ni suru** ~ をむだにする give one the cold shoulder

konsetsu ni 懇切に cordially; kindly

shinmi (da) 親身(だ) kindness (kind; warm)

> **~ ni naru** ~ になる Lincoln was a successful leader of men because he was able to *enter into people's feelings.*

> **~ ni sewa o suru** ~ に世話をする take affectionate care of

shitashii (mu) 親しい(親む) intimate; friendly; close (make friends with; get next to)

teinei na monogoshi de ていねいな物腰で *In a courteous manner* she asked me about my family.

yasashii 優しい gentle; kind; easy

> **kidate no yasashii hito** 気だての優しい人 *Being of a gentle disposition* (*Being gentle natured*), Abe pardoned many prisoners.

1, 160, 212

何よりもまず，互いに熱心に愛し合いなさい．愛は多くの罪をおおうからです．
つぶやかないで，互いに親切にもてなし合いなさい．
（ペテロ I 4 ^{8, 9}）

181 SHISŌ 思想
IDEA, THOUGHT

atama ni oku 頭に置く keep in mind
~ ni ukabu ~に浮かぶ come to mind
jukuryo (suru) 熟慮(する) deep consideration (think [a matter] over well)
KANGAE (ru) 考え(考える) idea; thought (think about; consider)
> **~ ga ukabu** ~が浮かぶ enters one's thoughts; an idea comes to mind; a thought occurs to one
> **~ ni ireru** ~に入れる I will *take* your suggestion *into consideration*.
> **~ o matomeru** ~をまとめる After that long discussion I'd better *collect my thoughts* (*form a definite idea*), and then answer.
> **[...no] ~ o suteru** [...の] ~を捨てる I've *given up the idea* of going to Europe.
> **asahaka na kangae** あさはかな考え absurd idea; shallow thought
> **dokusōteki na kangae** 独創的な考え original thought
> **hiyaku shita kangae** 飛躍した考え fuzzy thinking; reasoning which is difficult to follow
> **machigatta kangae** まちがった考え mistaken idea
> **shinkoku ni kangaeru** 深刻に考える think seriously [about]
> **sore wa ii kangae da** それはいい考えだ That's a good idea!
> **sujimichi tatete kangaeru** 筋道立てて考える think logically
kangaedasu 考え出す think out
kōsatsu(suru) 考察(する) consideration; contemplation (consider; contemplate; give thought to)
kannen(suru) 観念(する) conception; idea (conceive [of])
> **kotei kannen** 固定観念 fixed conception

kokoro no mochikata shidai 心の持ち方次第 Overcoming difficulties *is all in how you look at them* (*depends upon your attitude*).
okusoku no han'i o denai 憶測の範囲を出ない He has many ideas, but most of them *do not go beyond the realm of conjecture*.
> **~ suru dake** ~するだけ *It remains speculative*, but I guess they will go ahead with the project.
OMOI (u) 思い(思う) idea; thought (think)
> **[...no] ~ ni karareru** [...の] ~にかられる He's *got it in his head* that he wants to study overseas.
omoiataru 思い当たる flash upon one; occur to
omoichigai 思い違い misunderstanding
omoimegurasu 思いめぐらす ponder over; reflect upon; give thought to
Omoitatta ga kichinichi[P]思い立ったが吉日 Make hay while the sun shines [P]. Initiate action upon thinking of it.
shisaku(suru) 思索(する)contemplation (contemplate)
onaji kiban ni tatsu 同じ基盤に立つ Both parties *have the same viewpoint* concerning communism.
rensō (suru) 連想(する) association of ideas (make an association of ideas; be reminded of)
zengo no misakai mo naku 前後の見境もなく He made that rash statement *without considering the implications*.
⇨ 144, 174, 193
神よ、どうか、わたしを探って、わが心を知り、わたしを試みてわがもろもろの思いを知ってください。(詩篇 139 ²³)

182 SHITSUBŌ 失望
DISAPPOINTMENT

Akete kuyashii tamatebako [P] あけて悔やしい玉手箱 He was in great hopes of finding life enjoyable in Tokyo, but after a few weeks *was bitterly disappointed.*

akirameru あきらめる despair of; resign oneself to

Aona ni shio [P] 青菜に塩 He *is* really *down in the dumps lately.*

ate ga hazureru 当てがはずれる His *expectations* of taking first place *were disappointed*; he finished third.

chikara o otosu 力を落とす After failing the exam, he *has lost heart* in going on to college.

chikaranuke 力抜け disappointment

gakkari (suru) がっかり(する) disappointment (be disappointed; be discouraged)

hariai ga nai 張り合いがない It's *disappointing* to work for him; no matter what you do, he's dissatisfied.

hyōshinuke suru [C] ひょうし抜けする He worked out hard for the track meet but *was really let down (was disappointed)* when the other team failed to come.

ikan (da) 遺憾(だ) lament; regret (lamentable; deplorable)

KI ga nukeru 気が抜ける Knowing that he would have to quit school at the end of the term *took the edge off (made him spiritless in)* his studies.

   ~ o kusarasu ~ を腐らす feel depressed; feel rotten; be down in the dumps

   ~ o otosu ~ を落とす lose heart; be let down

genki o ushinau 元気を失う lose heart; become dispirited; lose one's pep

ikishōchin (suru) 意気消沈(する) dejection; low spirits (be dejected; be in low spirits; be depressed)

uchinomesareta yōna kimochi 打ちのめされたような気持ち When he heard the shocking news, he *felt completely at a loss (had the feeling of being knocked down flat).*

kitai ga hazureru 期待がはずれる Lincoln's *expectations* for ending the war quickly *were dashed to the ground* by McClellan's ineptness.

mikomi ga hazureru 見込みがはずれる expectations go wide of the mark

nasake nai 情けない discouraging; miserable; I feel sorry for myself

rakutan (suru) 落胆(する) dismay (be dismayed; lose heart; be discouraged; be cast down)

saiaku no jitai 最悪の事態 It is a desperate state of affairs. Things are at their worst.

shioreru しおれる be down in the dumps; have the blues

SHITSUBŌ (suru) 失望(する) disappointment (be disappointed)

   ~ no amari ~ のあまり in utter disappointment

ikiru nozomi o ushinau 生きる望みを失う The burden of it was far too heavy for us to bear, so heavy that we even *despaired of life.* (II Corinthians 1 : 8)

kibō o kujiku 希望をくじく The news of his book rejection *took the wind out of his sails.*

   ~ o kutsugaesu ~ をくつがえす upset hopes; frustrate hopes; upset the applecart

shitsui 失意 disappointment; despair; loss

shitsuren (suru) 失恋(する) disappointment in love (be disappointed in love)

zetsubō (suru) 絶望(する) despair (despair of; give up hope)

   ~ ni ochiiru ~ に陥る sink into despair

zetsubōkan ni osowareru 絶望感に襲われる General Grant at one time *was overcome with utter disappointment* and took to drink.

unadareru うなだれる one's head droops; be down at the mouth

⇨ 218, 221

わが魂よ，何ゆえうなだれるのか．何ゆえ わたしのうちに
思いみだれるのか，神を待ち望め，わたしはなお，わが助
け，わが神なる主をほめたたえるであろう．(詩篇 42 ⁵)

183 SHIYŌ 使用 USE

benri (da) 便利(だ) convenience (convenient)
　benrishugi 便利主義 utilitarianism
　yūri (da) 有利(だ) advantage (advantageous)
EKI [L]益 advantage; usefulness
　mueki (da) 無益(だ) uselessness (useless; profitless)
　yūeki (da) 有益(だ) usefulness (useful)
Obi ni mijikashi, tasuki ni nagashi [P] 帯に短し，たすきに長し [It] *is neither fish nor fowl.*
oharaibako ni naru [C] お払い箱になる He is looking for a job now, for he was *fired* (*laid off*) by that company.
SHIYŌ (suru) 使用(する) use (make use of; use)
　~ kinshi ~ 禁止 out of order; use is prohibited
　~ ni taeru ~ に耐える be usable; can be put to use
　aiyō (suru) 愛用(する) favorite (make constant use of)
fuyō no mono 不用のもの useless article
jitsuyō 実用 practical use
kōyō 効用 usefulness; usability
mochiiru 用いる make use of; employ
ōyō (suru) 応用(する) application; adaptation (apply; adapt)
riyō (suru) 利用(する) advantage; use (take advantage of; avail oneself of; make good use of)
riyōkachi 利用価値 utilitary value
tokuyō (da) 徳用(だ) economy size (economical use)
tsukaimichi ga nai 使い道がない That old tractor *is unusable.*

tsukau 使う use; utilize
yō ga tariru 用が足りる be enough; will satisfy; will answer the purpose [of]
　~ no sunda mono ~ の済んだもの Don't keep that engine anymore. *It's past its usefulness.*
　~ o tasu ~ を足す do one's business; fill one's need; turn to account
yūyō (da) 有用(だ) usefulness (useful; serviceable)
Takara no mochigusare [P] 宝の持ち腐れ It was thoughtful of them to give it to me, but it's really a *useless treasure* (*white elephant*).
toku (da) 得(だ) profit; gain (profitable; economical)
　~ ni naru ~ になる What *will* a man *gain* by winning the whole world, at the cost of his true self? (Matthew 16 : 26)
torie ga aru 取りえがある may come in handy; has some merits
　~ ga nai ~ がない *There is nothing useful about* me (*I have nothing to commend myself*), but I hope I can be of service here.
yaku ni tatsu 役に立つ be useful; be of service; will come in handy
　~ ni tatanaku naru ~ に立たなくなる The machine *has outgrown its usefulness.*
yakudatsu 役立つ be serviceable; be useful; will serve the purpose [of]

...たとい 私が持っている 物の全部を 貧しい人たちに
分け与え，また私のからだを焼かれるために渡しても，愛
がなければ，何の役にも立ちません．(コリント I 13 ⁸)

184 SHIZEN 自然 NATURE

nariyuki ni makaseru 成り行きに任せる We were concerned about the situation at first but decided to *let things take their course.*

shinra banshō 森ら万象 all of creation; all nature

SHIZEN 自然 nature

~ **genshō** ~ 現象 natural phenomenon

~ **ni junnō suru** ~ に順応する adapt to nature

~ **ni shitashimu** ~ に親しむ commune with nature; be at home in nature

~ **no bi** ~ の美 natural beauty

~ **no hōsoku** ~ の法則 natural law; laws of nature

~ **no mama** ~ のまま in the natural form

~ **no nariyuki** ~ の成り行き natural course of things

~ **no sugata** ~ の姿 natural form; state of nature

fushizen (da) 不自然(だ) unnaturalness (unnatural; forced; stilted)

shizenryoku no mōi 自然力の猛威 fury of the elements

~ **o riyō suru** ~ を利用する harness nature; make use of nature

shizenshugi (sha) 自然主義(者) naturalism (naturalist)

tōzen (da) 当然(だ) naturalness (natural)

~ **no kekka toshite** ~ の結果として *As a natural consequence* (*As a natural outcome*) the deforested areas became eroded by the rain.

seirai (no) 生来(の) natural; by birth

shiki 四季 the four seasons of the year

~ **no utsurikawari** ~ の移り変わり the changing of the seasons

sōzō (suru) 創造(する) creation (create)

sōzōryoku 創造力 creative power

TENCHI 天地 all nature; heaven and earth

bettenchi (da) 別天地(だ) different world; very pleasant place (out of this world)

tenchisōzō 天地創造 creation of the universe

tennen 天然 nature

tensei 天性 natural endowment

uchū 宇宙 universe; cosmos; space

~ **jidai** ~ 時代 space age

神の目に見えない本性，すなわち神の永遠の力と神性は，世界の創造された時からこのかた，被造物によって知られ，はっきりと認められるのであって，彼らに弁解の余地はないのです。（ローマ 1 [20]）

185 SHŌGAI 障害
OBSTACLE

anshō 暗礁 shoal

~ **ni butsukaru** ~ にぶつかる His economic plan *hit a snag* when some of the Cabinet men opposed it.

ashitematoi ni naru 足手まといになる She wants to help at the church, but the baby *has become a drag* on her.

atsui kabe ni butsukaru 厚い壁にぶつかる run up against a brick wall; find it hard going; be up against it

dotamba ni oikomareru どたん場に追い込まれる We *were in serious straits* (*were driven to the wall*) when the enemy sealed off our escape routes.

fusagu ふさぐ block; obstruct

gyakkyō o kirinukeru 逆境を切り抜ける surmount the difficulty

ha ga tatanai 歯が立たない Waseda practiced hard this year but *can't stand up to* Keio in baseball.

habamu はばむ hinder

hikitomeru 引き止める detain; buttonhole

itabasami ni naru 板ばさみになる I liked both parties, so when they asked me to join, I *was caught in the middle* (*was on the horns of a dilemma*).

JAMA (suru) 邪魔(する) intrusion; bother (intrude; bother; get in the way)

~ **ga hairu** ~ がはいる be interrupted

~ **o suru** ~ をする get in the way; obstruct; hinder

jamamono atsukai ni suru 邪魔物扱

いにする They always *treat me as a nuisance* there, so I don't like to go.

kanmon 関門 barrier

ki ni naru 気になる become irksome; become irritating; become a bother

kojiraseru こじらせる complicate; make complex

kongarakaru [c] こんがらかる *It becomes complicated (gets confused)* when two people are in charge.

kōsoku (suru) 拘束(する) restriction; limitation (restrict; limit)

kukyō 苦境 straits; difficulties

kushin (suru) 苦心(する) effort; pains (make an effort; take pains)

kyokumen o dakai suru 局面を打開する The attorney *turned the tables on them by* getting the witness to contradict himself.

kyūchi ni ochiiru 窮地に陥る have one's back to the wall; be really up against it

MEIWAKU (suru) 迷惑(する) bother; nuisance (be a nuisance; bother)

　～ **o kakeru** ～をかける be a bother; cause trouble

　tōwaku suru 当惑する be perplexed

mendō (da) めんどう(だ) trouble; bother (troublesome; bothersome)

　～ **na koto ni naru** ～なことになる become troublesome

mezawari (da) 目ざわり(だ) eyesore (offensive to the eyes)

　mimizawari (da) 耳ざわりだ disagreeable sound (offensive to the ears)

mizu o sasu 水を差す If you repeat what she said, you may *create a barrier between* them.

moteamasu 持てあます be at a loss; not know what to do

muzukashii むずかしい difficult; hard; hard going

NANGI 難儀 difficulty

　bannan o haisuru 万難を排する The captain told the troops to hold the line *at all costs.*

nankan 難関 barrier; obstacle

nampa (suru) 難破(する) shipwreck (be shipwrecked)

sainan 災難 disaster; calamity

　～ **ni au** ～に会う experience disaster; meet misfortune

　～ **o nogareru** ～をのがれる escape disaster

noppiki naranai jijō のっぴきならない事情 *Because of unavoidable circumstances (Due to circumstances beyond my control)* I could not attend the meeting.

nukisashi naranai hame ni ochiiru 抜き差しならないはめに陥る After having invested funds in the sinking firm, I *was in a sad plight (was in a fix).*

saegiru さえぎる obstruct; hinder; block; interrupt

　michi o saegiru 道をさえぎる obstruct the path; block the road

sashitsukae ga aru さしつかえがある there is a drawback; an obstacle appears; there is something which prevents [it]

shimatsu ni oenai 始末におえない there's no way to handle [it]; [one] gets out of hand

shochi ni komaru 処置に困る The National Railways *are having difficulty in dealing with* the increase of drunkenness on the trains.

SHŌGAI 障害 obstacle

　～ **ni butsukaru** ～にぶつかる hit a snag; meet obstacles

　～ **ni uchikatsu** ～に打ち勝つ surmount difficulties

　～ **o kirinukeru** ～を切り抜ける pass through a barrier

　bōgai (suru) 妨害(する) hindrance; obstruction (hinder; obstruct)

　saigai 災害 misfortune; disaster

　shintai shōgaisha 身体障害者 physically handicapped person

　shishō o kitasu 支障をきたす Your not

being there *was a hindrance* (*threw a spanner in the works*).

shōgaibutsu 障害物 obstacle; an interference

shōheki 障壁 barrier; obstacle

saku さく barrier

samatage (ru) 妨げ(妨げる) hindrance; interference (hinder; interfere)

~ **ni naru** ~になる I put up with all that comes my way rather than *offer any hindrance* to the gospel of Christ. (I Corinthians 9:12)

tesū 手数 trouble; care

tekozuru 手こずる have difficulty; have a bad time with

tōge o kosu 峠を越す Having passed the test, you *are over the worst part* (*are over the hump*).

yakkai (da) やっかい(だ) trouble (troublesome)

yakkaimono やっかいもの a bother

yokoyari ga hairu 横やりがはいる Just when we were proceeding nicely, some official *gummed up the works* by criticizing our methods.

⇨ **123, 130, 221**

見よ、わたしは主である．すべて命ある者の神である．わたしにできない事があろうか...「ああ主なる神よ あなたは大いなる力と伸べた腕をもって 天と地とを お造りになったのです．あなたのできないことはひとつもありません．」（エレミヤ 32 ²⁷, ¹⁷）

186 SHŌRI 勝利 VICTORY, TRIUMPH

bu ga yoi (warui) 歩が良い (悪い) In the coming tournaments the Japanese team *looks promising* in volleyball, but they (*are at a disadvantage*) in basketball.

fuminijiru ふみにじる trample under foot

gaika o sōsuru がい歌を奏する win a victory; bring home the bacon

gaisen (suru) がいせん (する) triumphal procession (make a victory parade)

gekkeikan 月桂冠 laurels

eikan o eru 栄冠を得る win the laurels; win the crown

gunbai ga agaru 軍配が上がる It was a close bout, but the umpire *gave the nod to* Taiho.

kisen o seisuru 機先を制する Just as we were about to put our product out, the other firm *beat us to the punch* (*got the jump on us*) and put theirs out first.

kōfuku (suru) 降伏 (する) surrender (surrender; capitulate)

MAKASU 負かす defeat; drub; put down

Makeru ga kachi [P] 負けるが勝ち To lose is to win.

makezugirai (da) 負けずぎらい (だ) [one] who hates to lose

uchimakasu 打ち負かす defeat; get the better of; trounce

ōza ni tsuku 王座に着く He *became* middleweight *champion* of the world.

seien o okuru 声援を送る cheer [the team]; root for [the team]

seifuku (suru) 征服 (する) conquest; subjugation (conquer; subjugate; subdue)

SHŌRI 勝利 victory; triumph

[...**no**] ~ **ni kisuru** [...の] ~ に期する The game *ended in victory for* Waseda.

~ **o eru** ~ を得る win; gain the victory

~ **o hokoru** ~ を誇る Lincoln felt it was not a time to *boast of victory* (*glory in victory*) over the South.

~ **o osameru** ~ をおさめる gain a victory; put [one] down; put [one] to flight; get the upper hand

attōteki shōri 圧倒的勝利 overwhelming victory; landslide victory

hanabanashii shōri はなばなしい勝利 brilliant victory

kagayakashii shōri 輝かしい勝利 brilliant victory

ketteiteki shōri 決定的勝利 decisive victory

seishinteki shōri 精神的勝利 moral victory

yasuyasu to shōri o shimeru やすやすと勝利を占める win an easy victory over

daishōri 大勝利 great victory; overwhelming victory

~ o eru ~を得る achieve a great victory; make a clean sweep

kachi 勝ち victory; a win

kachieru かち得る win; achieve; gain

kachihokoru 勝ち誇る exult; be triumphant

kachiki (da) 勝ち気 (だ) unyielding; determined to win

kachime ga nai 勝ち目がない They *have a slim chance of winning*.

kachitoru 勝ち取る go out and conquer; gain a victory

Kateba kangun 〔P〕勝てば官軍 Might is right.

katsu 勝つ overpower; win; beat; win the day

rakushō suru 楽勝 (する) win hands down; trounce

senshō o iwau 戦勝を祝う celebrate victory

senshōkoku 戦勝国 victor nation

shinshō (suru) 辛勝 (する) narrow victory (win by a narrow margin; edge out; eke out a win)

shōbu (suru) 勝負 (する) match; game; bout (have a match; play a game)

~ ga tsuku ~がつく the game is up

~ ni naranai ~にならない be no match for

~ o kessuru ~を決する This match *will decide the* volleyball *championship*.

shōrisha 勝利者 victor; conqueror

uchikatsu 打ち勝つ triumph over; conquer

yūshō (suru) 優勝 (する) victory; championship (win the championship)

⇨ 217

しかし，神に感謝します．神はいつでも，私たちを導いてキリストによる勝利の行列に加え，至る所で私たちを通して，キリストを知る知識のかおりを放ってくださいます．
(コリント II 2 ¹⁴)

187 SHŌRYO 焦慮
IMPATIENCE, FRETFULNESS

akuseku suru あくせくする busy oneself; tear around

aseru あせる be hasty; be in a hurry; jump the gun

awa o kuu あわを食う In the mixup he *became confused (was in a flurry)* and did some odd things.

AWATERU あわてる be hasty; fluster; tear around

awatete...suru あわてて...する If you want to do a good job of it, don't *go off half-cocked*, but take your time.

awatadashii あわただしい hustling; overhasty; bustling

awatefutameku あわてふためく be confused; become flustered

awatemono あわて者 hasty person; bustling person

dada o koneru だだをこねる When she told the child to come in the house, he stood outside, *stamping his feet.*

gō o niyasu 業を煮やす I *became impatient (was put out)* at the way he kept repeating his demands.

hagayui はがゆい I *was on edge* as the teams lined up to play.

harahara suru はらはらする feel worried about; be on edge

imaimashigaru いまいましがる one feels annoyed at; one is provoked at

iraira suru いらいらする become irritated; fret and fume

iradatsu いら立つ fret; chafe

ite mo tatte mo irarenai いても立ってもい

られない be beside oneself; can't keep still

jirettaku naru じれったくなる I *grew impatient* waiting for him at the station.

KI ga ki de nai 気が気でない I still *found no relief of mind*, for my colleague Titus was not there to meet me. (II Corinthians 2:13)

~ **no hayai hito** ～の早い人 impulsive person; person who rushes into things

~ **o momu** ～をもむ be in suspense; be rankled

shikiri ni ki ni suru しきりに気にする I'm *deeply concerned* (*chewing my finger nails*) wondering if he will get that job.

kuyashigaru 悔やしがる one feels vexed

kyūyo no issaku 窮余の一策 last resort; desperate measure

machikirenaku naru 待ち切れなくなる get out of patience; one's patience runs out

modokashigaru もどかしがる one is fretful; be in suspense; feel impatient

otchokochoi [C] おっちょこちょい Don't let him do it; he's *a bungler* (*scatterbrained*).

seikyū (da) 性急(だ) hastiness (hasty)

Seite wa koto o shisonjiru [P] せいては事を仕損じる Haste makes waste [P].

sekkachi (da) せっかち(だ) impetuous; rash

SHŌRYO (suru) 焦慮(する) impatience; fretfulness (be impatient; fret)

shōsō 焦燥 hastiness; fretfulness

sosokkashii そそっかしい careless; harumscarum

sowasowa suru そわそわする be fidgety; be restless

te o dashisugiru 手を出し過ぎる His business failed because he *had too many irons in the fire* (*was doing more than he could handle*).

uwatsuku うわつく be restless

ya mo tate mo tamaranai 矢も盾もたまらない I *was unable to contain myself* (*couldn't keep still*) waiting for news of

his safe return.

yaburekabure ni naru やぶれかぶれになる When he was jilted by his sweetheart, he *became reckless* (*became careless*) and took to drink.

yakimoki suru やきもきする feel nervous ⇨ **102, 150**

信ずる者はあわてることはない. (イザヤ 28 ¹⁶)

188　SHŪCHŪ 集中
CONCENTRATION

bottō suru 没頭する be absorbed in

CHŪMOKU (suru) 注目(する) attention (pay attention; watch; keep one's eyes on)

~ **ni atai suru** ～に価する be worthy of attention; be noteworthy

~ **o atsumeru** ～を集める catch the attention of

~ **o hiku** ～をひく attract attention

iki mo tsukazu ni 息もつかずに He was tired but went on to the next task *without a break.*

ki o torareru 気を取られる Lincoln, *occupied with* the papers on his desk, would stare at a caller before greeting him.

KIKU 聞く listen

jitto kiku じっと聞く listen avidly

seishuku ni kiku 静粛に聞く listen quietly

hitokoto mo kiki nogasumai to shite 一言も聞きのがすまいとして *Trying not to miss a single word*, we sat on the edge of our seats as he spoke.

karuku kikinagasu 軽く聞き流す briefly hear; just catch a few words; not pay much attention [to]

kikihoreru 聞きほれる listen with rapt attention

kikimimi o tateru 聞き耳を立てる He *pricked up his ears* to overhear what they were saying.

[...**ni**] **mi o ireru** [...に] 身を入れる Abe *threw himself into* (*devoted himself to*) studying English grammar at the age of twenty-three.

zenshin zenrei o uchikonde 全身全霊を打ち込んで devoting heart and soul to

mimi o sobadateru 耳をそばだてる When he began talking in whispers, I *strained my ears to catch* every word.

mitoreru 見とれる be lost in admiration; be enraptured by

[...**ni**] **nen o ireru** [...に] 念を入れる do extra carefully; put one's mind to

sennen (suru) 専念(する) close attention (give close attention)

Nito o ou mono wa itto o mo ezu [P] 二兎を追うものは一兎をも得ず You can't do two things at once.

SENSHIN (suru) 専心 (する) undivided attention (give one's undivided attention; concentrate upon)

isshin furan ni 一心不乱に The office force worked *intently* (*flat out; with all their hearts*) to get the job done in time.

senmon 専門 speciality; major; line

shinkei o tsukau 神経を使う The teacher complained that it *taxed her nerves* to be with rowdy children.

seishin tōitsu 精神統一 concentration of thought; collecting of one's thoughts

shinken (da) 真剣 (だ) seriousness (serious)

shinshoku o wasurete 寝食を忘れて *Forgetting sleeping and eating*, he kept working on his experiments.

SHŪCHŪ (suru) 集中(する) concentration (concentrate)

chūi o shūchū suru 注意を集中する The teacher told us to *concentrate our attention on* the grammar of the sentences.

seiryoku o shūchū suru 精力を集中する concentrate one's energies on; devote one's energies to

muchū (da) 夢中 (だ) absorption; rapture

muga muchū ni naru 無我夢中になる He *became wholly engrossed in* (*went hog wild over*) Western music.

netchū (suru) 熱中 (する) enthusiasm; zeal (be enthusiastic [over]; be engrossed in; put one's heart into)

shūketsu (suru) 集結 (する) concentration (amass; collect; gather)

toki no tatsu no mo wasureru 時のたつのも忘れる even forgetting the passing of time

wakime mo furazu ni わき目も振らずに After learning grammar, Abe studied *with undivided attention* (*wholeheartedly*) the Scriptures, books on science and books on the knowledge of men.

⇨ **23, 151, 176**

あなたは心をつくし, 精神をつくし, 力をつくしてあなたの神. 主を愛さなければならない. (申命記 6 ⁵)

189 SHUDAN 手段 MEANS, METHOD

gikō 技巧 technique

~ **o korasu** ~ を凝らす employ a special technique

HŌHŌ 方法 way; means; method

~ **o ayamaru** ~ を誤る do [it] the wrong way; mistake the means

~ **o kaeru** ~ を変える change methods; change the way

~ **o kōjiru** ~ を講じる employ some means; take some measure

~ **o miidasu** ~ を見いだす find a way

hoka ni hōhō ga nai ほかに方法がない We *have no alternative but* to do it his way.

ikagawashii hōhō de いかがわしい方

法で by questionable means; by doubtful methods

benpō 便法 easy method; expedient

hōsaku 方策 policy; plan; means

hōshiki 方式 system

shikata 仕方 way of doing; manner; method

yarikata やり方 way of doing

yobōhō 予防法 preventive means

kotsu o oboeru こつを覚える After studying on the side, Abe *got the knack* (*learned the tricks*) of surveying.

kufū 工夫 device

kyūyo no saku 窮余の策 last resort; desperate measure

taisaku 対策 countermeasure

mubō de wa nai 無謀ではない It may seem foolish to you, but *there's a method to his madness.*

nan toka shite 何とかして in one way or another

SHUDAN 手段 means; method

~ **ga tsukiru** ~が尽きる be at one's wits' end

~ **hōhō** ~ 方法 ways and means

~ **o ayamaru** ~ を誤る employ devious methods

~ **o erabazu** ~ を選ばず He is determined to make his fortune *by fair means or foul* (*by hook or by crook; by any means*).

~ **o toru** ~ をとる take measures; employ a measure for...

arayuru shudan o tsukusu あらゆる手段を尽くす exhaust every means

fusei shudan 不正手段 foul method; dishonest means

gaikō shudan 外交手段 diplomatic means

hijō shudan ni uttaeru 非常手段に訴える resort to extreme measures

mokuteki tassei no shudan 目的達成の手段 means to achieve the end

seitō na shudan 正当な手段 legal means; proper steps

saigo no shudan toshite 最後の手段として *As a last resort* the ambassador went to the president himself.

yūkō na shudan 有効な手段 effective method

dandori 段取り plan; order of doing; schedule; preliminaries

~ **o kimeru** ~ を決める fix the order of doing [work, etc.]

SOCHI 措置 step; action; measure

~ **o toru** ~ をとる take action; use measures

shochi (suru) 処置 (する) disposal; measure (dispose of; deal with)

TE o kae, shina o kae 手を変え品を変え The government was forced to *employ all sorts of material and means* to meet the pressing problem.

~ **o tsukusu** ~ を尽くす do one's utmost

~ **o utsu** ~ をうつ take action; take measures

happō te o tsukusu 八方手を尽くす We *used every available means* to search for him.

oku no te o dasu 奥の手を出す When he seemed to be outwitted, he then *used his trump card* (*showed he had an ace in the hole; used his last resources*).

tegiwa yoku yaru 手ぎわよくやる do skillfully

⇨ **174**

天が地よりも高いように、わが道は、あなたがたの道よりも高く、わが思いは、あなたがたの思いよりも高い。
(イザヤ 55 ⁹)

190 SHUKUMEI 宿命
DESTINY

akirame (ru) あきらめ(あきらめる) resignation (resign oneself to circumstances)

awa yokuba あわよくば The odds are heavily against us, but *if we get the breaks*, we might win against Waseda today.

detatoko shōbu 出たとこ勝負 Don't worry about it; *let matters take their course.*

gūzen (da) 偶然 (だ) chance; accident; coincident (by chance; accidentally)
　~ no itazura ~ のいたずら That's *the way the cookie crumbles (the way the ball bounces).*

INNEN 因縁 fate; destiny
　akuen 悪縁 ill fate; hapless love
　akuinnen 悪因縁 ill fate
　engi 縁起 omen; luck; portent
　~ ga warui (yoi) ~ が悪い(良い) be a bad omen (be a good omen)
　~ o katsugu ~ をかつぐ He is a college professor, but he *believes in omens (is superstitious).*
　inga 因果 Buddhist law of cause and effect (karma); cause of a turn of events
　~ o fukumeru ~ を含める The Buddhist priest told the bereaved mother to *accept* the child's death *as inevitable.*
　~ to akirameru ~ とあきらめる resign oneself to one's fate
　ma ga sasu 魔がさす He *was seized by a devilish impulse* and threw the book at his mother.
　~ ga warui ~ 魔が悪い I seem to *be jinxed*; every time I plan a picnic it rains.

meguriai めぐり会い chance meeting
　fushigi na meguriawase 不思議なめぐり合わせ *As luck would have it*, I just happened to meet him in the station.

mokke no saiwai もっけの幸い windfall; lucky break; streak of good luck

nazo o toku なぞを解く solve the riddle

uke ni iru うけに入る He's *been getting the breaks* lately and making plenty of money.

UNMEI 運命 one's lot; fate; destiny
　~ ni sakarau ~ にさからう go against fate
　~ no itazura ~ のいたずら trick of fate
　~ o sayū suru ~ を左右する affect the destiny of
　~ o shihai suru ~ を支配する control the destiny
　[...to]~ o tomo ni suru [...と] ~ を共にする cast in one's lot with; be in the same boat

fuun 不運 misfortune; bad luck
　~ ni mo ~ にも unfortunately; unluckily; have the misfortune of
　~ o nageku ~ を嘆く grieve over one's misfortune

hiun 非運 misfortune

kokuun 国運 nation's destiny

shukumei 宿命 destiny
　~ to akirameru ~ とあきらめる resign [oneself] to [one's] fate; accept [it] as one's destiny.

tenmei 天命 fate; destiny
　jinji o tsukushite tenmei o matsu 人事を尽くして天命を待つ She told him to *do his best on* the test *and leave the consequences to providence.*

un 運 fortune; luck; fate
　~ ga yoi (warui) ~ が良い (悪い) be lucky; be fortunate (be unlucky; be unfortunate; does not pan out)
　~ ga muku ~ が向く be in luck
　~ ga nai ~ がない be out of luck; have a bad break
　~ ni megumareru ~ に恵まれる *Fortune is smiling upon* him these days.
　~ no tsuki ~ のつき When they cornered the fugitive, he knew *the jig was up (he was all washed up).*
　~ o tamesu ~ をためす He *tried his luck* at the stock market.
　~ o ten ni makaseru ~ を天に任せる leave one's fate up to chance

unmeironsha 運命論者 fatalist

unmeizukerareru 運命づけられる I *was destined* to meet him.

uranai (u) 占い(占う) divination; fortune-telling (divine; tell one's fortune)

minoue o uranau 身の上を占う Those quacks around Shibuya station will *tell your fortune* if you pay them.

⇨ 2

主はわたしの嗣業, またわたしの杯にうくべきもの. あなたは わたしの分け前を守られる. 測りなわはわたしのために好ましい所に落ちた. まことにわたしは良い嗣業を得た. (詩篇 16 ⁵, ⁶)

191 SHŪKYŌ 宗教
RELIGION

bodai o tomurau ぼだいを弔う pray to Buddha for the happiness of the dead

bōsan (sōryo) 坊さん (僧侶) Buddhist priest

DENTŌ 伝統 tradition; convention

~ ni torawareru ~にとらわれる be controlled by tradition

~ o mamoru ~ を守る keep tradition; maintain tradition

~ o yaburu ~ を破る break with tradition

densetsu 伝説 legend

iitsutae (ru) 言い伝え(言い伝える) tradition; legend (pass on; relate)

ekō (suru) 回向 (する) Buddhist requiem mass (hold a requiem mass)

engi o katsugu 縁起をかつぐ believe in omens; be superstitious

gūzō 偶像 idol

~ sūhai ~ 崇拝 idol worship; idolatry

gūzōka suru 偶像化する make into an idol; idolize

inshū 因習 tradition; custom; convention

~ ni torawareru ~にとらわれる be conventional; be bound by tradition

~ o daha suru ~ を打破する break

with convention; do away with conventionalism

shūkan 習慣 custom

kaimyō o tsukeru 戒名をつける affix a Buddhist name to the deceased

kanrei 慣例 usage; custom; precedent

[...no] ~ ni shitagau [...の] 慣例に従う be in accordance with the custom [of]

matsuri (ru) 祭り(祭る) festival (enshrine; deify; worship)

saidan 祭壇 altar

meifuku o inoru めい福を祈る pray for the happy repose of the dead [Buddhist]

mo ga akeru 喪があける go out of mourning

~ ni fukusuru ~ に服する be in mourning

[...no] nagare o kumu [...の] 流れをくむ belong to the...school [caligraphy, etc.]

nenbutsu o tonaeru 念仏をとなえる pray to Buddha

ogamu 拝む worship; bow down to an object of worship

te o awasete ogamu 手を合わせて 拝む fold one's hands in prayer [before an idol or the dead]

reihai (suru) 礼拝 (する) worship (worship)

omairi (suru) お参り (する) worship (visit a temple; make a temple pilgrimage)

sankei (suru) 参けい (する) visit (visit a temple)

sanpai (suru) 参拝 (する) worship [Shintō] (visit a Shintō shrine)

(o) miya (お) 宮 Shintō shrine

(o) tera (お) 寺 Buddhist temple

SHINKŌ ni hairu 信仰にはいる enter the faith; profess religion

Nihon koyū no shinkō 日本固有の 信仰 indigenous religions of Japan

meishin 迷信 superstition

~ ni torawareru ~にとらわれる be superstitious

shinjinbukai furi o suru 信心深い振りをする …preserve the outward form of religion. (II Timothy 3 : 5)

Shintō 神道 Shintō (The Way of the gods)

jinja 神社 Shintō shrine

kannushi (shinkan) 神主 (神官) Shintō priest

shōkō suru 焼香する offer incense to the dead

SHŪKYŌ 宗教 religion

    gairai shūkyō 外来宗教 alien religion

Bukkyō 仏教 Buddhism

ikyō 異教 paganism

isshinkyō (yuiitsu shinkyō) 一神教 (唯一神教) monotheism

jakyō 邪教 perverse religion; diabolical religion

Jukyō 儒教 Confucianism

kaishū (suru) 改宗 (する) conversion to another religion (be proselytized)

kokkyō 国教 state religion; national religion

mushūkyō (da) 無宗教 (だ) without religious affiliation

shūkyōshin 宗教心 religious sentiment

    ~ ni tomu ~ に富む Men of Athens, I see that *in everything that concerns religion you are uncommonly scrupulous.* (Acts 17 : 22)

tashinkyō 多神教 polytheism

sosen sūhai 祖先崇拝 ancester worship

    ~ no rei o tomurau ~ の霊を弔う propitiate ancestral spirits

tatari (ru) たたり (たたる) evil spell; curse (bring evil upon; haunt)

⇨ **177**

ご承知のように，あなたがたが先祖から伝わったむなしい生き方から贖い出されたのは，銀や金のような朽ちる物にはよらず，傷もなく汚れもない小羊のようなキリストの，尊い血によったのです。(ペテロ I 1 ¹⁸﹐ ¹⁹)

192   SOTCHOKU 率直
FRANKNESS

ari no mama ni hanasu ありのままに話す *Tell us the plain facts* without any embellishing.

bukkirabō (da) 〔c〕 ぶっきらぼう (だ) He would be a better salesman if he didn't talk to people so *bluntly (point-blank).*

chūshin kara 衷心から from the bottom of one's heart

ENRYO naku iu 遠慮なく言う talk freely; speak out

    ~ naku hakkiri iu ~ なくはっきり言う I *won't mince words* when we talk about the problem.

tōmawashi na iikata o suru 遠回しな言い方をする When he talks he *uses a roundabout way of speech (beats around the bush).*

fukuzō naku hanasu 腹蔵なく話す speak without hiding anything; speak forthrightly; speak right out

habakaru koto naku はばかる事なく without reserve; openly; freely

hakkiri iu はっきり言う call a spade a spade; tell one off

hara o watte hanasu 腹を割って話す talk frankly; let down one's hair

hayai hanashi ga 早い話が in short; to make a long story short

hoka demo nai ga… ほかでもないが the point is…what I want to say is… ; what I'm driving at is…

kakene no nai tokoro 掛け値のないところ without any padding; things as they are

kakushidate shinai 隠し立てしない without holding anything back

kazarike no nai 飾り気のない unaffected; unadorned; simple

kokoro oki naku 心おきなく Please talk to us *without any mental reservations.*

men to mukatte 面と向かって I opposed

him *to his face,* because he was clearly in the wrong. (Galatians 2:11)

mukōmizu na hito 向こう見ずな人 devil-may-care person

okuba ni mono no hasamatta yōna ii-kata o suru 奥歯に物のはさまったような言い方をする He talked to the teacher *as if he were holding something back* (*as if he were not divulging all the implications*).

sappari shita taido さっぱりした態度 frank attitude

sekirara (da) 赤裸々 (だ) naked; bald; open; frank

SOTCHOKU (da) 率直 (だ) frankness (frank; candid)

  ~ ni iu to ~ に言うと speaking plainly; frankly speaking

  bakashōjiki (da) ばか正直 (だ) He is poor at dealing with people; he's *too honest and simple* (*too naive*).

  chokusetsu (da) 直接 (だ) directness (direct)

    ~ ni hanasu ~ に話す speak directly to

    ~ ni atte miru ~ に会ってみる Don't go around; *deal with* him *directly.*

  shōjiki (da) 正直 (だ) honesty; squareness (honest; straightforward; square)

    ~ ni ieba ~ に言えば To tell the truth, I...

    ~ no tokoro ~ のところ I confess that I...

TEMIJIKA (da) 手短 (だ) brief

  ~ ni iu ~ に言う And now, not to take up too much of your time, I crave your indulgence *for a brief statement of our case.* (Acts 24:4)

tettoribayaku iu to 手っ取り早く言うと to put it briefly; in other words

UCHIAKERU 打ち明ける open up to; take into confidence

  uchiakete iu 打ち明けて言う Since we had some time, I *got* that problem *off my chest,* and he listened understandingly.

akeppanashi no seishitsu [C] あけっ放しの性質 He has *a frank, open nature.*

akesuke ni mono o iu [C] 明けすけに物を言う He didn't hold back but *came right out with it* (*spoke freely; talked openly*).

wadakamari no nai わだかまりのない having no mental reservations; without mincing matters; have nothing weighing on one's mind

warubirezu ni iu 悪びれずに言う speak right out

zukezuke to ずけずけと plainly; outspokenly; bluntly

⇨ **142, 175**

そこで, 私たちは確信に満ちてこう言います。「主は私の助け手です。私は恐れません。人間が, 私に対して何ができましょう。」(ヘブル 13 ⁶)

193 SŌZŌ 想像
IMAGINATION

dokusō 独創 originality

  dokusōteki ni kangaeru 独創的に考える think creatively; do original thinking

jasui (suru) 邪推 (する) evil conjecture; groundless suspicion (mistrust; be suspicious)

KENTŌ 見当 guess; estimate; conjecture

  ~ ga tsukanai ~ がつかない I *can't imagine* what will be the situation when we get there.

  ~ o tsukeru ~ をつける guess; make a conjecture; speculate

  kentōchigai (suru) 見当違い (する) He *has the mistaken idea* (He *is off the beam* if he thinks) that liberty means everyone does as he pleases.

kūchū rōkaku o egaku [L] 空中楼閣を描く He is so unrealistic, always *building castles in the sky.*

mune ni egaku 胸に描く draw a mental picture; visualize; see in the mind's eye

~ ni ukabu ~に浮かぶ When I heard the weird call, " Nato-o-o! " our old days in Gumma *came back to me.*

OMOI (u) 思い(思う) thoughts; experience (think; conceive; believe)

    ~ mo yoranai ~もよらない Things beyond our seeing, things beyond our hearing, things *beyond our imagination,* all prepared by God for those who love him. (I Corinthians 2 : 9)

    omoimegurasu 思いめぐらす think over; mull over

SŌZŌ (suru) 想像 (する) imagination; guess; fancy (imagine; guess; fancy)

    ~ ga tsuku ~がつく one can guess

    ~ ni zessuru ~に絶する defy all imagination

    ~ o megurasu ~をめぐらす ponder over; cogitate; use one's imagination

    ~ o takumashiku suru ~をたくましくする imagine fully; well imagine

    gosōzō ni makaseru ご想像にまかせる We'll end the drama here, *leaving the rest to your imagination.*

    kūsō (suru) 空想 (する) fancy; fantasy; pipe dream (fancy; dream)

        ~ ni fukeru ~にふける have a flight of imagination; have a pipe dream

        ~ o takumashiku suru ~をたくましくする give reins to one's imagination; stretch one's imagination

    musō (suru) 夢想 (する) daydreaming (daydream)

    sōtei (suru) 想定 (する) hypothesis; supposition (hypothesize; suppose)

    sōzōryoku 想像力 imaginative power

        ~ ni toboshii ~に乏しい lacking in imagination

    sōzōsetsu 想像説 hypothesis

yosō (suru) 予想 (する) prediction (predict)

    ~ o yurusanai ~を許さない cannot predict; cannot anticipate

    yosōdōri ni naru 予想どおりになる The game *ended up as I predicted.*

SUISATSU (suru) 推察 (する) guess; surmise (guess; surmise)

    ~ o ayamaru ~を誤る make a wrong guess

    osasshi no tōri お察しのとおり You guessed right; As you guessed...

    sasshi ga tsuku 察しがつく surmise; make a conjecture

        ~ ga yoi ~が良い She *is sensitive to* the needs of others. He *catches on to hints quickly.*

    sassuru 察する guess; imagine; presume

satchi (suru) 察知 (する) surmise; inference (surmise; infer)

suiri (suru) 推理 (する) deduction; inference (deduce; infer)

suiryō (suru) 推量 (する) guess (guess; gather from)

    ~ ga ataru ~が当たる guess right

suisoku (suru) 推測 (する) presumption; conjecture (presume; conject)

yomitoru 読み取る perceive; catch the implied meaning; read between the lines

yume ni mo kangaerarenai 夢にも考えられない I *couldn't have dreamed* it happening to us. What happened to us *was beyond our wildest dreams.*

⇨ **144, 174**

どうか, 私たちのうちに働く力によって, 私たちの願うところ, 思うところのすべてを越えて豊かに施すことのできる方に,

教会により, またキリスト・イエスにより, 栄光が, 世々にわたって, とこしえまでありますように. アーメン.

(エペソ 3 ^{20, 21})

194   SUKUI 救い   SALVATION

aganai (u) あがない(あがなう) atonement; redemption; expiation (atone; redeem; expiate)

hogo (suru) 保護 (する) protection (protect; preserve)

hoken 保険 insurance

inochibiroi (suru) 命拾い(する) narrow escape (have a narrow escape; be snatched from death)

SUKUI (u) 救い (救う) salvation; rescue (save; rescue)

    ~ ni azukaru ~にあずかる be saved; partake of salvation

    ~ no te o sashinoberu ~の手を差し伸べる extend the arm of salvation; reach out to deliver

    ~ o miidasu ~を見いだす find salvation

    ~ o motomeru ~を求める seek salvation

    shinkō ni yotte sukuwareru 信仰によって救われる For it is by grace you *are saved, through trusting* him; it is not of your own doing. (Ephesians 2:8)

kyūgo (suru) 救護 (する) relief; rescue; salvage (relieve; rescue; salvage)

kyūjo (suru) 救助 (する) rescue; aid; deliverance (rescue; aid; deliver)

    jinmei o kyūjo suru 人命を救助する save a life

kyūjohō 救助法 life-saving

kyūmeibukuro 救命袋 life preserver

kyūsaijigyō 救済事業 relief work

kyūsaisaku 救済策 relief measure

kyūshutsu 救出 deliverance

sukuidasu 救い出す deliver out of; save from; redeem

sukuinushi 救い主 savior; redeemer; rescuer

shokuzai しょく罪 redemption; atonement; expiation

tasuke (ru) 助け (助ける) help; relief; support (help; relieve; support)

    ~ to naru ~となる be of help; be of service; contribute to

この方以外には, だれによっても救いはありません. 世界

中でこの御名のほかには, 私たちが救われるべき名としては, どのような名も, 人間に与えられていないからです.」(使徒行伝 4 ¹²)

195   TABEN 多弁
TALKATIVENESS

enzetsu 演説 speech

HANASHI ga yoko ni soreru 話が横にそれる get off the subject

    ~ ni abura ga noru ~に油が乗る Everyone was quiet at first, but after that witty remark, the *conversation got into full swing.*

    ~ ni hana ga saku ~に花が咲く They were *engaged in lively conversation.*

hanashizuki na hito 話好きな人 talkative person; chatterbox

jōzetsu (da) 〔L〕 じょう舌 (だ) loquacity (loquacious)

KUCHI ga tassha (da) 口が達者 (だ) have a clever tongue; be a good speaker

    ~ kazu no ōi ~数の多い talkative; verbose; have a big mouth

    ~ o hasamu ~をはさむ interrupt a conversation

    ~ o kiru ~を切る speak first; begin to speak

    ~ o suberasu ~をすべらす make a slip of the tongue

    ~ o suppaku shite iu ~をすっぱくしていう Her mother *drummed it into her* (*gave her a good talking to*) about not coming home late.

    ~ o tsugumu ~をつぐむ close one's mouth

kōkaku awa o tobasu 口角あわを飛ばす He rushed into the room and *talked a mile-a-minute* (*began shooting off his mouth*).

kuchiguse 口癖 pet phrase

mudaguchi むだ口 idle talk

    ~ o kiku ~をきく talk idly; talk on and on

mukuchi na hito 無口な人 man of few words

ōguchi 大口 big mouth

~ **o tataku** ~ をたたく talk big; sound off

kudokudo kurikaesu くどくどくり返す The landlord *kept harping* on the fact that we left the lights on in the house.

makushitateru [C] まくし立てる He *talked with such a barrage of words* that we couldn't answer back.

muteppō na koto o iu 無鉄砲な事を言う talk wildly; speak irresponsibly

muttsuriya [C] むっつり屋 silent person; glum fellow

roretsu ga mawaranai ろれつが回らない He has trouble speaking because he *cannot articulate well* (*cannot enunciate his words clearly*).

SHABERU しゃべる talk; chatter

berabera shaberu べらべらしゃべる speak volubly; gibber

nobetsu makunashi ni shaberu のべつまくなしにしゃべる They were *talking a mile-a-minute*, so I couldn't get a word in edgewise.

tateita ni mizu o nagasu yōni shaberu 立て板に水を流すようにしゃべる Graham *poured forth a torrent of words clearly* to thousands at the football stadium rally.

oshaberi おしゃべり chatterbox; windbag

shaberimakuru しゃべりまくる rattle on; prattle

shitsugen (suru) 失言 (する) slip of the tongue (pull a boner; put one's foot in one's mouth)

TABEN (da) 多弁 (だ) talkativeness (talkative; long-winded)

benron no sai 弁論の才 power of elocution

daben o rōsuru だ弁をろうする talk off the point; go babbling on

yūben (da) 雄弁 (だ) eloquent; fluent

tatami kakete kiku たたみかけてきく He tried to be evasive; but they *pressed* him *for an answer.*

zatsudan (suru) 雑談(する) conversation; bull session (talk things over; converse together; chat)

⇨ **127, 200**

神の前で軽々しく口をひらき，また言葉を出そうと心にあせってはならない．神は天にいまし，あなたは地にあるからである．それゆえあなたは言葉を少なくせよ．

(伝道の書 5 ²)

196　TAIKUTSU 退屈
BOREDOM

AKIRU 飽きる get tired of; get sick of

akiaki suru 飽き飽きする get fed up [with]; get bored [with]

akippoi あきっぽい easily tired of

akubi o kamikorosu あくびをかみ殺す stifle a yawn; try to keep from yawning

hima 暇 idleness; leisure

jikan o tsubusu 時間をつぶす We went for a walk just to *kill time.*

kentaikan けんたい感 fatigued feeling

nemuke ga sasu 眠気がさす grow sleepy

shibire o kirasu しびれを切らす I *became impatient* waiting so long.

shozainasa 所在なさ boredom; tedium; ennui

~ **sō ni suru** ~ そうにする We played records *to while away the time.*

TAIKUTSU 退屈 boredom; tedium

~ **no amari** ~ のあまり I was *bored stiff* at the meeting, so I left.

~ **o magirasu** ~ をまぎらす Having time on our hands, we went fishing to *fill in the hours.*

~ **shinogi ni** ~ しのぎに We took a walk to *kill time* (*relieve the boredom*).

tanchō (da) 単調 (だ) tedious; monotonous

TE ga aku 手があく be free; have time on one's hands

temochibusata (da) 手持ちぶさた (だ) I didn't like it there, for *I felt as if I had nothing to do* (*time hung heavy on my hands*).

tesuki 手すき spare time; leisure

unzari suru うんざりする I *am getting tired of* his same talk every morning.

あなたの若い日に, あなたの造り主を覚えよ. 悪しき日がきたり, 年が寄ってわたしには何の楽しみもないと言うようにならない前に, ... (伝道の書 12 ¹)

197 TAIMAN (TAIDA) 怠慢 (怠惰) NEGLIGENCE (LAZINESS)

abura o uru [C] 油を売る Every time those girls go to the water fountain, they *start loafing* (*start gabbing*).

an'itsu 安逸 idleness

an'i (da) 安易 (だ) He has an *easy-going* way of doing things.

ankan to shite irarenai 安閑としていられない If you want to get ahead here, you *can't let any grass grow under your feet*.

bushō (da) 無精 (だ) lazy; slothful

chūto hanpa (da) 中途半端 (だ) halfway; half done; half baked

dareru だれる get tired of; be bored [of]

fuchūi (da) 不注意 (だ) carelessness; thoughtlessness (careless; thoughtless)

gūtara (da) [C] ぐうたら (だ) loafer; goof-off [S] (idle; lazy)

guzutsuku ぐずつく loiter: dilly-dally; loaf

honeoshimi o suru 骨惜しみをする make a half-hearted attempt; begrudge effort

rō o oshimu 労を惜しむ stint one's efforts; begrudge work

jidaraku (da) 自堕落 (だ) slovenly; abandoned; untidy

[...ni] kakeru [...に] 欠ける be lacking in

michikusa o kuu 道草を食う The children are late because they *dilly-dallied* on

the way home. He got home late from work because he *detoured* into a bar along the way.

Mikka bōzu [P] 三日坊主 You can't count on him to finish the task; he *gives up easily* (he's *a quitter*).

minogasu 見のがす overlook; miss seeing; let pass

monogusa [C] ものぐさ He'll never succeed; he's a *lazybones* (*loafer; slacker*).

nageyari ni naru 投げやりになる do a sloppy job; do [it] any old way

naigashiro ni suru ないがしろにする make light of; treat lightly

namakeru なまける fool around; be lazy; stall

namakemono なまけ者 lazy person

naozari なおざり neglect

~ ni suru ~にする ...what escape can there be for us if we *ignore* a deliverance so great? (Hebrews 2 : 3)

nete kurasu 寝て暮らす fritter away one's time; idle away time

norakura suru のらくらする loaf; loiter; hang around

ōchaku (da) おうちゃく (だ) laziness (lazy)

okkūgaru おっくうがる stall; feel something is troublesome

orosoka (da) おろそか (だ) careless; negligent

~ ni suru ~にする neglect

Osokarishi Yuranosuke [P] 遅かりし由良之助 You came too late; the *show is all over*. You are a *Johnny-come-lately*.

saboru さぼる skip; neglect

TAIMAN 怠慢 negligence

shokumu taiman 職務怠慢 neglect of official duty; dereliction of duty

okotaru 怠る neglect; be negligent; be derelict

shokumu o okotaru 職務を怠る Lincoln's bodyguard Parker *was lying down on the job* (*was neglecting his duty*) when Boothe slipped into

Ford's Theater to assassinate him.

taida (da) 怠惰 (だ) slothful; sluggish; indolent

Tana kara botamochi [P] たなからぼたもち They just sit around, *expecting something for nothing.*

te o komanuite 手をこまぬいて When they told him his salary was lowered, he dropped his work and *stood there with folded arms.*

~ **o nuku** ~ 手を抜く skimp on one's work; cut corners in one's work

ukauka kurasu うかうか暮らす pass one's days in idleness

yukkuri (suru) ゆっくり (する) leisurely; slowly (take one's time)

⇨ 147

なまけ者よ、ありのところへ行き、そのすることを見て、知恵を得よ. ありはかしらなく、つかさなく、王もないが、夏のうちに食物をそなえ、刈入れの時にかてを集める.
(箴言 6 ⁶⁻⁸)

198 TANOSHIMI 楽しみ
PLEASURE, ENJOYMENT

asobi (bu) 遊び (遊ぶ) play; enjoyment (play; enjoy oneself; play around)
waruasobi 悪遊び questionable pleasure

etsu ni iru 悦に入る He *is in rapture* when listening to classical music.

kantai o ukeru 歓待を受ける We *were well entertained* at the party.

hōratsu ni sugosu 放らつに過ごす You have *lived* on earth *in wanton luxury,* fattening yourselves like cattle...(James 5 : 5)

ki mo ukitatsu yōna omoi 気も浮き立つような思い I had an *exhilarating feeling* walking through the forest.

me no hoyō ni 目の保養に We went to the department store *just to window shop* (*just for enjoyment*).

OMOSHIROI おもしろい interesting; enjoyable; pleasant

omoshiroku sugosu おもしろく過ごす We *spent an enjoyable time* at the beach last summer.

totemo omoshirokatta とてもおもしろかった I *enjoyed* the play *very much.*

oni no kubi demo totta yōni 鬼の首でも取ったように Just because he passed his entrance exams, he acted *as if he had the world by the tail on the downward pull* (*as if he had really done something*).

TANOSHIMI (mu) 楽しみ(楽む) pleasure; enjoyment (enjoy; take pleasure in)

omou zonbun tanoshimu 思う存分楽しむ enjoy oneself to the full

anraku (da) 安楽 (だ) comfort; ease (comfortable; easy)

dōrakumono 道楽者 fast liver; libertine; man of pleasure; hedonist

goraku 娯楽 amusement; entertainment; recreation; pastime

kairaku 快楽 pleasure

kanraku 歓楽 pleasure; merriment; mirth

~ **ni fukeru** ~ にふける indulge in pleasure; enjoy pleasure; revel; live it up; live wild

kōraku 行楽 pleasure trip; outing

kyōraku (suru) 享楽 (する) pleasure (take pleasure in; enjoy)

~ **kibun de** ~ 気分で On the Emperor's birthday everyone was *in a holiday mood* and went to the park.

kyōrakuteki (da) 享楽的 (だ) pleasure seeking

raku (da) 楽 (だ) ease (easy)

~ **o suru** ~ をする live an easy life; take life easy

rakuraku to 楽々と very easily

ureshii うれしい happy; joyful; glad

wakuwaku suru わくわくする Before the big occasion her *heart trembled* for joy.

yōki (da) 陽気 (だ) pleasant; jovial

yorokobashii 喜ばしい delightful; joyful; pleasant

yukai (da) 愉快 (だ) pleasantness (pleasant; jovial; merry; happy)

    kaikan 快感 pleasant sensation

yūkyō (shushoku) ni fukeru 遊興(酒色)にふける He *is addicted to wine and women.*

⇨**118, 210, 214**

遊興, 酩酊, 淫乱, 好色, 争い, ねたみの生活ではなく, 昼間らしい, 正しい生き方をしようではありませんか. (ローマ 13 ¹³)

199 TASŪ 多数 MAJORITY

DAIBUBUN (wa) 大部分 (は) the greater part (for the most part)

    daitai だいたい by and large; on the whole

    ōzei 大勢 crowd of people; a great number [of]

    taihan (wa) 大半 (は) greater part; majority (mostly; nearly all)

tairyō 大量 large quantity

imozuru shiki ni agerareru いもづる式にあげられる Under questioning they revealed their hideout, and the criminals *were rounded up one after another.*

issai (no) いっさい(の) everything; (every; entire; whole)

KAZU kazu no 数々の numerous; lots of

    ~ kagiri nai ~ 限りない numberless

    kazoekirenai hodo aru 数えきれないほどある more than can be counted; innumerable

kuchi o soroete 口をそろえて The mob shouted *with one voice*, " Crucify him! "

maikyo ni itoma ga nai [L] 枚挙にいとまがない too numerous to mention

moromoro no もろもろの all; every kind of

osuna osuna no ōnigiwai (da) 押すな押すなの大にぎわい(だ) During the Tanabata Festival in Sendai the streets are filled with *colorful crowds* (*jamming crowds*).

subete (no) すべて (の) all

takusan たくさん plenty; lot

TASŪ 多数 a great many

    ~ o seisuru ~ を制する obtain (command) a majority

    attōteki tasū o shimeru 圧倒的多数を占める show an overwhelming majority; have a big margin

    ketteiteki tasū 決定的多数 decisive majority

    zettai tasū de 絶対多数で Lincoln won the election *by an absolute majority.*

daitasū 大多数 great majority

kahansū 過半数 majority

    ~ o shimeru ~ を占める constitute a majority

ōi 多い many; plenty [of]

tasūketsu (de) 多数決 (で) majority decision (decision by majority)

zenbu 全部 all; the whole

狭い門からはいりなさい. 滅びに至る門は大きく, その道は広いからです. そして, そこからはいって行く者が多いのです. (マタイ 7 ¹³)

200 TAWAGOTO たわごと NONSENSE

atarisawari no nai koto o iu 当たりさわりのない事をいう The Missouri delegation was aggravated at Lincoln, for he *spoke in a non-committal way* (*spoke around the problem*).

BAKARASHII ばからしい nonsensical; absurd; foolish

    baka ie! ばか言え Don't be silly! You talk nonsense!

    bakageta koto ばかげたこと nonsense

bōgen o haku 暴言を吐く make reckless statements; speak rashly

chiguhagu na koto o iu ちぐはぐな事を言う He tried to explain things but really *made contradictory statements* (*talked at cross purposes*).

chinpun kanpun (da) [C] ちんぷんかんぷん

(だ) The language those physicists use *is all Greek to me*!

fuzaketa koto o iu ふざけた事を言う make a jesting remark

hen na koto o iu へんな事を言う talk strangely; say something odd

herazuguchi o tataku へらず口をたたく She *blabs about everything* she knows.

　mudaguchi o kiku むだ口をきく talk a lot of twaddle; talk nonsense

kumo o tsukamu yōna hanashi 雲をつかむような話 Don't take him seriously; that's just *pie-in-the-sky.*

muimi (da) 無意味 (だ) meaningless; senseless

ne mo ha mo nai 根も葉もない There *isn't an ounce of truth in* what he said about George.

negoto 寝言 nonsense

ōgesa ni iu 大げさに言う exaggerate; talk big

okashi na koto o iu おかしな事を言う talk foolishly

OROKA (da) 愚か (だ) foolish

　~ ni mo ~ にも foolishly

　gu ni mo tsukanai koto o iu 愚にもつかない事を言う talk plain foolishness; say something too silly for words

　guron 愚論 foolish opinion; absurdity

TAWAGOTO たわごと nonsense

　~ o iu ~ を言う talk nonsense

tawaketa たわけた silly; foolish

tohō mo nai koto o iu 途方もないことを言う make wild statements; talk absurdly

toritome no nai hanashi とりとめのない話 wild talk; rambling talk

uwagoto うわごと gibberish; rigmarole

　~ o iu ~ を言う talk deliriously

⇨ **48, 116, 195**

あなたがたの間では、聖徒にふさわしく、不品行も、どんな汚れも、またむさぼりも、口にすることさえいけません。また、みだらなことや、愚かな話や、下品な冗談を避けなさい。そのようなことは良くないことです。むしろ、感謝しなさい。 (エペソ 5 ³, ⁴)

201　TEKI 敵 ENEMY

ada あだ foe; enemy

　~ o utsu ~ をうつ take revenge on

AITE ni naru 相手になる Would you mind *playing against me* in tennis today?

　~ni shinai ~ にしない I advise you to *have nothing to do with* him.

　~ ni totte fusoku wa nai ~ にとって不足はない Kashiwado *is well pitted against* Taiho for the sumo match today.

fukushū (suru) 復しゅう (する) revenge (take revenge [on]; avenge [oneself])

Goetsu dōshū [P] 呉越同舟 *Like implacable enemies in the same boat,* the Socialists are taking the same position as the Democrats.

hamukau はむかう rise up against; turn on

　temukau 手向かう rise up against; set one's face against

hanmoku (suru) 反目(する) antagonism (set one's face against; be pitted against)

kataki かたき foe; adversary; enemy

shōbaigataki 商売がたき business rival; close competitor

niramiau にらみ合う glare at one another

omoishirasete yaru 思い知らせてやる Sherman wrote Lincoln: "...make them sick of war...*let them learn it well* that good citizens must obey as well as command."

shishi shinchū no mushi [L] 獅子身中の虫 Speaking about *the enemy within,* Lincoln said, " The enemy behind us is more dangerous to the country than the enemy before us."

tachiuchi dekinai たち打ちできない Waseda *is no match for* Keio in rugby.

taiji (suru) 対じ(する) confrontation (confront; stand face to face)

TEKI 敵 enemy; foe

　~ ni jōjirareru ~ に乗じられる They *were taken advantage of by the ene-*

my (were ambushed by the enemy).

~ no te ni ochiiru ~の手に陥る fall into the hands of the enemy

~ o kuitomeru ~を食い止める check the enemy; stop the enemy

~ o shire! ~を知れ *Know your enemy* before you fight him.

~ o tsukuru ~を作る Because of his coarse ways he *makes enemies (antagonizes people)* everywhere he goes.

shukuteki 〔L〕宿敵 long standing enemy; arch rival

tekigaishin 敵がい心 animosity; hostile feeling

~ o aoru ~をあおる stir up enmity against

tekigun 敵軍 enemy forces

tekihei 敵兵 enemy troops

tekii 敵意 enmity

tekijin 敵陣 the enemy's camp

~ o toppa suru ~を突破する break through the enemy's camp

tekimikata 敵味方 friend and foe

tekishi (suru) 〔L〕敵視〔する〕 hostility (be hostile toward)

tekitai (suru) 敵対（する）antagonism; hostility (be antagonistic to; be hostile to; clash with)

~ kōdō ~行動 hostilities; hostile act

⇨ **7, 172, 205**

では、これらのことからどう言えるでしょう．神が私たちの味方であるなら、だれが私たちに敵対できるでしょう．（ローマ 8 ³¹）

202 TEKITŌ 適当 FITNESS, APPROPRIATENESS

atehamaru 当てはまる apply [to]; suits; conform to

atehameru 当てはめる make application to; apply to one

atsuraemuki no あつらえむきの suitable for; just fits

AU 合う correspond with; agree with; fit

pittari au ぴったり合う exactly fits; be just cut out for; be well suited [for]

umaku au うまく合う be a perfect fit; just fits

niau 似合う match well; be becoming to; goes well with

deru maku dewa nai 出る幕ではない Please excuse me. Not being a member I've *no business* (I'm *out of place*) at this meeting.

do o sugosu 度を過ごす overdo

gendo o koeru 限度を越える exceed one's limitations

[...ni] fusawashii [...に] ふさわしい suitable for; fit for; appropriate for; worthy of

fusawashiku nai to omou ふさわしくないと思う When asked about his candidacy, Lincoln replied, " I must, in candor, say, *I do not think myself fit for* the presidency."

gara ni nai 柄にない It *was unlike* him to brag like that.

Hakidame ni tsuru 〔P〕はきだめにつる That old dump truck parked in the beautiful park *is quite out of place.*

kanau かなう suit; be compatible to; go along with; serves

mokuteki ni kanau 目的にかなう His plan will *serve our purpose (answer our purpose).*

Ki ni take o tsugu yōna 〔P〕木に竹をつぐような In this wooden house steel windows *are unbecoming (are out of place).*

mottekoi no もってこいの fitting; ideal

muri o suru 無理をする overdo something; do something beyond one's capability

nitsukawashii 似つかわしい becoming (to one) [clothes, etc.]

Oka ni agatta kappa 〔P〕陸にあがったかっぱ I'm *a fish out of water* among all those politicians.

ōyō (suru) 応用（する）application; adaptation (apply; adapt to; put [it] into practice)

sōō (da) 相応 (だ) suitable; appropriate

[...] rashiku nai [...] らしくない be unlike [one]

sessei (suru) 節制 (する) moderation (use moderation)

[...ni] sokushite [...に] 即して These plans *are in conformity* (*comply with*) our overall objectives.

TEKITŌ (da) 適当 (だ) fitness; suitability (suitable; proper)

  ~ na hōhō de ～な方法で with an appropriate method ⌈cise

  ~ na undō ～な運動 moderate exer-

  ~ ni suru ～にする I'll leave it up to you; *do as you think best* (*do as you see fit*).

  ~ to mitomeru ～と認める consider [it] fitting; think [it] best

  bun ni sugiru koto o suru 分に過ぎる事をする If he accepts the presidency of the bank, he'll *be biting off more than he can chew.*

futekitō (da) 不適当だ unsuitable; unfit

tekigō (suru) 適合 (する) conformity; appropriateness (be in conformity to; harmonize with; be appropriate)

  pittari tekigō suru ぴったり適合する Of Lincoln's Gettysburg Address the Gazette reported, "...this *was the right thing* in the right place..."

tekinin (sha) 適任 (者) suitability; fitness (suitable person; qualified person)

tekiō (suru) 適応 (する) adaptation; adjustment (be adapted to; be just the thing)

tekireiki 適齢期 marriagable age

tekisei (kensa) 適性 (検査) aptitude (aptitude test)

tekisetsu (da) 適切 (だ) appropriate; adequate; pertinent

tekisuru 適する fit; agree with

tekiyō (suru) 適用 (する) application [of a rule] (be applicable to)

tekizai tekisho 適材適所 He *is the right man in the right place.*

tekkaku 適格 fitness; competency

uttetsuke no kotoba うってつけの言葉 choice wording; words that hit home

yō o eru 要を得る be to the point; hit the nail on the head; give the essentials
⇨ 22

神が多くの子たちを栄光に導くのに、彼らの救いの創始者を、多くの苦しみを通して全うされたということは、万物の存在の目的であり、また原因でもある方として、ふさわしいことであったのです。（ヘブル 2 ¹⁰）

203 TSUMI 罪 SIN, CRIME

akuji 悪事 wrongdoing; misdeed

bassuru 罰する punish [sin, crime, etc.]

dappō kōi 脱法行為 law evasion

fugi 不義 iniquity; unrighteousness; sin

  ~ no ko ～の子 illegitimate child

fuhō kōi 不法行為 illegal act; illegality

  ihō 違法 unlawfulness

fusei (da) 不正 (だ) injustice (unjust)

  ~ na koto o suru ～な事をする You *commit a misdemeanor* when you use another person's pass on the trains.

  ~ shudan 手段 illegal means

HANKŌ 犯行 offense; crime

  dekigokoro de yatta hankō 出来心でやった犯行 unpremeditated crime

  chinōhan 知能犯 premeditated crime

  genkōhan o toraeru 現行犯を捕える They *caught* that criminal *redhanded* with the stolen goods on him.

  hanzai 犯罪 offense; crime

    ~ o mokuromu ～をもくろむ attempt to commit a crime; conceive a crime

    ~ o okasu ～を犯す commit a crime

    jūdai no hanzai 十代の犯罪 juvenile offense

  keihanzai 軽犯罪 misdemeanor

okasu 犯す commit [a sin, a crime, etc.]

satsujinhan 殺人犯 murder

ihan (suru) 違反 (する) violation (violate; make an infraction)

kōtsū ihan 交通違反 traffic violation

mi ni oboe ga nai 身に覚えがない I *had nothing to do with* the crime. I *am not guilty of* your allegation.

  seiten hakujitsu no mi ni naru 青天白日の身になる At the trial, *his innocence was proved* (he became perfectly free from any shadow of guilt).

sune ni kizu motsu mi すねに傷持つ身 Be careful of him; he *has a criminal past.*

nureginu ぬれぎぬ false charge

  ~ o kiserareru ~を着せられる be falsely accused [of]

toga とが fault

togameru とがめる blame; rebuke

TSUMI 罪 sin; crime

  ~ na koto o suru ~な事をする do a cruel thing; act wickedly

  ~ ni otoshiireru ~におとしいれる On the witness stand she tried to *incriminate* him, but he was proved innocent.

  ~ ni towareru ~に問われる be accused

  ~ o hinin suru ~を否認する deny one's guilt

  ~ o jikaku suru ~を自覚する be conscious of sin

  ~ o kabau ~をかばう cover up sin

  ~ o kakusu ~を隠す conceal one's guilt

  ~ o mitomerarenai ~を認められない ...happy is the man whose *sins* the Lord *does not count against* him. (Romans 4: 8)

  ~ o nogareru ~をのがれる escape punishment; get off easily; beat the rap

  ~ o tanin ni nasuritsukeru (kiseru) ~を他人になすりつける (着せる) He tried to *put the blame for* his crime on someone else.

jindō ni hansuru tsumi 人道に反する罪 Eichmann was convicted of *crimes against humanity.*

mujitsu no tsumi 無実の罪 false accusation; trumped up charge

harenchizai 破廉恥罪 felony; shameful crime; heinous crime

muzai (da) 無罪 (だ) innocence (innocent; guiltless)

  ~ ni naru ~になる be found not guilty

  ~ o iiwatasu ~を言い渡す The court *declared* the old man *not guilty.*

tsumibukai 罪深い sinful; corrupt

yūzai (da) 有罪 (だ) guilt (guilty)

  ~ to kimaru ~と決まる be condemned

zaiaku (kan) 罪悪感 vice; sin (sense of wrong)

zaigō 罪業 sin; iniquity

zaika 罪科 crime; wickedness

zenka ga aru 前科がある The judge was hard on him because he *had a previous offense* (had a criminal past).

⇨ **3, 10, 178**

神は、罪を知らない方を、私たちの代わりに罪とされました。それは、私たちが、この方にあって、神の義となるためです。 (コリント II 5 ²¹)

204 URAGIRI 裏切り
BETRAYAL, TREACHERY

ansatsu (suru) 暗殺(する) assassination (assassinate)

damashiuchi だまし討ち wicked plot; evil plan; sneak attack; foul play; dirty trick

  [...o] ~ ni suru [...を] ~にする stab one in the back

fushin kōi 不信行為 apostasy; falling away; treachery

hangyaku (suru) 反逆(する) rebellion; revolt (rebel against; rebel)

INBŌ 陰謀 plot; treachery

~ **o abaku** ~ をあばく expose a plot; reveal a conspiracy

~ **o kuwadateru** ~ を企てる make a conspiracy

bōryaku 謀略 intrigue; plot

kyōbō (suru) 共謀(する) plot; conspiracy (plot together; make a conspiracy)

sakubō (suru) 策謀(する) machination; artifice (frame up; contrive)

Kaiinu ni te o kamareru [P] 飼い犬に手をかまれる Criticizing the very professor who helped you graduate is *biting the hand that feeds you.*

KEIRYAKU 計略 plan; scheme; design

kankei [L] かん計 wicked plot; evil plan; foul piay

sakuryaku 策略 stratagem

kontan 魂胆 intrigue; plot

kūdetā クーデター coup d'etat

KUWADATERU 企てる plot; scheme

takurami (mu) たくらみ(たくらむ) scheme; intrigue (scheme; intrigue [against]; contrive)

akuji o takuramu 悪事をたくらむ devise something evil; hatch something evil

migoroshi ni suru 見殺しにする After being promoted, he forgot all about us. When we got in trouble, he *left us in the lurch* (*sold us down the river*).

muhon むほん rebellion; mutiny

~ **o okosu** ~ を起こす mutiny (against); make a rebellion (against); rise up against

naitsū (suru) 内通(する) collusion; double dealing (be in collusion with)

negaeri o utsu 寝返りをうつ double cross; go back on; go over to the other side

se o mukeru 背を向ける disown; forsake; turn one's back on

shitagokoro ga aru 下心がある He acts friendly but I don't trust him; I'm sure he *has some axe to grind* (*has an ulterior motive*).

teki ni tsuku 敵につく go over to the enemy; sell out to; defect to the enemy; play turncoat

uchimaku o nozoku 内幕をのぞく He *looked behind the scenes of* the political party and disclosed his findings in a magazine.

URAGIRI (ru) 裏切り(裏切る) betrayal; treachery (betray; deal treacherously; break faith with)

uragirimono 裏切り者 betrayer; traitor; heel

uraomote ga aru 裏表がある *There is double-dealing* in the real-estate business here.

⇨ **46**

しかし、見なさい。わたしを裏切る者の手が，わたしとともに食卓にあります。

人の子は，定められたとおりに去って行きます。しかし人の子を裏切るような人間はのろわれます。

(ルカ 22 ²¹, ²²)

205 URAMI うらみ GRUDGE, RESENTMENT

AKUI 悪意 malice; ill feelings

~ **atte...suru** ~ あって...する I shall *do* nothing *in malice.* What I deal with is too vast for malicious dealing. (Lincoln)

~ **o idaku** ~ をいだく have it in for; bear a grudge [against]; harbor malice

akkanjō 悪感情 animosity; bad feelings

tekii 敵意 enmity; hostility; animosity

fukushū (suru) 復しゅう(する) revenge; retaliation (take revenge; retaliate)

hōfuku (suru) 報復(する) retaliate; recompense; do justice to

haraise ni 腹いせに He did it to *get even with* (*take it out on*) him.

ikon ni omou 遺恨に思う harbor a grudge [against]; bear a grudge [against]

KATAKI o utsu かたきを討つ take revenge upon; settle an old score
Edo no kataki o Nagasaki de utsu [P] 江戸のかたきを長崎で討つ He won't oppose them directly but will *get even in a roundabout way.*
adauchi あだ討ち revenge
kuyashi magire ni くやしまぎれに He got piqued at everyone and *angrily did it without thinking (went on and did it anyway; did it out of vexation).*
MIKAESHITE yaru 見返してやる I want to *make him eat his words (get back at him)* by succeeding in the project. He has ridiculed it from the start.
ishugaeshi ni 意趣返しに in retaliation [...**ni**] **shikaeshi suru** [...に] 仕返しする settle accounts; get even with; give one some of his own medicine
niramiau にらみ合う glare at each other
ryūin ga sagaru りゅういんがさがる Corbett felt his *grudge was satisfied* by shooting Lincoln's assassin.
shūnenbukai 執念深い vindictive; deeply vengeful; tenacious
URAMI (mu) 恨み(恨む) grudge; resentment (bear a grudge against; resent; be bitter against)
[...**ni**] **~ ga aru** [...に] ~がある have a grudge against
~ ga tokeru ~がとける I got back at him; my *grudge is satisfied.*
~ kotsuzui ni tessuru ~骨髄に徹する Since being cheated out of his house by that broker, he *has deep-seated rancor (is bitter through and through)* against him.
~ ni omou ~に思う keep a score on wrongs
~ o harasu ~を晴らす take revenge upon
~ o iu ~を言う reproach
~ o kau ~を買う make an enemy of; incur the enmity of

shūsei no urami 終生の恨み long-standing grudge
urameshii 恨めしい resentful; spiteful; hateful
uramigamashii koto o iu 恨みがましい事を言う say something spiteful
⇨ **153, 201**

愛する人たち. 自分で復讐してはいけません. 神の怒りに任せなさい. それは, こう書いてあるからです. 「復讐はわたしのすることである. わたしが報いをする. と主は言われる,」 (ローマ 12 ¹⁹)

206 UWASA うわさ RUMOR

dema デマ rumor
~ o tobasu ~を飛ばす circulate an ugly rumor
FŪBUN 風聞 rumor; hearsay
fūhyō 風評 rumor; reports
fūsetsu 風説 rumor; talk of the town
gaibun 外聞 reputation; publicity
HANASHI ga hiromaru 話が広まる the story goes around; the story spreads
ohire o tsukete hanasu 尾ひれをつけて話す He always *exaggerates when he talks.*
sekenbanashi 世間話 gossip
wadai ni naru 話題になる become a popular topic; become a topic of conversation
HYŌBAN 評判 reputation; fame
~ ga hiromaru ~が広まる reputation grows; talk spreads
~ ga warui (yoi) ~が悪い(良い) of bad repute (well-thought-of)
~ ni naru ~になる be on everyone's lips; be talked about by all
moppara no hyōban もっぱらの評判 persistent rumor; widespread talk
fuhyōban (da) 不評判(だ) disreputable; unpopular
gebahyō 下馬評 everyone's feeling; everyone's hunch
sehyō 世評 public opinion

iifurasu 言いふらす spread around; circulate

kiku tokoro ni yoru to 聞くところによると from what I hear...; I hear reports that...

hitozute ni kiku 人づてに聞く hear by word of mouth; hear via the grapevine

kippō 吉報 good news

konkyo no nai 根拠のない groundless; without foundation

KUCHI kara moreru 口から漏れる He let the information *slip from his lips.*

~ **ni noboru** ~にのぼる The story *is making the rounds* that she broke off her engagement.

~ **ni suru** ~にする mention; talk about

kageguchi o kiku 陰口をきく She goes around *backbiting* people (*running people down).*

kuchisaganai [L] 口さがない What she said *was quite scandalous (was gossipy; was catty).*

tsugeguchi suru 告げ口する tell on; tell tales about

ryūgen 流言 rumors; false reports

~ **ni mayou** ~に迷う The people *were swayed by rumors* and mobbed the embassy.

torizata 取りざた comment; gossip; talk

toyakaku iu とやかく言う make petty criticisms; pick flaws in

ukeuri 受け売り second-hand information

UWASA うわさ rumor; story

~ **ga tatsu** ~が立つ rumor spreads; rumors start

~ **ni kiku** ~に聞く hear by rumor; get wind of

~ **ni noboru** ~にのぼる go the rounds; become the talk of the town

~ **ni yoreba** ~によれば according to rumor; rumor has it that...

~ **o hiromeru** ~を広める spread a rumor; circulate a story

~ **o momikesu** ~をもみ消す kill a rumor

~ **o nagasu** ~を流す spread a rumor

~ **o suru** ~をする gossip; spread tales about

~ **o sureba kage to yara** [P] ~をすれば影とやら Here he comes right now; *talk of the devil and he will appear.*

~ **o tateru** ~を立てる start a rumor; spread a rumor

Hito no uwasa mo shichijūgonichi [P] 人のうわさも七十五日 Don't worry about what they are saying about you; *it will soon be forgotten.*

machi no uwasa 町のうわさ the talk of the town

ne mo ha mo nai uwasa 根も葉もないうわさ groundless rumors

⇨ **25, 42, 195**

愚かな者のくちびるは争いを起し、その口はむち打たれることを招く。 愚かな者の口は自分の滅びとなり、その口びるは自分を捕えるわなとなる。 人のよしあしをいう者の言葉はおいしい食物のようで腹の奥にしみこむ. (箴言 18 [6, 7, 8])

207 WARAI 笑い
LAUGHTER

azakeri (ru) あざけり(あざける) ridicule (ridicule)

fukidasu 吹き出す burst out laughing

jōkigen de 上きげんで in good humor

nikoniko suru にこにこする beam; smile

WARAI (u) 笑い(笑う) laughter (laugh)

~ **ga tomaranai** ~が止まらない That was so funny I *couldn't stop laughing.*

~ **o osaeru** ~をおさえる suppress a smile

~ **wa hyakuyaku no chō** [P] ~百薬の長 Laughter is the best medicine [P].

kokoro kara warau 心から笑う laugh heartily

kusukusu warau くすくす笑う chuckle

nikkori warau にっこり笑う smile sweetly

nikoyaka ni warau にこやかに笑う make a beaming smile

niyaniya warau にやにや笑う grin; snicker; smirk

sokoiji waruku warau 底意地悪く 笑う give a contemptible laugh; snicker at; laugh sneeringly at

Warau kado ni wa fuku kitaru [P] 笑うかどには福きたる Laugh and grow fat [P].

bakawarai o suru ばか笑いをする laugh like a horse; laugh ridiculously

bakushō 爆笑 loud laughter

bishō (suru) 微笑(する) smile (smile; give a smile)

~ o ukabete ~ を浮かべて with a smile

fukumiwarai 含み笑い suppressed laughter

kushō (suru) 苦笑(する) forced smile (give a forced smile)

monowarai (no tane) 物笑い(の種) laughing stock

nigawarai (suru) にが笑い(する) grim smile; sardonic smile (give a grim smile)

oaisowarai おあいそ笑い forced laugh

ōwarai (suru) 大笑い(する) guffaw; roar; horse laugh (guffaw; roar)

reishō shite 冷笑して sneeringly; superciliously

shinobiwarai 忍び笑い giggle; smothered laugh

waraigoe 笑い声 laughter

shōshi (da) [L] 笑止(だ) laughable

karawarai から笑い empty laugh

takawarai 高笑い loud laugh

tsukuriwarai o suru 作り笑いをする give an artificial laugh

usuwarai 薄笑い faint smile

waraibanashi 笑い話 funny anecdote

waraidasu 笑い出す burst out laughing

waraigao 笑い顔 smiling face

waraigoto 笑い事 laughing matter

waraigusa 笑い草 laughing stock

waraijōgo 笑いじょうご laughing drunkard

waraikaeshite yaru 笑い返してやる He kidded me about my poor English, but *I got the last laugh on* him when I won the contest.

waraimono 笑い者 laughing stock ⇨ 11, 48, 214

心に楽しみがあれば顔色も喜ばしい. 心に憂いがあれば気はふさぐ. (箴言 15 ¹⁸)

208 YOKUBŌ 欲望 CRAVING, DESIRE

bonnō 煩悩 evil passion; lust

donyoku どん欲 ruthless greed; covetousness

dōraku 道楽 dissipation

HŌJŪ (da) 放縦(だ) self-indulgence; license (self-indulgent)

~ na seikatsu o suru ~ な生活をする lead a dissolute life

~ ni nagareru ~ に流れる He *is apt to be loose in his conduct.*

hōtō (suru) 放とう(する) prodigality; dissipation; loose living (live a fast life; have a fling)

mi o mochikuzusu 身を持ちくずす revel in reckless dissipation

fumimochi (da) 不身持ち(だ) dissipation; misconduct; fast life (dissolute)

midara na seikatsu o suru みだらな生活 をする lead a profligate life; sow one's wild oats

musabori (ru) むさぼり(むさぼる) craving (crave after; covet)

omoikogareru 思いこがれる burn with desire

shushoku ni fukeru 酒色にふける revel in sensual pleasures; carouse; indulge in wine and women

sokonuke sawagi 底抜け騒ぎ The youths were having *a wild revel* (*an orgy*) upstairs, so we called the police.

waisetsu (da) わいせつ(だ) obscenity (obscene; sexy)

YOKUBŌ 欲望 craving; desire
　~ **ni torawareru** ~ にとらわれる be gripped by ambition; be dying to; be in the clutches of desire
　~ **o mitasu** を満たす gratify desires
　~ **o osaeru** ~ を押える To succeed you must *curb the desire* for an easy life.

hossuru 欲する desire; want

jōyoku 情欲 lust
　~ **ni karareru** ~ にかられる be carried away by lust; be driven by passion
　~ **ni oboreru** ~ におぼれる drown in passionate lust
　~ **ni ochiiru** ~ に陥る caught up in inordinate lusts
　~ **o osaeru** ~ を押える suppress one's desires; control one's fleshly appetites
　osaekirenai jōyoku 押えきれない情欲 uncontrollable lusts

katsubō (suru) 渇望(する) craving; longing for (crave; long for; hunger after)

nikuyoku 肉欲 fleshly appetite
　~ **o sakeru** ~ を避ける *Abstain from the lusts of the flesh* which are at war with the soul. (I Peter 2 : 11)
　~ **to tatakau** ~ と戦う combat sensuality; struggle against one's fleshly appetite

seiyoku 性欲 sexual desire; sexual appetite
　hentai seiyoku 変態性欲 sexual perversion

shikiyoku 色欲 lust; carnal desire

yokkyū 欲求 craving; desire

~ **fuman** ~ 不満 unsatisfied desire
~ **o mitasu** ~ を満たす satisfy one's desires

yoku 欲 desire; greed
　~ **ga fukai** ~ が深い be avaricious; be greedy

yokubari (ru) 欲張り(欲張る) greed (be greedy; be covetous)

yokujō 欲情 passion; lust; indulgence ⇨ **209**

世と世の欲は滅び去ります．しかし，神のみこころを行なう者はいつまでもながらえます．(ヨハネ 2¹⁷)

209　YŌKYŪ 要求 DEMAND

hitsuzen (da) 必然(だ) necessity; inevitability (necessary; inevitable)

hossuru 欲する want; wish; desire
　hoshigaru ほしがる crave for; want; hanker after
　mono hoshisō na kuchiburi (da) 物ほしそうな口振り(だ) I don't know what, but he *talks as if he wants something* (*talks as if his heart is set on something*).
　shite hoshii してほしい I *want you to do this for me*.

musabori (ru) むさぼり(むさぼる) craving; covetousness (crave; covet; thirst after; one's heart is set on)

shinakereba naranai しなければならない have to; must; be obliged to; have got to

toritate (ru) 取り立て(取り立てる) collection (collect; exact from)

ueru 飢える hunger after

yodare ga deru hodo よだれが出るほど Seeing the neighbors beating out the hot rice made my *mouth water* for some omochi.

YŌKYŪ (suru) 要求(する) demand; request (demand; request)
　~ **ni kanau** ~ にかなう Your help *just*

fills the bill, and I know they will be satisfied.

[...no] ~ ni ōjiru [...の] ~ に応じる yield to one's demand

~ o hanetsukeru ~ をはねつける Lincoln *turned down* the South's *wish* to talk of peace terms that would recognize the secession.

~ o ireru ~ を入れる concede to the demand [of]

~ o kanaeru ~ をかなえる fulfill one's request; meet one's demand

~ shidai (da) ~ 次第(だ) on demand; upon request

muri na yōkyū 無理な要求 unreasonable demand

shikiri ni yōkyū suru しきりに要求する demand insistently that...

hitsuyō 必要 necessity; need

~ ijō (da) ~ 以上(だ) He kept helping them *beyond their necessity* (*to the excess*).

~ ni ōjite ~ に応じて as the need arises

~ ni semarareru ~ に迫られる He *was driven by necessity* to quit school and go to work.

~ na baai niwa ~ な場合には if necessary

~ o kanjiru ~ を感じる feel the need [of]

[...o] ~ to suru [...を] ~ とする We *are in need of* that book (*That book is required*) for the library.

[...o] suru hitsuyō wa nai [...を]する 必要はない Lincoln felt *there was no need* to be hard on the defeated Confederacy.

juyō 需要 demand; request

kokunai no juyō 国内の需要 national demands; domestic needs

motomeru 求める seek after; wish for; demand

enjo o motomeru 援助を求める seek aid

seikatsu hitsujuhin 生活必需品 necessities of life

seikyū (suru) 請求(する) claim; demand (make claim; demand payment)

tsuikyū (suru) 追求(する) pursuit (pursue; seek after; run after)

yokyū fuman 要求不満 unsatisfied desires

yōsei (suru) 要請(する) demand; request (demand; request)

⇨ **81, 208**

求めなさい．そうすれば与えられます．捜しなさい．そうすれば見つかります．たたきなさい．そうすれば開かれます．(マタイ 7 ⁷)

210   YOROKOBI 喜び
JOY, GLADNESS

iwai (u) 祝い(祝う) celebration (celebrate)

kokoro ga hazumu 心がはずむ I had *an exhilarated feeling* when we were on the picnic together.

~ ga odoru ~ がおどる My *heart danced with joy* when I got the news of my acceptance into Keio.

yume gokochi de 夢ごこちで as in a dream

mune o odorasu 胸をおどらす jump for joy

omedetō (gozaimasu) おめでとう(ございます) Congratulations!

uchōten 有頂天 ecstacy

~ ni naru ~ になる When he won first prize, he *became elated* (*felt as if he were on top of the world*).

ten ni mo noboru gokochi 天にも昇るごこち I *felt as if I were in seventh heaven* when he asked me to go to the concert with him.

URESHII うれしい happy; joyful; glad

ureshigaru うれしがる be happy about; show pleasure in

ureshinaki ni naku うれし泣きに泣く weep for joy

ureshiku omou うれしく思う I *am de-*

lighted to be able to speak to you all.

ureshikute shikata ga nai うれしくて仕方がない I *was pleased as punch (was extremely happy)* when I heard the good news.

YOROKOBI (bu) 喜び(喜ぶ) joy; gladness (rejoice [in]; be glad [in]; exult [in])

~ **ni afureru** ~ にあふれる be overjoyed

~ **no amari** ~ のあまり for the joy of

~ **no shirushi ni** ~ のしるしに This gift is *to congratulate you* on your success.

~ **o noberu** ~ を述べる offer congratulations

jibun no koto no yōni yorokobu 自分の事のように喜ぶ When he received that prize, I was *as delighted as if I* had received it myself.

jinsei no yorokobi 人生の喜び joys of life

koodori shite yorokobu 小おどりして喜ぶ dance with joy

tobitatsu bakari ni yorokobu 飛び立つばかりに喜ぶ jump for joy

tsutsumikirenai yorokobi つつみきれない喜び inexpressible joy

kanki (suru) 歓喜(する) delight; glee; gladness (delight in; rejoice)

kietsu [L] 喜悦 delight; gladness

kyōki suru 驚喜する be wild with joy

ōyorokobi de 大よろこびで in great joy

yorokobashii 喜ばしい delightful; joyful

yorokobasu 喜ばす please; bring joy to; make one happy

yorokobiisande 喜び勇んで in high spirits

yorokonde 喜んで with pleasure; gladly

⇨ **198, 214**

あなたがたはイエス・キリストを見たことはないけれども愛しており、いま見てはいないけれども信じており、ことばに尽くすことのできない、栄えに満ちた 喜びにおどっています。(ペテロ I 1 ⁸)

211 YOWASA 弱さ
WEAKNESS

ara あら flaw; fault

arasagashi o suru あら探しをする No matter what I do, he's always trying to *find fault with it (pick flaws in it).*

Ari no ana kara tsutsumi ga kuzureru [P] ありの穴から堤がくずれる You'd better take care of that small problem right away; remember that *a small leak will sink a ship* [P].

ashimoto o mirareru 足元を見られる If you show the slightest interest in the property, you'll *be taken advantage of* by that broker.

boro ga deru ぼろが出る one's weakness shows up

~ **o dasu** ~ を出す He claims to be proficient in English, but when he used poor grammar, he *showed his weakness.*

chikara ga nai 力がない He *is unable (is incompetent)* to meet the situation.

fubi ni jōjiru 不備に乗じる While the troops were digging in, the enemy *took them at a disadvantage* and attacked.

fujūbun (da) ふじゅうぶん(だ) insufficient

furi na tachiba ni oiyaru 不利な立場に追いやる put one at a disadvantage; drive one into an unfavorable position

hakanai はかない transitory; frail

hikeme 引け目 drawback; weak point

~ **o kanjiru** ~ を感じる feel small; feel reticent; feel inferior

itai tokoro o tsuku 痛いところをつく When you said that, you *hit where it hurts (struck my weak point).*

KETTEN 欠点 defect; fault; flaw

~ **no nai** ~ のない free from faults

~ **o bakuro suru** ~ を暴露する That report *exposed the faults* of the department.

~ **(ara) o sagasu** ~ (あら)を探す find fault with

kekkan 欠陥 shortcoming; defect
　~ no aru ~のある defective; faulty;
　not up to par
kowareyasui こわれやすい fragile; breakable
kyūsho 急所 vulnerable spot; the quick
　~ o tsuku ~をつく He *struck at the vulnerable part (hit the weak point)* of his argument.
mono tarinai tokoro ga aru 物足りない所がある Though your report is long, I feel *there is something lacking in it.*
moroi もろい frail; fragile
Tama ni kizu [P] 玉にきず The poor paint job in that beautiful chapel was the only *lump in the pudding.*
tsukeiru suki ga nai つけ入るすきがない Lincoln's opponents *could find no fault with* his personal integrity.
yasekoketa karada やせこけたからだ He came back from the prison camp *skin and bones (a bag of bones; skinny).*
YOWASA 弱さ weakness; frailty
　hakujaku (da) 薄弱(だ) debility (flimsy; frail)
　jakutai 弱体 weakness
　jakuten 弱点 weak point; Achille's heel
　　~ o tsuku ~をつく find the weak point; lay bare the Achille's heel
　kyojaku (da) 虚弱(だ) frail; delicate
　nanjaku 軟弱 weakness
　nyūjaku (da) 柔弱(だ) weakness (weak-kneed; effeminate)
　yowai 弱い He has a *weak (delicate)* body. When it comes to English conversation, I'*m poor* at it.
　　taishitsu no yowai 体質の弱い frail; of a weak constitution
　yowasa 弱さ faintheartedness; weak tendency
　yowameru 弱める weaken
　yowami ni tsukekomu 弱みにつけ込む take advantage of one's weakness
　yowamushi 弱虫 weakling; sissy

yowane o haku 弱音を吐く When he saw the strength of the opposition, he *drew in his horns (became weak-kneed).*
Yowarime ni tatarime 弱り目にたたり目 After losing his job, he got sick. *It never rains, but it pours* [P].
yowaru 弱る grow weak; get run down
yowayowashii 弱々しい weak; frail
⇨ **17**

しかし、主は、「わたしの恵みは、あなたに十分である。というのは、わたしの力は、弱さのうちに完全に現われるからである。」と言われたのです。ですから、私は、キリストの力が私をおおうために、むしろ大いに喜んで私の弱さを誇りましょう。（コリント II 12 ⁹）

212　YŪJŌ 友情 FRIENDSHIP

ashi ga tōku naru 足が遠くなる Since we had that argument, he *seldom comes around* to see us anymore.
Dōbyō aiawaremu [P] 同病相あわれむ Misery loves company [P].
kimyaku o tsūjiru 気脈を通じる be in communication with; conspire together; communicate with
kōi o yoseru 厚意を寄せる I think I can get you into that firm; I'*m in with* the manager (the manager *is favorable to me*).
kokoro to kokoro ga tsūjiru 心と心が通じる Though Lincoln and Grant seldom met, there *was mutual understanding between them (their hearts were united)* on the war effort.
kokoro yasui 心やすい intimate; easy going; chummy
MAJIWARI (ru) 交わり(交わる) fellowship (have fellowship with)
　~ o fukameru ~を深める deepen fellowship; strengthen fellowship
　~ o musubu ~を結ぶ form a fellowship
kōsai (suru) 交際(する) association; company; fellowship (associate with;

keep company with; fraternize with; rub shoulders with)

~ o tatsu ~ を絶つ have a falling out; have nothing more to do with each other; part company

kōyū 交友 friend; companion

kyōdai ai 兄弟愛 brotherly love

Kyōdai wa tanin no hajimari [P] 兄弟は他人の始まり Familiarity breeds contempt [P].

mizu kusai koto o suru 水臭いことをする We're the best of friends, so you don't need to *put on* like that. Be frank!

naka ga ii (warui) 仲がいい(悪い) be on good terms with (be on bad terms with)

kantan aiterasu naka 肝胆相照らす仲 They have been a help to each other because they *are on intimate terms* (*are bosom pals*).

shiriai 知り合い acquaintance

~ ni naru ~ になる make friends [with]; strike up an acquaintance [with]

SHITASHIMI (mu) 親しみ(親しむ) familiarity; intimacy; closeness (become familiar with; become intimate with; get close to)

shin'ai 親愛 affection

shimboku (kai) 親ぼく(会) friendliness; friendship (friendly get-together; social gathering)

shinmi ni naru 親身になる I didn't know who to go to, but my teacher *took my problem to heart* (*became thoughtfully considerate*).

shinyū 親友 intimate friend; close friend

muni no shinyū 無二の親友 close friend; intimate friend

shinzen (kankei) 親善(関係) goodwill; friendship (friendly relations)

shitashii 親しい intimate; close; friendly

[...to] shitashiku naru [...と]親しくなる become familiar with; get close

to; get in with

tayori ni naru hito 頼りになる人 someone to depend on

uchitokeru 打ちとける open up to; confide in

uchitoketa kūki 打ちとけた空気 The *ice was broken* at the meeting and they all talked freely.

wakiaiai to shite iru 和気あいあいとしている get along famously; get along smoothly

yoshimi よしみ friendship; bonds; intimacy

mukashi no yoshimi de 昔のよしみで I'm really too busy, but *for old times' sake*, I'll do what I can for him.

YŪJŌ 友情 friendship

~ ni atsui ~ に厚い Lincoln *was true to his friends*.

kyūkō o atatameru 旧交をあたためる He came back to *renew old friendships*.

tomo (dachi) 友(だち) friend; companion

yūai 友愛 friendly feeling; brotherly love

yūjin 友人 friend

yūkō 友交 friendship; amity

⇨ **1, 180**

人がその友のためにいのちを捨てるという, これよりも大きな愛はだれも持っていません. (ヨハネ 15 ¹³)

213 YŪJŪ FUDAN 優柔不断 INDECISION

aimai (da) あいまい(だ) vagueness (vague)

ayafuya (da) あやふや(だ) vague; inconclusive

chūburarin no [C] 宙ぶらりんの They couldn't agree, so the issue was left *up in the air*.

chū ni uku 宙に浮く be still up in the air; can't make heads nor tails of it

chūcho suru ちゅうちょする hesitate

chūto hanpa na koto o suru 中途半ぱな事をする do things by halves; do a mediocre job; do a halfway job [of it]
~ **hanpa ni shite oku** ~ 半ぱにしておく leave things unfinished; do a halfway job

dotchi tsukazu no どっちつかずの betwixt and between; on neither side

dōyō suru 動揺する waver; vascillate

fungiri ga tsukanai ふんぎりがつかない cannot make a decisive step; be on the fence

fushōbushō (da) 不承不承(だ) reluctant

futamata o kakeru 二またをかける In the East-West controversy, some neutrals *were playing both ends toward the middle* by accepting aid from both sides.

gen o sayū ni suru 言を左右にする prevaricate; use some pretext or another

GURATSUKU ぐらつく totter; waver
iken ga guratsuku 意見がぐらつく halt between two opinions
shinkō ga guratsuku 信仰がぐらつく one's faith wavers
guragura suru ぐらぐらする be shaky; wobble; be irresolute
guzuguzu suru ぐずぐずする hesitate; dawdle; dilly-dally

hakkiri shinai はっきりしない be not clear; be indefinite

hiyorimi 日より見 wait and see policy
hiyorimishugisha 日より見主義者 opportunist; fence rider

kimagure 気まぐれ whim; caprice; vagary

iikagen (da) いいかげん(だ) half-way; half-hearted; mediocre; expedient

ikuji ga nai いくじがない weak-willed; having no backbone; spaghetti-spined
ishi hakujaku (da) 意志薄弱(だ) weak-minded; willy-nilly; wishy-washy

itabasami ni naru 板ばさみになる I *was caught in between (was torn two ways; was in a predicament; was in a dilemma)*

and couldn't take action.

KESSHIN ga tsukanai 決心がつかない can't make up one's mind
ketsudanryoku ni toboshii 決断力に乏しい lack decision; be irresolute; indecisive
miketsu-jikō 未決事項 matters to be decided; pending issue

kyoshū ni mayou 去就に迷う I'm *at a loss as to how to act* in the situation.

mura no aru むらのある unsteady; capricious

muteiken (da) 無定見(だ) inconsistency (inconsistent; wavering; vascillating)

nama hanka (da) 生半可(だ) superficial; shallow; half-baked
nama henji o suru 生返事をする give a vague answer

niekiranai taido 煮え切らない態度 You can't go into the conference with *a half-baked attitude.*

omoikiri ga warui 思い切りが悪い You're wasting your time with him; he's too *irresolute (lacks decisiveness; he has trouble making up his mind).*

seikan suru 静観する Don't do anything now; just *wait and see.*

shiburu しぶる hesitate; hang back
iishiburu 言いしぶる hesitate to say

sono mama no jōtai ni shite oku そのままの状態にしておく I wanted to settle the matter, but he wanted to *leave it open.*

tamerau ためらう hesitate; have misgivings

te o kaesu yōni 手を返すように We thought he was with us, but at the last moment he *did an about-face* and voted against the move.

utsurigi 移り気 fickleness; inconsistency

uyamuya ni owaru うやむやに終わる There was much talk of a new treaty, but it *ended up in smoke (came to nothing).*
~ **ni suru** ~にする The government

tried to *hush up* the affair.

ただし、少しも疑わずに、信じて願いなさい。疑う人は、風に吹かれて揺れ動く、海の大波のようです。そういうのは、二心のある人で、その歩む道のすべてに安定を欠いた人です。(ヤコブ 1 ^{6, 8})

214 YUKAI 愉快 PLEASANTNESS

aiso no yoi hito 愛想の良い人 charming person; pleasant person

hyōkin (da) ひょうきん(だ) comical; facetious

jōdan 冗談 joke; jest

　~ o iu ~ を言う joke; crack a joke; wisecrack 〔C〕

kigeki 喜劇 comedy

KIMOCHI ga harebare suru 気持ちが晴れ晴れする He's *been in high spirits* since he passed the exam.

　~ ga yoi ~ が良い pleasant; have a good feeling [about]

　hareyaka na kimochi 晴れやかな気持ち bright feeling; cheerful spirit

kigaru ni 気軽に light-heartedly; casually; nonchalantly

kokkei (da) こっけい(だ) humor; witticism (humorous; witty; comical)

kokoro ga ukiuki suru 心が浮き浮きする feel buoyant; feel high

odokeru おどける joke; crack jokes; play the fool

　odoketa kakko o suru おどけたかっこうをする He kept us laughing, *clowning (acting silly)* like a monkey.

okashii おかしい funny; laughable; amusing; strange; bizarre

　okashikute namida ga deru おかしくて涙が出る I *laughed till I cried* when he dropped the basket of eggs.

omoshiroi おもしろい delightful; interesting; amusing

onaka no kawa ga yojireru おなかの皮が

よじれる I *split my sides* when I heard that joke.

tanoshimu 楽しむ enjoy; take delight in

　tanoshii 楽しい enjoyable; entertaining; pleasant

uchitokete うちとけて friendly

ureshii うれしい happy; joyful; pleasant

YUKAI(da) 愉快(だ) pleasantness; merriment (pleasant; delightful)

　~ ni toki o sugosu ~ に時を過ごす have a good time; pass the time enjoyably

　fukai (da) 不快 (だ) discomforting; disagreeable

　fuyukai (da) 不愉快(だ) unpleasant; unhappy

　　~ ni omou ~ に思う feel unpleasant; be displeased

　kokoroyoi 快い agreeable; pleasant; cheerful

yūmoa ga aru ユーモアがある humorous; witty; funny

　~ o majieru ~ を交える Lincoln would *add a touch of humor* to his conversation to clinch arguments or disarm opponents.

⇨ 198

笑う時にも悲しみがあり、喜びのはてに憂いがある。(箴言 14 ¹³)

215 YŪKI 勇気 COURAGE

aete...suru あえて...する Would you *dare to do (venture to do)* that before his face?

bōryoku ni taikō suru 暴力に対抗する brave violence; stand against violence

DAITAN (da) 大胆(だ) daring; boldness (boldly; fearlessly)

　~ ni kataru ~ に語る speak boldly; speak fearlessly

　tanryoku 胆力 pluck; courage; audacity

eiyū 英雄 hero

dōdō toshita taido 堂々とした態度 manly courage

dokyō 度胸 nerve; pluck

~ **o sueru** ～をすえる muster courage; brace up; become fixed in purpose

fukutsu no tōshi 不屈の闘志 indomitable courage

futoppara no 太っ腹の broadminded; bold; big-hearted

haisui no jin o shiku 背水の陣を敷く Sherman *burned his bridges behind* him as he slipped behind Confederate lines and marched to the sea.

KI o ōkiku suru 気を大きくする muster courage; take the larger view of things; think big; have a broader outlook

~ **ga ōkiku naru** ～が大きくなる After a few drinks, he *began to feel big.*

~ **o torinaosu** ～を取り直す take fresh courage; brace up; keep a stiff upper lip

genki 元気 spirit; pluck; vigor

~ **o dasu** ～を出す take heart

genkizukeru 元気づける cheer one up; bolster; brace one up

ikiyōyō toshite 意気揚々として triumphantly

kiryoku 気力 get up and go; push; vitality

kimottama no chiisai [C] 胆っ玉の小さい He backed down in front of the boss because he's so *lily-livered.*

~ **no futoi** ～の太い brave-souled

Kiyomizu no butai kara tobioriru [P] 清水の舞台から飛びおりる I've decided to *run the risk (take the plunge)* and invest all my funds in the project.

Koketsu ni irazumba koji o ezu [P] 虎穴に入らずんば虎児を得ず Let's give it a try; *nothing ventured, nothing gained* [P].

ōde o futte 大手を振って With a secret knock, little Tad would come *strutting* into Lincoln's office *with nothing to fear.*

otokorashiku suru 男らしくする It will be hard, but I want you to *do it like a man (show yourself a man).*

seikan (da) [L] 精かん (だ) dauntless; intrepid

shikkari suru しっかりする take heart; pull oneself together

YŪKI 勇気 courage

~ **ga kujikeru** ～がくじける After the fall of Richmond Lee's *spirit was broken.*

~ **o ataeru** ～を与える inspire courage

~ **o dasu** ～を出す take courage; screw up one's courage

gōyū 剛勇 bravery; valor

isamashii 勇ましい valiant; courageous; brave

isamitatsu 勇み立つ take courage; muster fresh courage

shiki o kobu suru 士気を鼓舞する He came to *raise the morale* of the troops.

yūkan (da) 勇敢(だ) bravery (brave; gallant; courageous; bold)

yūkizukeru 勇気づける instil courage

yūō maishin suru [L] 勇往まい進する The small platoon *plunged forward (dashed ahead)* against the withering fire of the enemy.

yūshi 勇士 hero

Yūshō no moto ni jakusotsu nashi [L] 勇将のもとに弱卒なし Where you have *brave officers* you *have brave soldiers.*

yūsō (da) 勇壮 (だ) bravery (brave; heroic; gallant)

yūyaku shite 勇躍して *Taking heart* from the control tower's encouragement, Glenn continued in orbit.

⇨ **110**

悪しき者は追う人もないのに逃げる。正しい人はししのように勇ましい。(箴言 28 ¹)

216 YURUSHI 許し
FORGIVENESS

dōzo ashikarazu どうぞ悪しからず I didn't answer your letter, but please *think nothing of it.*

ashikarazu omotte kudasai 悪しからず思って下さい no offense was meant

hoshaku (suru) 保釈(する) bail (bail out)

kanben suru 勘弁する forgive; excuse; let me out [of]

MENJIRU 免じる exempt; pass over

   gomen nasai! ご免なさい I'm sorry! Forgive me, won't you?

   hōmen (suru) 放免(する) acquittal; reprieve; release (acquit; grant a reprieve; release)

      muzai hōmen to naru 無罪放免となる stand acquitted of the charge; get off scot free

   menjo (suru) 免除(する) exemption (exempt [from])

   menkyo 免許 license

      unten menkyosho 運転免許証 driver's license

   shamen (suru) 赦免する pardon; remission; amnesty; clemency (pardon; remit; grant amnesty; grant clemency; let off)

minogasu 見のがす overlook; stretch a point; look the other way

TSUMI o kiru 罪を着る bear the sins of; hold oneself blameable

   ~ o nuguu ~ をぬぐう Repent and turn to God that your *sins may be wiped out.* (Acts 3 : 19)

   ~ o ou ~ を負う In his own person, he *carried our sins* to the gallows...(I Peter 2 : 24)

   ~ o yurusu ~ を許す forgive sin

   shazai (suru) 謝罪(する) pardon; apology (apologize; ask forgiveness)

yōsha (suru) 容赦(する) forgiveness (forgive)

YURUSHI (su) 許し(許す) pardon; forgiveness; permission (pardon; forgive; permit)

   ~ o ataeru ~ を与える Lincoln was criticized for *granting forgiveness to* (*pardoning*) so many soldiers.

   ~ o eru (ete) ~ を得る(得て) secure permission; get permission [by permission]

   ~ o ukeru ~ を受ける receive forgiveness; be forgiven

   kyoka (suru) 許可(する) permission; approval (grant permission; give approval)

   yurushigatai 許しがたい hard to forgive; almost beyond forgiveness

⇨ 9, 97, 141

私たちは、この御子のうちにあって、御子の血による贖い, すなわち罪の赦しを受けているのです. これは神の豊かな恵みによることです. (エペソ 1 ⁷)

217 YŪSHŪ 優秀
SUPERIORITY

ashimoto nimo oyobanai 足元にも及ばない Most Northern generals *could not hold a candle to* Lee in military strategy.

bannō no 万能の all around [person]; outstanding in every way

   ~ senshu ~ 選手 all around athlete

batsugun (da) 〔L〕抜群(だ) distinguished; pre-eminent

danchigai (da) 段違い(だ) far above; head and shoulders above

dare ni mo makenai だれにも負けない be second to none; yield to no one

hanarewaza 離れわざ extraordinary feat

hike o toranai 引けを取らない He *is on the same level as* the others in golf.

hiideru 秀でる excel [others in]; tower above [others]

   nukinderu 抜きんでる stand above others; surpass others; excel [in]

hirui no nai 比類のない incomparable

hitome o hiku 人目を引く attract attention

hitokado no ningen ひとかどの人間 splendid person; a somebody; respectable person

hitokiwa medatsu ひときわ目立つ be conspicuous; stand paramount

ishoku no 異色の unique

  isai o hanatsu 異彩を放つ There is something about him which *makes him stand out from others* (*is conspicuous*).

ittōchi o nuku 一頭地を抜く be by far the best; be the cream of the crop

  tōkaku o arawasu 頭角を現わす Through his hard work he quickly *came to the fore* (*distinguished himself; rose above his peers*).

JŌZU (da) じょうず(だ) skillful; adept; proficient; good at

  jōi no 上位の superior

  kono ue nai この上ない incomparable; above all

  hito no ue ni tatsu 人の上に立つ You will have to work and study hard if you want to *become a leader*.

kata o naraberu mono wa nai 肩を並べる者はない Lincoln *has an unrivalled position* in American history because he saved the Union.

kencho (da) 顕著(だ) distinguished; outstanding

kessaku 傑作 masterpiece

kisen o seisuru 機先を制する That company *has the edge* (*took the lead; got the jump*) on us, but we will catch up.

kurōto hadashi [c] くろうとはだし The way that little girl can play the piano! She's enough to *put the professionals to shame*.

kūzen zetsugo no 空前絶後の an unheard of thing; the first and probably the last

masaru まさる surpass [others]; be better than [others]; outshine [others]

[...no] migi ni deru mono ga nai [...の]右に出る者がない *No one can approach him* (*No one can come near him*) in English speech.

migoto (da) みごと(だ) splendid; superb; brilliant

mizugiwadatta 水ぎわ立った out of the ordinary; striking

nami hazureta 並みはずれた extraordinary

rippa (da) りっぱ(だ) superb; splendid; excellent

saikō (no) 最高(の) maximum; highest; paramount

  saidai 最大 maximum; greatest

subarashii すばらしい splendid; wonderful; remarkable

sugureru すぐれる excel; surpass; have the advantage over

suteki (da) すてき(だ) great; terrific; swell

ta no tsuizui o yurusanai 他の追随を許さない He *is peerless* in his knowledge of Japanese art.

taishita mono たいしたもの He is *really something*—the way he can speak all those languages!

takuetsu (suru) [L] 卓越(する) excellence (excel [in]; be distinguished)

tasai (da) 多才(だ) versatile

tenka o fūbi suru 天下を風びする That musical troupe *took the world by storm* with their music.

YŪSHŪ (da) 優秀(だ) superiority; excellence (superior; excellent)

  shūitsu no 秀逸の the very best; paramount

  yūetsu (kan) 優越(感) superiority (superiority complex)

  yūretsu o arasou 優劣を争う compete; strive for the mastery

  yūryō (da) 優良(だ) good quality (choice)

  yūsei (da) 優勢(だ) leading; ahead; winning

  yūseigachi (da) 優勢勝ち(だ) winning on points

yūtōsei 優等生 honor student
yūsū no 有数の foremost; prominent
zubanukeru ずば抜ける be outstanding; be by far the best
  tobinukete iru 飛び抜けている be way ahead; be head and shoulders above
  zunukete ずぬけて by far
⇨ **186**
あなたがたの間で人の先に立ちたいと思う者は，あなたがたのしもべになりなさい．(マタイ 20 ²⁷)

218 YŪUTSU 憂うつ
MELANCHOLY

fusagu ふさぐ be in low spirits; be dejected
  ki ga fusagu 気がふさぐ be dejected; be downcast; feel depressed
genki ga nai 元気がない spiritless; no life in
INKI (da) 陰気(だ) gloominess (gloomy; dismal)
  ~ na kaotsuki o suru ~ な顔つきをする So too when you fast; do not *look gloomy* like the hypocrites..." (Matthew 6:16)
inkikusai 陰気臭い gloomy; blue
in'utsu (da) 陰うつ(だ) moody; sullen; melancholy
jimejime shita kimochi じめじめした気持ち dull feeling; low spirits
KANSHŌTEKI ni naru 感傷的になる have the blues
  kanshō ni fukeru 感傷にふける He likes to *stew in his own juice*, so you'd better leave him alone.
  kurai kanji ga suru 暗い感じがする feel gloomy; pull a long face
  kyodatsukan 虚脱感 aching void; despondency
KI o kusarasu 気を腐らす He *has gone sour* (*become jaundiced*) on parties.
  ~ ga hareru ~ が晴れる After a good night's rest I *feel fine* again.

omoi kibun 重い気分 be dismal; have a heavy heart
kumoru 曇る be dismal; have a heavy heart
kurai kimochi ni osowareru 暗い気持ちに襲われる When he told that sad story, I *was overcome with gloom.*
meiru めいる feel gloomy; mope
  ki ga meiru yōna 気がめいるような gloomy; dejected; depressed
muttsuriya [C] むっつりや silent fellow; glum person; crape-hanger
nigamushi o kamitsubushita yōna kao o suru 苦虫をかみつぶしたような顔をする He *made a sour face* when they told him he would have to clean up the room.
otsūya no kyaku no yōna kao o suru お通夜の客のような顔をする What's the matter with you? You *look as if you were at a funeral.*
shioeru しおれる be down in the dumps; feel depressed
  uchishiorete iru mono 打ちしおれている者 But God, who brings comfort to the *downcast*... (II Corinthians 7:6)
shizumu 沈む become downcast; sink; droop
  ki ga shizumu 気が沈む After repeated Union defeats Lincoln *felt very dejected* (*felt depressed*).
ukanu kao 浮かぬ顔 gloomy face; sourpuss
usa o harasu うさを晴らす His cheery way always *dispels the gloom.*
uttōshii うっとうしい depressing; gloomy
YŪUTSU 憂うつ melancholy; depression
  ~ ni naru ~ になる become melancholy; have the blues
  yūshū [L] 憂愁 melancholy; grief
⇨ **89, 111, 182**
シオンの中の悲しむ者に喜びを与え，灰にかえて冠を与え，悲しみにかえて喜びの油を与え，憂いの心にかえてさんびの衣を与えさせるためである．(イザヤ 61 ³)

219 YŪWAKU 誘惑
TEMPTATION

amai kotoba o kakeru 甘い言葉をかける
He makes a lot of sales by *talking
smoothly* (*stringing people along; soft-
soaping people*).

keshikakeru けしかける incite; egg on

KOKORO o azamuku 心をあざむく ...they
seduce the minds of innocent people
with smooth and specious words.
(Romans 16: 18)
~ **o madowasu** ~ を惑わす deceive
~ **o sosoru** ~ をそそる tempt

KOKOROMI (ru) 試み(試みる) test; trial;
temptation (test; try; tempt)
shiren 試練 trial; temptation; ordeal
~ **o ukeru** ~ を受ける be tried; go
through an ordeal

[...ni] me ga kuramu [...に]目がくらむ
Lincoln was concerned about Northern
businessmen, *blinded by* war profiteer-
ing.

netsu ni ukasareta (yōni) 熱に浮かされた
(ように) She *has been carried away by the
craze* for rock-and-roll music and
listens to nothing else.

madowasu まどわす seduce; mislead

nōsatsu (suru) 悩殺(する) charm; steal the
heart [of]; fascinate; enchant

obikiyose (ru) おびきよせ(おびきよせる) lure;
decoy (lure; bait)

sendō (suru) 扇動(する) instigation; abet-
ting (instigate; abet; egg on)
[...ni] sendō sarete [...に]扇動されて
The students *were instigated* (*egged
on*) by the communists to demonstrate.

shigeki (suru) 刺激(する) goading; stimulation; excitement (goad on; stimulate;
excite)

sosonokasu そそのかす seduce; incite; egg
[one] on

warujie o tsukeru 悪知恵をつける insti-

gate; abet; make a sly suggestion

YŪWAKU (suru) 誘惑(する) temptation;
enticement (tempt; entice)
~ **ni au** ~ に会う be tempted; face
temptation
~ **ni katsu** ~ に勝つ overcome temptation
~ **ni makeru** ~ に負ける yield to
temptation; succumb to temptation
~ **ni ochiiru** ~ に陥る ...every man
is tempted, when he is drawn away
of his own lust, and enticed.
(James 1 : 14 AV)
~ **ni otoshiireru** ~ におとし入れる lead
one into temptation
~ **ni taeru** ~ に耐える resist temptation
~ **o kirinukeru** ~ を切り抜ける struggle through temptation; overcome
temptation

sasoi (u) 誘い(誘う) invitation; temptation (invite; tempt; entice; allure)
~ **ni noru** ~ に乗る succumb to temptation; go along with the suggestion
~ **o kakeru** ~ をかける try to tempt

yūdō (suru) 誘導(する) inducement
(induce; lead; incite)
yūdō jinmon 誘導尋問 The police
asked him a *leading question* and he
divulged the gang's whereabouts.

試練に耐える人は幸いです。耐え抜いて良しと認められ
た人は、神を愛する者に約束された、いのちの冠を受け
るからです。(ヤコブ 1 ¹²)

220 ZANKOKU 残酷
CRUELTY

gokuaku hidō no 極悪非道の unspeak-
ably cruel

iji ga warui 意地が悪い mean; snarly
tempered; nasty

ijimeru いじめる torment; be hard on

jaken (da) じゃけん(だ) merciless

jūsei 獣性 bestiality
kokoro nai shiuchi 心ない仕打ち That was a *very inconsiderate thing* to do to your mother.
mugoi むごい cruel; merciless
  mugotarashii むごたらしい outrageous; inhuman
mujihi (da) 無慈悲(だ) pitiless; merciless; cruel; ruthless
mushi mo korosanai kao o shite 虫も殺さない顔をして He *looks as if he wouldn't hurt a flea (is innocent looking)*, but he has been cruel to his children.
muzan ni mo 無惨にも mercilessly; cruelly
GŌMON (suru) 拷問(する) torture (torture; inflict pain)
  ~ ni kakeru ~ にかける Others *were tortured* to death, disdaining release, to win a better resurrection. (Hebrews 11 : 35)
gyakutai (suru) 虐待(する) cruel treatment; mistreatment (treat cruelly; mistreat; abuse)
  bōgyaku (da) 〔L〕暴虐(だ) atrocity (atrocious)
HIDOI ひどい cruel
  ~ me ni awaseru ~ 目に合わせる treat cruelly
  ~ shiuchi o suru ~ 仕打ちをする treat unfairly and cruelly
ZANKOKU (da) 残酷(だ) cruelty (cruel)
  ~ na kōi ~ な行為 atrocity; cruel act
  ~ ni toriatsukau ~ に取り扱う treat cruelly
reikoku (da) 冷酷(だ) inhuman; heartless; hard-hearted
zangyaku (da) 残虐(だ) brutality (brutal)
zannin (da) 残忍(だ) cruelty; brutality (cruel; brutal)
zanninsei 残忍性 bloodthirstiness
⇨ **6**
いつくしみある者はおのれ自身に益を得，残忍な者はお

のれの身をそこなう。(箴言 11 [17])

221   ZASETSU ざ折
FRUSTRATION

agattari da! 〔C〕あがったりだ The bottom has dropped out of the market; my business *is on the rocks (is ruined)*.
banji fushubi (da) 万事不首尾(だ) *Everything went wrong* today.
jiremma ni ochiiru ジレンマに陥る be put in a dilemma
dotanba ni oikomareru どたん場に追い込まれる He *was driven into a corner*; the deadline was up and he didn't have the money.
fukyō 不況 depression; slump
fusagu ふさぐ block; check
  happō fusagari (da) 八方ふさがり(だ) I want to solve the problem, but right now *things look dark (there is no way out)*.
fushin no 不振の inactive; slow; dull [business, etc.]
habamu はばむ thwart; block; impede; countervail
isshō o dainashi ni suru 一生をだいなしにする You may *ruin your whole life* by going around with that gang in Shinjuku.
KUJIKERU くじける be thwarted; be discouraged; be disillusioned
  ikigomi ga kujikeru 意気込みがくじける After that set-back *his enthusiasm was dampened (his spirit was broken; he was disillusioned)*.
kujiku くじく stop; baffle; disappoint; crush
  debana o kujiku 出鼻をくじく Chase aspired to replace Lincoln, but his party *stopped him in his tracks (snubbed him; thwarted him)* by renominating Lincoln.

kyūsuru 窮する be at a loss; be at one's wits' end

kyūchi ni ochiiru 窮地に陥る He *found himself in serious straits (was up a tree)* when they questioned him about it.

migoroshi ni suru 見殺しにする He encouraged us in the project then *left us holding the bag (sold us down the river; left us high and dry).*

mizu no awa to naru 水のあわとなる When the depression hit, all his plans *burst like a bubble.*

moto no mokuami (da) 元のもくあみ(だ) He made a small fortune then *lost all he had gained* through drink.

nozomi o ushinau 望みを失う abandon hope; lose hope for; be disillusioned

oshitsukeru 押し付ける crush; smash

shintai kiwamaru 進退窮まる be driven into a corner; have no way to turn; be in a dilemma

shippai (suru) 失敗(する) failure (fail)

tatsuse ga nai 立つ瀬がない When you said that to my friends, I *was put on the spot.*

te mo ashi mo denai 手も足も出ない I *am powerless* to do anything about the problem.

tohō ni kureru 途方にくれる I *was at my wit's end,* but he came along and offered to help.

toritsuku shima ga nai 取りつくしまがない The boss is so busy that *there's no way to get to him (it's hard to get his ear).*

tōwaku suru 当惑する be perplexed; be confused

YUKIZUMARI (ru) 行き詰まり(行き詰まる) deadlock; impasse (reach a dead end; come to a standstill; come to an impasse)

~ o dakai suru ~を打開する break the deadlock

hata to yukizumaru はたと行き詰まる suddenly find oneself in a jam

zasetsu (suru) ざ折(する) frustration (be frustrated)

⇨ **123, 182, 185**

私たちは、四方八方から苦しめられますが、窮することはありません. 途方にくれていますが、行きづまることはありません.
いつでもイエスの死をこの身に帯びていますが、それは、イエスのいのちが 私たちの身において明らかに 示されるためです. (コリント II 4 [8, 10])

222 ZOKUAKU 俗悪
VULGARITY, WORLDLINESS

arai 荒い He offends people because his talk *is rough (is coarse).*

doronuma ni ochiiru どろ沼に陥る He fell in with a bad crowd in Tokyo and *hit the skids.*

gebita げびた ill-bred

hanashi ga ochiru 話が落ちる When the *conversation got rough,* I excused myself and left the room.

hanatsumami (da) 鼻つまみ(だ) The way he cheats people *is disgusting (is loathsome).*

iyashii 卑しい base; mean

mibun ga iyashii 身分が卑しい He was born in *humble circumstances* but rose above it and has become a success.

kudaranai くだらない cheap; off-color; risqué; worthless [books, magazines, etc.]

gehin (da) 下品(だ) vulgar; coarse; unrefined

midara (da) みだら(だ) obscene; unbridled; indecent

ryūkō ni kokoro o ubawareru 流行に心を奪われる be caught up in the rage [of]; be captivated by fleeting fashions [of]

seko ni taketa hito 世故にたけた人 worldly-wise person; man about town; one who knows his way around

ukiyobanare shita 浮き世離れした He is devoting his energies to biological research and *is really unconcerned about the daily humdrum of life* (*couldn't care less about daily trivia*).

teikyū (da) 低級(だ) vulgar [conversation, movie, etc.]

waisetsu (da) わいせつ(だ) obscenity; indecency; pornography (obscene; indecent; pornographic; suggestive)

yahi (da) 野卑(だ) unrefined; ill-mannered; uncouth

ZOKUAKU (da) 俗悪(だ) vulgarity; worldliness (vulgar; worldly)

　sezokuteki (da) 世俗的(だ) worldly; secular; mundane

　warui nakama 悪い仲間 bad company

　warujare 悪じゃれ off-color joke

　zokka (suru) 俗化する vulgarization (vulgarize)

zokuakka suru 俗悪化する vulgarize

zokubutsu 俗物 vulgar person; worldly-minded person; man of the world

zokugo 俗語 slang; vulgarism

zokunen 俗念 worldliness

zokuppoi 俗っぽい cheap; vulgar

zokushū ni somaru 俗習に染まる Living among those rough workers, he *was contaminated by worldly habits* (*he was corrupted*).

zonzai (da) ぞんざいだ impolite; rough; coarse

⇨ 3

世をも，世にあるものをも，愛してはなりません．もしだれでも世を愛しているなら，その人のうちに御父を愛する愛はありません．

すべての世にあるもの，すなわち，肉の欲，目の欲，暮らし向きの自慢などは，御父から出たものではなく，この世から出たものだからです．（ヨハネ I 2 15, 16)

LIST OF MEDICAL TERMS

abnormal ijō 異常; byōteki 病的; hentai 変態

abortion datai 堕胎

abscess haremono はれ物; nōshu 膿腫

acid dyspepsia isankatashō 胃酸過多症

adenoids adenoido アデノイド; senbyō 腺病

airsickness kōkūbyō 航空病

alcoholism arukōru chūdoku アルコール中毒; arukōru chūdoku shō-jō アルコール中毒症状

allergy arerugī アレルギー

anemia hinketsu 貧血

anesthesia mahi マヒ; mukankaku 無感覚; masui 麻酔

antidote gedokuzai 解毒剤; doku-keshi 毒消し

appendicitis chōsuien 虫垂炎; mō-chō 盲腸

appetite shokuyoku 食欲

arteriosclerosis dōmyaku kōkashō 動脈硬化症

artery dōmyaku 動脈

arthritis kansetsuen 関節炎

artificial respiration jinkōkokyū 人口呼吸

asthma zensoku ぜん息

athlete's foot mizumushi 水虫

atrophy ishuku 委縮; shōmōshō 消耗症

bacteria saikin 細菌

baldness hage atama はげ頭; toku-tōbyō とく頭病

birth shussan 出産; shussei 出生; tanjō 誕生

bladder bōkō ぼうこう

blind person mōjin 盲人

blindness mōmoku 盲目

blister suihō 水ほう; kihō 気ほう; mizubukure 水ぶくれ; hibukure 火ぶくれ

blood ketsueki 血液; chi 血

blood bank ketsueki ginkō 血液銀行

blood pressure ketsuatsu 血圧

blood test ketsueki kensa 血液検査

blood vessel kekkan 血管

boil dekimono でき物; haremono はれ物

bone hone 骨

bowels naizō 内臓; chō 腸

bowel movement otsūji お通じ

brain nō 脳

brain concussion nōshintō 脳震とう

breast chibusa 乳房; mune 胸

breast bone kyōkotsu 胸骨

bronchitis kikanshien 気管支炎

bruise uchikizu 打ち傷; uchimi うちみ

bunion sokomame そこまめ

burn yakedo やけど

caesarean operation shikyū sekkai 子宮切開; teiō sekkai 帝王切開

cancer gan ガン

breast cancer nyūgan 乳ガン

lung cancer   haigan 肺ガン
skin cancer   hifugan 皮膚ガン
stomach cancer   igan 胃ガン
canker   kaiyōka かいよう化 gakōsō が口そう；kōgan ロガン
caries   kariesu カリエス
cataract   hakunaishō 白内障
cathartic   gezai 下剤
cavity   kūdō 空洞
cerebral hemorrhage nōshukketsu 脳出血
cerebral anemia   nōhinketsu 脳貧血
cerebral hyperemia nōjūketsu 脳充血
chicken pox   mizubōsō 水ぼうそう
chill   samuke 寒気
cholera   korera コレラ
cleft palate   kōgai haretsu 口ガイ破裂
clot (blood) ketsueki gyōko 血液凝固
cold   kaze かぜ kanbō 感冒
colic   fukutsū 腹痛
coma   konsui こん睡
color blindness   shikimō 色盲
constipation   benpi 便秘
contraception   hinin 避妊
cramp   keiren けいれん
dandruff   fuke ふけ
decayed tooth   mushiba むし歯
deafness   tsunbo つんぼ
delirium   genkaku 幻覚；sakkaku 錯覚 mōsō もう想
dentist   shikai (shi) 歯科医 (師)
diabetes   tōnyōbyō 糖尿病
diarrhea   geri 下痢
digestion   shōka 消化；shōka sayō 消化作用
diptheria   jifuteria ジフテリア
dizziness   memai めまい
dislocation   dakkyū 脱きゅう

dysentery   sekiri 赤痢
ear   mimi り
external ear   gaiji 外耳
middle ear   chūji 中耳
internal ear   naiji 内耳
ear ringing   miminari 耳鳴り
electrocardiogram   shindenzu 心電図
embryo   taiji 胎児
empyema   chikunō 蓄のう
encephalitis   nōen 脳炎
exhaustion   hirō 疲労；shōmō 消耗
eye   me 目
farsightedness   enshi 遠視
nearsightedness   kinshi 近視
astigmatism   ranshi 乱視
sty   monomorai ものもらい
trachoma   torakōma トラコーマ；torahōmu トラホーム
first-aid   ōkyū teate 応急手当
flat foot   henpeisoku 偏平足
fracture   kossetsu 骨折
frostbite   tōshō 凍傷
gallstone   tanseki 胆石
glands . . . sen . . . 腺
gonorrhea   rinbyō リン病
gum   haguki 歯ぐき；haniku 歯肉
halitosis   kōshū 口臭
harelip   mitsukuchi みつ口
heart failure   shinzōmahi 心臓マヒ
heartburn   muneyake 胸焼け
hemorrhoids   ji じ
high blood pressure kōketsuatsu 高血圧
immunity   men'ekisei 免疫性
infection   kansen 感染；densen 伝染
insomnia   fuminshō 不眠症
insulin   inshurin インシュリン
itch   kayui koto かゆいこと
the itch   kaisen かいせん；hizen ひぜん

kidney jinzō じん臓
leprosy raibyō ライ病
leukemia ʰkakketsubyō 白血病
liver kanzō 肝臓
low blood pressure teiketsuatsu 低血圧
lung haizō 肺臓
malaria mararia マラリア
malnutrition eiyō furyō 栄養不良；eiyō shitchō 栄養失調
mastoiditis nyūyōtokkien 乳様突起炎；nyūtotsuen 乳突炎
measles hashika はしか
meningitis nōmakuen 脳膜炎
menopause gekkei heishiki 月経閉止期
menstruation gekkei 月経
miscarriage ryūzan 流産
mumps otafuku kaze おたふくかぜ ryūkōsei 流行性；jikasenen 耳下腺炎
narcotic masuiseino 麻酔性の；masuizai 麻酔剤；mayaku 麻薬；jōyōsha 常用者
nausea hakike 吐き気
nerve shinkei 神経
nervous exhaustion shinkei suijaku 神経衰弱
nervous system shinkeikei 神経系
ointment nankō 軟こう nurigusuri 塗り薬
operation shujutsu 手術
opium ahen アヘン
occulist meisha 目医者；ganka'i 眼科医
optometrist kengan'i 検眼医；shiryoku sokutei'i 視力測定医
organic disease kishitsusei shikkan 器質性疾患
orthopedics seikei geka 整形外科
osteopath seikotsu senmon'i 整骨専門医

ovary ransō 卵巣
ovulation hairan 排卵
oxygen sanso 酸素
pain itami 痛み
pancreas suizō すい臓
paralysis mahi マヒ
Parkinson's disease pakinsonshibyō パーキンソン氏病
penis inkei 陰茎
perspiration ase 汗
pharynx intō いん頭；nodo のど
pile ji じ
pimples nikibi にきび
plastic surgery seikeigeka 整形外科
pneumonia haien 肺炎
poison doku 毒；chūdoku 中毒
poliomyelitis sekizui kaihakushitsuen せき髄灰白質炎
infantile paralysis shōni mahi 小児マヒ
prescription shohōsen 処方せん
prostate zenritsusen 前立腺
psychiatry seishin igaku 精神医学
puberty shishunki 思春期
pulse myaku 脈
pus umi うみ
quarantine ken'eki 検疫；ken'eki kikan 検疫期間
rabies kyōkenbyō 狂犬病
reaction hannō 反応
rectum chokuchō 直腸
reflex hansha 反射
rehabilitation kaifuku 回復；shakkai fukki 社会復帰
renal calculus jinzō kesseki 腎臓結石
reproduction seishoku (sayō) 生殖（作用）
respiratory kokyūki 呼吸器
rheumatic fever ryūmachi (netsu) リューマチ（リューマチ熱）

Rh factor Rh inshi Rh 因子
ringworm tamushi たむし
scarlet fever shōkōnetsu しょうこう熱
schizophrenia seishin bunretsubyō 精神分裂病
sedative chinseizai 鎮静剤
smallpox tennentō 天然痘
sore haremono はれ物
specimen hyōhon 標本
spine sebone 背骨; sekizui kotsu せきづい骨
spleen hizō ひ臓
staphylococcus budōjōkyūkin ぶどう状球菌
sterility funinshō 不妊症
streptococcus rensajōkyūkin 連鎖状球菌
stool (feces) ben 便; haisetsubutsu 排せつ物
sulfa drugs surufazai スルファ剤
swelling haremono はれ物
symptom shōjō 症状
syphilis baidoku 梅毒
temperature ondo 温度
  body temperature taion 体温
thyroid kōjōsen 甲状腺
tonsillitis hentōsen へんとう腺
tourniquet shiketsuki 止血器
trachoma torakōma トラコーマ torahōmu; トラホーム

tranquilizer chinseizai 鎮静剤
transfusion yuketsu 輸血
trauma gaishō 外傷
tuberculosis kekkaku 結核
pulmonary tuberculosis haikekkaku 肺結核
tumor haremono はれもの; shuyō しゅよう
typhoid chōchifusu 腸チフス
typhus hasshinchifusu 発しんチフス
ulcer kaiyō かいよう haremono; gastric ulcer ikaiyō 胃かいよう
urinalysis nyōbunseki 尿分析; kennyō 検尿
urine nyō 尿
uterus shikyū 子宮
vaccination shutō 種痘
  preventative injection yobōchūsha 予防注射
venereal disease seibyō 性病
virus birusu ビールス
vitamin bitamin ビタミン
vomiting ōto おう吐
whooping cough hyakunichizeki 百日ぜき
worm, parasite mushi 虫; kiseichū 寄生虫
wound gaishō 外傷
yellow fever ōnetsubyō 黄熱病

GENERAL JAPANESE INDEX

bankon 125.1
bankurawase 151.2
bannan 221.1
bannō 253.2
bansaku 188.2
banzen 8.2, 114.2
barabara 148.2
bariki 25.2
bassuru 150.2, 239.2
batō 33.2
batsu 63.1, 150.2, 197.2
batsugun 253.2
bengo 10.2
bengoshi 213.1
benkai 54.2, 213.1
benkyō 122.1, 160.2
benpō 226.1
benri 219.1
benrishugi 219.1
benron 54.2, 233.1
benzetsu 152.2
beppin 16.1
besshi 121.1
betsu 196.2
bettenchi 220.1
bi 16.1
bibō 16.2, 119.2
bidan 16.2
bifū 16.2
bigaku 16.2
biganjutsu 16.2
bihin 99.1
biishiki 16.2
bijin 16.2
bijireiku 16.2, 154.2
bijutsu 16.2
bika 16.2
bikan 16.2
bikkuri 83.1, 164.2
bikubiku 159.1
bimbō 79.2
bimbōgurashi 79.2
bimbōkusai 79.2
bimbōnin 79.2
bimbōsho 79.2
bimbōyusuri 143.1
bimei 57.2
bimyō 110.2
binanshi 16.2
binjō 34.2

binkan 111.1
binkatsu 17.2, 105.1
binshō 17.2, 104.2
binsoku 17.2
bishō 119.2, 244.1
biten 39.2
biteki 16.2
bitoku 39.2
bōanki 137.2
bodai 228.1
bōdo 20.1
bōfū 20.1
bōgai 221.2
bōgen 20.2, 33.2, 236.2
bōgo 8.2
bōgyaku 257.1
bōgyo 8.2
boin 188.1
bōjaku 59.2
bōkan 20.2
bōken 133.1
bokin 136.1
bōkō 20.2
bokumetsu 67.1
bōkun 20.2
bōkyaku 19.1
bōkyo 20.2
bonjin 69.2
bonnō 244.2
bonyari 36.1
bonyō 69.2
boro 247.2
bōryaku 241.1
bōryoku 20.1, 251.2
bōryokudan 20.2
bōsan 228.1
boseiai 3.2
bōto 20.2
bōtō 65.1
botsuraku 66.2
bottō 224.2
bōzen 36.1, 167.1
bu 222.1
buchikowasu 67.2
buenryo 190.1
buji 8.2
bujoku 34.1, 64.1, 121.1
bukka 101.2
bukkirabō 190.1, 229.2
Bukkyō 229.1

bummei 21.2
bun 239.1
bunan 8.2
bungaku 160.2
bungei 160.2
bunka 21.1
bunkajin 21.2
bunkasai 21.2
bunkatsubarai 135.2
bunkateki 21.2
bunkazai 21.2
bunkyō 21.2, 161.2
bunretsu 10.2
bunsai 185.1
bunseki 160.2
bunshō 154.2
burabura 167.1
burei 190.2
bureikō 123.2
buru 59.2
buryoku 20.2, 25.2, 205.1
busahō 191.1
bushi 183.1
bushō 234.1
busō 205.1
buta 101.1
butsu-butsu 44.1
byōin 22.1
byōjō 22.1
byōki 22.1
byōkon 22.1
byōmei 22.2
byōnin 22.2
byōsei 22.2
byōshō 22.2
byōteki 22.2

chakasu 16.1
chakuchaku 115.1, 214.2
chakufuku 57.2
chakujitsu 185.2
chakushu 66.2
chakusō 208.1
chansu 131.2
chanto 115.1
chi 36.2, 124.1, 143.1,
  158.1, 159.1, 180.2
chie 24.1, 32.2, 124.1,
  208.1
chigai 14.2, 195.2

dentō 伝統 228.1
deru maku 238.2
detarame 51.2
detatoko 227.1
detchiageru 51.2
dō 45.2, 115.1, 194.1
do 238.2
dōbyō 13.1, 248.2
dōdō 54.2, 84.1, 252.1
dogaishi 176.2
dōgan 120.1
dōgi 39.2
dogimagi 143.2
dōgishin 39.2, 195.2
dōi 90.1, 197.2
dōigo 152.2
dōitsu 194.1
dōji 92.1
dōjiru 159.1
dōjō 13.1
dōjōshin 13.1
dōka 53.1
dōkan 90.2, 197.2
doko 121.1, 193.2
dōkei 194.1
dōki 動き 42.2
dōki 動機 49.1, 173.2
doki 85.2
dokitto 42.2, 83.1
dokudan 35.2
dokugaku 160.2
dokuji 35.2
dokuritsu 35.2
dokuritsudokkō 35.2
dokuritsudoppo 35.2
dokuritsukoku 35.2
dokuritsusai 35.2
dokuritsushin 35.2
dokuryoku 35.2
dokusenteki 36.1
dokusō 230.2
dokuzen 93.2
dokuzenteki 94.1
dokuzetsu 34.1
dokuzuku 77.1, 121.1
dokyō 185.2, 252.1
dōmei 163.1
dōmo 190.1
donaru 85.1
dondon 17.2, 91.1

donguri 193.2
donkan 36.1, 111.1
donna me 157.1
donyoku 244.2
donzumari 188.2
dōraku 244.2
dōrakumono 235.2
dōran 70.2
dorei 121.1
dōri 40.1, 192.2
doro 146.2
doronuma 258.2
doryō 119.1, 191.2
doryoku 37.1
dōsa 144.2
dōsatsu 38.2
dōsatsuryoku 38.2
dōshi 90.2
dōshiuchi 10.2
dotamba 220.2, 257.2
dotchi tsukazu 176.2, 250.1
dōtō 194.1
dōtoku 39.2
dōtokugaku 40.1
dōtokujō 40.1
dōtokuritsu 40.1
dōtokushin 40.1
dowasure 19.1
dōyō 194.2, 250.1
dōzo 253.1

egao 120.1
eien 40.2
eiga 81.2, 171.1
eikan 171.1, 222.2
eikō 171.1
eikyō 41.1
eikyū 40.2
eikyūteki 40.2
eimin 206.2
eisei 127.2
eiyo 171.2
eiyōeiga 81.2
eiyū 251.2
eizokusei 41.1
eki 219.1
ekibyō 22.2
ekken 126.1
ekō 228.1

ekoji 48.1
emman 35.1, 70.2
emmusubi 124.2
en 111.2, 171.2
endan 124.2
endōi 111.2, 117.1
engi 227.1, 228.1
engumi 124.2
enjo 163.2
enjuku 184.1
enkatsu 30.2
enkyoku 102.1
enryo 128.2, 190.1, 229.2
enryobukai 128.2, 190.1
enryogachi 128.2
entsuzuki 112.1
enzetsu 232.2
erabu 129.1, 196.1
eragari 171.2
eragaru 59.2,
erai 84.1, 144.2
erasō ni 100.1
eri 123.1, 190.1
ete 46.1
etoku 191.2
etsu 235.1

fu 47.1, 53.1
fuan 42.2
fubi 247.2
fubin 13.2
fūbun 242.2
fubunritsu 139.1
fuchin 71.1
fuchō 23.1
fuchūi 14.2, 234.1
fudōtoku 40.1
fūfu 125.2
fūfuai 3.2
fufuku 44.2
fūgawari 47.1
fugi 7.1, 239.2
fugō 90.1
fugū 142.2
fūha 147.2
fuhai 40.2, 66.2
fuhei 44.1
fuhō 239.2
fuhon'i 89.1
fūhyō 242.2

harai 135.2
harainokeru 103.2
haraise 241.2
harebare 165.1
harenchizai 240.2
hareru 8.1
hariai 218.1
hasan 67.1
hashi 端 188.2
hashi はし 101.2
hashiru 17.2
hashitagane 136.1
hason 67.1
hassei 65.2
hatairo 10.2
hatan 67.1
hataraki 37.2
hatasu 115.1, 203.1
hate 188.2
hateshi 41.1, 188.2
hatsu 65.1
hatsuho 65.1
hatsukoi 4.1, 65.2
hatsumei 208.1
hatsumono 65.2
hatsunetsu 23.1
hatsuon 153.1, 188.1
hatsuratsu 104.2
hatten 214.2
hattensei 214.2
hayagatten 191.2
hayai 17.2, 229.2
hayame 91.1
hayameru 18.1
hayaoki 18.1
hazukashigaru 63.2
hazukashii 63.2
hazukashime 63.2
hazumi 131.2
hazumu 143.2, 246.2
hei 205.1
heibon 69.2
heifuku 211.2
heigai 7.1
heihei 69.2
heii 118.2
heiji 71.1
heikai 188.2
heiki 36.2, 176.2, 185.2
heimin 69.2

heion 7.2, 71.1, 185.2
heisei 7.2, 71.1, 185.2
heishi 205.1
heishin 211.2
heitai 205.1
heiwa 70.1, 70.2
heiwateki 71.1
heizen 71.1, 185.2
hekotareru 62.1
hema 15.1
hemmei 71.2
hen 47.1, 237.1
hendō 71.2
henji 27.1
henjiru 71.2
henka 71.1, 71.2
henkaku 71.2
henkei 71.2
henken 196.1
henkō 71.2
henkutsu 47.1, 48.1
henrei 81.2
henseiki 72.1
hensen 72.1
henshitsukyō 162.2
henshitsusha 162.2
henshoku 72.1
hensō 72.1
hensoku 72.1
hentai 72.1
henten 72.1
hentetsu 70.1
herazuguchi 237.1
herikudaru 128.2
herikutsu 11.1, 192.2
hesokuri 135.2
hesomagari 78.2
heta 117.2, 184.2
hetabaru 62.2
hetsurai 73.1, 73.2
hi 日 12.1, 122.1, 200.1
hi 火 49.2, 79.2
hi 非 15.1, 115.1
hiai 107.2
hibiki 187.2
hibō 34.1
hibuta 65.2, 205.1
hidarimae 67.2
hidoi 122.1, 147.2, 257.1
hifun 85.1

higai 158.1
higashi 12.2
hige 121.2, 128.2
higeki 107.2
higekiteki 107.2
higō 206.2
higure 12.1
hihan 74.1
hihanteki 74.1
hihō 107.2, 177.2
hihyō 74.1
hihyōka 74.1
hiideru 253.2
hijōshiki 24.2, 29.1
hikaeme 128.2
hikaku 196.2
hikan 167.2
hikareru 4.2, 117.1
hikari 74.2, 75.1, 170.1
hike 196.1, 253.2
hikeme 247.2
hiketsu 76.1
hikin 70.1
hikitomeru 220.2
hikkomijian 63.2, 186.2
hikō 144.2
hikōshiki 123.1
hikutsu 64.1, 78.1
hikyō 186.2
hima 91.1, 233.2
himei 107.2, 187.2
himitsu 75.2, 170.2
himmin 79.2
himotsuki 112.1
himpu 79.2
himpyōkai 74.1
hin 79.2
hinagata 193.2
hinammin 167.2
hinan 非難 77.1
hinan 避難 102.2
hinanjo 102.2
hinekure 78.1
hinekureta 78.1
hin'i 84.1
hinikkuta 79.1
hiniku 78.2, 79.1
hinikuya 79.1
hinjaku 79.2
hinkaku 40.2

mugotarashii 257.1
muhihan 74.2
muhon 241.1
muimi 175.2, 237.1
mujaku 118.2
mujihi 257.1
mujinzō 81.1
mujō 72.2
mujun 192.1
mukachi 101.2
mukandō 36.2
mukankaku 36.2
mukankei 112.2
mukanshin 175.2
mukappara 85.2
mukashi 93.1, 138.1
muki むき 110.2
muki 向き 121.1
mukiryoku 105.2
mukō 42.1, 175.2
mukōmizu 61.2, 230.1
mukuchi 27.2, 233.1
mukui 82.1
muikyu 41.1
mumei 172.2
munakuso 182.2
munasawagi 43.2, 180.1
munashii 176.1
mune 23.1, 89.2, 108.1,
 109.1, 138.1, 144.1,
 146.2, 158.2, 177.2,
 180.1, 230.2, 246.2
munō 184.2
mura 250.2
muraki 73.1, 135.1
muri 56.1, 215.1, 238.2
muryō 137.1
musekinin 204.1
musabori 244.2, 245.2
mushakusha 86.1
mushi 虫 45.1 95.1,
 135.1, 182.2, 257.1
mushi 無視 177.1
mushinkei 36.2
mushizu 182.2
mushō 57.1
mushūkyō 229.1
musō 231.1
musubareru 125.2
musubi 188.2

muteikan 250.2
muteppō 124.2, 233.1
mutonjaku 36.2, 176.2
muttsuriya 27.2, 233.1,
 255.2
muyō 175.2
muyūbyōsha 168.1
muzai 214.1, 240.2
muzan 257.1
muzukashii 221.1
myaku 131.1
myō 47.2
myōan 208.1
myōban 12.1
myōnichi 12.1
myōrei 17.1

na 172.2
naburimono 16.1
naburu 16.1
nadakai 172.2
nadameru 179.1
nadamesukasu 179.1
nagai 5.2
nagaiki 203.1
nagameru 114.2, 169.1
nagare 228.2
negekawashii 178.1
nageki 177.2
nageyari 234.2
nagori 138.1
naguriai 11.2
naguru 20.2
nagusame 178.2, 179.1
nagusami 179.1
naibukōsaku 76.2
naien 124.2
naigashiro 177.1, 234.2
naihō 76.2
naikōsei 96.2
naimitsu 76.1
nainai 76.2
nasake 13.2
naisei 173.1
naishin 43.2
naisho 76.2
naishobanashi 76.2
naitsū 241.1
najiru 77.2
naka 仲 90.2, 249.1

naka 中 11.2, 35.1
nakama 112.2
nakanaori 30.2, 71.1
nakatagai 11.2
nakayasumi 165.2
nakidasu 178.1
nakifusu 178.1
nakigara 206.2
nakigoe 178.1
nakigoto 45.1
nakikanashimu 178.1
nakikuzureru 178.1
nakimane 178.1
nakimono 67.2
nakimushi 178.1
nakineiri 178.1, 183.2
nakiotosu 178.1
nakisakebu 178.1
nakitsura 108.1
nakōdo 125.2
naku 108.1, 178.1
nakunaru 206.2
namahanka 29.1, 250.2
namahenji 69.1
namaiki 60.1
namakemono 234.2
namakeru 234.2
namanurui 105.2
nami 70.1
namida 108.1, 109.2,
 178.1
namidagumashii 78.1,
 109.2, 178.2
namidagumu 178.2
namihazureta 254.2
namitaitei 157.2
nampa 221.2
nan 226.1
nandai 147.2
nangi 148.1, 221.1
nangyō 148.1
nanifusoku 81.1
nanige 36.2
nanjaku 248.1
nanji 何時 92.2
nanji 難事 148.1
nankan 221.2
nankyoku 148.1
naore 64.2
naoru 23.1

senzai 77.1
senzairyoku 26.1
seppa-tsumaru 113.2
seron 87.1
seserewarau 15.2, 79.1, 121.1
sesse to 157.2
sessei 156.2, 239.1
sesshō 56.1
sesuji 160.1
setchūan 35.2
setogiwa 132.2
setsumei 193.1
setsunai 14.1, 108.2
settoku 42.2, 56.2, 191.2
sewa 216.1
sewazuki 216.1
sezokuteki 259.1
shaberimakuru 233.1
shaberu 233.1
sha'i 116.2
shakkin 136.2
shaku 86.1
shakuhō 98.1
shamen 253.1
share 154.2
sharei 116.2
shasuru 116.2
shayōzoku 80.2
shazai 253.1
shi 死 206.2, 207.1
shi 詩 154.2
shiage 115.1
shiai 11.2
shian 209.1
shiawase 143.1
shibaiki 141.2
shibai 59.1
shibaraku 93.2
shibetsu 207.1
shibire 36.2, 184.1, 233.2
shibō 死亡 207.1
shibō 志望 131.1
shibōtodoke 207.2
shiburu 250.2
shibutoi 48.2
shichi 67.2
shidai 93.2
shidō 162.1

shidoro-modoro 150.1
shigeki 143.2, 256.1
shigo 207.2
shigokugenki 127.2
shigoto 38.1, 204.2, 211.1
shihai 127.1
shiharai 82.2, 135.2
shihei 135.2
shihō-happō 71.1
shihon 137.1
shiin 188.1
shiitageru 10.1
shiji 163.2, 198.1
shijū 93.2
shika'i 23.1
shikamettsura 69.1, 120.2
shikaritobasu 77.2, 86.1
shikaru 77.2, 151.1
shigata 5.2, 176.1, 226.1
shikaeshi 242.1
shikatsu 100.2
shikei 150.2, 207.2, 213.2
shiken 162.1
shiki 式 123.2
shiki 四季 220.1
shiki 士気 135.1, 252.2
shikibetsu 39.1, 197.1
shikii 64.2
shikijō 4.1
shikin 136.2
shikiyoku 245.1
shikkari 96.2, 107.1, 252.2
shikō 207.2, 208.2
shikōryoku 209.1
shikujiri 15.1
shikuhakku 157.2
shikyo 207.2
shimai 189.2
shimatsu 104.2, 221.2
shimbō 172.2
shimboku 249.1
shimei 204.2
shimekiri 189.2
shimekukuri 189.2
shimen-soka 9.2

shimesu 171.1
shimetsu 67.2
shimmai 122.2
shimmei 57.1
shimon 33.2
shimpai 43.2, 160.1, 180.1
shimpi 76.1
shimpu 126.1
shimpuku 信服 56.2
shimpuku 心服 46.2
shin'ai 3.2, 249.1
shinakereba naranai 245.2
shinbō 184.1
shinbōzuyoi 184.1
shindai 81.2
shindan 23.2
shindansho 23.2
shindō 188.1
shingi 56.2, 214.1
shingichū 56.2
shin'i 89.2
shinikakaru 207.2
shinikata 207.2
shinin 207.2
shin'i 174.1
shinitaeru 207.2
shiniwakareru 207.2
shinja 212.1
shinjidai 214.2
shinjigatai 45.2, 212.1
shinjin 212.1
shinjinbukai 212.1, 229.1
shinjiru 212.1
shinjitsu 信実 212.2
shinjitsu 真実 209.1, 209.2
shinjō 心情 146.2
shinjō 信条 212.2
shinka 真価 101.2
shinka 進化 215.2
shinkaron 215.2
shinkei 111.2, 163.1, 206.1, 225.1
shinken 210.1, 211.1, 225.1
shinkenmi 211.1
shinketsu 38.2, 211.1
shinki 新規 66.1